# GRAHAM KERR'S BEST

## OTHER BOOKS BY GRAHAM KERR

*Graham Kerr's Smart Cooking*
*Graham Kerr's Minimax™ Cookbook*
*Graham Kerr's Creative Choices Cookbook*
*Graham Kerr's Kitchen*

# GRAHAM KERR'S BEST

## A Low-Fat, Heart-Healthy Cookbook

G. P. PUTNAM'S SONS
NEW YORK

G. P. Putnam's Sons
*Publishers Since 1838*
200 Madison Avenue
New York, NY 10016

Minimax™ is a registered trademark of the Treena and Graham Kerr Corporation.

Library of Congress Cataloging-in-Publication Data

Kerr, Graham.
Graham Kerr's best : a low-fat, heart-healthy cookbook.
p.   cm.
Includes index.
ISBN 0-399-14076-X
1. Cookery. 2. Low-fat diet—Recipes. 3. Low-calorie diet—Recipes.
4. Nutrition—Requirements.   I. Title.
TX714.K4782   1995              95-13581 CIP
641.5'638—dc20

*Book design by H. Roberts*

Printed in the United States of America
3  5  7  9  10  8  6  4

This book is printed on acid-free paper.  ∞

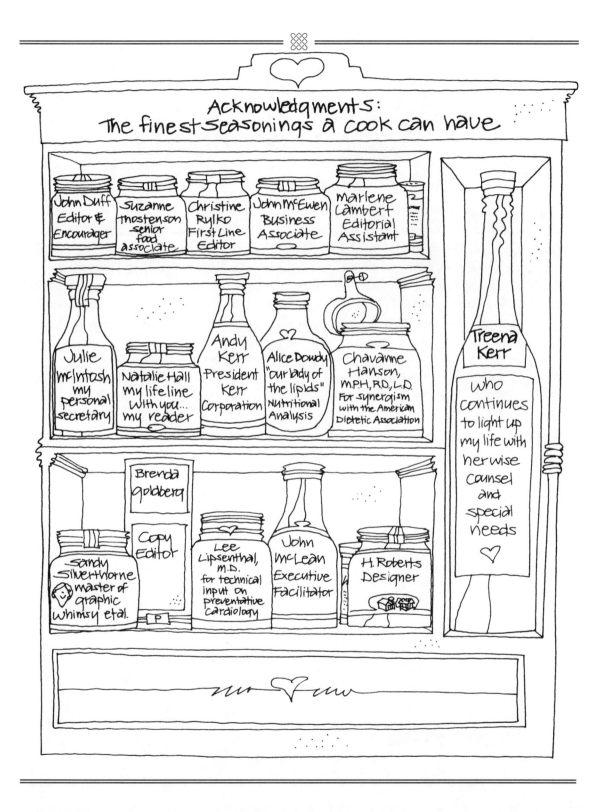

Acknowledgments:
The finest seasonings a cook can have

# *Acknowledgments*

I'm always eager to recognize the great team that gives me such valuable help with my books. I've grown accustomed to using the visual metaphor of a pantry to describe their value as "intellectual seasonings." But in this book, I want to add two special words of thanks.

Suzanne Thostenson has been my Senior Food Associate since 1992, when I moved my Research Kitchen to Camano Island, Washington. My respect for Suzanne's love of good food and her healthy response to change in her own life is so great that I asked her to review and revise fifty new recipes in this book. When I read through the changes she proposed, I knew she had made the right decisions. So, if you notice some substantial changes from some of the recipes you see on television, you can attribute it to Suzanne's synergistically special seasonings!

Second, throughout all my books since 1991, Christine Andrews Rylko has been my first line editor. That's a job a little like winding a ball of wool after the cat's got at it. Chris kept everyone on deadline and reviewed every sentence for measure and meaning, inevitably in rushed and complicated times. She has always given me the "best of care," and I'm grateful.

# Contents

# Introduction

After twenty-two years of helping people change their life-styles to include the healthiest and most enjoyable way of eating possible, I have surveyed my recipes and offer you what I believe to be the most vital collection to date.

*Fat implicated as a critical factor*

Without doubt the key issue for all our eating has proven to be the amount of fat we consume, kept track of on a daily basis. Fat has been implicated as a critical factor in the number one killer in America, heart disease; a key in the development of what may be the most feared disease, cancer; and a general indicator of danger to one's waistline and overall weight.

*But I have found that most people still have no idea how much fat is the right amount for their personal needs.*

I use a sophisticated computer software program to give you an accurate nutritional analysis for each recipe presented in all of my books, however, for the first time, I want to present you with a short list of simple questions to help you determine what your general goal of daily fat intake *should* be. Then I have divided this book into specific collections of recipes based on three levels of fat intake so you can easily turn to that section and see the full range of creative eating that's available to you at every level of fat intake. A complete listing of all the recipes in this book, organized by categories such as appetizers, entrées, desserts, etc., is also available on page xviii, for those who wish a more traditional approach to recipe browsing.

You will see as you read through the recipes that selecting food based on a daily percentage of calories from fat does not mean a gradual reduction in pleasure. Rather, it's the most useful framework I can offer to give you creative food choices to increase your quality of life. It's about discovering ingredients rich in aromas, colors, and textures that you can use in your cooking every day to enhance your eating enjoyment. It's about finding new cooking techniques that allow you to prepare all your favorite foods in a healthier and just as pleasurable style, meeting your need for comfort, satisfaction, creativity, and variety.

*Graham's sophisticated software program*

So please answer the questions to determine your optimum fat intake and use my recipes for your health and enjoyment. Of course, I highly recommend that you verify your results with your personal doctor in association with a registered dietitian. The checklists were compiled in association with experts in several medical fields, especially Chavanne Hanson, M.P.H., R.D., L.D., of the University Hospitals of Cleveland Synergy Program (a leader in the field of preventative cardiology) and Lee Lipsenthal, M.D., the Director of the Preventive Medicine Research Institute in San Francisco.

*Amazing! What a discovery!*

Remember, if you cook for others, you should also have them read through the short lists to determine their fat levels.

*If you cook for others*

## Daily Health and Eating Checklists

I believe that one of the most important things you can do when cooking for yourself and those you love is to determine your optimum level of daily fat intake. I have made this as easy as possible by giving you simple questions to which you answer "yes" or "no." More "yes" than "no" answers indicate that you could maximize your eating and possibly help to reduce your health risk at that fat level. Please always verify your results with a doctor and a registered dietician.

**Easy Steps Toward Maximum Goals**

After each checklist I have suggested the easiest steps possible to *start you on the road* to attaining your complete life-style change goals. May I warmly suggest (with a big smile of encouragement) after reading through these checklists that you also check out the recipes that match your level of fat. Then, having whetted your appetite, begin by cooking an easy recipe. I am sure that spurred on by one success, you will see how a successful change is within your reach.

*With a big smile of encouragement.*

LEVEL 1: 30% of Daily Calories from Fat

For people who are "well," 25 to 30 percent of daily calories from fat is the maximum amount recommended by the American Heart Association for the general populace. Of course, this group can enjoy dishes from any of the fat levels in this book.

**1.** Do you have a family history free of cancer, heart disease, hypertension, or diabetes? ❑ YES ❑ NO
   **2.** Are you satisfied with your personal weight? ❑ YES ❑ NO
      **3.** Is your cholesterol under 200? ❑ YES ❑ NO
      **4.** Are you a nonsmoker? ❑ YES ❑ NO
      **5.** Do you seldom feel short-tempered or impatient? ❑ YES ❑ NO
      **6.** Do you eat four or more servings (1/2 cup) of vegetables or fruit every day? ❑ YES ❑ NO
      **7.** Do you exercise at least three days per week for at least 20 minutes? ❑ YES ❑ NO
   **8.** Do you want to make your diet healthier? ❑ YES ❑ NO

STEP ONE

Start to reduce meat and fish portions to 6 ounces per day. Increase servings of fresh vegetables, fruit, and grains to 9 1/2-cup servings each day.

STEP TWO

Use low-fat cheese and dairy products. Try 1 tablespoon of freshly grated Parmesan cheese on top of a dish before serving.

STEP THREE

Cook food for four people in no more than 1 teaspoon of olive oil. Salad dressings should use 2 parts vinegar to 1 part olive oil.

Plus, walk briskly four times a week for at least 20 minutes. (As recommended by your physician.)

*For Your Information:* At this 30% level, an average 2,000-calories-a-day diet gives you 600 calories from fat each day, which translates to 66 grams, or 13 teaspoons of fat. (See the Recipes on page xviii.)

LEVEL 2: 20% of Daily Calories from Fat
For people who want to "stay well"—to go beyond simply maintaining their health, to preventing possible health problems in the future, 16 to 24 percent of daily calories from fat is recommended.

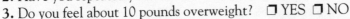

1. Do you have a parent or sibling who has developed either cancer, heart disease, diabetes, or hypertension?  ❐ YES ❐ NO
2. Have you repeatedly tested for blood cholesterol levels at over 200?   ❐ YES ❐ NO
3. Do you feel about 10 pounds overweight?   ❐ YES ❐ NO
4. Do you seriously crave sweet or fatty foods, alcohol, or tobacco?   ❐ YES ❐ NO
5. Do you eat four or less servings (1/2 cup) each day of fruit or vegetables?
   ❐ YES ❐ NO
6. Do you find you can't exercise three to four times a week for at least 20 minutes?
   ❐ YES ❐ NO
7. Do you want to make healthy diet changes and practice disease prevention?
   ❐ YES ❐ NO

STEP ONE
   Enjoy smaller meat and fish portions, about 4 ounces a day. Start alternating vegetables, legumes, and grains in place of meat.

STEP TWO
   Experiment with replacing amounts of butter, cheese, and mayonnaise with strained yogurt (page 288) and fat-free, low-sodium condiments. Try low-sugar frozen yogurt and fruit ices instead of ice cream.

STEP THREE
   Try salsa as a topping and low- or nonfat salad dressings. Plus, walk briskly four times a week for at least 20 minutes. (As recommended by your physician.)
   *Bonus:* Keep your eyes open for people in difficulty, then be kind in a creative way. This exercises your compassion and helps to keep you from getting too self-focused.
   *For Your Information:* At this level, an average 2,000-calories-a-day-diet gives you 400 calories a day from fat, which equals 44 grams of fat, or about 9 teaspoons. (See the Recipes on page xviii.)

LEVEL 3: 10% of Daily Calories from Fat
For people who want to "be well," limiting fat level to up to 15 percent of daily calories from fat is the ideal target for those who have already experienced health problems, who want to prevent further disease and restore damaged body systems.

**1.** Do you, personally, have heart disease, cancer, diabetes, or hypertension?  ❐ YES ❐ NO
**2.** Do you feel that you are about 25 pounds overweight?  ❐ YES ❐ NO
**3.** Does repeat testing of your blood cholesterol levels come in over 250; or over 200 even though you're consuming cholesterol-lowering medication?  ❐ YES ❐ NO
**4.** Are you a cigarette smoker, or have you given it up within the last 12 months?  ❐ YES ❐ NO
**5.** Do you find it difficult to exercise due to breathlessness, weakness, or chest or leg pain?  ❐ YES ❐ NO
**6.** After considering all the above, are you unhappy with how you feel?  ❐ YES ❐ NO
**7.** Do you want to change the way you eat?  ❐ YES ❐ NO

STEP ONE

Meat in the minor key or *garnish* your dishes with meat.
Savor small meat, poultry, cold cuts, and fish portions of 1 ounce per day.
Creatively use herbs, juices, peppers, and nonfat cheese.

STEP TWO

Become a virtual vegetarian. Increase amounts of vegetables, fresh fruits, legumes, and whole grains. Become a "soupy groupy." Soups provide comfort, nourishment, and pleasure as a main meal.

STEP THREE

Trade high-calorie snacks and candy for low-calorie vegetables and fruits, like carrot sticks and grapes. Replace soda with carbonated unsweetened water. Replace caffeinated drinks with decaffeinated.

Plus, walk briskly four times a week for at least 20 minutes (with approval from your physician).

*Bonus:* Take quality time on a daily basis to meditate, reflect, consider, and pray about your personal faith and the impact that it has upon your relationship with others less fortunate than yourself.

*For Your Information:* At this level, an average diet of 2,000 calories a day would give you 200 calories a day from fat, which equals about 22 grams of fat, or 4.5 teaspoons. (See the Recipes on page xviii.)

## Stretching Fat Percentages

This entire book revolves around the idea that each plate of food can be measured to find its fat content and then grouped according to the percentage of calories it derives from that fat. This is all very neat and orderly, but unfortunately, life and recipes are not always that simple.

*Categories*

It's possible, for example, the nutritional numbers for a healthy salad with a low-fat vinaigrette dressing could be 100 calories and 5 grams of fat per portion. This is quite acceptable in even the most stringent low-fat eating plans. However, it works out to 45 percent of calories from fat—so high a percentage that it's off the scale in my book into forbidden territory.

On the opposite end of the scale, a dish with lots of calories, like pasta in sausage sauce, could be 696 calories and 10 grams of fat per serving. The percentage of calories from fat works out to 13 percent. But 10 grams of fat is almost half of the amount you should consume in one day.

*I will alert you . . .*

When these aberrations take place, I will alert you with two simple symbols:

An arrow pointing up ⬆ means that a low amount of total calories makes a low amount of fat grams appear as a high percentage. So even if the percentage of fat is high, I'm placing it in a healthy "10 percent of daily calories from fat" group.

An arrow pointing down ⬇

means that the total calories make the fat percentage look good, but the recipe should be used cautiously. So I'll place that recipe in a "30 percent calories from fat" category.

This is the reason why you will find a large range of percentage calories from fat numbers in categories labeled simply 30%, 20%, and 10%. It's also the reason why the percentage used on food labels these days is expressed as that product's contribution to the entire day's food intake or daily value (D.V.).

## Fat and Food in the Future

Lowering fat, especially from animal sources, seriously impacts large and sensitive segments of our society. The percentage of butterfat contained in milk, for example, determines its cash value. The higher the fat content, the better the farmer's profit margin.

*Getting the issue before the public*

When the government of *all* the people, including sensitive cattle farmers, determined what level of fat consumption was best for the population as a whole, they balanced known science with a gut feeling about what was achievable, and added an appropriate margin to assuage the farmers' pain. Essentially the recommendation to consume a maximum of 30 percent of your daily calories from fat was a mix of good science, guesswork, and compromise that has nonetheless had the beneficial effect of getting the issue before the public.

As the story unfolds and scientists begin to prove their points, the buzzword is out that maybe 20 percent of your daily calories from fat is a healthier overall goal, especially for those who want to practice a life-style that actively tries to prevent disease.

This is, of course, a sensitive matter for everyone connected to the production, distribution, and sale of fats from all sources, and it's perfectly natural that those with vested interests should fund studies and public-relations efforts that evaluate the issues from a different perspective.

At the publication date of this book, a level of 10 percent of daily calories from fat is seen as a goal for those who want to potentially reverse the effects that a high animal fat and cholesterol diet has had upon their overall health.

## The Middle-of-the-Road Position

The concept of being healthier by eating less fat is hardly new, since it can be traced back to the traditional diet of many cultures that have their roots in lower fat consumption and large amounts of vegetables, fruits, and whole grains. The American pioneer in this field, Nathan Pritikin, knew this as he began his search back in 1976.

In 1985, Dr. Dean Ornish turned the same page in a progressively more analytical way. His purpose was to try to prove scientifically that a "cluster" of life-style changes could make a considerable difference in a wide range of physical ailments, including overweight. Essentially Dr. Ornish's work promotes a virtually

*The middle-of-the-road approach*

vegan vegetarian diet (no animal products other than some nonfat dairy and egg whites), stress reduction through nonspecific religious yoga and meditation, a wide range of regular exercise options, and finally, small-group support discussions.

Those who are aware of their own very personal exposure to risk, including genetic factors, have so benefited from Dr. Ornish's research-oriented philosophy that they extol its virtues with almost evangelical fervor. Critics and skeptics have said that Dr. Ornish asks for "too many changes all at once." There is also some concern about small reductions in "good" cholesterol (HDL) along with the benefit of considerably reduced "bad" cholesterol (LDL) and in some cases a heightening of triglycerides because of the increased consumption of carbohydrates. So far, from my personal observations, I find Ornish's arguments interesting and with very minor adjustments for our own individual needs, Treena and I are in the midst of our own measured evaluation.

In the meantime, this book simply stays more or less in the middle of the nutritional debate. I include quite a few dishes that fall within the 10 to 15 percent of fat range, for those, like my wife, Treena, who find themselves at high health risk. Some of these are vegetarian; however, most are not.

So, how could you use this book for someone you love, and keep them at low risk? Since I have included a wide range of recipes already collected under the broad headings of 30%, 20%, or 10% calories from fat, all you need to do is actively embrace the twin ideas of compassion and creativity in order to make it work for you.

## Wrap Caring Cuisine in Pleasure

I believe that regardless of the level of need, all of us want to continue to eat and enjoy our food in a guiltfree and healthy manner. My contention is that this is only possible by accepting certain limits as a frame within

*A frame within which an individual can be creative . . .*

which every individual can be creative with the foods and seasonings that he or she likes and can eat. Therefore, the focus of this book is not on what one can't eat but, rather, on using creatively what one can.

This means a deemphasis in fats, sugars, salts, and portion sizes, and an increase in a wide range of vegetables, fruits, whole grains, fresh herbs, and seasonings. I hope that you will quickly realize that deprivation is not the key. I don't take the pleasure out at every level with increasing vigor since that is neither creative nor compassionate!

By "creative," I mean the virtual opposite of destructive. For example, in 1971, I received the Broken Spoon Award from the Weight Watchers organization because they considered my "Galloping Gourmet" television show the number one enemy to weight loss. It's odd now, but at that time I honestly thought I was just encouraging good creativity. My sole creative purpose in those days was to provide pleasure for those happy folk who enjoyed good food and good friends. I took it for granted that these same people, perhaps you or your parents, just naturally provided the "caring side" of cooking for their family on a day-to-day basis, which I never talked about on television.

Over the years, I have gradually come to see that our entire cooking experience for both friends and family is actually a continual balancing act between pleasing and caring. If the sole purpose of cooking is to please, then the pleasure you create will strongly reinforce a desire for a repeat performance.

If your sole purpose in cooking is caring, to the exclusion of pleasure, then the food could wind up being dull, bland, and colorless, thus bringing your loved ones to the point of rebellion, as happened in some of my earliest attempts at culinary change within my own family.

*Continual balancing act*

I have found that the secret of lasting success, to changing habits, is to wrap caring cuisine in pleasure. I have come to think of our sensual reaction to food as five individual experiences: aroma, appearance, texture, sizzle (hearing), and, of course, taste. Although taste always seems to rule the others, reacting strongly to sweet, sour, bitter, salt, and fat's tantalizing "mouthroundfulness," all my testing has shown that the other senses of smell, sight, touch, and even hearing are an essential "quartet backing for the taste-soloist." Even though these sensual reactions leave the mouth swiftly, they now can reinforce a positive habit pattern.

### A Large Dollop of Compassion

I'm convinced that for a personal life-style change to take place, there must be a large dollop of compassion shown along with both personal and medical care.

Compassion comes from the Greek word *splangisnomae*, from which is derived the word *spleen*, an organ found under the rib cage in the very middle of our bodies. This could well be the source of the phrase "gut reaction," and could easily explain why some people call compassion "a fellowship of suffering."

Compassion in and of itself does have a remarkable healing effect, and when it is missing, the results can be tragic. Last year, at a University Hospital of Cleveland seminar, a woman visiting from out of state told me that she recently had been hospitalized for an extended period. She said: "I felt like a disease that they wanted to go away, and if it didn't, then I represented a potential malpractice suit. All I wanted was to be treated like a human being who wanted to get well."

I hear so often from my medical friends that the real problem they face with either prevention or rehabilitation is compliance: a patient's willingness or ability to stick to a diet that includes exercise and behavioral change. My view is that compliance takes place only when it is encouraged with a mix of compassion and individual creativity.

## The Minimax Method

"Minimax," a term you'll see used throughout this and my previous books, describes two very different courses of action in preparing food, both of which must take place together.

MINI stands for minimizing known health risks because you care.

MAX stands for maximizing eating enjoyment by adding aroma, color and texture because you want to *please*.

*Minimizing risks* is an objective, scientific process that some might consider unpleasant. It may sound to you like a wrist-slapping, eat-it-up-it's-good for-you experience. Taken by itself it seems to ban such delights as cheese, cakes, cookies, pastries, hamburgers, fries and ice cream.

*Maximizing enjoyment*, on the other hand, is a subjective, emotional experience that feels good. We love the idea of warm aromas, bright, fresh colors and crisp, crunchy textures, as well as what I call "mouthroundfulness"—the luscious textural sense of smooth flowing richness that we *usually* associate with fat.

During my first years of experimenting with MINI, I made some major mistakes. I read scientific studies copiously and, as a result, developed a kind of food phobia. There seemed to be nothing left to eat that wasn't somehow contaminated. My family objected to the loss of enjoyment at our table.

In 1987, my wife, Treena, suffered a mild stroke and later, a spasm heart attack. During these events, we also discovered a number of genetic factors that put her at considerable health risk. I resolved to figure out how to help her enjoy the dietary and life-style changes she needed to make. It was at this precise moment that compassion joined with creativity to meet the needs of a specific individual. Soon after this, in 1988, Treena and I produced our first television series, designed to communicate my new cooking philosophy, called "Simply Marvellous."

## Your Food Preference List, First

In my book *Graham Kerr's Kitchen*, I included an innovative idea, a Food Preference List, that focused attention not so much on isolating foods that could have negative impacts, but upon those ingredients that you like and that also provide enjoyment and creativity from their aromas, colors, and textures. Taped to your refrigerator, it's a constant reminder of all the great ingredients at your disposal for enhancing cooking.

I present it to you again because it truly does provide information that can make diet change successful and delicious and, best of all, make it yours! Please take the time to read this list on page xvii.

## But Do You Want to Change?

After filling out all the lists and answering the questions, it's important that you ask yourself the staggering question, "Do I want to change?"

The answer to this question involves three elements. First is a willingness to eat less volume of certain specific foods. Second is the acceptance that there are far, far more foods and seasonings that you can add to your life than those you will take away. Third is to count the cost. No it won't cost you more in dollars and cents, it could even cost you less. What will change dramatically is the quality time you devote to the table.

It is true that we have shrunk our time at the dining table and transitioned it from a soothing hammock where both refreshment and relaxation occur, to a jarring trampoline upon which we take a microwave minute just to bounce en route to something else that we judge to be more important.

When you decide to change, your table habits will become very important. Your priorities will shift so that the time you spend cooking and eating is amply rewarded because it is now a significant act of creativity, compassion, and kindness.

So with that as a promise to you and your loved ones, let's get cracking and start experimenting with the recipes that will serve you best.

Let me know how you get on!

## Food Preference List

The Food Preference List is designed to give you a one-page snapshot of your eating

*Tape to your refrigerator*

habits. It helps you assess exactly what it is that you love about the foods you eat. You will notice that there are far more ingredients that have little or no fat than those that do—that's just the way it is!

If you fill one out for the people you most commonly cook for, then all you'll have to do is avoid the "dislikes." Start by trying to cut the fatty food portions in half, and adding more of the foods that have appealing flavors, colors, and aromas and no fat. With this one simple step, you will immediately cut your risk, and at the same time increase your enjoyment, because you've added more of the foods you love!

For instance, the other day I made a brown onion and wild mushroom sauce with de-alcoholized red wine. At my wife, Treena's, suggestion, I added an ingredient that we both really like, fresh ripe pear, to replace all the classic butter and bacon fat. It was delicious, and yet, nowhere to be found in the traditional kitchen.

This is a new era in food preparation, and we are all responsible for making healthier food taste really wonderful for those we love. So please, make photocopies of the Food Preference List, and have everyone in your family fill it out. Then write up a master list that highlights their likes and dislikes, and tape it to your refrigerator door.

Next time you start to cook one of your standard favorite recipes, remember the idea: Halve the fat and double the nonfat foods that they love.

# FOOD PREFERENCE LIST

*Check what you like, cross out what you don't like.*

## 1. Seasonings and Flavors

❑ Allspice ❑ Almond Extract ❑ Anchovies ❑ Basil ❑ Bay Leaf ❑ Canadian Bacon ❑ Capers ❑ Caraway Seed ❑ Cardamom ❑ Cayenne Pepper ❑ Chili Powder ❑ Chives ❑ Cilantro ❑ Cinnamon ❑ Cloves ❑ Cocoa ❑ Coconut Essence ❑ Coriander ❑ Cumin ❑ Curry Powder ❑ Dijon Mustard ❑ Dill Weed/Seed ❑ Fish Sauce ❑ Flowers—Edible ❑ Garam Masala ❑ Garlic ❑ Gingerroot ❑ Juniper Berries ❑ Kaffir Lime Leaves ❑ Lemon Grass ❑ Maple Syrup ❑ Mint ❑ Molasses ❑ Nutmeg ❑ Nuts ❑ Oregano ❑ Paprika ❑ Parmesan Cheese ❑ Parsley ❑ Pepper ❑ Rosemary ❑ Saffron ❑ Sage ❑ Salt—Sea ❑ Savory ❑ Sesame Oil ❑ Shallots ❑ Soy Sauce ❑ Strained Yogurt ❑ Sun-dried Tomatoes ❑ Tarragon ❑ Thyme ❑ Turmeric ❑ Vanilla ❑ Vinegars ❑ Worcestershire Sauce ❑ Zests of Citrus

## 2. Vegetables

❑ Artichokes ❑ Asparagus ❑ Beans—dried ❑ Beans—fresh ❑ Beets ❑ Bok Choy ❑ Broccoli ❑ Brussels Sprouts ❑ Cabbage ❑ Carrots ❑ Cauliflower ❑ Celery ❑ Corn ❑ Cucumbers ❑ Eggplants ❑ Fennel ❑ Green Onions ❑ Greens—Salad ❑ Jicama ❑ Kale ❑ Leeks ❑ Mushrooms ❑ Okra ❑ Onions ❑ Parsnips ❑ Peas—Dried ❑ Peas—Green ❑ Peppers—Hot ❑ Peppers—Sweet Bell ❑ Potatoes ❑ Radishes ❑ Rutabagas ❑ Spinach ❑ Sprouts ❑ Squash—Summer ❑ Squash—Winter ❑ Sweet Potatoes ❑ Swiss Chard ❑ Tomatillos ❑ Tomatoes ❑ Turnips ❑ Water Chestnuts ❑ Other

## 3. Fruit

❑ Apples ❑ Apricots ❑ Avocados ❑ Bananas ❑ Berries ❑ Cherries ❑ Cranberries ❑ Dates ❑ Figs ❑ Grapefruit ❑ Grapes ❑ Kiwifruit ❑ Lemons ❑ Limes ❑ Mangoes ❑ Nectarines ❑ Oranges ❑ Papayas ❑ Peaches ❑ Pears ❑ Persimmons ❑ Plums ❑ Prunes ❑ Raisins ❑ Rhubarb ❑ Tangerines ❑ Other

## 4. Main Ingredients

❑ Bacon ❑ Beans ❑ Beef ❑ Chicken ❑ Duck ❑ Eggs ❑ Egg Substitute ❑ Fish ❑ Game ❑ Game Hen ❑ Goose ❑ Grains ❑ Ham ❑ Lamb ❑ Pasta ❑ Pork ❑ Rice ❑ Sausage ❑ Shellfish ❑ Tofu ❑ Turkey ❑ Other

## 5. Food Styles

❑ Asian ❑ British ❑ Caribbean ❑ Chinese ❑ French ❑ Greek ❑ Indian ❑ Italian ❑ Japanese ❑ Northern European ❑ South American ❑ Spanish ❑ Thai ❑ USA/Northeast ❑ USA/Northwest ❑ USA/Southern ❑ USA/Southwest ❑ Other

## 6. Cooking Techniques

❑ Bake ❑ Boil ❑ Braise ❑ Broil ❑ Casserole ❑ Deep-Fry ❑ Étoufée ❑ Grill/Barbecue ❑ Microwave ❑ Poach ❑ Pressure-Cook ❑ Reduce Liquids ❑ Shallow-Fry/Sauté ❑ Skewer ❑ Smoke ❑ Soup/Stew ❑ Steam ❑ Stir-Fry ❑ Wrap Cookery

## Favorite Main Dishes and Desserts

*Write in the space provided your three favorite main dishes and desserts.*

_____

_____

_____

# The Recipes

### 20% Calories from Fat  139

Seafood
    Fish 'n' Chips 'n' Peas
    Salmon China Moon
    The Peacemaker
    Smoked Chilean Sea Bass
      with Thai Vinaigrette
    Salmon Mummies
Poultry
    Braised Turkey and
      Celery
    Chicken and Red Bell
      Pepper Pasta
    Chicken English Mehson
    Chicken Stir-Boil
    Coq au Vin
    Crêpes Antonin Carême
    Pizza Polese
    Pheasant & Chestnuts
    Evil Jungle Princess
    Pollo di Prince
    Poulet Basquaise
    Roast Chicken and
      Vegetables
    Roast Turkey with Apple-
      Orange Gravy, Swiss
      Chard, and Sweet
      Potatoes
    Sloppy Joes
Beef
    Fillet of Beef Meurice
    Broiled Hamburgers
    Hard-Hat Pizza
    Karewai Steak Piscatella
    Meat Loaf with Mushroom
      Sauce
    Steak Diane
    Scottish Beef Collops
Pork, Lamb, Veal & Venison
    Kare Poaka

Pirogen with Beet Salad
Lobscouse
Stuffed Pork Chops
Pork Tenderloin with Glazed
    Pears
Veal Buco with Saffron
    Risotto
Veal Pizzaiola with Fennel
    Risotto
Veal Risotto
Veal Sutton
Veal Weyerhaeuser
Venison with Spiced Pears
Pasta, Vegetables & Legumes
    Gold Medal Beans and Rice
    Christmas Risotto
    Orzo Pasta with Chicken
      and Red Peppers
    Sweet Stuff Pasta
    Vegetable Lasagne Roll-ups
    Radiatore
    Spaghetti Salmonara

### 30% Calories from Fat  227

Seafood
    Broiled Salmon Steak and
      Creamy Cucumber Sauce
    British Clay Bowl Salmon
      Pie and Sweet Corn Sauce
    Baked Herb-Garden Salmon
    Smoked Salmon with
      Barley Pilaf
    Thai-Style Sardines
Poultry
    Braised Chicken with
      Pepper Sauce and Polenta
    Chicken Fantengo
    Chicken Kebabs with
      Peanut Butter
      Spreadin'dipity

Chicken Polese
Chicken Yankova
Chicken Ultraburger
Crunchy-Top Turkey
Enchiladas Fina Cocina
Rock Cornish Game Hens
    & Pilaf Kirkland
Beef
    Roast Beef & Yorkshire
      Pancakes
    Slow Beef Curry
    Sancocho
    Steak and Oyster Pie
Pork, Lamb, Veal & Rabbit
    Harvest Succotash
    Hawke's Bay Lamb
    Lamb Shanks in a Polenta
      Pie
    Moussaka
    Hoppin' Skippin' John
    Pancit Luglug Palabok
    Orange-Braised Pork Chops
    Roast Pork with Fiesta Beans
      and Rice
    Roast Lamb with Apple-
      Orange Gravy
    Rabbit Casserole
    Rogan Josh
    Soul-Food Pork Roast with
      Glazed Vegetables
    Toltott Kaposzta
    Veal Hampshire
Pasta, Vegetables & Legumes
    Fondue and Salad
    Golden Threads Squash
    Spaghetti Carbonara
    Roasted Vegetable
      Quesadillas
    Cannelloni
    Tortellini Metropolitan

# 10% calories from fat

⊠

# Appetizers
# &
# Soups

# GARLIC HERB SPREAD

*A savory, Italian-style hors d'oeuvre dip or terrific spread on the toasted slices of Italian bread.*

*Time Estimate: Hands-on, 20 minutes; unsupervised, 45 minutes*

*Serves 8 (yields 1 1/4 cups)*

1 whole head garlic
4 dry-packed sun-dried tomato halves
1 cup strained yogurt (page 288)
1/2 teaspoon maple syrup
2 tablespoons chopped fresh basil
1/2 teaspoon red pepper flakes
1/4 teaspoon freshly ground sea salt
1 loaf hearty Italian bread

Preheat the oven to 375°F (190°C). Slice the top off the garlic head, about 1/2 inch (1.5 cm) from the top. Wrap the garlic in aluminum foil and bake in the preheated oven for 35 minutes. Lower temperature to 325°F (165°C). Remove the aluminum foil and allow to cool. Press the roasted garlic until all the flesh squeezes out. You will get 1 generous tablespoon of purée.

Bring the sun-dried tomatoes to a boil in a small amount of water in a small saucepan. Let sit for 15 minutes, then drain and lay on paper towels to dry. Chop finely.

Combine all the ingredients except the bread with a wire whisk in a medium bowl. Allow to sit for at least 30 minutes to let the flavors marry.

Slice sixteen 1/4-inch (2.25-cm) slices from the Italian loaf. Cut the slices in half if they're too big. Spread out on a baking sheet and bake at 325°F (165°C) for 15 minutes. They should be lightly toasted but not hard.

**To serve:** Offer the spread with the toasted bread as an hors d'oeuvre. It also makes a tasty vegetable dip, sandwich spread, or dressing for baked potatoes.

Nutritional Profile per Serving: Calories—97; % calories from fat—8%; fat (gm)—1 or 1% daily value; saturated fat (gm)—0; sodium (mg)—249; cholesterol (mg)—1; carbohydrates (gm)—17; dietary fiber (gm)—1.

# MASALA DOSA
## (INDIAN BEAN AND POTATO PANCAKES)

*This is southern India's answer to the American hamburger, the British sausage roll, and the Australian floater and peas. They are wonderfully delicious, full of flavor, and very low in fat. I owe the basic idea to Mrs. Usha Reddy and her team at The Bite of India, an excellent restaurant in Bellevue, Washington.*

*Time Estimate: Hands-on, 60 minutes; unsupervised, 11 hours*

*Serves 6*

DOSA (THE PANCAKE)

1¼ cups warm water
1¼ cups rice flour
1/2 cup split black lentils, washed, soaked for 3 hours in 3 cups water, and drained
1/2 cup water
1/8 teaspoon freshly ground sea salt

MASALA (THE FILLING)

1/2 teaspoon light olive oil with a dash of toasted sesame oil
2 large onions, peeled and thinly sliced
1 teaspoon finely chopped gingerroot
1/2 teaspoon whole cumin seeds
1/2 teaspoon whole black or yellow mustard seeds
2 jalapeño peppers, seeded and finely chopped
1/2 teaspoon turmeric
1 cup water
3 large potatoes, peeled, cut into 1/4-inch (.75-cm) cubes, boiled, and drained
1/4 teaspoon freshly ground sea salt
1/2 teaspoon garam masala (see below)
6 tablespoons mango chutney

GARNISH

1 mango, peeled and sliced
1 lime, cut into wedges

The night before serving, start the dosa: In a medium bowl, beat together the 1¼ cups warm water and rice flour. In a food processor, purée the lentils, the 1/2 cup water, and the salt. Add the rice flour mixture and purée again. Transfer the batter to a 6-quart bowl, cover, and put in a warm place, 80°F (27°C), overnight.

The day of serving, continue with the masala: In a 10-inch (25-cm) skillet, heat the oil and cook the onions until slightly translucent, about 2 minutes. Add the gingerroot, cumin and mustard seeds, and cook 8 minutes, stirring frequently to prevent scorching the mustard seeds. Stir in the jalapeño peppers and turmeric and cook 5 minutes. Add the water, stirring to deglaze the bottom of the pan. Add the boiled potatoes, stirring to combine, and cook 5 minutes. Season with the salt and garam masala and just heat through to allow the flavors to meld. Remove from the heat and set aside.

Finish the dosa: Spray a medium skillet with a little olive oil cooking spray and heat over medium-high. Whisk the batter until it's the consistency of a thin pancake batter, then spoon 1 cup into the center of the skillet and spread evenly to cover the bottom. Cook for 3 minutes or until the dosa starts to turn brown underneath and the top surface is just set. Do not flip it over, just remove and set aside. Repeat this process until you have 6 dosas. **Caution:** Do not stack the dosas!

To assemble: Spread each dosa with 1 tablespoon of the mango chutney and spoon 1/6 of the masala down the center. Fold the sides over and roll tightly into a cylinder.

To serve: Slice each filled pancake into 5 equal pieces and fan the pieces out on a plate in the shape of a star. Garnish with the mango and lime on the side. You can also eat Masala Dosa whole . . . as fast food.

Nutritional Profile per Serving: Calories—329; % calories from fat—5%; fat (gm)—2 or 5% daily value; saturated fat (gm)—0; sodium (mg)—153; cholesterol (mg)—0; carbohydrates (gm)—71; fiber (gm)—7.

Garam masala is an Indian condiment of mixed warming spices that is sprinkled on just like salt and pepper to give a great last-minute kick to curry or any strongly flavored dish. You can find this in specialty food stores or make your own in an electric coffee mill. Whiz together a 2-inch (5-cm piece of thin cinnamon stick—about 1/4 inch (.75 cm) diameter; 6 allspice berries, 1/4 teaspoon freshly ground nutmeg, and 4 whole cloves. The mixture does not include the coloring of turmeric or the heat of cayenne pepper whose sole purpose is to enhance aroma.

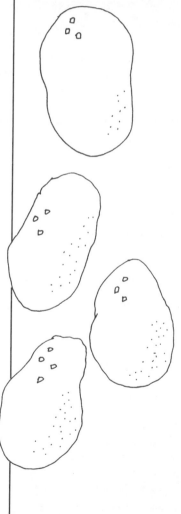

# Fava Bean Soup Procaccini

※

*This is the recipe that took away the dreaded "Broken Spoon Award!" Back in 1970, Weight Watchers gave me this "badge of dishonor" because of my liberal use of . . . well . . . everything! I created this dish for Nina Procaccini, who was head of recipe research for Weight Watchers, to demonstrate my new style of cooking. Fava beans are one of her favorite ingredients, and now, I hope, they will become one of yours!*

*Time Estimate: Hands-on, 30 minutes*
*Serves 6*

1 teaspoon light olive oil with a dash of toasted sesame oil
8 ounces (225 gm) sweet onions (I prefer Walla Walla), peeled and cut into 1/2-inch (1.5-cm) cubes
2 large cloves garlic, bashed, peeled, and thinly sliced
1/2 cup thinly sliced bulb fennel
1 (6-ounce or 175-gm) can no-salt tomato paste
1 quart water
Bouquet Garni (page 289)
1 (19-ounce or 540-gm) can fava beans
1/2 cup arugula
1/2 cup mustard greens
1 pound (450 gm) plum tomatoes, peeled and coarsely chopped
Freshly ground black pepper to taste

Heat the olive oil in a large soup pot over medium heat and fry the onions and garlic until soft. Add half the fennel, the tomato paste, and the water; stir and bring to a boil. Drop in the bouquet garni and fava beans, and simmer for 30 minutes.

Drop the arugula and mustard greens into a large pot of boiling water and blanch for 30 seconds. Plunge immediately into cold water to refresh. Slice the arugula and mustard greens and add them to the soup.

Push the chopped tomatoes through a sieve with a wooden "mushroom" or the back of a spoon. At the last minute, add the remaining fennel and the fresh tomato purée. Season with pepper to taste and serve.

Remember to remove the bouquet garni before serving the soup . . . it could get nasty if a wide-mouthed, talkative guest swallowed it!

Nutritional Profile per Serving: Calories—152; % calories from fat—10%; fat (gm)—2 or 2% daily value; saturated fat (gm)—.25; sodium (mg)—78; cholesterol (mg)—0; carbohydrates (gm)—29; dietary fiber (gm)—8.

---

To peel tomatoes, drop them into a pot of boiling water for a minute or two. The skin will split and start to peel back. Remove the tomatoes from the water. The skin will come off easily.

Sweating the vegetables: In practically all my soups, sauces, stocks, and casseroles, I use a standard technique called "sweating"—a process that involves cooking the vegetables in a small amount of olive oil, never more than 1 teaspoon. Sweating raises the temperature of the vegetables enough to release their aromatic and flavorful volatile oils.

# MINESTRONE

⁂

*Minestrone may be the world's best-known soup. In Italy, the recipe changes from region to region. The northern versions are unusually light, possibly due to the heavier main dishes that follow. In the south, they add sausage, ham, and pig's trotters with meat broth. I've adapted the Genoa method for a delicious main-dish soup.*

*Time Estimate: Hands-on, 45 minutes*
*Serves 6*

## BASIL PESTO

2 tablespoons chopped fresh basil leaves
2 tablespoons pine nuts
I clove garlic, peeled and bashed
I tablespoon freshly grated Pecorino Romano cheese

### OR

## PARSLEY PESTO

2 tablespoons chopped fresh parsley
I tablespoon dried basil
1/8 teaspoon light olive oil with a dash of toasted
   sesame oil
2 tablespoons pine nuts
I clove garlic, peeled and bashed
I tablespoon freshly grated Pecorino Romano cheese

## SOUP

I teaspoon light olive oil with a dash of toasted sesame oil
I onion, peeled and diced into 1/4-inch (.75-cm) pieces
2 stalks celery, finely diced
4 carrots, finely diced
8 ounces (225 gm) red new potatoes, quartered
7 cups water
4 ounces (115 gm) uncooked, small pasta shells
2 zucchini, quartered and sliced
2 tablespoons pesto (see recipes below)
I (15-ounce or 425-gm) can low-sodium cannellini
   (white kidney) beans, drained and well rinsed
2 cups peeled, seeded, and chopped plum tomatoes
1/2 teaspoon freshly ground sea salt
1/4 teaspoon freshly ground black pepper

## GARNISH

I tablespoon chopped fresh basil
6 tablespoons freshly grated Pecorino Romano cheese

**The basil pesto:** Place the basil on a cutting board. Smash the pine nuts and press together with the back of a knife to form a thick paste. Using the back of the knife, scrape and mix the basil, pine nuts, garlic, and cheese together into a well-combined paste.

### OR

**The parsley pesto:** On a cutting board, use a knife to chop the parsley, basil, and oil together into a paste. Smash the pine nuts, pressing with the back of the knife to form a thick paste and add to the parsley, along with the garlic and cheese.

**The soup:** In a large pot or Dutch oven, heat the oil and sauté the onion over medium-high heat until soft, about 2 minutes. Add the celery and carrots and cook 3 minutes. Add the potatoes and water and bring to a boil. Add the pasta shells and simmer for 10 minutes. Add the zucchini and simmer for another 10 minutes.

Transfer 1 cup of the soup to a small bowl. Sitr in the pesto until blended, then return this mixture to the soup pot. Add the beans, tomatoes, salt, and pepper and cook until heated through.

**To serve:** Spoon the Minestrone into individual serving bowls. Garnish with the basil and cheese.

Nutritional Profile per Serving: Calories—280; % calories from fat—16%; fat (gm)—4 or 13% daily value; saturated fat (gm)—2; sodium (mg)—294; cholesterol (mg)—8; carbohydrates (gm)—50; fiber (gm)—10.

# Seattle Clam Chowder

*New England clam chowders are velvet experiences—very dense, very white, very creamy. This was the standard we set out to match! I hope you like this creative alternative. It is very crisp, fawn colored, and almost Asian in its sweet and sour style. Serve with warm bread and salad, and it's a soul-satisfying meal.*

*Time Estimate: Hands-on, 60 minutes*
*Serves 6*

1 teaspoon light olive oil with a dash of toasted sesame oil
1 cup diced onion
3 tablespoons fresh thyme leaves
3 bay leaves
1 cup de-alcoholized white wine
3 cups fish stock (page 287)
6 pounds (2.7 kg) clams (yields 10 ounces [285 gm] meat)
3 cups peeled and diced potatoes
1½ cups chopped leeks
2 cups fresh or frozen corn kernels
3 tablespoons cornstarch mixed with 6 tablespoons water (slurry)
1 cup strained yogurt (page 288)
4 ounces (115 gm) Canadian bacon (5 thin slices), diced
1/4 teaspoon freshly ground black pepper
2 tablespoons chopped fresh parsley

Heat the olive oil in a high-sided casserole and sauté the onion, thyme, and bay leaves over medium-high heat until the onions are translucent, about 2 minutes. Stir in the de-alcoholized wine and a third of the fish stock and bring to a fierce boil. This becomes your steaming base.

Drop in the clams, making sure the steaming base stays at a boil. Cover and boil for 3 minutes. Using pot holders, lift the casserole, holding the lid tightly in place. Give a vertical shake, which will distribute the steaming base evenly throughout the clams. Place the casserole back on the burner and boil for another 3 minutes. Uncover and the clams will be wide open.

Discard any that remain firmly closed. Pour the clams and steaming base into a strainer or colander set over a large bowl to catch the juices. Shuck the clams, chop in half, and set aside.

Wash out the casserole, return it to the hot burner, and turn heat to high. Add the remaining 2 cups fish stock. Pour the reserved cooking juices through a strainer lined with muslin (this removes any sand particles from the juice) into the stock and boil for for 10 minutes. (You should have about 5 cups total, after boiling.) Strain once more, and return the reduced liquid to a large stock pot. Add the diced potatoes and simmer for 5 minutes. Stir in the leeks and simmer for 5 more minutes. Add 3/4 of the corn and cook for another 5 minutes. Transfer 1 cup of the broth from the chowder to a small bowl. Stir in the cornstarch slurry and the yogurt and mix thoroughly. Pour mixture back into the casserole, bring to a boil, and cook, stirring, for 30 seconds to thicken. Add the Canadian bacon, clams, and the remaining corn and simmer for 5 minutes. Season with the freshly ground pepper and parsley, and serve in bowls.

Nutritional Profile per Serving: Calories—297; % calories from fat—11%; fat (gm)—4 or 6% daily value; saturated fat (gm)—1; sodium (mg)—381; cholesterol (mg)—35; carbohydrates (gm)—45; dietary fiber (gm)—5.

# SHRIMP GUMBO

### ✦

*The Minimax version of this Creole classic is based on the marvelous rendition served by Chef Leah Chase at her fabulous restaurant in New Orleans, "Dooky Chase." One food critic called Leah's gumbo "the kind of dish that makes you want to throw down your spoon, rush into the kitchen and kiss the cook!" I hope this Minimax version inspires similar emotions—it could be the beginning of world peace!*

*Time Estimate: Hands-on, 55 minutes*
*Serves 4*

1 pound (450 gm) fresh uncooked shrimp, peeled (save shells), deveined, and cut into 3 pieces
6 cups water
1 cup uncooked long-grain rice
4 tablespoons all-purpose flour
2 (14-ounce or 400-gm) cans cut okra, drained
4 teaspoons light olive oil with a dash of toasted sesame oil
1 (6-ounce or 175-gm) can no-salt tomato paste
1 large white onion, peeled and chopped
3 stalks celery, chopped
2 green bell peppers, seeded and chopped
2 cloves garlic, bashed, peeled, and chopped
6 sprigs thyme
2 bay leaves
1/2 teaspoon cayenne pepper

GARNISH

Chopped green onions
Fresh chopped parsley

Put the shrimp shells into a medium saucepan and cover with 2 cups of the water. Bring to a boil and simmer for 2 minutes. Strain, discarding the shells, and return the cooking liquid to the saucepan. Add the rice and bring to a boil. Cover, reduce the heat, and simmer for 20 minutes or until all the liquid has been absorbed. Keep warm until serving.

Put the flour in a saucepan and cook over medium-high heat, stirring constantly until it turns light brown, about 6 minutes. Remove from the heat and cool. This step is crucial in developing a nice, toasty flavor and brown color for your gumbo.

Put the drained okra in a large plastic bag. Pour in the cooled flour. Seal the top and shake until the okra is completely coated with flour.

Heat 1 tablespoon of the oil in a large pot on medium-high heat. Add 1/2 of the flour-coated okra and the flour and cook until really brown, about 4 to 5 minutes. Repeat with the remaining okra. Push the okra to one side of the pot. On the other side of the pot, add the tomato paste and cook, stirring often, until it turns a dark brown, about 3 minutes. Now stir the tomato paste into the cut okra and turn it out onto a plate, scraping up all the tasty brown pan residue.

Add the remaining oil to the same pot and cook the onion, celery, green pepper, and garlic high heat for 5 minutes. Stir in the cooked okra, the remaining 4 cups of water, the thyme, bay leaves, and cayenne pepper and simmer 30 minutes.

Just before you're ready to serve, stir in the shrimp and cook until just heated through, about 4 minutes. The shrimp should not be overdone.

**To serve:** Spoon the cooked rice into bowls and sprinkle with the chopped green onion. Top with the shrimp gumbo and sprinkle with the chopped parsley.

Nutritional Profile per Serving: Calories—447; % calories from fat—14%; fat (gm)—7 or 11% daily value; saturated fat (gm)—1; sodium (mg)—184; cholesterol (mg)—107; carbohydrates (gm)—77; dietary fiber (gm)—14.

# POT OF GOLD, SPOON OF COMFORT

*Keep this in the refrigerator and use it whenever you want a delicious, low-fat method of thickening soups, pasta sauces, and so on. It will keep for two weeks.*

*Time Estimate: Hands-on, 15 minutes; unsupervised, 15 minutes*

*Makes 2 cups; about 16 2-tablespoon servings*

1 teaspoon light olive oil
1/4 teaspoon toasted sesame oil
1/2 yellow onion, peeled and finely chopped
1 (1-inch or 2.5-cm) cube fresh gingerroot, peeled and finely chopped
1 clove garlic, bashed, peeled, and minced
8 ounces (225 gm) dried red lentils
4 fresh sage leaves, finely sliced
1 teaspoon fresh thyme leaves
2 cups water

Pour the oils into a hot pressure cooker, add the onion, ginger, and garlic and fry for 30 seconds over medium-high heat. Add the lentils, herbs, and water, stirring to make sure nothing is sticking to the bottom of the pan and every lentil is scraped from the sides. Fasten the lid and bring to a boil. When the cooker starts to hiss, turn the heat down and let the lentils simmer for 15 minutes. Remove from the heat, release the steam, and unfasten the lid.

Spoon the lentils into a bowl or cover and keep on hand in the refrigerator, adding about 2 tablespoons to bowls of stew or soup or whenever you feel you need a "golden spoonful of comfort."

*Nutritional Profile per Serving: Calories—53; % calories from fat—9%; fat (gm)—1 or 1% daily value; saturated fat (gm)—.07; sodium (mg)—1; cholesterol (mg)—0; carbohydrates (gm)—9; dietary fiber (gm)—2.*

# 10% calories from fat

⌘

# Entrées

# Catfish with Orange Sauce

⬚

*This ginger-infused orange sauce is an elegant touch for many dishes. Try it with a boneless chicken breast and rice pilaf.*

Time Estimate: Hands-on, 35 minutes
Serves 4

## SAUCE

1/4 teaspoon light olive oil
1/4 teaspoon toasted sesame oil
4 green onions, separated into white parts, finely chopped, and dark green parts, minced and reserved for garnish
8 quarter-size slices peeled gingerroot
1 clove garlic, bashed, peeled, and chopped
1½ cups freshly squeezed orange juice
2 teaspoons cornstarch mixed with 4 teaspoons orange juice (slurry)
1 orange, peeled and divided into segments, zest reserved for garnish, pith removed (if you separate the segments over a small bowl, you can use the excess juice to make the cornstarch slurry)

## CATFISH

4 (4-ounce or 115-gm) catfish fillets
1/2 teaspoon sesame oil
1/4 cup freshly squeezed orange juice
1/8 teaspoon freshly ground sea salt
1/8 teaspoon freshly ground black pepper

## SIDE DISHES

12 red new potatoes
8 ounces (225 gm) carrots, coarsely chopped
8 ounces (225 gm) broccoli florets

**The orange sauce:** Pour the oils into a small saucepan over medium heat and cook the white parts of the chopped green onions for 1 minute. Add the ginger and garlic and cook 2 minutes. Pour in the orange juice and bring to a boil. Reduce the heat and simmer 8 minutes. Remove from the heat and set aside.

**The catfish:** Pour 1/2 inch (1.5 cm) of water into the bottom of a roasting pan. Lay the catfish on the rack in the roasting pan, brush with the sesame oil and orange juice, sprinkle with the salt and pepper, and pop under the broiler for 8 minutes [the rack should be 4 inches (10 cm) from the heat source].

**The side dishes:** While the catfish is broiling, start the potatoes steaming. After 4 minutes, add the carrots; 3 minutes later, add the broccoli and cook another 5 minutes, for a total steaming time of 12 minutes.

Just before serving, strain the orange sauce into a small bowl, pressing firmly on the solids to extract the pulp from the vegetables; return to the same saucepan. Pour in a little of the cornstarch slurry, bring to a boil, and stir until thickened, adding more of the cornstarch slurry until the sauce coats the back of a spoon, about 30 seconds. Remove from the heat, stir in the orange segments, and set aside.

**To serve:** Divide the fish, potatoes, and vegetables among 4 dinner plates. Spoon the sauce over the fish and sprinkle with the minced dark green onion tops and orange zest slivers.

Nutritional Profile per Serving: Calories—522; % calories from fat—6%; fat (gm)—3 or 5% daily value; saturated fat (gm)—1; sodium (mg)—244; cholesterol (mg)—69; carbohydrates (gm)—91; dietary fiber (gm)—9.

# Orange Roughy Poached in Vinaigrette

*The wonderful fresh flavors of mint and lime are brightened with fresh ginger, spicy chili paste, and balsamic vinegar. Then the pineapple smooths it all out and pulls it together. Use vinaigrette ice cubes (page 144–45) or just whip it up fresh in minutes.*

*Time Estimate: Hands-on, 25 minutes*
*Serves 4*

1/2 teaspoon light olive oil with a dash of toasted
    sesame oil
1 yellow onion, peeled and chopped
2 cubes (1/4 cup) frozen Vinaigrette (page 144–45)
1/4 cup low-sodium chicken stock (page 286)
1 cup chopped pineapple
8 thin quarter-size slices fresh gingerroot, finely diced
1/4 teaspoon roasted chili paste
1 tablespoon balsamic vinegar
4 (4-ounce or 125-gm) orange roughy fillets
4 cups cooked long-grain white rice
2 tablespoons shredded fresh mint
1/2 teaspoon red chili flakes

Heat the oil in a small skillet over medium heat and fry the onion for 3 minutes or until wilted but not brown. In a large skillet, heat the vinaigrette cubes until melted, then stir in the cooked onion, chicken stock, pineapple, ginger, chili paste, and balsamic vinegar. Place the fish fillets on top, cover, and simmer gently for 8 minutes.

Serve the fish and vegetables immediately with the rice, sprinkled with the fresh mint and chili flakes.

Nutritional Profile per Serving: Calories—359; % calories from fat—8%; fat (gm)—3 or 5% daily value; saturated fat (gm)—1; sodium (mg)—117; cholesterol (mg)—62; carbohydrates (gm)—53; dietary fiber (gm)—2.

# Couscous

*In North Africa, there is a wealth of wonderful, colorful, and aromatic dishes. I took a classic couscous, served with local Mediterranean tuna, and made it possible to fix this version after just one trip to a good supermarket. The result could be a breakthrough for both your family and your friends.*

*Time Estimate: Hands-on, 60 minutes*

Serves 6

## HARISSA SEASONING

6 dried red chili peppers
1/4 teaspoon caraway seeds
1/4 teaspoon cumin seeds
1/2 teaspoon coriander
1 clove garlic

## COUSCOUS

1 teaspoon light olive oil with a dash of toasted sesame oil
2 medium onions, peeled and thickly sliced
2 cloves garlic, bashed, peeled, and diced
1 green bell pepper, seeded and thickly sliced
1 red bell pepper, seeded and thickly sliced
1 yellow bell pepper, seeded and thickly sliced
1 fresh jalapeño pepper, seeded and chopped
1/2 teaspoon chopped fresh thyme
1 zucchini, cut into 1/2-inch (1.25-cm) cubes
2 cups instant couscous
6 cups low-sodium fish stock (page 287)
3 large tomatoes, peeled, seeded, and coarsely chopped
1/4 cup chopped fresh parsley
1 pound (450 gm) fresh sole fillets, cut diagonally across the fillets into 1-inch (2.5-cm) slices
1/4 teaspoon freshly ground sea salt

**The Harissa seasoning:** In a small coffee grinder or food processor, whiz the dried red peppers, caraway seeds, cumin seeds, coriander, and garlic. Spoon into a small bowl and set aside. If you have any difficulty finding these spices in their whole form, purchase them ground. The result will lack some pungency, but not enough to discourage one from trying this recipe.

**The couscous:** Heat the oil in a large Dutch oven or pot over medium heat and fry the onions for 1 minute. Add the garlic and cook 2 minutes longer. Stir in the bell peppers, the jalapeño, thyme, and zucchini and cook 5 minutes. Add the instant couscous, 3½ cups of the fish stock, and half of the tomatoes; stir well and bring to a boil. Cover, remove from the heat, and let stand for 5 minutes. Uncover and add the remaining tomatoes and the parsley. Stir gently, cover, and set aside.

**The sauce:** In a saucepan, bring the remaining 2½ cups of fish stock to a boil. Stir in 1 teaspoon of the Harissa seasoning and the sole slices. Cover, remove from the heat, and let stand for 3 minutes; drain, reserving the stock. Mix the remaining Harissa seasoning into the fish stock to make a sauce.

**To serve:** Spoon the couscous into 6 individual soup bowls. Spoon 1/6 of the sole on top of the couscous and serve the Harissa sauce on the side, allowing your guests to choose the amount of spice they would like to add to their life—or at least their couscous.

Nutritional Profile per Serving: Calories—388; % calories from fat—9%; fat (gm)—4 or 6% daily value; saturated fat (gm)—1; sodium (mg)—231; cholesterol (mg)—35; carbohydrates (gm)—63; dietary fiber (gm)—6.

# CREOLE FISH DUMPLINGS

*This fusion of Southern United States and traditional Jewish cooking comes from Ratner's Restaurant in New York City. With its pungent spices and herbs mellowed in a tomato and bell pepper sauce, it's perfect for our purposes. The tender, little fish balls remind me of* quenelles *but without the traditional use of cream.*

*Time Estimate: Hands-on, 45 minutes*
*Serves 4*

1⅓ cups uncooked long-grain white rice
1/8 teaspoon freshly ground sea salt

## SAUCE

1 teaspoon light olive oil with a dash of toasted sesame oil
1 onion, finely chopped
3 cloves garlic, bashed, peeled, and chopped
1 green bell pepper, seeded and chopped
1/2 cup sliced mushrooms
1¾ cups low-sodium diced tomatoes, in juice
1 cup fish stock (page 287)
1 tablespoon fresh thyme leaves
1/4 teaspoon crushed red pepper flakes
1/2 teaspoon ground cumin
1 tablespoon freshly squeezed lemon juice
2 teaspoons grated lemon zest
1/4 teaspoon freshly ground sea salt
1/4 teaspoon freshly ground black pepper
1 bay leaf

## FISH DUMPLINGS

1/4 cup nonfat milk
1 slice country-style white bread, torn into small pieces
1/4 pound (115 gm) raw shrimp meat
3/4 pound (350 gm) rockfish or red snapper
1/4 cup finely chopped green pepper
1/4 cup finely chopped onion
1 large egg white, slightly beaten
1/4 teaspoon freshly ground sea salt
1/4 teaspoon freshly ground black pepper

## GARNISH

2 tablespoons chopped fresh parsley

Bring 4 cups of water to a boil in a large saucepan, add the rice and salt, and boil for 15 minutes. Strain in a metal sieve, put the rice-filled sieve over a pan of boiling water, and steam, covered, for 5 minutes.

**The sauce:** Heat the oil in a high-sided skillet over medium-high heat and fry the onion for 1 minute. Add the garlic and cook for 30 seconds more. Toss in the green peppers and mushrooms and cook for 2 minutes. Add the remaining ingredients and simmer, uncovered, for 15 minutes.

**The fish dumplings:** While the sauce is simmering, pour the milk over the bread pieces in a small bowl. Cut the shrimp and fish into small chunks and pulse in a food processor until coarsely ground but not a fine paste. Scrape out into a mixing bowl and add the remaining dumpling ingredients, including the milk-soaked bread. With slightly moistened hands to prevent sticking, mix well and form into 16 small balls. Lay the dumplings on top of the sauce, cover, and simmer for 10 minutes. Turn and cook for another 5 minutes.

**To serve:** Divide the rice among 4 warm plates. Cover the rice with the sauce and arrange 4 dumplings on the side. Sprinkle the parsley over all.

Nutritional Profile per Serving: Calories—442; % calories from fat—8%; fat (gm)—4 or 6% daily value; saturated fat (gm)—1; sodium (mg)—442; cholesterol (mg)—86; carbohydrates (gm)—70; dietary fiber (gm)—4.

# CRÊPES FRUITS DE MER

*This dish comes from my past! My parents opened Gravetye Manor near East Grinstead, in England, in 1958. We originally invented this dish for the head of the seafood company Young's. He was delighted! Now it is re-invented for you.*

*Time Estimate: Hands-on, 60 minutes*
*Serves 4*

## CRÊPE BATTER (YIELDS 8 CREPES)

1/2 cup all-purpose flour
1 whole egg
1 egg yolk
1 cup nonfat milk
1 teaspoon light olive oil with a dash of toasted sesame oil
8 fresh sprigs dill

## SEAFOOD FILLING

1 (15-ounce or 425-gm) can cooked butter beans, drained and rinsed
1/2 cup de-alcoholized white wine
3 cups nonfat milk
12 ounces (350 gm) sole, preferably Petrale, cut in finger-size strips
6 ounces (175 gm) sea scallops
3/4 cup button mushrooms, quartered, unless very small
2 tablespoons arrowroot mixed with 4 tablespoons de-alcoholized white wine (slurry)
1 teaspoon finely chopped fresh dill
1/8 teaspoon cayenne pepper
6 plum tomatoes, peeled, seeded, and chopped
1 tablespoon chopped fresh parsley
6 ounces (175 gm) small, precooked salad shrimp
2 tablespoons freshly grated Parmesan cheese

## GARNISH

1 lemon, cut into wedges
Chopped fresh parsley

**The crêpe batter:** In a medium bowl, combine the flour, eggs, and milk and let stand for 30 minutes.

Swish the oil around a hot crêpe pan over medium-high heat to prepare the surface, then pour the excess oil into the batter. Mix in well. This will make each crêpe self-releasing.

Pour a small ladle of the batter into the hot crêpe pan. When it begins to bubble and look waxy, gently loosen the edges. Place a fresh dill sprig on the cooked surface and flip the crêpe over. Cook for 30 seconds, then transfer to a dish. Cook the remaining crêpes in the same manner. Cover them with a damp towel to await filling.

**The seafood filling:** Purée the butter beans and 1/4 cup of the wine in a food processor to make a paste. Set aside and reserve.

Heat the milk in a large skillet over medium heat. Place the sole strips, sea scallops, and mushrooms in the milk. Poach for 4 to 5 minutes; do not boil. Remove seafood and mushrooms from the milk and keep warm.

Take out 1 cup of the poaching milk and place it in a small saucepan. Add half the arrowroot slurry, place over medium heat, and cook until thickened. This is the finishing sauce.

Add remaining 1/4 cup wine to the milk in the large skillet. Stir in the remaining arrowroot mixture to thicken and add 1/2 cup of the butter bean paste. Return the poached fish mixture to the sauce along with the dill and cayenne. Gently stir in the tomatoes and chopped parsley for color and the small shrimp for flavor.

Lay the reserved crêpes in an ovenproof pan, dill side down. Fill each one with an equal amount of the fish mixture and fold. Turn seam side down. Pour the sauce over the herbed tops—they should just show through. Sprinkle with the Parmesan cheese and place under the preheated broiler until the cheese melts and browns, about 2 minutes.

**To serve:** Place 2 crêpes on each plate with the sliced lemons on the side and a good scattering of the chopped parsley.

Nutritional Profile per Serving: Calories—542; % calories from fat—14%; fat (gm)—8 or 13% daily value; saturated fat (gm)—2; sodium (mg)—741; cholesterol (mg)—250; carbohydrates (gm)—61; dietary fiber (gm)—11.

# EASTERN-EXPOSURE SQUID

*The future will undoubtedly see the squid become one of the world's most popular foods. There is only 28 percent preparation waste, the flesh is super lean and 18 percent protein. Already the quantity of squid eaten is staggering, with a catch of between 100 and 300 million tons a year. So why not start in on the future today and try this recipe?*

*Time Estimate: Hands-on, 35 minutes*
*Serves 4*

8 ounces uncooked spaghetti
2 teaspoons light olive oil with a dash of toasted sesame oil
8 ounces (225 gm) calamari, cleaned and cut into 1/4-inch (.75-cm) rings
1 clove garlic, bashed, peeled, and chopped
1 (2-inch or 5-cm) piece of gingerroot, finely chopped
1/2 teaspoon red pepper flakes
1 (5-ounce or 150-gm) can sliced water chestnuts, drained and rinsed
3 stalks bok choy, leaves separated from stalks and reserved separately, both thinly sliced
6 green onions, sliced diagonally
1 large red bell pepper, seeded and very finely sliced
1 tablespoon brown sugar
3 tablespoons low-sodium soy sauce
1 teaspoon toasted sesame oil
1 teaspoon arrowroot mixed with 1/4 cup rice wine vinegar (slurry)

GARNISH

1 tablespoon toasted sesame seeds
2 tablespoons chopped fresh cilantro

Bring 6 quarts of water to a boil and cook the pasta according to package directions until just tender. Drain and set in a colander over a pot of hot water to keep warm.

Pour half of the oil into a wok or large skillet over medium heat and cook the squid ringlets, tossing continuously, for 2 minutes. You will notice the squid turning white and the edges curling gently. Be careful not to overcook the squid or the meat will turn rubbery. Remove the squid from the pan and set aside.

Add the remaining oil to the same wok or skillet over medium heat and cook the garlic, ginger, and red pepper flakes for 15 seconds. Add the water chestnuts, bok choy stalks, and green onions and cook, stirring frequently, for 3 minutes. Add the red bell pepper and cook for 1 minute. Add the brown sugar and soy sauce and cook just until the sugar is dissolved.

Add the reserved squid and heat through. Add the cooked pasta and the bok choy leaves, sprinkle with the sesame oil, and toss gently. Remove from the heat and stir in the arrowroot slurry. Return to the heat and stir until the pasta is a glossy brown and all ingredients are well incorporated.

**To serve:** Spoon onto dinner plates and sprinkle with the sesame seeds and chopped cilantro. This dish can be served as an elegant main course, or as an appetizer by cutting the portion size in half.

Nutritional Profile per Serving: Calories—385; % calories from fat—15%; fat (gm)—7 or 10% daily value; saturated fat (gm)—1; sodium (mg)—508; cholesterol (mg)—136; carbohydrates (gm)—63; dietary fiber (gm)—5.

To toast sesame seeds, place them in a heavy-bottom skillet over medium-high heat. Cook, shaking pan and stirring, until they turn golden brown, about 2 or 3 minutes. They can also be toasted in a 350°F oven. Place seeds in a pie tin and bake in the preheated oven, shaking pan occasionally, for 5 minutes.

# Fresh Tuna in Nectarine Sauce

*A tuna steak is a hearty, juicy piece of fish, great for grilling or broiling. I've chosen a nectarine "salsa" as the tuna's zesty, colorful sauce. And by all means, if you can't find tuna, substitute a boneless chicken breast.*

*Time Estimate: Hands-on, 30 minutes; unsupervised, 12 minutes*

*Serves 2*

3 medium nectarines, pitted and chopped (papaya may be substituted)
6 tablespoons green onions, white and green parts, thinly sliced
1 jalapeño pepper, finely chopped (seeded if you like it mild; seeds left in if you like it hot)
3 tablespoons freshly squeezed lime juice
4 tablespoons chopped fresh cilantro
1/4 teaspoon freshly ground sea salt
1 teaspoon brown sugar (optional, depending on the sweetness of the nectarines)
1 teaspoon light olive oil with a dash of toasted sesame oil
12 ounces (350 gm) fresh tuna, preferably yellowfin
2 cups hot cooked white rice
3 cups shredded fresh spinach

**The salsa:** Combine the chopped nectarines, 1/4 cup of the onions, jalapeño, 2 tablespoons of the lime juice, 2 tablespoons of the cilantro, 1/8 teaspoon of the salt, and the brown sugar. Set aside to mellow while you prepare the rest of the meal.

**The tuna:** Heat the broiler or barbecue. Pour the oil, the remaining tablespoon of lime juice, and the rest of the salt on a plate and gently mop it up with the tuna, making sure each piece is lightly oiled on both sides. Broil or grill the tuna steaks about 6 minutes on each side. While the tuna is cooking, stir the remaining 2 tablespoons of green onions and 1 tablespoon of the cilantro into the hot rice.

**To serve:** Scatter the shredded spinach over each warm plate. Make a circle of rice on top of the spinach and place a tuna steak in the center. Spoon the nectarine salsa across the top. Sprinkle the rest of the cilantro over the whole plate.

Nutritional Profile per Serving: Calories—552; % calories from fat—10%; fat (gm)—6 or 9% daily value; saturated fat (gm)—1; sodium (mg)—473; cholesterol (mg)—82; carbohydrates (gm)—87; dietary fiber (gm)—7.

# GLAZED HALIBUT FILLETS

*Snow-white halibut fillets are served with brightly colored vegetables and glazed with a buttery-yellow saffron sauce. Everything is steamed in one pot and ready at exactly the same time.*

*Time Estimate: Hands-on, 25 minutes;*
   *unsupervised, 8 minutes*

*Serves 4*

4 (4-inch or 10-cm) sprigs fresh dill
1 bay leaf
4 (4-inch or 10-cm) sprigs fresh thyme
3 whole cloves
4 (6-ounce or 175-gm) fresh halibut fillets
1/4 teaspoon ground cumin
1/2 teaspoon chopped fresh dill
Zest of 1/2 lemon, grated
1/2 cup chopped onion
4 medium zucchini (6 inches or 15 cm), coarsely
   chopped
1 cup (1/2 large) coarsely chopped sweet red pepper
1 cup (1/2 large) coarsely chopped sweet yellow pepper
1/8 teaspoon freshly ground sea salt
1/4 teaspoon freshly ground black pepper
3 cups hot cooked white rice tossed with 2 tablespoons
   chopped fresh dill

## GLAZE

1/2 cup cooking liquid (from above)
1/2 cup de-alcoholized dry white wine
1 tablespoon freshly squeezed lemon juice
1/16 teaspoon saffron powder
2 teaspoons cornstarch mixed with 1 tablespoon de-
   alcoholized white wine (slurry)

## GARNISH

Chopped fresh dill
Freshly ground black pepper

Pour about 1/2 inch (1.25 cm) of water into a large steamer pot, add the dill, bay leaf, thyme, and cloves and bring to a vigorous boil for 2 minutes.

Arrange the halibut on a plate that will fit into a steamer tray. Sprinkle with the cumin, dill, and lemon zest and set the plate in the first steamer tray.

Spread the vegetables in a second steamer tray and sprinkle with the salt and pepper. Put the halibut tray into the hot steamer first and top with the vegetable tray. Cover and steam for 8 minutes. Remove the trays and set aside while you make the glaze.

**The glaze:** Strain the water from the steamer into a bowl. Pour 1/2 cup of the steaming liquid, the wine, lemon juice, and saffron back into the steamer pot. Cook over high heat for 3 minutes. Remove from the heat, stir in the cornstarch slurry, return to the heat, and cook to clear and thicken, about 30 seconds.

**To serve:** Arrange the halibut, vegetables, and cooked rice on warm dinner plates. Brush the fish and vegetables with the glaze and garnish with the dill and pepper.

Nutritional Profile per Serving: Calories—346; % calories from fat—6%; fat (gm)—2 or 2% daily value; saturated fat (gm)—1; sodium (mg)—193; cholesterol (mg)—74; carbo-hydrates (gm)—49; dietary fiber (gm)—5.

# HALIBUT A-2-VAY

—— ✦ ——

*The French call this method poêle or poêlage or étuvée (pronounced "A-2-Vay"). The idea is simply to sauté in a covered pan so that the steam and fat combine to cook the food. In this case, I've created a leek, mushroom, and lemon bed spiked with cayenne, mustard, and white wine to cook the fish—absolutely delicious! The vegetables blend well and make a complete dinner in just over 10 minutes cooking time.*

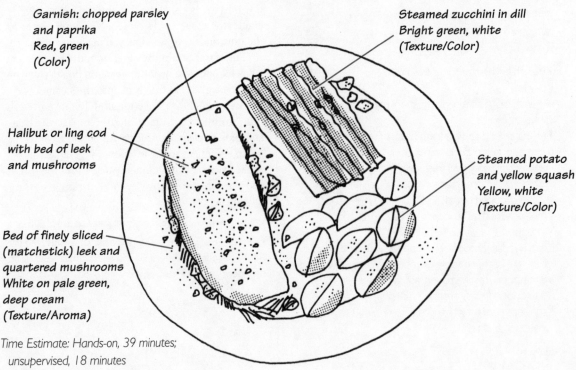

**Garnish: chopped parsley and paprika**
Red, green
(Color)

**Steamed zucchini in dill**
Bright green, white
(Texture/Color)

**Halibut or ling cod with bed of leek and mushrooms**

**Steamed potato and yellow squash**
Yellow, white
(Texture/Color)

**Bed of finely sliced (matchstick) leek and quartered mushrooms**
White on pale green, deep cream
(Texture/Aroma)

Time Estimate: Hands-on, 39 minutes;
unsupervised, 18 minutes
Serves 4

2 leeks, root ends trimmed and discarded
1 teaspoon light olive oil with a dash of toasted sesame oil
12 ounces (350 gm) white mushrooms, quartered
2½ teaspoons coarsely chopped fresh dill or 2 teaspoons dried dill
1/8 teaspoon cayenne pepper
2 tablespoons freshly squeezed lemon juice
4 (6-ounce or 175-gm) halibut steaks, with skin on
1/8 teaspoon freshly ground sea salt
1/4 teaspoon freshly ground black pepper
2/3 cup de-alcoholized white wine

2 large russet potatoes, peeled and sliced into 1/4-inch (.75-cm) rounds
2 medium yellow summer squash, trimmed to equal lengths and sliced into 1/4-inch (.75-cm) rounds
4 medium zucchini, trimmed to equal lengths and cut in half lengthwise
1 teaspoon arrowroot mixed with 2 teaspoons de-alcoholized white wine (slurry)

GARNISH

1 tablespoon finely chopped fresh parsley
Paprika

Cut the trimmed leeks into two parts: the light green stem and the dark top. Slice the light green part into long, fine matchsticks (a hand-held mandolin works very well for this) and set aside. Save the dark green tops for other uses.

Heat the oil in a large skillet over medium heat and shallow-fry the leeks, mushrooms, 1 teaspoon of the dill, and the cayenne pepper for 4 minutes. Stir in the lemon juice and spread the cooked vegetables out to make a "bed."

Lay the halibut fillets on the vegetable bed and sprinkle with the salt and pepper. Pour half of the wine around the outside edge of the pan and swirl around to mix thoroughly; cover and cook over medium heat for 6 minutes.

Bring the water in a large pot to a full boil. Place the potato slices in a steamer tray and cook for 8 minutes. After 4 minutes, place the squash and zucchini in a second steamer tray and sprinkle with 1/2 teaspoon of the dill. Add to the steamer and cook for 4 minutes. Remove from the heat.

Remove the halibut from the pan, cover to keep warm, and set aside. To the leeks and mushrooms, add the remaining 1/3 cup wine and the rest of the dill and "deglaze" the pan, scraping the bottom of the pan to lift any pan residue flavor into the vegetables, about 1 minute. Stir in the arrowroot slurry and cook until thickened. Remove from the heat.

**To serve:** Make a bed of the cooked leeks and mushrooms on one side of each dinner plate and nestle a halibut piece on top. Alternate the white, yellow, and green slices of potatoes and squash on the side. Sprinkle with the sparkling green parsley and bright red paprika as a final touch.

| Nutritional Profile per Serving | | | |
|---|---|---|---|
| | Classic | Minimax | Daily Value |
| Calories | 973 | 358 | |
| Calories from fat | 75% | 12% | |
| Fat (gm) | 81 | 5 | 8% |
| Saturated fat (gm) | 11 | 1 | 5% |
| Sodium (mg) | 409 | 200 | 8% |
| Cholesterol (mg) | 120 | 74 | 25% |
| Carbohydrates (gm) | 20 | 49 | 16% |
| Dietary fiber (gm) | 6 | 12 | 48% |
| Classic compared: Halibut Salad | | | |

# HALIBUT CALIENTE

——— ✜ ———

*I'm using an old recipe here with a new twist—springboarding! Try it yourself with
your favorite seasonings and vegetables.*

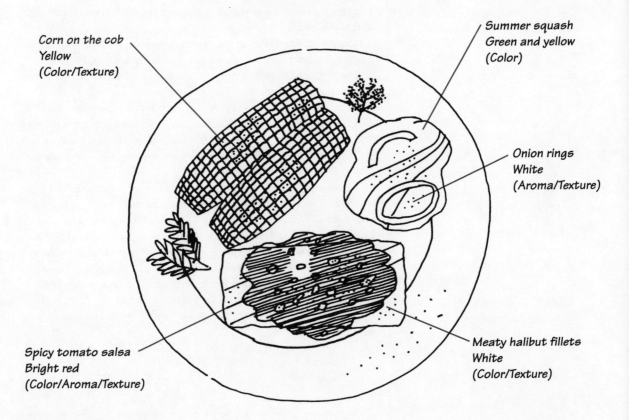

**Corn on the cob
Yellow
(Color/Texture)**

**Summer squash
Green and yellow
(Color)**

**Onion rings
White
(Aroma/Texture)**

**Spicy tomato salsa
Bright red
(Color/Aroma/Texture)**

**Meaty halibut fillets
White
(Color/Texture)**

*Time Estimate: Hands-on, 25 minutes;
  unsupervised, 12 minutes*
*Serves 2*

6 tablespoons low-sodium salsa, your choice of hotness
1/8 teaspoon freshly ground sea salt
2 (6-ounce or 175-gm) halibut fillets
4 small ears fresh or frozen corn
1 thick slice sweet onion, separated into rings
1 medium zucchini, sliced

1 medium yellow summer squash, sliced
1/8 teaspoon freshly ground sea salt
1 teaspoon arrowroot mixed with 2 teaspoons water
  (slurry)
1 tablespoon chopped fresh cilantro

Pour about 1 inch of water in the bottom of a large pot, cover, and bring to a rapid boil. Spoon 2 tablespoons of the salsa onto a plate that will just fit into a steamer tray. Set the halibut fillets on the plate and drizzle with 2 more tablespoons of the salsa. Set the plate in the steamer tray.

Lay the corn around the outside of a second steamer tray and the onion in the middle. Set the first steamer tray into the pot and put the second tray on top; cover and cook for 5 minutes. Remove the cover and scatter the sliced zucchini and squash over the top of the onion. Sprinkle with salt and top with the last 2 tablespoons of salsa; cover and cook for 5 more minutes.

**To serve:** Place 2 pieces of the cooked corn, 1 halibut fillet, and half the zucchini, yellow squash, and onion on each warm plate. Pour the liquid from the halibut steaming plate into a small saucepan and bring to a boil; remove from the heat. Stir in the arrowroot slurry, return to the heat, and cook until it clears and thickens. This will happen almost instantly. Pour the sauce over the corn, sprinkle the cilantro on the fish, zucchini, and squash and serve.

| Nutritional Profile per Serving | | | |
|---|---|---|---|
| | **Classic** | **Minimax** | **Daily Value** |
| Calories | 638 | 363 | |
| Calories from fat | 30% | 6% | |
| Fat (gm) | 21 | 2 | 3% |
| Saturated fat (gm) | 11 | 1 | 5% |
| Sodium (mg) | 576 | 273 | 11% |
| Cholesterol (mg) | 138 | 74 | 25% |
| Carbohydrates (gm) | 74 | 55 | 18% |
| Dietary fiber (gm) | 12 | 7 | 28% |
| Classic compared: Fish with Parsley Sauce | | | |

# JAMBALAYA

*This famous Creole dish from the southeastern United States is always served as it cooks, from pot to plate. From 704 calories and 41 grams of fat in the classic recipe, you have before you a dish with just 332 calories and 5 grams of fat. Enjoy it with a crisp green salad tossed in a tangy vinaigrette.*

Time Estimate: Hands-on, 75 minutes;
  unsupervised, 75 minutes
Serves 6

1 teaspoon fresh thyme leaves
1/8 teaspoon whole cloves
1/2 teaspoon cayenne pepper
1 pound (450 gm) smoked ham hocks
4 bay leaves
1¾ pounds (800 gm) uncooked shrimp/prawns, in their
  shells
2 cups boiling water
1½ cups uncooked Louisiana or converted long-grain
  rice, rinsed
1 teaspoon light olive oil with a dash of toasted sesame oil
1 onion, peeled and chopped
2 cloves garlic, bashed, peeled, and chopped
1/2 cup chopped celery
1 tablespoon no-sodium tomato paste
1 (28-ounce or 800-gm) can plum tomatoes, drained
  and coarsely chopped
1/4 cup chopped fresh parsley

Place the thyme, cloves, and cayenne pepper in a coffee grinder or a small food mill and grind the spices to a powder. Set aside.

Place the ham hocks in a large pot, cover with cold water, and bring to a boil; boil 5 minutes. Strain the hocks and discard the water.

Place the cooked ham hocks in a large pot. Pour in 4 cups of fresh water, stir in the bay leaves, and simmer 1 hour, or pressure-cook for 20 minutes. Remove the ham hocks and cut away all the lean meat. Chop meat into small pieces and set aside. Boil the reserved liquid until reduced to 2 cups. Skim off any fat that rises to the surface.

Cook the shrimp for 3 minutes in 2 cups of boiling water. Strain the shrimp, pouring the cooking liquid into the ham hock cooking liquid. Submerge the cooked shrimp directly in ice water; when cool enough to handle, peel, devein, and slice in half lengthwise. Return the shells to the ham hock stock and boil until reduced to 3 cups. Stir in half of the spice powder.

Pour the reduced stock into a saucepan and bring to a boil. Stir in the rice and simmer, covered, for 20 minutes, or until all the liquid has been absorbed. Never stir the rice while cooking as it can break its texture into mush.

In a large skillet, heat the oil and fry the onion, garlic, and celery for 2 minutes. Stir in the tomato paste and cook 1 minute. Add the ham hock meat, the remaining half of the spice powder, the cooked rice, tomatoes, and the cooked shrimp and heat through. Sprinkle the top with fresh parsley and bring it to the table to serve.

Nutritional Profile per Serving: Calories—332; % calories from fat—15%; fat (gm)—5 or 8% daily value; saturated fat (gm)—2; sodium (mg)—500; cholesterol (mg)—133; carbohydrates (gm)—49; dietary fiber (gm)—3.

# SCALLOP STIR-FRY

*Here's a dinner in less than half an hour—bursting with fresh color and flavor.*

*Time Estimate: Hands-on, 20 minutes*
*Serves 4*

2 teaspoons light olive oil with a dash of toasted sesame oil
1 clove garlic, bashed, peeled, and finely chopped
8 dime-size paper-thin slices peeled gingerroot, cut into thin matchsticks
8 ounces (225 gm) snow peas
8 ounces (225 gm) sweet red bell pepper, cut into thick matchsticks
1/4 teaspoon toasted sesame oil
12 ounces (350 gm) sea scallops
2 tablespoons minced fresh cilantro
1 cup vegetable stock (page 288)
1 cup de-alcoholized white wine
2 tablespoons cornstarch mixed with 4 tablespoons de-alcoholized white wine (slurry)
1/4 teaspoon freshly ground black pepper
4 cups hot cooked white rice

Heat half the olive oil in a large wok or skillet and sauté the garlic and ginger over medium heat for 1 minute. Turn up the heat to medium-high, add the vegetables, and toss vigorously until just crisp-tender, about 4 minutes. Transfer to a bowl and set aside.

Add the remaining olive oil and the toasted sesame oil to the same wok and cook the scallops over medium-high heat for 2 minutes. Transfer to a bowl, sprinkle with the cilantro, cover, and set aside.

Return the vegetables to the hot wok. Pour in the stock and wine and heat through. Remove from heat. Add the cornstarch slurry, return to heat, and stir until thickened, about 30 seconds. Remove from the heat, stir in the scallops, and sprinkle with the pepper.

**To serve:** Spoon the scallops and vegetables over the rice on dinner plates.

Nutritional Profile per Serving: Calories—387; % calories from fat—11%; fat (gm)—5 or 7% daily value; saturated fat (gm)—1; sodium (mg)—246; cholesterol (mg)-—27; carbohydrates (gm)—59; dietary fiber (gm)—3.

# Paella

*One of the greatest contributions to "real food" is this classic dish which comes from the Spanish coast around Valencia. A regional favorite, it combines rice, saffron, and a wide variety of fish and shellfish, as well as chicken and ham. This reduced-fat version uses shrimp stock as the liquid to add flavor. And the method is so much simpler than the traditional way that the threat of failure is removed. However, since 39 grams of fat per serving have been removed, the rice will stick unless it is cooked in another pot.*

*Time Estimate: Hands-on, 60 minutes*
*Serves 6*

## SHRIMP STOCK

4½ cups water
2½ pounds (1.1 kg) raw jumbo shrimp (16 to 20 per pound)

## PAELLA

1 teaspoon light olive oil with a dash of toasted sesame oil
1/2 onion, peeled and chopped
1 clove garlic, bashed, peeled, and chopped
1 teaspoon grated fresh gingerroot
1 bay leaf
2 cups uncooked pearl rice
4 cups shrimp stock (see above)
1/2 cup de-alcoholized white wine
1/8 teaspoon powdered saffron
1/4 teaspoon freshly ground sea salt
1/4 teaspoon freshly ground black pepper

## SAUCE

1 teaspoon light olive oil with a dash of toasted sesame oil
1/2 onion, peeled and sliced
1 red bell pepper, seeded and cut into 1/2-inch (1.5-cm) slices
1 green bell pepper, seeded and cut into 1/2-inch (1.5-cm) slices
1 teaspoon grated fresh gingerroot
1 clove garlic, bashed, peeled, and chopped
1 cup de-alcoholized white wine

1 cup low-sodium tomato purée
2 teaspoons capers
1 cup quartered fresh mushrooms
3 tablespoons chopped black olives
1 cup frozen green peas, thawed
3 tablespoons chopped fresh basil

## GARNISH

Freshly squeezed lemon juice
Chopped fresh mint leaves

**The shrimp stock:** In a saucepan, bring the water to a boil. Drop in the shrimp and cook for 3 minutes. Strain, reserving the liquid. Plunge the shrimp into ice water to prevent further cooking and to make them easy to handle. Peel and devein the shrimp, returning the shells to the reserved liquid. Set the shrimp aside.

Bring the reserved liquid and shrimp shells to a boil, reduce the heat, and simmer 20 minutes. Strain—you should have 4 cups of shrimp stock.

**The paella:** In a high-sided skillet, heat the oil and cook the onion and garlic over medium-high heat for 1 minute. Add the ginger, bay leaf, and pearl rice, stirring until the rice is well coated. Add the shrimp stock, wine, saffron, salt, and pepper, stirring until combined. Bring to a boil, reduce the heat, and simmer over very low heat for 25 minutes, stirring every 3 minutes.

**The sauce:** In another high-sided skillet, heat the oil and sauté the onion, bell peppers, ginger, and garlic for 3 minutes over medium-high heat. Stir in the wine and tomato purée and bring to a boil. Reduce the heat and simmer 10 minutes. Add the mushrooms, olives, capers, peas, and fresh basil.

**To assemble:** Remove the bay leaf from the paella. Fold the sauce into the rice, then gently fold in the cooked shrimp. Remove the paella from the heat, cover, and let stand for 10 minutes to allow the flavors to mingle.

**To serve:** Spoon the paella into serving bowls. Sprinkle with fresh lemon juice and chopped mint.

Nutritional Profile per Serving: Calories—431; % calories from fat—9%; fat (gm)—4 or 7% daily value; saturated fat (gm)—1; sodium (mg)—568; cholesterol (mg)—178; carbohydrates (gm)—67; dietary fiber (gm)—5.

# River Café Succotash

*The food at David Burke's River Café in New York has to compete with an unobstructed view of the New York skyline, so David's cuisine is remarkable for its display. This dish is somewhat altered, but owes its concept to David's genius for presentation.*

Time Estimate: Hands-on, 30 minutes;
  unsupervised, 60 minutes
Serves 4

4 mini pumpkins (or 1 medium-sized pumpkin)
2 cups shrimp stock (page 287)
1 teaspoon light olive oil with a dash of toasted sesame oil
12 large shrimp, shelled
1 cup diced red bell pepper
1 cup diced yellow bell pepper
1/2 cup de-alcoholized white wine
1 cup cooked corn kernels
1 cup cooked lima beans
1 tablespoon chopped fresh sage
1/4 teaspoon freshly ground sea salt
4 cups fresh spinach fettuccine
1/4 cup chopped fresh chives

Cut the stem and top off each pumpkin. Remove the seeds and stringy material. (I toast the seeds and use them on my breakfast cereal, Kerrmush page 208.) Scoop the pumpkin flesh out with a melon baller, leaving the shell 1/4 inch (.75 cm) thick. Place the balls in a saucepan with the shrimp stock and bring to a boil. Then reduce the heat and simmer until the pumpkin balls are tender, about 20 minutes. Purée in a food processor until smooth.

Preheat the oven to 350°F (180°C). Place the hollowed-out pumpkins on a rack in a roasting pan with a small amount of water in the bottom. Cover with foil and bake for 35 minutes.

Heat the oil in a large skillet over medium-high heat and sauté the shrimp and peppers until the shrimp are lightly brown. Place in a small bowl and set aside. Pour the wine into the skillet. Add the

corn, lima beans, and sage and cook 30 more seconds. Add the pumpkin purée and simmer another 1 to 2 minutes. Season with the freshly ground salt.

Bring a large pot of water to a full rolling boil. Drop in fresh pasta and stir to separate strands. Boil for 3 minutes. Drain.

**To serve:** On a large platter, place the medium pumpkin shell or place 1 mini-pumpkin per individual plate. Place 2 shrimp in the bottom of each pumpkin and pour in the succotash. Top with 1 more shrimp and a sprinkle of the chives. Serve with spinach fettuccine fresh from the pot.

Nutritional Profile per Serving: Calories—353; % calories from fat—8%; fat (gm)—3 or 5% daily value; saturated fat (gm)—1; sodium (mg)—241; cholesterol (mg)—40; carbohydrates (gm)—66; dietary fiber (gm)—7.

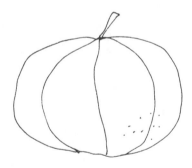

# SCALLOPS & SHRIMP VINCENT

⌘

*Chef de Cuisine Vincent Guerithault of the restaurant Vincent's at Camelback in Phoenix, Arizona, gave me permission to adapt his popular scallops and shrimp appetizer to provide a quick and elegant main dish. As you'll see, the recipe utilizes an unusual method: one in which the shrimp and scallop juices make up a lovely fresh orange sauce in only a matter of minutes.*

*Time Estimate: Hands-on, 45 minutes*
*Serves 2*

2 cups water
1/2 cup uncooked basmati rice
1/2 teaspoon light olive oil with a dash of toasted sesame oil
1 shallot, peeled and finely sliced
1 teaspoon freshly grated gingerroot
Zest of 1/2 orange, grated
1 tablespoon finely sliced fresh basil
1 cup de-alcoholized white wine
6 medium raw shrimp, peeled, deveined, and the shells reserved
6 scallops
1 tablespoon arrowroot mixed with 2 tablespoons de-alcoholized white wine (slurry)
1 orange, segmented, pitted, and pith removed

GARNISH

Finely sliced fresh basil
Freshly ground white pepper

Put the water in a medium saucepan and bring to a boil. Add the basmati rice and cook for 10 minutes. Drain in a metal sieve or colander. Fill the saucepan about a quarter full with hot water. Put the sieve or colander filled with rice over the saucepan, cover, and steam for 15 minutes.

Heat the oil in a pot large enough to hold a steamer platform to cook the seafood. Add the shallot, gin-gerroot, orange zest, and basil and stir. Add the de-alcoholized wine and the reserved shrimp shells. Put the steamer platform in place, cover, and bring to a boil. Place the shrimp and scallops on the steamer tray, cover, and steam for 5 minutes. Remove the shrimp and scallops and keep warm.

Strain the steaming liquid into a small saucepan. Add the arrowroot slurry, place over medium-high heat, heat, and stir until thickened.

Return the shrimp, scallops, and orange pieces to the thickened steaming liquid.

**To serve:** Spoon the glistening, fragrant seafood on top of a nest of the steamed rice, and sprinkle with the basil and white pepper to taste.

Nutritional Profile per Serving: Calories—321; % calories from fat—7%; fat (gm)—2 or 4% daily value; saturated fat (gm)—.4; sodium (mg)—156; cholesterol (mg)—44; carbohydrates (gm)—56; dietary fiber (gm)—2.

# SEA BASS BAKED IN PARCHMENT*

⌘

*Affectation or a real benefit? I admit I've asked this question about foods baked in parchment. Now that every scrap of food is important, I've decided that it really works wonders. The food is sealed and cooks in the aromatic steam created in the confines of the parchment, without the need of fat-laden pastry or obscuring sauces. I cook up to four portions in a single wrap and then cut along the straight folded edge so that the contents can be slipped out onto a serving platter to receive their final garnish. I don't try to serve wrapped portions as single servings; there's too much inedible paper left on the plate and it winds up looking messy.*

*Time Estimate: Hands-on, 45 minutes*
*Serves 2*

4 green onions

1 red bell pepper, seeded and cut into matchsticks

1 tablespoon lime zest, in strips

3¾ cups fish stock (page 287)

1/2 cup uncooked long-grain white rice

1/4 cup uncooked wild rice

2 teaspoons fish sauce

1⅛ teaspoons light olive oil with a dash of toasted sesame oil

4 thin slices gingerroot

1 large turnip, peeled and cut into matchsticks

4 inches of lemon grass, cut into 2 X 1/8-inch (5 X 0.5-cm) pieces, or substitute 1 tablespoon very narrow strips of lemon zest

1 dried red chili pepper, finely chopped

2 (4-ounce or 115-gm) white fish fillets (sea bass is preferable)

1 tablespoon arrowroot mixed with 2 tablespoons water (slurry)

Cut a 2-foot (60-cm) piece of parchment paper and fold it in half. Starting at the top of the folded edge, cut a half circle that uses as much paper as possible. Unfold, and you have an oval.

Starting with the bulb, slice the green onions on the diagonal, up to 3 inches (8 cm) from the end of the green part. Chop the remaining 3 inches (8 cm) of the green part into very thin strips, equal in length to the lemon grass.

In a small bowl, combine the thin green onion strips, red pepper matchsticks, and lime zest and divide the mixture in half: half for the fish topping and half for the sauce.

Preheat the oven to 350°F (180°C). In a large saucepan, heat 1½ cups of the fish stock, add the white rice, and bring to a boil. Stir once and cover. Reduce the heat to low and cook for 25 minutes.

In another saucepan, heat 1 cup of the fish stock, add the wild rice and 1 teaspoon of the fish sauce, and bring to a boil. Reduce the heat, cover loosely, and cook for 45 minutes. Drain, add to the cooked white rice, and set aside.

In a large frying pan, heat 1 teaspoon of the oil over medium-high heat and sauté the ginger, turnip, lemon grass, the diagonal slices of green onion, and the red chili pepper for about 2 minutes. Pour in the remaining 1¼ cups of fish stock and the remaining fish sauce, bring to a boil, and reduce by half. Remove from the heat and strain, reserving the broth and cooked vegetables separately.

Lay the parchment paper oval on a baking sheet. On half of the circle, near the center fold, make a bed out of the reserved vegetables and place the fish fillets on top. Sprinkle with half of the red pepper–green onion mixture. Fold the parchment paper over the fish and turn the whole thing so that the open edges face you. Starting at one end, fold over about 3 inches (8 cm) of the edge. Crease the middle of the fold, and make another 3-inch (8-cm) fold that overlaps the first one. Continue this overlapping folding around the entire edge. Finish off the last fold with a slight twist to secure it all together. Make sure you leave some air space inside the paper packet, allowing steam to expand but remain contained. Bake the fish in the preheated oven for 15 minutes.

While the fish cooks, heat the reserved fish broth in a small saucepan over medium-high heat. Remove from the heat and add the arrowroot slurry; return to the heat and stir until thickened. Add the remaining red pepper–green onion mixture and heat through.

**To serve:** Tear open the parchment packet along the folds. Slip each fillet out onto a dinner plate and coat with the sauce. Spoon out the vegetables and the rice and serve on the side.

Nutritional Profile per Serving: Calories—505; % calories from fat—11%; fat (gm)—6 or 10% daily value; saturated fat (gm)—1; sodium (mg)—486; cholesterol (mg)—60; carbohydrates (gm)—76; dietary fiber (gm)—6.

# Seafood Burgers

*With the arrival of the food processor, a brave new world has emerged for the old-fashioned hamburger. The high-speed blades literally melt all kinds of "meats" and seasonings to form an incredibly attractive dish.*

*Time Estimate: Hands-on, 15 minutes;
  unsupervised, 10 minutes*

*Serves 4*

8 ounces (225 gm) medium-sized shrimp, boiled for 30
  seconds, peeled, and deveined
8 ounces (225 gm) orange roughy, cut into small pieces
1/4 teaspoon freshly ground sea salt
1/4 teaspoon cayenne pepper
3 green onions, finely chopped
4 medium white mushrooms
1 tablespoon chopped fresh dill
2 egg whites
1/4 cup bread crumbs

Preheat the oven to 400°F (205°C). Place half of the shrimp and half of the orange roughy in a food processor and process 10 pulses; transfer to a large bowl. Repeat with the remaining shrimp and fish. Sprinkle with the salt and cayenne pepper.

Place the onions, mushrooms, and dill in the processor and pulse 5 times; add to the seafood. Pour in the egg whites and mix well. Form into 4 patties and set aside.

Spread the bread crumbs out on a plate. Place the patties on top and press firmly, coating both sides with the crumbs; transfer to a baking sheet. Bake for 10 minutes in the preheated oven.

**To serve:** Serve in buns, like a sandwich, or solo, with steamed vegetables and potatoes on the side.

Nutritional Profile per Serving: Calories—112; % calories from fat—10%; fat (gm)—1 or 2% daily value; saturated fat (gm)—.31; sodium (mg)—306; cholesterol (mg)—85; carbohydrates (gm)—5; dietary fiber (gm)—1.

## Using the Food Processor

If you use fairly small portions and pulse the motor rather than run it flat out, you retain control over the texture to a finer degree.

Also, although it may seem like an inconvenient step, I really do recommend that you combine the vegetable seasonings separately from the meat and then hand-mix the two . . . the overall texture balance is far superior.

# SEAFOOD PIE

⁂

*This dish is hearty and comforting as well as elegant. The rice and cheese crust used in this pie makes it an extremely desirable alternative to a rich traditional crust. Experiment with your favorite fillings.*

*Time Estimate: Hands-on, 45 minutes; unsupervised, 40 minutes*

*Serves 6*

1 (1-pound or 450-gm) bunch fresh spinach, washed and stemmed (to be used in crust and filling)

RICE CRUST

1/4 teaspoon light olive oil with a dash of toasted sesame oil (for the pie dish)
2 cups cooked long-grain white rice
1/4 cup freshly grated Parmesan cheese
1/8 teaspoon freshly ground sea salt
1/4 teaspoon freshly ground black pepper
1 lightly beaten egg white

FILLING

1 cup liquid egg substitute
1/2 cup evaporated skim milk
1 tablespoon Dijon mustard
1/4 teaspoon freshly ground black pepper
1/2 teaspoon dried dill
Zest of 1/2 lemon, grated
1/4 teaspoon red pepper flakes
1 teaspoon light olive oil with a dash of toasted sesame oil
3 ounces (90 gm) shallots, peeled and finely chopped
1 clove garlic, bashed, peeled, and chopped
12 ounces (350 gm) medium shrimp, peeled and deveined
12 ounces (350 gm) small scallops
1 tablespoon freshly grated Parmesan cheese

Preheat the oven to 350°F (180°C). Wash the spinach thoroughly and discard the stems. Steam just until the spinach wilts. Run under cold water to cool quickly and wring all the water from it with your hands. Chop finely.

**The crust:** Brush the oil on the bottom and sides of a high-sided 9-inch (23-cm) pie dish. Combine all the remaining crust ingredients and 2 tablespoons of the chopped spinach. Press into the prepared pie dish. The crust should extend about 1/2 inch (1.5 cm) above the top of the pan.

**The filling:** Whisk together the egg substitute, milk, mustard, pepper, dill, lemon zest, and red pepper flakes and set aside.

Heat the oil in a large frying pan over medium heat and fry the shallots until they wilt, about 2 minutes. Add the garlic and continue cooking for about 1 minute. Add the shrimp and scallops and toss for 3 minutes or until the shrimp starts to turn pink. Transfer the seafood to a plate.

**To assemble:** Layer the remaining spinach on the bottom of the crust and spoon the cooked seafood on top. Pour the milk and egg mixture over all. Sprinkle with the cheese and bake in the preheated oven for 30 to 40 minutes or until the custard is set. Let stand for 10 minutes before serving.

Nutritional Profile per Serving: Calories—241; % calories from fat—15; fat (gm)—4 or 6% daily value; saturated fat (gm)—1; sodium (mg)—493; cholesterol (mg)—76; carbohydrates (gm)—23; dietary fiber (gm)—2.

# SIMPLY "SQUISITO" SOLE

*It's important to know that squisito is Italian for "exquisite"—a word that I hope you'll use often after sampling dishes from this book.*

*Time Estimate: Hands-on, 20 minutes*
*Serves 4*

1/2 teaspoon light olive oil with a dash of toasted sesame oil
4 (6-ounce or 175-gm) fresh sole fillets
1/4 teaspoon freshly ground sea salt
1/4 teaspoon freshly ground black pepper
2 cups very clear fish stock (page 287)
8 small red new potatoes, steamed until tender
8 ounces (225 gm) fresh green beans
1/16 teaspoon powdered saffron
1 teaspoon chopped fresh dill weed (not the stalks)
1 tablespoon arrowroot mixed with 2 tablespoons reserved fish stock (slurry)
1/2 teaspoon freshly squeezed lemon juice

Brush a 9 X 13-inch (23 X 33-cm) baking sheet with the oil. Lay the sole fillets on the sheet and sprinkle with half the salt and half the pepper. Brush the fillets with a little of the fish stock.

Pour a small amount of water into the bottom of a steamer pot and bring to a boil. Put the potatoes in the first rack; insert rack in the pot, cover, and steam for 10 minutes. Now add the beans to the second rack and steam both for another 5 minutes, until done.

Preheat the broiler. Pour the fish stock into a medium skillet, bring to a boil, and reduce by half to 1 cup, about 5 minutes. Remove from the heat.

While the stock is reducing, pop the fish under the broiler to cook until tender, about 5 minutes.

Add the saffron, dill, and arrowroot slurry to the reduced stock; return to medium heat and stir until thickened. Stir in the lemon juice and the remaining salt and pepper for a golden, "buttery" sauce!

**To serve:** Divide the fish and steamed vegetables among 4 dinner plates and coat liberally with the sauce. Serve *very hot*, please!

Nutritional Profile per Serving: Calories—363; % calories from fat—8%; fat (gm)—3 or 5% daily value; saturated fat (gm)—1; sodium (mg)—306; cholesterol (mg)—80; carbohydrates (gm)—49; dietary fiber (gm)—5.

# SMOKED CATFISH ON A RAFT

*Smoking is such a flavorful cooking technique, with virtually no added fat. Once you get the hang of it, I think you'll find it perfect for many light fish and poultry uses.*

*Time Estimate: Hands-on, 45 minutes*
*Serves 4*

1/4 teaspoon olive oil
4 (4-ounce or 115-gm) catfish fillets
Basic Tea Smoke ingredients (page 40)

YOGURT PURÉE

1/2 cup strained yogurt (page 288)
1/4 cup finely chopped pimiento
12 fresh basil leaves, very finely sliced
1 teaspoon creamy prepared horseradish
1/8 teaspoon freshly ground sea salt

GARNISH

1 head iceberg lettuce, cut into 1/2-inch (1.5-cm) thick slices
Finely chopped pimiento
2 tablespoons finely sliced fresh basil leaves
Juice of 1/2 lemon

Oil 2 stacking steamer platforms with the 1/4 teaspoon olive oil. Place the catfish fillets on the platforms and cook in the Basic Tea Smoke (page 40), about 10 minutes. Remove the fish with tongs and set aside.

**Yogurt purée:** In a food processor or blender, purée the strained yogurt, half of the pimiento, the basil, and horseradish until smooth. Stir in the remaining pimiento and the salt.

**To serve:** Place a lettuce "raft" on each of 4 individual serving plates and spread with 2 tablespoons of the yogurt purée. Top each "raft" with 1 fillet and garnish with a little of the chopped pimiento, basil, and fresh lemon juice. Use any remaining pimiento and basil to scatter decoratively around the plate.

Nutritional Profile per Serving: Calories—168; % calories from fat—10%; fat (gm)—2 or 3% daily value; saturated fat (gm)—.5; sodium (mg)—234; cholesterol (mg)—71; carbohydrates (gm)—7; dietary fiber (gm)—1.

# SOLE WITH SAFFRON SAUCE

*The classic recipe for this dish featured moist, thick Dover sole stuffed with highly seasoned butter, nestled in a bath of butter sauce. Today, I have used no butter at all! I can almost hear you gasp sharply, saying, "No, it isn't possible!" But it may be that you won't even miss the butter. Let your taste buds be the judge!*
*Great accompaniments to this dish are tiny, steamed new potatoes and green beans sprinkled with a touch of nutmeg, parsley, and mint.*

*Time Estimate: Hands-on, 30 minutes; unsupervised, 30 minutes*
*Serves 6*

6 (6-ounce or 175-gm) sole fillets

SAFFRON SAUCE

2 cups fish stock (page 287)
1/4 teaspoon chopped fresh tarragon
1/2 teaspoon chopped fresh dill
1 tablespoon chopped fresh parsley
2 tablespoons chopped green onions
2 anchovy fillets, mashed to a paste
1 tablespoon capers
1 clove garlic, bashed, peeled, and chopped
2 teaspoons English mustard
1 tablespoon freshly squeezed lemon juice
Pinch of saffron threads
1 tablespoon arrowroot mixed with 1/4 cup de-alcoholized white wine (slurry)

When you get the sole fillets home from the market, put them in ice cold, salted water. This Scottish crofter's technique, called "crimping," will remove the "woofy" smell.

Boil the fish stock in a medium saucepan over medium-high heat until reduced to 1 cup. Set aside.

Preheat the oven to broil.

Just anoint your broiler pan with a touch of olive oil. Place the sole fillets on the broiler. Position the pan 4 inches (10 cm) from the broiler's heat source for about 6 minutes. Remove the fish while it's tender and snowy white. Don't wait until it browns or becomes crisp. Keep warm.

**The saffron sauce:** In a small saucepan over medium heat, mix the reduced stock with the tarragon, dill, parsley, green onions, anchovies, capers, garlic, mustard, and lemon juice. Stir in a pinch of saffron to give it that buttery color. Take the saucepan from the heat and stir in the arrowroot slurry. Return to the heat and stir until thickened.

**To serve:** Present the fish on a warmed serving plate and ladle with the golden saffron sauce.

Nutritional Profile per Serving: Calories—161; % calories from fat—14%; fat (gm)—3 or 4% daily value; saturated fat (gm)—1; sodium (mg)—233; cholesterol (mg)—81; carbohydrates (gm)—3; dietary fiber (gm)—.3.

# SWEET LIME & BROILED SEAFOOD SALAD

━━━ ✕ ━━━

*This is a dish that uses several new ideas: a lime vinaigrette salad dressing tossed with a tangle of salad greens and inter-mingled with fresh herbs; the textures of tender broiled fish with blistered, crunchy skin and stiffly whipped potatoes; and a radically new glaze of lime marmalade and wine, colored with radicchio.*

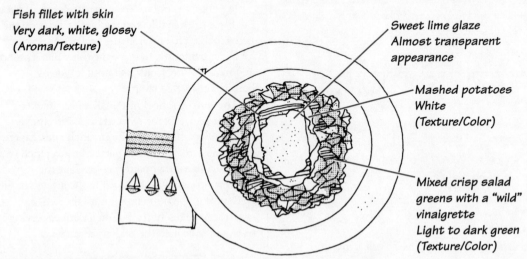

**Fish fillet with skin
Very dark, white, glossy
(Aroma/Texture)**

**Sweet lime glaze
Almost transparent
appearance**

**Mashed potatoes
White
(Texture/Color)**

**Mixed crisp salad
greens with a "wild"
vinaigrette
Light to dark green
(Texture/Color)**

*Time Estimate: Hands-on, 40 minutes;
    unsupervised, 6 minutes*
*Serves 4*

## MASHED POTATOES

1½ pounds (675 gm) russet potatoes, peeled and cut in
    2-inch (5-cm) pieces
1/2 teaspoon plus 1/8 teaspoon freshly ground sea salt
1/2 to 1 cup 2%-fat milk
1/8 teaspoon freshly grated nutmeg
1/8 teaspoon freshly ground white pepper

## SALAD

1 tablespoon coarsely chopped fresh dill, mixed with 3
    tablespoons coarsely chopped fresh parsley
5 cups of at least four varieties of lettuce (for example,
    red leaf, romaine, radicchio, iceberg, or arugula), torn
    into bite-size pieces

## LIME VINAIGRETTE

1 clove garlic, bashed, peeled, and chopped
2 tablespoons light olive oil with a dash of toasted
    sesame oil
Juice of 1 lime
5 tablespoons rice wine vinegar
1/2 teaspoon ground mustard
2 tablespoons brown sugar
1/8 teaspoon cayenne pepper (use 1/4 teaspoon if you
    like things hot)

## FISH

1 teaspoon light olive oil with a dash of toasted sesame oil
1/4 teaspoon freshly ground sea salt
1/4 teaspoon freshly ground black pepper
4 (6-ounce or 175-gm) red snapper or halibut fillets,
    with skin

## LIME GLAZE

2 tablespoons lime marmalade, preferably Rose's
1/4 cup de-alcoholized white wine
2 tablespoons very finely chopped radicchio, red leaves only
1 teaspoon arrowroot mixed with 2 teaspoons de-alcoholized white wine (slurry)

## GARNISH

2 tablespoons very finely chopped radicchio, red leaves only
1 teaspoon chopped fresh parsley
Freshly ground black pepper

**The mashed potatoes:** Bring the potatoes to a boil in a large pot of water, add the 1/2 teaspoon of salt, and cook for 20 minutes; drain. Return potatoes to the same pot over low heat, cover with a kitchen towel, and let steam dry for 15 minutes. This will prevent a watery consistency in your final product. Mash together the boiled potatoes, milk, the remaining salt, the nutmeg, and white pepper until lump free.

Spoon the mashed potatoes into a large piping bag with a 1/2-inch (1.5-cm) nozzle (a star shape would look decorative). To keep the potatoes warm, place the filled piping bag in a bowl over a pot of simmering water and cover with a lid until needed.

**The salad:** In a large bowl, toss the herbs and the torn lettuce leaves together until thoroughly mixed. Transfer to a salad spinner.

**The lime vinaigrette:** Combine all the ingredients in a blender until the garlic is dissolved, about 1 minute. Pour over the salad in the spinner, drenching the leaves thoroughly. Spin and drain off any excess vinaigrette (save for another use).

**The fish:** Preheat the broiler and position a broiler rack to within 4 inches (10 cm) of the heat source. Pour the oil onto a large plate, dust with the salt and pepper and wipe with the fish fillets, coating both sides. Lay the fillets on the broiler rack, skin side up, and broil for 6 minutes or until the skin has blistered and crisped.

**The lime glaze:** In a small saucepan over low heat, mix the lime marmalade with the wine until it forms a smooth syrup, stirring occasionally, about 3 minutes. Stir in the chopped radicchio and mix well. Remove from the heat and add the arrowroot slurry; return to the heat and stir until clear, about 1 minute. Remove from the heat and strain to remove the radicchio, leaving a soft pink hue.

**To serve:** Place a quarter of the salad greens on each of 4 cold serving plates. Pipe the warm mashed potatoes on top to form a bed and top with a fish fillet. Brush with the glaze and sprinkle with the chopped radicchio, parsley, and black pepper.

### Nutritional Profile per Serving

|  | Classic | Minimax | Daily Value |
| --- | --- | --- | --- |
| Calories | 829 | 356 |  |
| Calories from fat | 66% | 15% |  |
| Fat (gm) | 61 | 6 | 9% |
| Saturated fat (gm) | 10 | 2 | 3% |
| Sodium (mg) | 800 | 497 | 21% |
| Cholesterol (mg) | 154 | 79 | 26% |
| Carbohydrates (gm) | 50 | 44 | 15% |
| Dietary fiber (gm) | 6 | 3 | 12% |

Classic compared: Salmon and Potato Salad

# ALL-AMERICAN PICNIC: OVEN-FRIED CHICKEN AND POTATO SALAD

Fried chicken and potato salad have to be the ultimate American picnic food. I set out to find a way to make them available to the heart-conscious eater who loves picnics, fresh air, and mossy banks beside sylvan streams. With about 12 percent of its calories from fat, this version meets the need and tastes great! Don't forget the insect repellent.

Time Estimate: Hands-on, 30 minutes; unsupervised, 35 minutes

Serves 4

POTATO SALAD

1½ pounds (750 gm) red new potatoes, steamed and quartered
1/4 cup finely chopped green onions
1 tablespoon finely chopped parsley stalks
1 tablespoon finely chopped parsley leaves
1/4 red onion, peeled and finely diced
1 stalk celery, finely diced
3/4 cup strained yogurt (page 288)
4 teaspoons Dijon mustard
1 teaspoon dark brown sugar
1/4 teaspoon freshly ground black pepper

CHICKEN

1/2 cup cornmeal
1/2 teaspoon cayenne pepper
1/2 cup bread crumbs
1/2 teaspoon dried tarragon
1/2 teaspoon ground ginger
1/4 teaspoon freshly ground sea salt
3/4 cup liquid egg substitute
1/2 cup all-purpose flour
1 (3-pound or 1.4-kg) fryer chicken, quartered (1 whole breast, split, and 2 whole legs), skin and fat removed

**The potato salad:** In a large bowl, combine the potatoes, green onions, parsley stalks and leaves, red onion, and celery.

In a small bowl, mix the strained yogurt, Dijon mustard, and brown sugar and stir into the potatoes until well combined. Stir in the black pepper.

**The chicken:** Preheat the oven to 350°F (180°C). Line a baking sheet with parchment paper to help keep the batter from sticking to the baking sheet. In a medium bowl, combine the cornmeal, cayenne pepper, bread crumbs, tarragon, ginger, and salt. Pour the egg substitute into a small bowl and place it next to the bowl with the cornmeal mixture. Put the flour in a large bowl.

Dip the chicken pieces in the flour, turning until they are completely covered. Next dip the chicken in the egg substitute and then in the cornmeal. When completely coated with the cornmeal, place the chicken pieces on the baking sheet, round side down.

Bake chicken in the preheated oven for 20 minutes. Turn the pieces over, return to the oven, and cook 15 minutes more.

You can eat Oven-Fried Chicken hot out of the oven along with the Potato Salad, or save them for a picnic. To prepare the chicken for later use, cool it rapidly on a rack in the refrigerator. When cold, put the chicken and potato salad into sealed plastic containers and refrigerate until ready to leave for your picnic.

Nutritional Profile per Serving: Calories—547; % calories from fat—12%; fat (gm)—7 or 11 % daily value; saturated fat (gm)—2; sodium (mg)—474; cholesterol (mg)—77; carbohydrates (gm)—77; dietary fiber (gm)—5.

# APRICOT CILANTRO CHICKEN

I love this simple breast adorned with a chutneylike sauce, using apricots, cilantro, and a special spice mix. This is a recipe you must try—full of aroma, color, and texture, almost the perfect Minimax dish!

Time Estimate: Hands-on, 75 minutes; unsupervised, 90 minutes

Serves 6

## CHICKEN AND MARINADE

2 tablespoons freshly squeezed lemon juice
1 tablespoon Dijon mustard
1/8 teaspoon cayenne pepper
1/8 teaspoon freshly ground black pepper
2 tablespoons de-alcoholized white wine
1 tablespoon chopped fresh thyme
6 (6-ounce or 175-gm) chicken breasts with skin, fat trimmed and deboned

## APRICOT CILANTRO SAUCE

1½ cups hot water
1 cup dried apricots, without sulfites
2 whole cloves
1 (1-inch or 2.5-cm) piece of cinnamon stick
1/4 teaspoon coriander seeds
1/4 teaspoon whole black peppercorns
1 teaspoon light olive oil with a dash of toasted sesame oil
1 medium onion, peeled and diced
1 tablespoon finely cut gingerroot strips
12 plum tomatoes, seeded and diced
2 tablespoons chopped fresh cilantro
2 tablespoons apricot preserves

## RICE

1 quart water
Bouquet garni (see below)
1¼ cups uncooked long-grain rice
Pinch of saffron (enough to color the rice *pale* yellow)

## BOUQUET GARNI

4 whole cloves
6 black peppercorns
6 coriander seeds
1 (2-inch or 5-cm) piece of cinnamon stick
1 (1-inch or 2.5-cm) square piece of gingerroot
2 sprigs fresh cilantro

## GARNISH

8 cups kale leaves
Chopped fresh cilantro

**The marinade:** In a medium bowl, mix all the ingredients. Add the chicken breasts, cover, and refrigerate for 3 hours.

**The sauce:** Pour the hot water over the dried apricots and let plump for 1 hour. Strain, reserving the water. Finely dice 4 of the apricots and set aside to use later in the rice. Chop the remaining apricots.

In a small spice mill, or using a mortar and pestle, grind the cloves, cinnamon, coriander seeds, and black peppercorns for the sauce. Push the spice powder through a sieve, trapping any large particles.

Heat the oil in a medium saucepan over medium-high heat and cook the onion and ginger for 2 minutes. Stir in the tomatoes and apricots. Strain the apricot and tomato juices into the saucepan and bring to a rapid boil. Stir in the spice powder and apricot preserves to add a lovely gloss. Keep warm.

**The rice:** Pour the water into a medium saucepan, add the bouquet garni, and bring to a boil. Add the rice and saffron, cover, and boil for 10 minutes. Strain through a metal sieve, or colander with very small holes. Place the sieve with the rice over the saucepan, which has been filled one-quarter full with boiling water. Stir in the 4 chopped apricots. Cover and steam for 15 minutes.

**The chicken:** Remove the chicken breasts from the marinade and place them in a skillet, skin side down, over medium-high heat. Brown for 1 minute, then reduce the heat to low and continue cooking for 5 minutes on each side. Remove and set aside. Pour 1 cup of the reserved apricot soaking water into the skillet to deglaze the pan residues. Bring to a boil, scraping up the residues, and reduce by half.

Strip the skin off the chicken breasts and return the chicken to the original skillet. Coat with the sauce and keep warm over medium heat.

Just before serving, steam the kale leaves for 3 to 4 minutes.

**To serve:** Place 1 cup of the kale leaves on each dinner plate. Spoon 1/2 cup of rice in the center in the shape of a nest. Pour a spoonful of sauce on the rice and top with a sauce-coated chicken breast. Sprinkle with the chopped cilantro and serve hot!

Nutritional Profile per Serving: Calories—424; % calories from fat—11%; fat (gm)—5 or 8% daily value; saturated fat (gm)—1; sodium (mg)—97; cholesterol (mg)—62; carbohydrates (gm)—64; dietary fiber (gm)—7.

# BANGERS & MASH

——— ✕ ———

One of my television viewers, Marilyn Schermerhorn, wrote to tell me that she loves sausage and my brown onion sauce. I paired her up with a lower-fat sausage and, because Marilyn also likes Chinese food, I adapted a dish I had in Hong Kong called Silver Cloud Pierced with a Thousand Golden Arrows—which turned out to be sausages (bangers) and mashed potatoes!

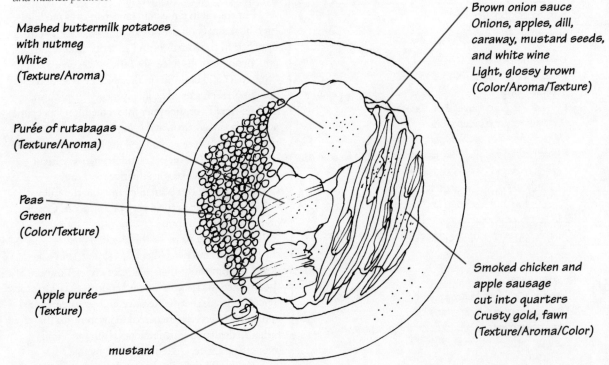

**Mashed buttermilk potatoes with nutmeg**
White
(Texture/Aroma)

**Brown onion sauce**
Onions, apples, dill, caraway, mustard seeds, and white wine
Light, glossy brown
(Color/Aroma/Texture)

**Purée of rutabagas**
(Texture/Aroma)

**Peas**
Green
(Color/Texture)

**Smoked chicken and apple sausage**
cut into quarters
Crusty gold, fawn
(Texture/Aroma/Color)

**Apple purée**
(Texture)

**mustard**

Time Estimate: Hands-on, 40 minutes;
   unsupervised, 45 minutes
Serves 4

3 lower-fat smoked chicken-apple sausages (preferably Aidell's)
4 sweet apples (such as Jonagold, Rome, or Winesap), whole, cored, peel intact
4 medium rutabagas, peeled and quartered
4 large russet potatoes, peeled and quartered
1/2 teaspoon freshly ground sea salt
1/2 cup 1%-fat buttermilk
1/8 teaspoon freshly grated nutmeg
1/8 teaspoon freshly ground white pepper

## ONION-APPLE SAUCE

1 teaspoon light olive oil with a dash of toasted sesame oil
2 medium onions, peeled and thinly sliced
1 teaspoon dill seeds
1 teaspoon caraway seeds
1 teaspoon yellow mustard seeds
1 sweet apple (Jonagold, Rome, or Winesap), peeled, cored, and sliced
1 cup low-sodium chicken stock (see page 286)

1 cup de-alcoholized dry red wine
1 tablespoon arrowroot mixed with 2 tablespoons
   de-alcoholized red wine (slurry)

MINTY PEAS

1/4 cup water
1 tablespoon mint leaves
1 tablespoon brown sugar
2 cups frozen or fresh peas

GARNISH

2 tablespoons chopped fresh parsley
4 teaspoons dry English mustard mixed with 4
   teaspoons 2%-fat milk

Preheat the oven to 350°F (180°C). Place the sausages and apples together in a shallow baking pan and bake for 30 minutes. Remove the peel from the apples and mash four, reserving one for the sauce below.

In a medium saucepan, boil the rutabagas in water to cover for 30 minutes. Drain, return to the same pot, and mash until smooth.

In another medium saucepan, bring the potatoes to a boil in water to cover, add 1/4 teaspoon of the salt, and cook for 20 minutes. Drain, return to the same pot over low heat, cover with a kitchen towel, and let steam dry for 15 minutes. Mash the boiled potatoes with the buttermilk, nutmeg, white pepper, and the remaining 1/4 teaspoon salt until smooth.

**The onion-apple sauce:** While the bangers and mash are cooking, heat the oil in a high-sided skillet over medium-high heat. Add the onions, dill, caraway, and mustard seeds, and cook, uncovered, 5 minutes without stirring. Add the sliced apple; stir once, cover, and cook for 5 minutes. Pour in the stock and wine, stirring and scraping all the pan residues up into the liquid until the bottom of the pan is perfectly clean, and simmer 5 minutes. Remove from the heat; stir in the arrowroot slurry, return to the heat, and bring to a boil to thicken. Peel and mash the reserved baked apple; stir into the sauce and set aside.

**The minty peas:** In a medium saucepan, bring the water, mint, and sugar to a boil and simmer the peas until they are tender, about 5 to 10 minutes for fresh, 3 minutes for frozen.

**To serve:** Place one scoop each of the mashed potatoes, apple, and rutabaga down the center of each serving plate. Slice each sausage into quarters lengthwise. Ladle some sauce on one side of the mash and top the sauce with three quarters of sausage. Spoon some minty peas on the other side of the mash. Garnish with the parsley and a tablespoon of the mustard mixture next to the sausage.

| Nutritional Profile per Serving | | | |
|---|---|---|---|
| | Classic | Minimax | Daily Value |
| Calories | 748 | 696 | |
| Calories from fat | 70% | 13% | |
| Fat (gm) | 58 | 10 | 15% |
| Saturated fat (gm) | 21 | 3 | 15% |
| Sodium (mg) | 2,606 | 820 | 34% |
| Cholesterol (mg) | 124 | 60 | 20% |
| Carbohydrates (gm) | 43 | 118 | 39% |
| Dietary fiber (gm) | 6 | 15 | 60% |
| Classic compared: Pork Sausages and Mashed Potatoes | | | |

# Blushing Chicken Fettuccine with Basic Tomato Sauce

⌘

*Blushing from the tomatoes, of course, not the shame of high fat content.*

*Time Estimate: Hands-on, 60 minutes*
Serves 4

## BASIC TOMATO SAUCE

1/2 teaspoon light olive oil with a dash of toasted sesame oil
2 tablespoons low-sodium tomato paste
1 medium onion, peeled and finely diced
2 cloves garlic, bashed, peeled, and finely diced
1 (28-ounce or 700-gm) can crushed tomatoes
2 tablespoons fresh oregano, 1 tablespoon chopped, 1 left whole
1 tablespoon arrowroot mixed with 2 tablespoons water (slurry)
2 tablespoons chopped fresh parsley stalks
1/4 teaspoon freshly ground black pepper
1/4 cup de-alcoholized wine (optional)

## CHICKEN

4 (6-ounce or 175-gm) boneless chicken breasts, with skin
1 teaspoon light olive oil with a dash of toasted sesame oil
8 ounces (225 gm) uncooked spinach fettuccine
1/4 cup de-alcoholized white wine
Chopped fresh oregano leaves

**The tomato sauce:** Over medium-high heat, brush a large skillet with the oil to coat. Add the tomato paste and cook until the color darkens, stirring to prevent scorching, about 5 minutes.

Stir in the onion and garlic, and cook 5 minutes, stirring occasionally to prevent scorching. Add the tomatoes with the tablespoon of chopped oregano; bring to a boil, reduce the heat, and simmer 10 minutes. Remove

from the heat; stir in the arrowroot slurry, parsley stalks, pepper, and remaining oregano. A last aromatic splash of de-alcoholized wine is your choice.

**The chicken:** Pat the chicken breasts dry with a paper towel. Pour the oil into a large skillet over medium heat. Place the chicken breasts in the skillet, skin side down, and brown for 10 minutes, turning them every 2 minutes. Resist the temptation to turn the heat up just to cook them quickly. The hotter the pan, the more the surface moisture evaporates and the stringier the meat. Low-heat cooking will retain maximum tenderness and juiciness. Remove the chicken from the pan and set aside.

While the chicken browns, cook the fettuccine in boiling water according to directions on the package until just tender, about 9 to 11 minutes. Drain. Pour half of the tomato sauce into a large pot; add the cooked pasta, toss well, and keep warm until ready to serve.

Remove the skin from the cooked chicken, dipping your fingers in a bowl of ice water every few seconds to keep them cool. Using a paper towel, blot the breasts to remove residual fat.

Blot the chicken-browning skillet with a paper towel to remove excess fat. Pour in the remaining tomato sauce and the wine; add the browned breasts, cover, and let them heat through.

**To serve:** Divide the pasta among individual dinner plates. Spoon a small pool of the sauce on the side and lay a chicken breast on top of it, coating with another spoonful of sauce. Garnish the pasta with the remaining sauce and a sprinkle of the fresh oregano leaves.

Nutritional Profile per Serving: Calories—443; % calories from fat—13%; fat (gm)—7 or 10% daily value; saturated fat (gm)—1; sodium (mg)—390; cholesterol (mg)—62; carbohydrates (gm)—61; dietary fiber (gm)—5.

Note on chicken breasts: To get boneless chicken breasts with skin, you can buy whole or split fryer breasts and debone them. However, from an economic point of view, you will experience greater financial savings over the long run by purchasing a whole chicken and freezing the other parts for later use. An added benefit for low-fat cooks is that you will also be able to use the bones for chicken stock (page 286).

# CHICKEN ANNA SKYE

*This dish honored the birth of Anna Skye, first daughter of my first line editor, Chris Rylko, and her husband, Michael.*

*Onion, garlic, and ginger are used to produce a flavorful, aromatic marinade which is injected into the chicken breasts. The result is a moist, tender chicken breast that melts in your mouth.*

Time Estimate: Hands-on, 38 minutes
Serves 4

GINGER GARLIC MARINADE

1/4 teaspoon toasted sesame oil
4 green onions, separated into white and green parts, finely chopped
10 quarter-size slices of peeled gingerroot
1 clove garlic, bashed, peeled, and chopped
1 cup de-alcoholized white wine
1 tablespoon low-sodium soy sauce

CHICKEN

4 (4-ounce or 115-gm) boneless chicken breasts, with skin
20 ounces (565 gm) baby bok choy
1/2 teaspoon cardamom
1/4 teaspoon freshly ground sea salt
1 cup de-alcoholized white wine
2 teaspoons arrowroot mixed with 1 tablespoon low-sodium soy sauce (slurry)
1/8 teaspoon freshly ground black pepper
4 cups hot cooked white rice

GARNISH

2 tablespoons chopped fresh parsley
Crushed red peppers (optional)

**The marinade:** Pour the oil into a medium saucepan over medium heat, add the white parts of the green onions, the ginger, and garlic, and cook, stirring, for 2 minutes. Pour in the wine; bring to a boil and cook for 10 minutes to reduce the liquid to 1/4 cup. Strain into a small bowl, pressing very lightly on the solids to extract their juices.

**The chicken:** Put the flavor injector needle into the marinade and draw it into the barrel. Place the chicken breasts on a large plate and inject small amounts of the juice throughout the meat. If you don't have a flavor injector, marinate the chicken in the marinade for at least 1/2 hour.

Heat a large nonstick skillet over medium heat; add the chicken breasts, skin side down, and fry for 8 minutes, turning every 2 minutes.

Cut the bok choy in half lengthwise, then crosswise, thus separating the leaves from the bottoms. Lay the bottoms in the first "floor" of a 2-platform steamer and the leaves in the second. Sprinkle with cardamom and salt, and cook over boiling water for 5 minutes.

Transfer the cooked chicken to a plate and remove the skin. To make an easy sauce, blot the skillet with a paper towel to remove excess fat, then deglaze the pan with the wine, scraping up all the pan residues. Strain into a small bowl, stir in the arrowroot slurry and any excess marinade, return to the skillet, and bring to a boil to thicken.

**To serve:** Mix the green parts of the green onions and the pepper with the hot rice and divide among 4 warm plates. Slice the chicken breasts on the diagonal and place on top of the rice. Spoon the sauce over the chicken and rice. Sprinkle the chopped parsley and crushed red peppers over the top. Arrange the bok choy tops and bottoms attractively on each plate.

Nutritional Profile per Serving: Calories—331; % calories from fat—8%; fat (gm)—3 or 5% daily value; saturated fat (gm)—1; sodium (mg)—521; cholesterol (mg)—41; carbohydrates (gm)—51; dietary fiber (gm)—3.

# CELEBRATION SMOKED CHICKEN WITH PASTA

*I urge you to try this smoking technique for your favorite poultry and fish. Its flavors are complex, the presentation lovely, and much of it can be prepared ahead of time. A wonderful dish to celebrate a happy occasion—pop the cork on the (de-alcoholized) champagne!*

*Time Estimate: Hands-on, 1 hour*
*Serves 4*

## SEASONING RUB

1 teaspoon dried oregano
1 teaspoon dried basil
1/4 teaspoon dried thyme
1 teaspoon hot Hungarian paprika
1/4 teaspoon freshly ground black pepper
4 (6-ounce or 175-gm) boneless, skinless chicken breasts

## BASIC TEA SMOKE

2 tablespoons uncooked rice
4 whole cloves
Tea leaves from 2 Earl Grey tea bags, removed from packets

## SAUCE

1 teaspoon light olive oil with a dash of sesame oil
1 small onion, finely chopped
1 teaspoon hot Hungarian paprika
2 cloves garlic, bashed, peeled, and chopped
2 large red bell peppers, roasted and finely chopped (see sidebar recipe)
1 tablespoon balsamic vinegar
1 cup low-sodium or homemade chicken stock (page 286)
1/4 teaspoon freshly ground sea salt

## PASTA

8 ounces uncooked linguini
6 leaves kale, cut in fine shreds (collard greens or spinach may be substituted)
2 cloves garlic, bashed, peeled, and finely chopped
2 tablespoons freshly grated Parmesan cheese

## GARNISH

2 tablespoons chopped fresh parsley

**The seasoning rub:** Crush the oregano, basil, and thyme with your hands as you place them in a small bowl. Mix in the paprika and pepper. Rub the mixture on each of the chicken breasts, using it all. Lay the chicken on a stainless steel, expanding steamer platform.

**The smoke:** Cut 3 sheets of heavy-duty aluminum foil into 15-inch (38-cm) squares. Lay them on top of each other and roll the sides under to form a circle that fits in the bottom of a Dutch oven. Cast-iron or cast-aluminum pans work fine. You should have a foil "saucer" approximately 5 inches (13 cm) in diameter. When the edge is rolled to about 1 inch (2.5 cm) high, stop and flatten the foil. Depress the center to hold the smoke ingredients.

In the depression of the aluminum foil saucer, sprinkle the rice on the bottom, cloves, and then the contents of the tea bags. Place the foil dish in the bottom of the Dutch oven, cover the pan tightly, and cook over high heat until the ingredients in the foil start smoking, about 5 minutes.

When there is plenty of smoke, place the steamer platform with the chicken into the pot; cover and cook for 10 minutes. Remove from the heat and set aside.

**The sauce:** Heat the oil in a medium saucepan over medium-high heat and fry the onions until they wilt, about 2 minutes. Add the garlic and cook for 1 minute. Now add the peppers, paprika, balsamic vinegar, and chicken stock, and simmer very gently until you are ready to use it. If it gets thicker than you want, add more stock.

**The pasta:** Cook the linguini according to package directions until just tender, about 10 minutes. Put the kale in a colander and pour the boiling pasta water and cooked pasta over the top. Toss the drained pasta and kale with the garlic and Parmesan cheese. Set aside and keep warm over a pan of hot water.

**To serve:** Divide the pasta among four warm plates. Slice the chicken breasts on the diagonal and fan out on top of the pasta. Spoon the sauce over the chicken and garnish with a dusting of the chopped parsley.

Nutritional Profile per Serving: Calories—492; % calories from fat—15%; fat (gm)—8 or 13% daily value; saturated fat (gm)—2; sodium (mg)—302; cholesterol (mg)—95; carbohydrates (gm)—54; dietary fiber (gm)—4.

## ROASTED RED PEPPERS

Position a cooking rack 2 inches (5 cm) from the broiler heat source. Cut the top and bottom off the peppers, remove and discard seeds, and cut each one into 4 large flat pieces. Place on a baking sheet, skin side up, and press to flatten. Broil until blistered and black, about 10 minutes. Remove from the oven and immediately transfer to a paper bag. Seal well and let peppers steam for 20 minutes. Pinch-peel off the skin and they're ready to use.

When you don't have time to roast, use the roasted sweet red peppers bottled in glass jars. They are very rustic with charred flecks on the flesh, but they taste wonderful and cost only a fraction more than roasting your own in season.

# CHICKEN PILAF

—— ⋈ ——

*I love it when this happens: I've reduced the fat in this popular dinner dish from 30 grams in the classic to just 6 grams in this version. Enjoy it often!*

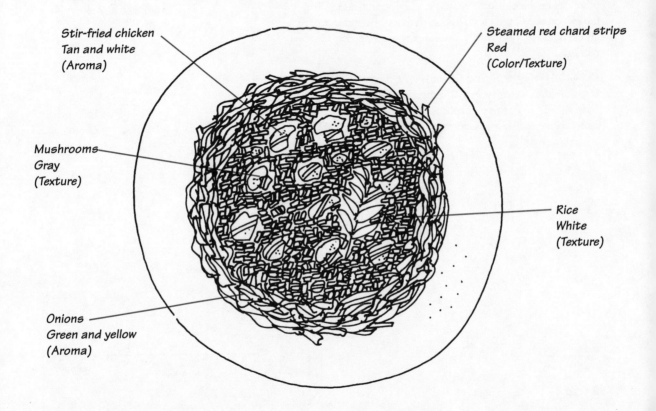

**Stir-fried chicken**
**Tan and white**
**(Aroma)**

**Steamed red chard strips**
**Red**
**(Color/Texture)**

**Mushrooms**
**Gray**
**(Texture)**

**Rice**
**White**
**(Texture)**

**Onions**
**Green and yellow**
**(Aroma)**

*Time Estimate: Hands-on, 25 minutes; unsupervised, 15 minutes*
*Serves 4*

1 teaspoon light olive oil with a dash of toasted sesame oil
8 ounces (225 gm) chicken meat, a breast and whole leg, all visible fat trimmed, cut into very small pieces
1/2 large yellow onion, peeled and finely chopped
2 cups uncooked white rice
4 cups low-sodium chicken stock (page 286)
1 bay leaf
1 branch tarragon with 12 fresh leaves

1/4 teaspoon freshly ground sea salt
1/2 teaspoon freshly ground black pepper
8 ounces (225 gm) mushroom caps, quartered
1/4 cup minced green onions
1 teaspoon finely chopped fresh tarragon
1 bunch red chard, very finely sliced
Balsamic vinegar or freshly squeezed lemon juice to taste (optional)

Preheat the oven to 450°F (230°C). Pour the oil into a large casserole over medium heat and brush it around to cover the bottom. Add the chicken and cook for 7 minutes, turning often, to cook all the sides. Transfer chicken to a bowl and set aside.

Add the onion and rice to the same casserole, stirring to coat with the oil and chicken residue. Pour in the stock; stir in the bay leaf, tarragon branch, salt, and pepper. Bake in the preheated oven, uncovered, for 20 minutes.

Take the casserole from the oven, remove the tarragon and bay leaf, and stir in the cooked chicken, the mushrooms, and green onions, burying them in the rice. Smooth the top and return to the oven for 5 minutes to just heat through. Remove and stir in the finely chopped tarragon.

While the pilaf is heating through, pour about 1 inch (2.5 cm) of water into a large pot and bring to a boil. Spread the chard on a steamer tray and steam for 1 minute. Remove from the heat and set aside.

**To serve:** Spoon a mound of pilaf onto the center of each dinner plate and encircle in a dark red wreath of the chard. The chard taste is brightened by a sprinkle of the balsamic vinegar or fresh lemon juice.

| Nutritional Profile per Serving | | | |
|---|---|---|---|
| | Classic | Minimax | Daily Value |
| Calories | 608 | 512 | |
| Calories from fat | 44% | 10% | |
| Fat (gm) | 30 | 6 | 9% |
| Saturated fat (gm) | 14 | 1 | 7% |
| Sodium (gm) | 1,162 | 347 | 14% |
| Cholesterol (mg) | 194 | 34 | 11% |
| Carbohydrates (gm) | 49 | 89 | 30% |
| Dietary fiber (gm) | 4 | 5 | 2% |
| Classic compared: Chicken Fricassée | | | |

# CHOP SUEY

※

*This dish could well be the source of worldwide enthusiasm for the stir-fry as we know it today. As with all speedily cooked dishes using fresh foods, your time will be taken up beforehand, cutting and slicing, but the sheer fun of putting it all together is well worth it. Simply make sure that the family is seated before you begin to cook, since the process goes so quickly. Serve with a good deep bowl of boiled rice on the side. I love to eat Chop Suey with chopsticks and share good conversation!*

Time Estimate: Hands-on, 30 minutes
Serves 4

RICE

1 cup uncooked short-grain white rice
1½ cups cold water

CHOP SUEY

1 tablespoon light olive oil with a dash of toasted sesame oil
6 green onions, trimmed, green part cut into 1-inch (2.5-cm) pieces and white part into 1½-inch (4-cm) pieces
1 teaspoon freshly grated gingerroot
2 cloves garlic, bashed, peeled, and chopped
1 (8-ounce or 225-gm) boneless, skinless chicken breast, cut in thin strips across the breast
1 large onion, peeled and thinly sliced
1 large green bell pepper, seeded and sliced
1/2 cup canned sliced bamboo shoots
1 (5-ounce or 150-gm) can whole water chestnuts, rinsed, each sliced into 3 pieces
1 cup quartered fresh mushrooms
2 cups bean sprouts
2 red pimientos, sliced
1/4 cup frozen green peas
1 tablespoon cornstarch mixed with 1 cup chicken stock (page 286) and 2 tablespoons low-sodium soy sauce (slurry)

**The rice:** Rinse the rice gently until the water is quite clear of all milkiness and drain well in a sieve or colander. Put the drained rice in a heavy 2½-quart saucepan. Pour in the 1½ cups water and bring to a boil. Cover, reduce the heat, and simmer gently for 15 minutes. Turn off the heat and let stand 15 minutes. Check to make sure all the water has been absorbed.

**The chop suey:** Heat 1 teaspoon of the oil in a large wok or skillet over medium-high heat and sauté the green onion ends, ginger, and garlic for 30 seconds. Turn out onto a plate and set aside.

Heat another teaspoon of oil in the wok over medium-high heat and sauté the chicken, stirring constantly, for 1 minute. Add the remaining oil and stir in the white bulbs of the green onion, the onion, and green pepper, and cook for 2 minutes. Add the cooked green onions, ginger, and garlic; the bamboo shoots; water chestnuts; and mushrooms; and cook for 2 minutes. Sprinkle the bean sprouts, pimientos, and peas over the top, and cook for 1 more minute.

Pour in the cornstarch slurry and stir gently until evenly combined. Cook until the sauce boils and thickens.

**To serve:** Spoon the Chop Suey onto warm dinner plates with the cooked rice on the side.

Nutritional Profile per Serving: Calories—377; % calories from fat—15%; fat (gm)—6 or 9% daily value; saturated fat (gm)—1; sodium (mg)—370; cholesterol (mg)—31; carbohydrates (gm)—60; dietary fiber (gm)—5.

# "I REMEMBER" CHICKEN WITH RICE

*After tasting this dish, my senior food assistant assured me that it was a taste he remembered from his childhood—the kind of dish he craved after a hard soccer practice. This Minimax version is the real thing, folks: heartwarming sauce, comforting chicken, colorful peas and carrots.*

Time Estimate: Hands-on, 35 minutes;
   unsupervised, 75 minutes
Serves 4

## CHICKEN

1 (3½-pound or 1.6-kg) whole chicken
1 bouquet garni (page 289)

## BASIC WHITE SAUCE

3 cups chicken stock (reserved from cooking chicken)
3 tablespoons cornstarch mixed with 6 tablespoons de-alcoholized white wine (slurry)
1 cup strained yogurt (page 288), at room temperature
1 tablespoon finely chopped fresh parsley
1/8 teaspoon freshly grated nutmeg
1/8 teaspoon freshly ground sea salt
1/8 teaspoon freshly ground white pepper

## SIDE DISHES

8 ounces (225 gm) diced carrots, diced the same size as the peas
8 ounces (225 gm) frozen peas
2 tablespoons chopped fresh parsley
6 cups hot cooked white rice

**The chicken:** Rinse the chicken, put it in a large saucepan, and cover with cold water. Add the bouquet garni; bring to a boil, reduce the heat, and simmer gently for 1 hour and 15 minutes, occasionally skimming the surface. Drain, reserving both the stock and the chicken. For this recipe, pour 3 cups of the stock into a fat-strainer cup and freeze the rest for later use.

To serve 4 ounces (115 gm) of chicken per person, remove the chicken meat from the bone, discarding the fat, skin, and bones. The thigh meat will fall naturally into the muscles of which it's comprised. Take the breast meat and break it into roughly 2-inch (5-cm) pieces. Set aside.

**The sauce:** Pour the reserved and defatted chicken stock into a medium saucepan; bring to a boil and reduce by half, about 10 minutes. Remove from the heat; whisk in the cornstarch slurry, return to the heat, and boil for 30 seconds, stirring constantly, until clear and thick. Remove from the heat and let the sauce cool.

Put the yogurt in a small bowl and stir gently until all the lumps are gone. Stir the yogurt into the cooled sauce. Reheat the sauce slowly over low heat and add the parsley, nutmeg, salt, and white pepper.

**The side dishes:** Steam the carrots for 6 minutes, add the frozen peas, and steam for an additional 2 minutes. The carrots should be cooked, but crunchy.

**To assemble:** Pour the sauce into a large saucepan and stir in the cooked chicken meat, steamed vegetables, and the parsley, and heat slowly over low heat.

**To serve:** Divide the rice among 4 warm dinner plates and spoon on the sauced chicken and vegetables.

Nutritional Profile per Serving: Calories—686; % calories from fat—12%; fat (gm)—9 or 14% daily value; saturated fat (gm)—3; sodium (mg)—376; cholesterol (mg)—96; carbohydrates (gm)—95; dietary fiber (gm)—6. ↑

# Roast Turkey Breast

⁂

*Here is a recipe for a wonderful Thanksgiving feast! Roast Turkey Breast served with Stuffing Loaf (page 89). You'll find the recipe for a terrific pumpkin dessert on page 115. Have a great holiday!*

*Time Estimate: Hands-on, 20 minutes; unsupervised, about 1 hour, 5 minutes, depending on the size of the breast*

Serves 12

ROAST TURKEY BREAST

1 (4-pound or 1.8-kg) whole turkey breast
4 fresh sage leaves
4 (3-inch or 8-cm) fresh thyme sprigs
2 cloves garlic, bashed, peeled, and chopped
1/4 teaspoon freshly ground white pepper
1/8 teaspoon freshly ground sea salt

GRAVY

1 cup low-sodium chicken stock (page 286)
1 tablespoon arrowroot mixed with 2 tablespoons de-alcoholized white wine (slurry)
1 tablespoon chopped fresh parsley
1 recipe Thanksgiving Stuffing Loaf (page 89)

Preheat the oven to 325°F (165°C). Remove the skin from the turkey and set it aside. Carefully remove the center breast bone, keeping the two sides of the breast connected. Remove the tenderloin pieces of turkey that form the inner muscles of the breast and save them for other dishes. By removing them you make room for the herb dressing.

Spread the two boned sides out flat on a cutting board. Place the sage leaves on top of one and the thyme sprigs, garlic, pepper, and salt on the other. Fold the two sides together, enclosing the seasonings. Place the breast in a standard-size meat loaf pan. Cover the top with the reserved turkey skin.

Roast the turkey for 25 minutes per pound. Remove the cooked turkey to a serving platter, reserving the juices in the pan.

**The gravy:** To give the gravy a nice, toasty color, put the meat loaf pan with the turkey juices on a hot burner for several minutes until the pan juices are browned. Pour the chicken stock into the meat loaf pan and dredge up any turkey residue. Now pour the stock into a saucepan and bring to a boil. Remove from the heat and pour into a fat strainer. Let the fat rise to the surface, about 5 minutes, then pour the clear, fat-free stock back into the saucepan. Stir in the slurry then return to the heat and stir until thickened, about 30 seconds. Add the parsley.

**To serve:** Slice the turkey breast and serve on a warm plate with the gravy. Place a slice of Thanksgiving Stuffing Loaf and a green vegetable of your choice on the side.

Nutritional Profile per Serving: Calories—241; % calories from fat—5%; fat (gm)—5 or 8% daily value; saturated fat (gm)—1; sodium (mg)—348; cholesterol (mg)—55; carbohydrates (gm)—25; dietary fiber (gm)—4.

# SUPER BURRITOS

⁂

*I'm not as practiced with Mexican food as I would like to be, but I've traveled in Mexico and eaten in some truly wonderful restaurants. I had missed out on burritos and therefore was delighted to "have a go." What a happy combination this recipe turned out to be.*

Time Estimate: Hands-on, 30 minutes;
  unsupervised, 12 minutes
Serves 4

4 (10-inch or 25-cm) flour tortillas
1 teaspoon light olive oil with a dash of toasted sesame oil
1 cup chopped onion
2 cloves garlic, chopped
1 jalapeño chili (seeded if you like it mild; seeds left in if you like it hot), finely chopped
8 ounces (225 gm) skinless chicken breast meat, chopped
1/4 teaspoon ground cumin
1 tablespoon chili powder
1¾ cups low-sodium pinto beans
3/4 cup low-sodium chicken stock (page 286)
1 cup cooked brown rice
3 tablespoons diced green chilies
1/4 teaspoon freshly ground sea salt

SALSA

5 plum tomatoes, seeded and chopped
1/4 cup chopped fresh cilantro
1/4 cup chopped green onions

GARNISH

4 cups mixed leaf and romaine lettuce, shredded

1/2 cup strained yogurt (page 288)

Preheat the oven to 350°F (180°C). Stack the tortillas and wrap tightly in foil. Heat in the preheated oven for 10 minutes to soften.

Heat the oil in a large, high-sided skillet and fry the onions for 2 minutes. Add the garlic and jalapeño pepper, and fry 1 minute. Toss in the chopped chicken, cumin, and chili powder, and fry until the chicken turns white, about 3 or 4 minutes. Stir in the pinto beans, mashing a little with a spoon. Add the stock, brown rice, diced chilies, and salt, and stir to mix.

Divide the chicken and bean mixture among the flour tortillas. Fold the opposite sides in until they meet. Fold the bottom and top edges just over the filling and turn over on a baking sheet so that all the folds are underneath. Bake in the preheated oven 8 to 10 minutes or until they are warmed through.

Combine the salsa ingredients.

**To serve:** Divide the shredded lettuce among 4 serving plates. When the burritos are hot, lay one on each bed of lettuce. Spoon the salsa over the top with a dollop of strained yogurt on top of that.

Nutritional Profile per Serving: Calories—572; % calories from fat—15%; fat (gm)—10 or 15% daily value; saturated fat (gm)—2; sodium (mg)—540; cholesterol (mg)—32; carbohydrates (gm)—90; dietary fiber (gm)—11. ⬆

---

You can use commercially prepared salsa for this recipe, but read the label to make sure it doesn't contain more salt than you want.

# THAI CHICKEN SALAD

*Here's a radically different main-dish chicken salad, combining some Asian ideas with the Western love of lettuce and tomatoes. Salads are usually associated with light diet eating, but in reality an amazing amount of fat is often carried in the salad dressing. Let's get smart together on delicious, low-fat salads like this one.*

Time Estimate: Hands-on, 30 minutes
Serves 4

DRESSING

1/2 cup rice wine vinegar
1/2 cup water
2 tablespoons sugar

CHICKEN SALAD

6 ounces (175 gm) uncooked Chinese rice noodles
1/2 head iceberg lettuce, finely shredded
4 plum tomatoes, seeded and finely diced
1 tablespoon chopped fresh cilantro
1/4 teaspoon freshly ground sea salt
1 teaspoon light olive oil with a dash of toasted sesame oil
4 green onions, separated into white and green parts, both cut into 1/4-inch (0.75-cm) pieces
4 quarter-size slices fresh gingerroot, chopped
2 cloves garlic, bashed, peeled, and chopped
12 ounces (350 gm) boneless, skinless chicken breast, sliced lengthwise into 1/4 X 2-inch (.75 X 5-cm) strips
1/8 teaspoon red pepper flakes
1 cup bean sprouts
Juice of 1 large lime

GARNISH

1/2 cup uncooked long-grain white rice
1 thin (3 X 1/4-inch or 8 X .75-cm) slice fresh gingerroot
1 tablespoon chopped fresh cilantro

**The dressing:** In a medium bowl, combine the ingredients for the dressing and set aside.

**The chicken salad:** Cook the rice noodles according to the package instructions. Drain and run under cold water to stop the cooking process; keep moist. Let the noodles sit in a sieve or colander for 5 minutes, allowing any excess moisture to drain.

Combine the noodles with the lettuce, half of the tomatoes, half of the dressing, the cilantro, and the salt.

Pour the oil into a large skillet or wok over medium-high heat. Add the white parts of the green onions, the gingerroot, and garlic, and cook for 1 minute. Add the chicken strips and red pepper flakes, and cook for 6 minutes. Add the green onion tops, the remaining tomatoes, and the bean sprouts, and cook for 1 minute, stirring frequently. Add the remaining dressing and the lime juice, and remove the pan from the heat.

**The garnish:** Add the rice and ginger to a small, dry pan and cook over medium heat, stirring frequently, until the rice turns nutty brown. Transfer to a small coffee mill, grind to a coarse texture, and set aside.

**To serve:** Divide the noodle mixture among 4 deep bowls and top with equal amounts of the chicken salad. Now sprinkle each portion with the cilantro and 1 teaspoon of the ground rice garnish.

Nutritional Profile per Serving: Calories—442; % calories from fat—10%; fat (gm)—5 or 8% daily value; saturated fat (gm)—1; sodium (mg)—201; cholesterol (mg)—47; carbohydrates (gm)—71; dietary fiber (gm)—4.

# Turkey Mountain

*This recipe combines Basic Brown Onion Sauce with mashed potatoes and leftover meats for incredible comfort food. It appears to pack a few calories, but please note that there are only 6 grams of fat, which is only 14 percent of total calories from fat.*

*Time Estimate: Hands-on, 15 minutes;*
*  unsupervised, 20 minutes*
*Serves 4*

## TURKEY MOUNTAIN

4 (8-ounce or 225-gm) russet potatoes, peeled and cut
  into chunks
1/2 cup 1%-fat buttermilk, at room temperature
1 teaspoon freshly grated nutmeg
1/4 teaspoon freshly ground white pepper
1/4 teaspoon freshly ground sea salt
4 thin slices leftover ham, warmed
4 thin slices leftover turkey breast, warmed

## BASIC BROWN ONION SAUCE

1/4 teaspoon light olive oil with a dash of toasted
  sesame oil
2 large onions, peeled and thinly sliced
1 teaspoon dill seed
1 teaspoon caraway seeds
1 cup low-sodium beef stock (page 286)
1 cup de-alcoholized dry red wine
1 tablespoon arrowroot mixed with 2 tablespoons de-
  alcoholized red wine (slurry)

## GARNISH

4 tablespoons chopped fresh parsley

Boil the potatoes for 30 minutes, drain, and return to the same pot over low heat. Put a kitchen towel over the top of the pot and let them dry out. This will prevent a watery consistency in your final product.

In a medium bowl, mash together the boiled potatoes, buttermilk, and seasonings. Set aside and keep warm.

**The sauce:** Pour the oil into a large skillet over medium-high heat, and cook the onions, dill, and caraway, uncovered, for 5 minutes, without stirring. Add the stock and wine, scrape up all the pan residues into the liquid, and simmer 5 minutes. Remove the pan from the heat and stir in the arrowroot slurry. Return to the heat and stir until thickened. (This sauce is also great on your favorite steak or chop, or on chicken or turkey.) Keep warm until ready to use.

**To assemble:** To give your leftovers an elegant presentation, create an informal mold; rub the ham around the inside of a soup bowl to lubricate the surface. Layer the ham and turkey to cover the inside of the bowl. Spoon in the hot potatoes, completely covering the meat to about 1/4 inch (0.75 cm) from the top of the rim, and smooth out the top. Invert the bowl over the middle of a large serving plate, grasp the edges firmly, and give it a couple of sharp shakes. The potatoes should unmold in a graceful, meat-covered mound. If you don't feel up to this procedure, you can always mound the potatoes on the plate and lay the meats decoratively on top. Whichever way, it tastes wonderful!

**To serve:** Make a depression in the center of each serving, pour on the warm onion sauce, and sprinkle with the parsley. Surround with a wreath of vegetable leftovers and your meal is complete.

Nutritional Profile per Serving: Calories—371; % calories from fat—14%; fat (gm)—6 or 9% daily value; saturated fat (gm)—2; sodium (mg)—659; cholesterol (mg)—61; carbohydrates (gm)—50; dietary fiber (gm)—4.

# Turkey & Brown Onion Chutney Salad

⚝

The idea for this recipe came from the fertile mind of my former food assistant, Robert Prince, and fits into what he calls a "composed" salad: it's not tossed, but the ingredients are artfully placed on serving plates. By adding a few pine nuts for texture, we have actually turned the Basic Brown Onion Sauce into an onion chutney that (in my humble opinion) comes very close to rivaling Crosse & Blackwell's Branston pickle at only a fraction of the price.

Time Estimate: Hands-on, 15 minutes;
  unsupervised, 30 minutes
Serves 4

2 cups Basic Brown Onion Sauce (see preceding recipe)
2 tablespoons pine nuts
1 teaspoon arrowroot mixed with 2 teaspoons de-
  alcoholized red wine (slurry)

TURKEY SALAD

4 tablespoons strained yogurt (page 288)
2 teaspoons balsamic vinegar
8 leaves Bibb lettuce
4 leaves red lettuce
12 ounces (350 gm) sliced cooked turkey breast
8 red new potatoes, about 2 inches (5 cm) in diameter,
  steamed until tender and halved
1 teaspoon chopped fresh dill

Prepare the Basic Brown Onion Sauce. Simmer the sauce until it reduces to a glaze, about 15 minutes. Remove from the heat and stir in the pine nuts and arrowroot slurry. Transfer to a small bowl and refrigerate until cool.

**The turkey salad:** In a small bowl, stir the yogurt and vinegar until the mixture turns tawny brown.

In a large bowl, toss the lettuces with the dressing until well coated.

**To compose the salad:** On one half of a dinner plate, lay out 2 leaves of the dressed Bibb lettuce and 1 leaf of the dressed red lettuce. On the other half of the plate, artfully arrange 2 slices of the turkey next to a small mound of the onion sauce and a quarter of the potatoes. Sprinkle with the dill and it's ready to be uncomposed (eaten, that is)!

Nutritional Profile per Serving: Calories—421; % calories from fat—14%; fat (gm)—6 or 10% daily value; saturated fat (gm)—2; sodium (mg)—119; cholesterol (mg)—66; carbohydrates (gm)—57; dietary fiber (gm)—6.

# Turkey Treenestar

⚝

This recipe is named for my wife, Treena. It came about on the day she came home from the hospital after giving birth to our first child, Tessa. All I had was a very small turkey, a can of tiny shrimp, and some Swiss asparagus soup powder. From such humble and romantic beginnings came a memorable meal.

Time Estimate: Hands-on, 60 minutes;
  unsupervised, 1 hour, 20 minutes
Serves 6

1 (5-pound or 2.3-kg) turkey breast with ribs and backbone, to yield 1 pound (450 gm) cooked turkey meat
4 sprigs immature thyme
8 fresh sage leaves
1/4 teaspoon freshly ground black pepper
1/8 teaspoon freshly ground sea salt

## SAUCE

7 ounces (200 gm) asparagus, fresh, or frozen if out of
   season
2 cups warm low-sodium turkey stock (page 286)
1 cup evaporated skim milk
1/4 cup cornstarch mixed with 4 tablespoons de-
   alcoholized white wine (slurry)
Pinch of freshly ground white pepper
4 ounces (115 gm) cooked bay shrimp
1 teaspoon dried dill weed

## RICE PILAF

1 teaspoon light olive oil with a dash of toasted sesame oil
1 onion, peeled and thinly sliced
1½ cups uncooked long-grain rice, well rinsed and
   drained
6 stalks parsley
1 sprig thyme
1 bay leaf
3 cups low-sodium turkey stock (page 286)
4 ounces (115 gm) tiny shrimp
1/2 teaspoon dried dill weed
1/8 teaspoon freshly ground sea salt

## GARNISH

Chopped fresh parsley
Paprika

Preheat the oven to 375°F (190°C). Using a sharp
knife, cut the backbone and ribs out of the whole
turkey breast. Remove the inner fillet, known as the
supreme. Set the bones aside for the stock. Cut the
breast into 2 even sections. You should have approximately 2¼ pounds (1 kg) of uncooked meat.

Set the meat skin side down on a board. Place the
thyme sprigs and the sage leaves down the center of
one side. Sprinkle with the fresh pepper and salt. Now
place the other breast section on the seasoned section
so that the skin is on the outside and the thick muscles are at either end, to make a more evenly sized
package. Wrap the turkey in butcher's net or tie with
kitchen twine.

Place the prepared turkey on a trivet or rack in a
roasting pan and roast for 1 hour 15 minutes, or until

the center of the turkey has reached 185°F (85°C) on
a meat thermometer.

**The rice pilaf:** Heat the oil in a small ovenproof
saucepan over medium-high heat and fry the onion
until soft, about 5 minutes. Add the rice and cook for
1 to 2 minutes, stirring to coat the rice with oil. Add
the herbs and turkey stock, and bake with the turkey,
for 30 minutes. Remove the herbs and use a fork to
fluff up the rice. Stir in the shrimp, dill weed, and salt.

**The sauce:** Cut the asparagus tips from the spears
and cut through the tips a few times just to break them
up without mashing them. The tips will be added to
the sauce. Cut the rest of the asparagus into 1/2-inch
(1.5-cm) slices and steam to serve as a side dish.

Approximately 25 minutes prior to the turkey being
fully cooked, combine the heated stock and the evaporated skim milk in a large saucepan over medium heat,
and bring to a boil. Stir in the cornstarch slurry, return
to a boil, and stir until thickened. Lower the heat, add
a pinch of white pepper, the shrimp, reserved asparagus
tips, and the dill weed and keep warm.

**To serve:** Remove the turkey from the oven, cut
off the butcher's net or twine, and slice into twelve
1/3-inch (1-cm) slices. Press the pilaf into a slim loaf
pan and turn out onto a platter. Lay the turkey slices
on the rice and coat with the sauce. Dust with the
parsley and paprika. Serve with the steamed asparagus.

Nutritional Profile per Serving: Calories—519; % calories
from fat—13%; fat (gm)—7 or 11% daily value; saturated fat
(gm)—2; sodium (mg)—359; cholesterol (mg)—170;
carbohydrates (gm)—54; dietary fiber (gm)—2.

# TURKEY VEGETABLE ROAST

*In this recipe, the turkey breast stays moist and tender under its skin while the flavors of the vegetables intensify as they roast. Paprika used in the herb rub gives the meat an appealing color when the skin is removed.*

Time Estimate: Hands-on, 25 minutes;
  unsupervised, 1 hour
Serves 6

2 teaspoons dried thyme
1 teaspoon dried tarragon
1 teaspoon dried rosemary
1 teaspoon dried sage leaves
1 teaspoon hot Hungarian paprika
1/4 teaspoon freshly ground black pepper
1/4 teaspoon freshly ground sea salt
1/2 whole turkey breast (1½ pounds or 680 gm)
12 medium red potatoes, quartered
3 small parsnips, peeled and quartered lengthwise
6 carrots, peeled and quartered lengthwise
1 large sweet onion, peeled and cut into 12 wedges
1 teaspoon light olive oil with a dash of toasted sesame oil

SIDE DISH

3 pounds (1.4 kg) Swiss chard, washed and stemmed

SAUCE

1½ cups unsweetened apple juice
1/4 teaspoon dried sage leaves
1 tablespoon plus 1 teaspoon arrowroot mixed with 2
  tablespoons unsweetened apple juice (slurry)

Preheat the oven to 325°F (170°C). Crumble the thyme, tarragon, and rosemary into a small bowl. Add the paprika, pepper, and salt, and mix well.

Take the skin off the turkey in one piece and set aside. Trim any fat off the breast meat. Rub half the herb-spice mixture over the breast. Re-cover well with the skin, tucking it in around the edges. Place on a rack in an 8 X 8-inch (20 X 20-cm) baking pan.

Arrange the vegetables on a large baking sheet.

Brush all sides with the oil and sprinkle with the remaining herb-spice mixture.

Roast the turkey and the vegetables side by side in the center of the preheated oven for 55 minutes. At that point the turkey will be moist and the vegetables firm but tender. Remove the turkey, transfer to a carving board, and cover to keep warm. Pour the accumulated cooking juices through a strainer into a small saucepan. Turn the heat off and leave the vegetables in the oven.

**The side dish:** Place the Swiss chard in a steamer tray over boiling water, cover, and steam for 4 minutes.

**The sauce:** Pour the apple juice and sage into the saucepan with the strained meat juices and bring to a boil. Remove from the heat; stir in the arrowroot slurry, return to the heat, and cook over high heat to clear and thicken, about 30 seconds.

Take the vegetables out of the oven. Discard the turkey skin and cut the meat into thin slices.

**To serve:** Arrange the vegetables on warm dinner plates along with the turkey slices and Swiss chard. Spoon the sauce over the turkey and roasted vegetables.

Nutritional Profile per Serving: Calories—448; % calories from fat—8%; fat (gm)—4 or 6% daily value; saturated fat (gm)—1; sodium (mg)—540; cholesterol (mg)—53; carbohydrates (gm)—76; dietary fiber (gm)—11.

# Cottage Pie

*Like any great comfort food, this English classic has hundreds of local variations. Mine reduces the meat and adds bulgur wheat, and, in my judgment, does no disservice to the flavor of the original.*

Time Estimate: Hands-on, 45 minutes;
  unsupervised, 20 minutes
Serves 6

MASHED POTATOES

3 pounds (1.4 kilos) baking potatoes, peeled and cut into
  2-inch pieces
1/4 teaspoon freshly ground sea salt
1/4 teaspoon freshly ground white pepper
1 cup 1%-fat buttermilk

FILLING

1/4 cup uncooked bulgur wheat
3 cups low-sodium beef stock (page 286)
3/4 pound (0.4 kilo) leanest ground beef (9% fat)
1/2 teaspoon freshly ground sea salt
3 tablespoons low-sodium tomato paste
1 teaspoon light olive oil with a dash of toasted sesame oil
1 cup chopped onion
1 cup chopped carrots
1/4 cup chopped celery
2 cloves garlic, bashed, peeled, and chopped
1 tablespoon chopped fresh thyme
1 tablespoon chopped fresh parsley
1/2 teaspoon marjoram
1 tablespoon low-sodium soy sauce
1 tablespoon prepared horseradish
1 tablespoon arrowroot mixed with 2 tablespoons beef
  stock (slurry)

**The potatoes:** Boil the potatoes in a large pot of water for 20 minutes with the salt. Drain; return to the pot, cover with a clean kitchen towel, and let steam dry for 15 minutes over very low heat. Add the pepper and buttermilk, and mash until smooth. Set aside until needed.

**The filling:** Preheat the oven to 350°F (180°C). Place the bulgur in a medium bowl. Heat 2 cups of the stock in a small saucepan, pour over the bulgur, and set aside for 10 minutes to soften.

Brown the ground beef with 1/4 teaspoon of the salt in a frying pan over high heat until brown. Push the meat to one side, reduce the heat to medium, add the tomato paste to the hot pan, and stir until it starts turning dark. Pour the remaining cup of beef stock into the pan, stirring to free all the flavorful bits, then transfer the filling to a bowl and set aside.

Without washing the pan, heat the oil over medium heat and start frying the onions. When they begin to wilt, add the rest of the vegetables, garlic, herbs, and the remaining salt, and cook for 2 minutes. Add the soy sauce, horseradish, bulgur, and beef stock, and simmer for 10 minutes or until the carrots are tender. Add the cooked meat mixture and stir in the arrowroot slurry. Bring to a boil and pour into a 9 X 9-inch (23 X 23-cm) baking dish. Spread the mashed potatoes over the top of the hot filling or pipe them on, using a large star tip. Bake in the preheated oven for 20 minutes, then place under the broiler for 2 minutes to brown the potatoes slightly.

Nutritional Profile per Serving: Calories—374; % calories from fat—15%; fat (gm)—6 or 3% daily value; saturated fat (gm)—2; sodium (mg)—509; cholesterol (mg)—34; carbohydrates (gm)—60; dietary fiber (gm)—7.

I make the best whipped potatoes from large, mature baking potatoes. They have a dry, mealy texture that is much better than waxy new potatoes for this purpose. To remove any lumps, I mash them with a ricer, which looks like a large garlic press.

# Hearty Vegetable Stew Seasoned with Beef

—— ✕ ——

*Is there anything more basic than a hearty meat stew? This version has switched the traditional ratio of beef to vegetables and winds up with three-quarters vegetables to one-quarter meat. Then it comforts and cares for you with familiar aromas and textures.*

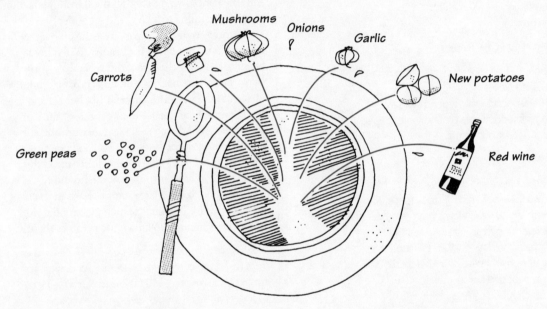

Time Estimate: Hands-on, 20 minutes;
  unsupervised, 1 hour, 15 minutes
Serves 4

8 ounces (225 gm) beef bottom round, all visible fat removed, cut into 1/2-inch (1.5-cm) pieces
1½ teaspoons light olive oil with a dash of toasted sesame oil
2 medium onions, peeled and thickly sliced
3 ounces (90 gm) low-sodium tomato paste
2 cloves garlic, bashed, peeled, and chopped
4 tablespoons de-alcoholized red wine
3 cups enhanced canned low-sodium beef stock (page 286), reduced to 2½ cups
16 ounces (450 gm) carrots, peeled and cut into 1-inch (2.5-cm) pieces

12 small red new potatoes, scrubbed
12 medium mushrooms, quartered
2 cups frozen peas, thawed
2 tablespoons arrowroot mixed with 4 tablespoons de-alcoholized red wine (slurry)
2 tablespoons chopped fresh parsley
1/4 teaspoon freshly ground black pepper
1/4 teaspoon freshly ground sea salt

GARNISH

Chopped fresh parsley

Pat the meat dry with a paper towel. Heat 1 teaspoon of the oil in a large skillet over medium-high heat and brown the meat on one side, about 3 minutes. Remove and set aside.

In the same hot skillet, heat the remaining 1/2 teaspoon oil and cook the onions and tomato paste, scraping the brown meat residue into the mixture, for 5 minutes. Stir in the garlic and set aside. (This step accomplishes three important functions at one time: the onions and garlic release their aromatic volatile oils; the tomato paste caramelizes the mixture; and a flavor-filled glaze builds up on the pan— all of which add depth of taste without fat.)

Transfer the browned meat to a medium saucepan. Add the tomato and onion mixture, wine, and beef stock; bring to a boil, reduce the heat to its lowest setting, and simmer, covered, for 30 minutes. Add the carrots and potatoes, and simmer for 30 minutes. Stir in the mushrooms and simmer for 5 minutes.

Remove from the heat; add the peas and the arrowroot slurry, return to the heat, and stir until thickened. Add the parsley, pepper, and salt.

**To serve:** Ladle into bowls and sprinkle with a little of the fresh parsley.

| Nutritional Profile per Serving | | | |
|---|---|---|---|
| | Classic | Minimax | Daily Value |
| Calories | 579 | 576 | |
| Calories from fat | 41% | 10% | |
| Fat (gm) | 26 | 6 | 9% |
| Saturated fat (gm) | 10 | 2 | 10% |
| Sodium (mg) | 1,142 | 232 | 10% |
| Cholesterol (mg) | 125 | 48 | 16% |
| Carbohydrates (gm) | 37 | 100 | 33% |
| Dietary fiber (gm) | 8 | 14 | 56% |
| Classic compared: Old-Fashioned Beef Stew | | | |

# QUINOA AND BEEF CONQUISTADOR

——— ✕ ———

*The light, fresh taste and slightly crunchy texture of quinoa goes very well with beef, chicken, or fish. In addition, quinoa offers more iron than any other grain and is a good source of potassium, riboflavin, magnesium, zinc, copper, manganese, and folacin. I use it in this dish as an "extender," allowing us to use less red meat per person and still have a dish that is high in protein.*

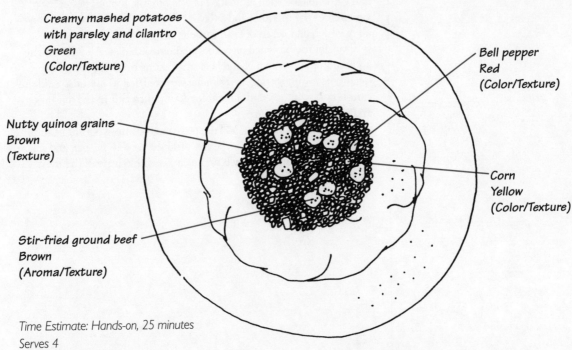

Creamy mashed potatoes
with parsley and cilantro
Green
(Color/Texture)

Bell pepper
Red
(Color/Texture)

Nutty quinoa grains
Brown
(Texture)

Corn
Yellow
(Color/Texture)

Stir-fried ground beef
Brown
(Aroma/Texture)

*Time Estimate: Hands-on, 25 minutes*
*Serves 4*

## GREEN MASHED POTATOES

4 large potatoes, peeled and cut into chunks
1/2 cup 1%-fat buttermilk
1/8 teaspoon freshly ground sea salt
1/4 teaspoon freshly ground white pepper
1/4 cup finely chopped fresh cilantro, mixed with
   1/8 cup finely chopped parsley

## BEEF CONQUISTADOR

2 cups water
1 cup raw quinoa
1/2 teaspoon light olive oil with a dash of toasted
   sesame oil

1 small yellow onion, peeled and finely chopped
3 cloves garlic, bashed, peeled, and chopped
8 ounces (225 gm) ground beef bottom round
1 tablespoon low-sodium tomato paste
2 tablespoons low-sodium soy sauce
1 cup low-sodium beef stock (page 286)
1 red bell pepper, seeded and finely chopped
1 cup frozen corn, thawed
2 tablespoons chopped fresh parsley
2 tablespoons chopped fresh cilantro
1/2 teaspoon cayenne pepper
1/4 teaspoon ground cumin
1 tablespoon arrowroot mixed with 2 tablespoons
   water (slurry)

**The potatoes:** Boil the potatoes for 30 minutes, drain, and return to the same pot over low heat. Put a kitchen towel over the top of the pot and let the potatoes dry out. This will prevent a watery consistency in your final product.

In a medium bowl, mash together the potatoes, buttermilk, salt, and pepper. Stir in the cilantro-parsley mixture until well incorporated. Set aside and keep warm.

**The beef:** In a medium saucepan, bring the water to a boil. Add the quinoa, bring to a boil, reduce the heat, and simmer 10 minutes. Remove from the heat and set aside.

Pour the oil into a large casserole over medium heat and cook the onion and garlic until the onion is translucent, about 4 minutes. Add the beef and cook until fully browned, stirring often, about 3 minutes. Turn the heat to high and stir in the tomato paste until completely incorporated and deepened in color, about 2 minutes. Stir in the cooked quinoa, the soy sauce, stock, red pepper, corn, parsley, cilantro, cayenne pepper, and cumin, and mix well. Remove from the heat; stir in the arrowroot slurry, return to the heat, and stir until thickened. Remove from the heat and set aside.

**To serve:** For an elegant presentation, spoon the potatoes into a pastry bag and pipe a wreath on each dinner plate. Otherwise, spoon a mound onto each plate and make a hollow in the middle. Ladle the beef filling into the center.

| Nutritional Profile per Serving | | | |
|---|---|---|---|
| | **Classic** | **Minimax** | **Daily Value** |
| Calories | 386 | 469 | |
| Calories from fat | 66% | 11% | |
| Fat (gm) | 28 | 6 | 9% |
| Saturated fat (gm) | 13 | 1 | 7% |
| Sodium (gm) | 294 | 463 | 19% |
| Cholesterol (mg) | 197 | 31 | 10% |
| Carbohydrates (gm) | 11 | 83 | 28% |
| Dietary fiber (gm) | 1 | 7 | 28% |
| Classic compared: Beef Lindstrom | | | |

# Sauerbraten

*One of the world's greatest classics is the "sour meat" pot roast that is about as German in style as a dish can get. I have used a flavor injector to increase the flavor and a pressure cooker to decrease the cooking time in my lower-risk version.*

*Time Estimate: Hands-on, 1 hour, 40 minutes; unsupervised, 90 minutes*

*Serves 8*

MARINADE

6 tablespoons raisins
1¾ cups de-alcoholized red wine
2 tablespoons arrowroot
1/2 teaspoon light olive oil with a dash of toasted
   sesame oil
1 onion, peeled and finely chopped
1 stalk celery, finely chopped
1 carrot, peeled and finely chopped
1/2 leek, finely chopped
2 whole cloves
1 bay leaf
6 black peppercorns
6 juniper berries
1/4 cup red wine vinegar

BEEF

3 pounds (1.4 kg) bottom round beef
1 teaspoon light olive oil with a dash of toasted sesame oil
3 tablespoons low-sodium tomato paste

MASHED POTATOES

3 pounds (1.4 kg) potatoes, peeled and quartered
1/2 cup 1%-fat buttermilk
1 tablespoon chopped leek
1/4 teaspoon freshly grated nutmeg
1/4 teaspoon caraway seeds
1/8 teaspoon freshly ground sea salt
1/4 teaspoon freshly ground black pepper

BROILED TOMATOES

4 large tomatoes
8 teaspoons chopped fresh dill
8 teaspoons bread crumbs

GARNISH

1 tablespoon chopped fresh parsley

**The marinade:** Soak the raisins in 1/4 cup of the red wine until plump, approximately 1 hour. Drain through a sieve, reserving the wine. Set the raisins aside. Mix the reserved raisin-soaking wine with the arrowroot to form a slurry and set aside.

In a medium saucepan, heat the oil over medium-high heat and sauté the onion, celery, carrot, and leek until the onion is translucent, about 5 minutes. Add the cloves, bay leaf, peppercorns, juniper berries, the remaining 1½ cups red wine, and the vinegar, and bring to a boil. Remove from the heat, cover, and let it sit for 30 minutes. Strain, reserving the marinade and the vegetables and spices separately.

**The beef:** Wash the beef, dry completely with paper towels, and place on a cutting board. Pour 1/4 cup of the strained marinade into a flavor injector (see below). Inject tiny amounts all over the beef's surface until the injector is empty. Fill the flavor injector with another 1/4 cup of strained marinade and repeat the process. Reserve the leftover marinade.

In a large pressure cooker, heat the oil and brown the marinated beef and the tomato paste. Remove the beef and set aside.

Deglaze the pressure cooker with the reserved marinade and add the reserved spices and vegetables. Add the beef, secure the lid, and cook for 25 minutes.

**The side dishes:** While the beef is cooking, boil the potatoes in a medium saucepan for 20 minutes. Drain, cover with a clean towel, and set over low heat for 5 minutes. Transfer to a large bowl and mash. Add the buttermilk and whip thoroughly. Stir in the chopped leeks, nutmeg, caraway seeds, and half of the salt and pepper. Cut the tomatoes in half and sprinkle with the dill, bread crumbs, and remaining salt and pepper. Just before serving, put the tomatoes on a baking tray and pop under the broiler for 5 minutes.

Transfer the cooked beef to a carving board. Strain the marinade from the pressure cooker through a sieve and into a saucepan. Add the plumped raisins and the arrowroot slurry and stir over medium heat until thickened.

**To serve:** Carve the beef into 1/4-inch (.75-cm) slices. Place 2 slices on each dinner plate and serve with a broiled tomato half and 1 cup of the mashed potatoes. Drizzle with the marinade-gravy and dust with the chopped fresh parsley.

Nutritional Profile per Serving: Calories—406; % calories from fat—15%; fat (gm)—7 or 10% daily value; saturated fat (gm)—2; sodium (mg)—164; cholesterol (mg)—83; carbohydrates (gm)—51; dietary fiber (gm)—5.

This recipe uses a flavor injector. If you do not have one, you can marinate the beef the traditional way. Wash the beef and place it in a small bowl. Pour in the marinade, including the spices and vegetables, making sure that the meat is completely immersed. Put the beef in the refrigerator and marinate for three to five days, turning the meat once every day. Remove from the marinade and dry completely with paper towels. It will only soften the outside and won't flavor the inside, but the sauce is delicious.

# TEXAS CHILI

*This one's for all you hearty beef lovers who thought you couldn't enjoy Texas-style chili anymore. The Minimax version has great flavor and texture, and I feel fortunate to have been able to bring the fat down to 6 grams and the fiber up to 14.*

Time Estimate: Hands-on, 25 minutes;
  unsupervised, 1 hour
Serves 6

1 teaspoon light olive oil with a dash of toasted sesame oil
1/2 pound (225 gm) beef bottom round
1/2 pound (225 gm) leanest ground turkey breast

1 large onion, peeled and chopped
3 cloves garlic, peeled, bashed, and chopped
2 jalapeño peppers, seeded and chopped (leave the seeds in if you like it hot)
1 (6-ounce or 175-gm) can no-salt tomato paste
1 teaspoon cayenne pepper
1 tablespoon powdered cumin
1 teaspoon dried oregano
1 (4-ounce or 115-gm) can diced green chilies
1½ cup water
1½ cups de-alcoholized red wine
3 cups cooked brown rice
2 (15-ounce or 425-gm) cans low-sodium pinto beans, drained

GARNISH

6 tablespoons diced raw onions
6 teaspoons freshly grated Parmesan cheese
6 tablespoons chopped fresh cilantro

Trim the beef of all visible fat and cut into 1/4-inch (.75-cm) cubes. Heat the oil in a large, high-sided skillet over high heat. Drop the meat into the hot pan and brown on all sides. When the beef cubes are brown, add the turkey and cook until browned. Add the onions, garlic, and jalapeños, and cook for 2 minutes. Add the tomato paste and now you will see the Maillard reaction: a darkening color change in the tomato paste that is the source of a deep, smoky taste. Stir in the cayenne pepper, cumin, oregano, green chilies, water, and wine, carefully scraping up all of the flavorful residue from the bottom of the pan. Bring to a boil, cover, and simmer over very low heat for 1 hour, or until the meat is very tender.

While the chili is cooking, keep the beans and rice warm, in separate skillets.

**To Serve:** Place 1/2 cup of the brown rice in each dish and top with 1/2 cup each of the beans and the chili. Sprinkle with the onions, cheese, and cilantro.

Nutritional Profile per Serving: Calories—469; % calories from fat—11%; fat (gm) 6 or 9% daily value; saturated fat (gm)—2; sodium (mg)—325; cholesterol (mg)—44; carbohydrates (gm)—72; dietary fiber (gm)—14.

# STROGANOFF WITH BROWN RICE

*"Meat in the minor key" (reducing the portion size of the meat) is one of the most useful techniques in my way of cooking. However, if meat moves from center stage, something must always take its place! Here, I've added an aromatic kick with the dill and the de-alcoholized red wine, but it's really the color and texture from the red peppers and snow peas that do the trick.*

Time Estimate: Hands-on, 35 minutes
Serves 4

## MEAT AND VEGETABLES

6 ounces (175 gm) beef tenderloin
1 teaspoon light olive oil with a dash of toasted sesame oil
Freshly ground black pepper, to taste
1 medium onion, peeled and thinly sliced
2 cloves garlic, bashed, peeled, and chopped
1 red bell pepper, seeded and cut into thin strips
1/4 cup low-sodium tomato paste
1 tablespoon Worcestershire sauce
2 tablespoons chopped fresh parsley, including stems
2 cups snow peas, cut on the diagonal into thirds
4 cups fresh mushrooms, cut into 1/4-inch (.75-cm) slices

## SAUCE

1½ cups enhanced low-sodium beef broth (page 286)
1/2 cup de-alcoholized red wine
2 tablespoons cornstarch mixed with 4 tablespoons de-alcoholized red wine (slurry)
3/4 cup strained yogurt (page 288)
1 teaspoon dried dill
3 cups cooked brown rice tossed with 1½ teaspoons chopped fresh dill or 1/2 teaspoon dried

**The meat and vegetables:** Pound the beef tenderloin until it's about 1/4 inch (.75 cm) thick. Slice into thin strips, 5 inches long and 1/4 inch wide (13 X .75 cm). Brush a large, high-sided, nonstick skillet with 1/4 teaspoon of the oil. When the pan is hot, brown the beef slices on one side for 1 minute over high heat. Transfer to a bowl and sprinkle with the pepper.

Pour the remaining oil into the same pan and fry the onions for 3 minutes over medium-low heat. Add the garlic and peppers, and cook for 3 more minutes. Stir in the tomato paste, turn the heat up to medium-high, and cook until it darkens slightly. Add the Worcestershire sauce, parsley, peas, and mushrooms, and stir-fry for 1 minute. Remove the pan from the heat.

**The sauce:** Stir the stock and wine together in a medium saucepan over low heat. Remove from the heat; stir in the cornstarch slurry, return to the heat, and bring to a boil to thicken, about 30 seconds. Remove from the heat and pour about 1 cup of the hot liquid into the strained yogurt, stirring to combine. Slowly pour the yogurt mixture into the thickened broth, stirring with a wire whisk. This will keep the sauce from breaking or curdling.

Pour the sauce over the vegetables in the other pan, add the meat, and heat through, scraping the bottom of the pan to deglaze it. Stir in the dill and taste for seasoning.

**To serve:** Present this glossy, colorful Stroganoff with a mound of steamed rice or over noodles.

Nutritional Profile per Serving: Calories—432; % calories from fat—15%; fat (gm)—7 or 11% daily value; saturated fat (gm)—2; sodium (mg)—310; cholesterol (mg)—26; carbohydrates (gm)—68; dietary fiber (gm)—9.

# GOULASH

*My version of the Hungarian favorite with much less fat but no less appeal—this is a deliciously satisfying meal to serve those you love.*

*Time Estimate: Hands-on, 35 minutes;*
*unsupervised, 1 1/2 hours*
Serves 4

1 teaspoon light olive oil with a dash of toasted sesame oil
12 ounces (350 gm) bottom round beef, fat trimmed
   and cut into small cubes
1 onion, peeled and chopped
3 cloves garlic, bashed, peeled, and chopped
1/2 cup chopped celery
1½ cups chopped carrots
2 green bell peppers, seeded and chopped
1/2 teaspoon thyme
1/4 teaspoon marjoram
2 tablespoons plus 1 teaspoon Hungarian hot paprika
1 teaspoon caraway seeds
1/4 teaspoon freshly ground sea salt
1/2 teaspoon freshly ground black pepper
3/4 cup tomato purée
3 cups low-sodium beef stock (page 286)
2 large potatoes, peeled and cut into 1/2-inch (1.5-cm)
   cubes

GARNISH

1/2 cup strained yogurt (page 288)

Heat 1/4 teaspoon of the oil in a large, high-sided skillet over high heat. Drop the cubed meat into the hot pan and brown all sides. Reduce the heat to medium-high, add the remaining oil and the onions, and cook for 1 minute. Add the garlic, celery, 1/2 cup of the carrots, 1/2 of the peppers, the thyme, marjoram, 1 tablespoon of the paprika, the caraway seeds, salt, and pepper. Stir and cook for 2 to 3 minutes, until the onions are transparent. Add the tomato purée and cook until it begins to darken. Pour in the beef stock, scraping the flavorful brown bits off the

bottom of the pan. Simmer, uncovered, for 1 hour.

Add the potatoes, the remaining carrots and peppers, and 1 more tablespoon of paprika, and cook for 30 minutes more or until the vegetables are tender. Stir in the remaining 1 teaspoon of paprika.

**To serve:** Dish up in individual serving bowls and top the goulash with a healthy dollop of the strained yogurt.

Nutritional Profile per Serving: Calories—318; % calories from fat—15%; fat (gm)—5 or 8% daily value; saturated fat (gm)—1; sodium (mg)—498; cholesterol (mg)—46; carbohydrates (gm)—42; dietary fiber (gm)—6.

# YANKEE POT ROAST

⌗

*Here it is: instant nostalgia, the kind of food that fogs up the kitchen windows on a winter's day. The sort of food that Dad carves at one end of the table, while Mum sends the vegetables around from the other. I love low-risk nostalgia, so I've tweaked the classic, by largely reducing the meat and increasing the vegetables.*

Time Estimate: Hands-on, 45 minutes; unsupervised, 60 minutes

Serves 8

2½ pounds (1.1 kg) rump beef roast
3 tablespoons low-sodium tomato paste
1 teaspoon light olive oil with a dash of toasted sesame oil
3 onions, peeled and finely chopped
6 carrots, finely chopped
8 stalks celery, finely chopped
1 bouquet garni (page 289)
3½ cups low-sodium beef stock (page 286)
2 tablespoons cider vinegar
6 carrots, chopped into 2-inch (5-cm) pieces
1½ cups cubed turnips
1¼ pounds (625 gm) new red potatoes
10 small boiling onions, peeled
1½ cups fresh mushrooms
4 teaspoons horseradish
1 tablespoon chopped fresh parsley
4 tablespoons arrowroot mixed with 8 tablespoons de-alcoholized red wine (slurry)

Put a large pot or Dutch oven over high heat. When the pot is very hot, brown the beef and the tomato paste. Transfer the beef to a plate and set aside. Heat the oil over medium heat in the same pot and sauté the onions, finely chopped carrots, and celery for 10 minutes. This establishes a fragrant aromatic base.

Return the browned beef to the bed of vegetables. Add the bouquet garni, beef stock, and vinegar, and bring to a boil. Reduce the heat, cover, and simmer gently for 30 minues. Remove the roast and set aside.

Remove the vegetables and reserve, leaving the liquid in the pot.

Return the roast to the pot and add the roughly chopped carrots, turnips, the potatoes, and boiling onions. Cover and cook over low heat for 20 minutes. Add the mushrooms and cook 10 minutes.

While the roast continues cooking, purée the reserved cooked vegetables in a food processor. Stir in the horseradish and parsley. Set aside as a side dish for your roast.

Transfer the roast to a carving board. Leave the vegetables and beef stock in the pot to keep warm. Carve the beef into thin slices. Take the pot off the heat and remove the bouquet garni. Stir in the arrowroot slurry, return to the heat, and stir until the stock thickens.

**To serve:** Place 2 slices of roast on each dinner plate. Place cooked vegetables to the side and drizzle with the thickened beef juices. Serve the puréed vegetables at room temperature in a small side dish.

Nutritional Profile per Serving: Calories—374; % calories from fat—15%; fat (gm)—6 or 9% daily value; saturated fat (gm)—2; sodium (mg)—208; cholesterol (mg)—75; carbohydrates (gm)—46; dietary fiber (gm)—8.

# BEAN AND BACON BURRITO WITH MEXICAN RICE

⚜

*This is a good dish to make with the entire family. There is a job for everyone.*

Time Estimate: Hands-on, 45 minutes
Serves 4

## SALSA

8 ounces (225 gm) plum tomatoes, peeled, seeded, and diced
1 tablespoon finely chopped onion
1/4 teaspoon dried oregano
1 teaspoon red wine vinegar
1 jalapeño pepper, seeded and chopped
2 tablespoons chopped fresh cilantro

## MEXICAN RICE

1 cup uncooked long-grain white rice
1 teaspoon light olive oil with a dash of toasted sesame oil
1/2 large onion, peeled and chopped
1 clove garlic, bashed, peeled, and chopped
1 jalapeño pepper
8 ounces (225 gm) roma tomatoes
2 cups low-sodium chicken stock (page 286)
1/4 teaspoon freshly ground sea salt
1/4 cup chopped fresh cilantro

## REFRIED BEANS

1 teaspoon light olive oil with a dash of toasted sesame oil
1/2 large onion, peeled and chopped
1 clove garlic, bashed, peeled, and chopped
1 jalapeño pepper, seeded
3 ounces (90 gm) Canadian bacon, diced
2 cups canned, low-sodium pinto beans, drained and rinsed
1 cup low-sodium chicken stock (page 286)

4 whole-wheat tortillas

## GARNISH

1/2 cup strained yogurt (page 288)
1 tablespoon chopped fresh cilantro

**The salsa:** In a medium bowl, combine all the ingredients and set aside.

**The rice:** Pour hot water over the rice in a bowl and set aside for 15 minutes. (This step gives the rice a texture more like authentic Mexican rice. If you're short on time, it can be eliminated.) Drain thoroughly, shaking until all the water is gone. Heat the oil in a saucepan over medium-high heat and fry the onion until it wilts, about 2 minutes. Add the garlic and drained rice, and fry for 10 minutes, stirring often to keep the onions from browning. Stir in the jalapeño, tomatoes, stock, and salt, and simmer, uncovered, for 15 minutes, without stirring. Cover and keep warm until ready to serve. Just before serving, stir in the cilantro.

**The refried beans:** Heat the oil in a medium non-stick skillet over medium-high heat and fry the onion until wilted, about 2 minutes. Add the garlic, jalapeño pepper, and Canadian bacon, and fry for another minute. Add the beans and mash well. Pour in 1/2 cup of the stock and continue mashing and frying, scraping the bottom of the pan often to release the brown bits forming there. Fry for about 5 minutes, adding stock when you need it to achieve the consistency you like.

**To serve:** Heat the tortillas in the oven or microwave. Divide the refried beans among the 4 tortillas, roll, and garnish with the salsa, yogurt, and cilantro. Serve the Mexican rice on the side.

Nutritional Profile per Serving: Calories—529; % calories from fat—12%; fat (gm)—7 or 10% daily value; saturated fat (gm)—2; sodium (mg)—659; cholesterol (mg)—11; carbohydrates (gm)—94; dietary fiber (gm)—11.

# LAMB THERESA

⬧

*This dish is named after our eldest daughter, Tessa, who is very colorful and a pure delight—just like this dinner. It's a great use for leftover meat.*

*Time Estimate: Hands-on, 30 minutes*
*Serves 4*

1 teaspoon light olive oil with a dash of toasted sesame oil
2 cloves garlic, bashed, peeled, and finely chopped
4 tablespoons low-sodium ketchup
1 tablespoon finely chopped fresh parsley stalks
1¼ cups low-sodium tomato juice
8 ounces (225 gm) cooked roast lamb, cut into 1/2-inch (1.5-cm) cubes
1 (12-ounce or 350-gm) can whole peeled Italian tomatoes, drained
1 (15-ounce or 425-gm) can low-sodium kidney beans, drained and rinsed
2 tablespoons arrowroot mixed with 1/4 cup de-alcoholized white wine (slurry)
1 cup chopped broccoli florets
1/4 teaspoon freshly ground black pepper

### SIDE DISH

2 cups water
1/4 teaspoon turmeric
1½ cups uncooked long-grain rice

Heat the oil in a large skillet over medium-high heat and sauté the garlic for 1 minute. Add the ketchup and cook until the color darkens. Add the parsley stalks and tomato juice, and cook for 2 minutes. Add the lamb, tomatoes, and beans; bring to a boil, reduce the heat, and simmer for 5 minutes.

Remove from the heat; stir in the arrowroot slurry, return to the heat, and stir until thickened. Stir in the broccoli florets, making sure they are submerged; bring to a boil, reduce the heat, and simmer 5 minutes. Stir in the black pepper and keep warm.

**The side dish:** In a medium saucepan, bring the water and the turmeric to a boil. Add the rice and boil 10 minutes. Strain through a metal sieve, then place the rice-filled sieve over a pan of boiling water and steam, covered, for 5 minutes.

**To serve:** This is a very simple food and is served literally "as is"—just a mound of yellow rice and a ladle of meat and vegetable sauce.

Nutritional Profile per Serving: Calories—614; % calories from fat—11%; fat (gm)—8 or 12% daily value; saturated fat (gm)—2; sodium (mg)—206; cholesterol (mg)—52; carbohydrates (gm)—102; dietary fiber (gm)—13. ⬆

# PORK TENDERLOIN IN RED-WINE ONION SAUCE

⬧

*Quick, juicy, tender, full of flavor, lots of great colors . . . frankly, it's hard to imagine a better plateful. Here is a complete dinner for guests or family, with under 500 calories per serving and only 8 grams of fat.*

*Time Estimate: Hands-on, 80 minutes*
*Serves 4*

### POTATOES

1 teaspoon light olive oil with a dash of toasted sesame oil
1 large onion, peeled and sliced
1 clove garlic, bashed, peeled, and chopped
1 tablespoon finely chopped fresh thyme
1/4 teaspoon freshly ground black pepper
1/2 teaspoon freshly ground sea salt
4 large red new potatoes, thinly sliced
1/2 cup low-sodium beef stock (page 286)

## ONION SAUCE

1 teaspoon light olive oil with a dash of toasted sesame oil
2 large onions, peeled and sliced
1 teaspoon caraway seeds
1 teaspoon dill seed
1/4 cup dark raisins
3/4 cup de-alcoholized red wine
1 cup low-sodium beef stock (page 286)

## PORK TENDERLOIN

1/4 teaspoon freshly ground black pepper
1/4 teaspoon freshly ground sea salt
1/4 teaspoon light olive oil with a dash of toasted
   sesame oil
2 (1/2-pound or 225-gm) pork tenderloins, fat and
   silverskin trimmed
1/4 cup de-alcoholized red wine
2 tablespoons arrowroot mixed with 4 tablespoons de-
   alcoholized red wine (slurry)

## SIDE DISH: SPINACH-STUFFED RED PEPPER

1 large sweet red bell pepper, seeded and cut in half
   lenghwise
5 ounces (150 gm) spinach leaves, washed
1/16 teaspoon freshly ground sea salt
1/16 teaspoon freshly ground black pepper
1/8 teaspoon freshly grated nutmeg

## GARNISH

1 tablespoon chopped fresh parsley

**The potatoes:** Preheat the oven to 350°F (180°C). In a large skillet, heat the oil over medium-high heat and sauté the onion and garlic until the onion is slightly soft, about 3 minutes. Stir in the thyme, pepper, and salt; heat through and set aside.

Layer the bottom of an 8 X 8-inch (20 X 20-cm) baking pan with a quarter of the potato slices. Spoon a third of the sautéed onion and garlic on top. Continue the layering process, finishing with a neat layer of potatoes on top. Pour the beef stock over the potatoes and bake in the preheated oven for 50 minutes.

**The onion sauce:** Heat the oil in a skillet over medium heat and cook the onions, caraway, and dill,

without stirring, for 5 minutes. Stir once, then cover and cook for 5 minutes. Add the raisins, wine, and stock, and cook for 5 minutes more. Remove from the heat and set aside.

**The pork tenderloin:** Sprinkle the pepper and salt on a large plate. Drizzle the oil over the pepper and salt, and stir together. Dredge the pork pieces through the seasoned oil.

Heat a large ovenproof skillet over high heat and quickly brown the pork on all sides to seal in the juices, about 5 minutes. Place the skillet in the preheated oven and bake for 15 minutes. (You can time this to bake with the potatoes for that dish's last 15 minutes.) Remove and carve each tenderloin into 6 even slices. Deglaze the skillet with the wine and add the liquid to the reserved onion sauce.

Return the onion sauce to the stove, and over medium-high heat, bring to a simmer. Remove from the heat, add the arrowroot slurry, and stir to thicken.

**The stuffed pepper:** In a stack-and-steam unit, place the red peppers on the lower platform and the spinach on the upper rack; or steam red peppers and spinach in two separate steamers. Cook each for 3 minutes or until spinach is slightly limp. Remove and chop the spinach coarsely; season with the salt, pepper, and nutmeg. Fill each pepper half with some of the spinach and cook for 2 more minutes. Remove and cut each pepper half in two.

**To serve:** Spoon a quarter of the potatoes on each dinner plate. Make a bed of the onion sauce and place 3 pork slices on top. Garnish with a sprinkle of the chopped parsley and serve with a stuffed pepper quarter on the side.

Nutritional Profile per Serving: Calories—487; % calories from fat—14%; fat (gm)—8 or 12% daily value; saturated fat (gm)—2; sodium (mg)—546; cholesterol (mg)—72; carbohydrates (gm)—72; dietary fiber (gm)—7.

# LAMB IN PITA

*Such a satisfying sandwich: redolent with garlic and laughing with yogurt. Perhaps the tastiest and best use for leftover lamb.*

*Time Estimate: Hands-on, 45 minutes*
*Serves 4*

1 cup uncooked bulgur wheat
1 cup boiling water
1/2 teaspoon light olive oil with a dash of toasted
   sesame oil
1 yellow onion, peeled and finely chopped
3 cloves garlic, bashed, peeled, and finely chopped
8 ounces (225 gm) ground leg of lamb
1 cup lamb or low-sodium beef stock (page 286)
1 teaspoon finely chopped fresh oregano leaves
4 teaspoons mango chutney, preferably Major Grey's
2 teaspoons cumin seeds
1/4 teaspoon cayenne pepper
1/2 teaspoon dried rosemary
1/8 teaspoon freshly ground sea salt
1 teaspoon cornstarch mixed with 2 teaspoons water
   (slurry)
2 tablespoons finely chopped fresh parsley
1/2 cup strained yogurt (page 288)
4 whole-wheat pita breads, cut in half
8 Chinese cabbage leaves, shredded

Place the bulgur in a small bowl, pour in the water, and steep for 10 minutes.

Pour the oil into a large hot skillet and cook the onion and garlic over high heat until the onion browns, about 4 minutes. Add the lamb, cooking and stirring until completely browned, about 4 minutes. Stir in 1 cup of the cooked bulgur, the stock, oregano, chutney, cumin seeds, cayenne pepper, rosemary, and salt; bring to a boil, reduce the heat, and simmer 9 minutes. Remove from the heat; stir in the cornstarch slurry, bring to a boil, and stir until thickened, about 30 seconds. Transfer to a plate, sprinkle with the parsley, and spread the mixture out to cool quickly before stirring in half of the yogurt.

**To serve:** Spoon the lamb mixture into the pita halves and top with 1 tablespoon of the remaining yogurt and some of the shredded cabbage. Each guest gets 2 halves.

Nutritional Profile per Serving: Calories—468; % calories from fat—13%; fat (gm)—7 or 11% daily value; saturated fat (gm)—2; sodium (mg)—434; cholesterol (mg)—40; carbohydrates (gm)—78; dietary fiber (gm)—15.

# SWEDISH MEATBALLS

⌘

*This dish must take the prize for plate appeal: the wreath of red cabbage filled with cream-coated potatoes, mushrooms, and meatballs. Nothing else is needed.*

Time Estimate: Hands-on, 1 hour
Serves 6

3 pounds (1.4 kilos) small red new potatoes
1 cup low-sodium chicken stock (page 286)
1/4 cup de-alcoholized white wine
1/2 teaspoon dried dill
1/4 teaspoon cayenne pepper
24 medium mushrooms

MEATBALLS

6 ounces (175 gm) lean veal shoulder
6 ounces (175 gm) lean pork shoulder
1 cup cooked bulgur wheat
1½ teaspoons light olive oil with a dash of toasted
   sesame oil
1/4 cup finely chopped onion
1/2 teaspoon dried dill
1/4 teaspoon freshly grated nutmeg
1/4 teaspoon freshly ground sea salt
1/4 teaspoon freshly ground white pepper
1 egg white

VEGETABLES

1 medium onion, peeled and sliced
1 large red cabbage, finely sliced
1/2 teaspoon light olive oil with a dash of toasted
   sesame oil
1 (8¼-ounce or 235-gm) can pickled beets, drained, cut
   into matchsticks, juice reserved
1/4 teaspoon freshly ground sea salt
1/4 teaspoon freshly ground black pepper

SAUCE

1 cup strained yogurt (page 288)
2 tablespoons cornstarch
1 tablespoon prepared horseradish
Reserved potato cooking liquid

GARNISH

2 tablespoons chopped fresh parsley

Place the potatoes in a high-sided skillet with the stock, de-alcoholized wine, dill, and cayenne; cover, bring to a boil, and cook for 15 minutes. Add the mushrooms and cook 5 minutes more. Drain the liquid into a small bowl to use in the sauce and keep the potatoes and mushrooms warm in their cooking pan.

**The meatballs:** Cut the meat into small chunks and mince in a food processor or food grinder. Place the ground meat in a bowl with the bulgur wheat. Heat 1/2 teaspoon of the oil in a small frying pan; fry the onions over medium-high heat until slightly translucent and add to the meat. Add the seasonings and egg white, and mix well. Make 18 meatballs by squeezing and rolling the mixture between slightly moistened hands. Heat the remaining teaspoon of oil over medium-high heat in a medium fry pan and brown the meatballs for 10 minutes, shaking the skillet frequently to prevent them from sticking. Add them to the potatoes and mushrooms to keep warm while you finish the vegetables and sauce.

**The vegetables:** Heat the oil in a large Dutch oven over medium-high heat and fry the onions and cabbage until the onions are translucent, about 2 minutes. Add the beet juice, salt, and pepper; cover and cook for 10 minutes. Stir in the beets.

**The sauce:** Combine the yogurt, cornstarch, horseradish, and potato cooking liquid in a small bowl. If the reserved potato cooking liquid does not measure a full cup, add more stock. Pour over the meatballs, potatoes, and mushrooms; stir gently and bring to a boil for 30 seconds to cook the cornstarch.

**To serve:** Make a wreath of the red cabbage on each individual plate, divide the meatballs, potatoes, and mushrooms and place in the center of each cabbage nest. Sprinkle the parsley over the top.

Nutritional Profile per Serving: Calories—498; % calories from fat—12%; fat (gm)—8 or 12% daily value; saturated fat (gm)—2; sodium (mg)—418; cholesterol (mg)—44; carbohydrates (gm)—84; dietary fiber (gm)—11.

# Scottish Irish Stew

— ✕ —

*If such a thing as a classic Irish stew exists (for every home there's a variation), then surely it would have potatoes in the pot, right? In fact, it's true to say the Scots have an almost identical favorite made with pot barley. In the continued interest of fusion (a combination of cultures), I've taken a leaf from each book and used both potato and barley. It really is delicious, especially with the completely new wilted-spinach garnish.*

**Scottish-Irish stew, with lamb, carrots, potatoes, onions, pot barley**
**Pale yellow with orange and brown relief**
**(Texture/Aroma)**

**Large raw spinach leaves**
**Dark green**
**(Color/Texture)**

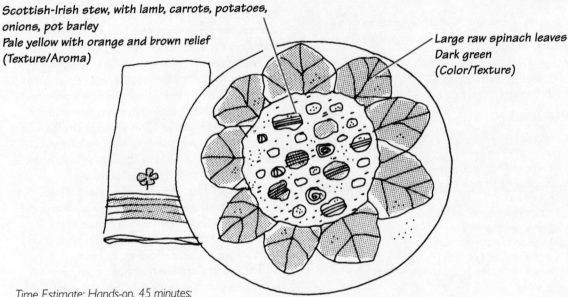

*Time Estimate: Hands-on, 45 minutes;*
*    unsupervised, 3 hours, 30 minutes*
*Serves 4*

ENHANCED STOCK

2 (14-ounce or 400-gm) cans low-sodium chicken
    broth (or fresh, page 286)
1 (14-ounce or 400-gm) can beef broth (or fresh, page
    286)
1 cup water
1 bouquet garni (page 289)
1 potato, unpeeled, cut into thin slices

STEW BASE

1 teaspoon light olive oil with a dash of toasted sesame oil
4 small yellow onions, peeled and roughly chopped
1½ cups enhanced stock (see above)
1¼ pounds (565 gm) lamb necks

1/4 cup barley, well rinsed
3/4 cup boiling water

STEW

2 carrots, peeled and cut into 1/2-inch (1.5-cm) chunks
3 yellow potatoes, peeled and cut into 1/2-inch (1.5-
    cm) chunks
16 boiling onions, 1½ inches (4 cm) in diameter, peeled
1/8 teaspoon freshly ground black pepper
1 (3-inch or 8-cm) sprig fresh rosemary
16 whole mushrooms, to match onion size
1 pound (450 gm) fresh spinach leaves, well rinsed and
    stems removed

**The broth:** In a large saucepan, bring the canned broths, water, bouquet garni, and potato to a boil; reduce the heat and simmer 30 minutes. Strain and return to the saucepan. (Throw out the potato, which was there to absorb the excess salt.)

**The stew base:** Heat the oil in a large saucepan over medium heat and cook the onions until slightly limp, about 5 minutes. Add the stock and lamb necks, and bring to a boil. Reduce the heat and simmer for 2½ hours, or until the meat falls off the bone.

While the lamb necks are cooking, in a separate small saucepan, mix the barley with the boiling water; stir once, cover, and return to a boil. Reduce the heat and simmer for 30 minutes. Drain and discard the water.

When the lamb is cooked, remove it from the broth, strip off the meat, and set aside. Strain the broth into a fat separator cup.

**The stew:** Return the defatted broth to the large saucepan and add the carrots, potatoes, boiling onions, and pepper, and bring to a boil. Reduce the heat so that it just bubbles, add the rosemary and lamb, and simmer for 10 minutes. Stir in the cooked barley and simmer for 10 minutes more. Finally, add the mushrooms and cook for 5 minutes.

**To serve:** Line four large soup bowls with several of the spinach leaves. Ladle the hot stew on top and serve with the uncooked spinach leaves sticking up around the side of the bowl like a garland.

| Nutritional Profile per Serving | | | |
|---|---|---|---|
| | **Classic** | **Minimax** | **Daily Value** |
| Calories | 700 | 328 | |
| Calories from fat | 42% | 15% | |
| Fat (gm) | 33 | 5 | 8% |
| Saturated fat (gm) | 14 | 1 | 5% |
| Sodium (mg) | 974 | 154 | 6% |
| Cholesterol (mg) | 327 | 28 | 9% |
| Carbohydrates (gm) | 31 | 56 | 19% |
| Dietary fiber (gm) | 5 | 10 | 40% |
| Classic compared: Blanquette of Lamb à l'Ancienne | | | |

# Bosnbeans Pasta Salad

⧉

*One of the most requested recipes from my television audience: "a pasta salad coated with a creamy, cheese dressing . . . and, oh . . . low fat, please." By George, I think we've done it, and with only 7 grams of fat.*

*Time Estimate: Hands-on, 30 minutes*

*Serves 4*

SALAD

1/2 pound (225 gm) uncooked farfalle (bow tie) pasta
1 (15-ounce or 425-gm) can low-sodium kidney beans, rinsed and drained
3/4 cup sliced green onions
3/4 cup chopped red bell pepper
3 tablespoons chopped fresh parsley

DRESSING

1/2 cup low-sodium garbanzo beans, rinsed and drained
1/2 cup 1%-fat cottage cheese
1/2 cup strained yogurt (page 288)
1/2 cup freshly grated Parmesan cheese
1/4 cup rice vinegar
1 tablespoon Dijon mustard
1/4 teaspoon freshly ground white pepper
1/4 teaspoon dried dill
1/4 teaspoon cumin
1/8 teaspoon cayenne pepper

GARNISH

6 cups hand-torn red leaf and romaine lettuce leaves
4 teaspoons freshly grated Parmesan cheese
1 tablespoon chopped fresh parsley

**The salad:** Cook the pasta in a large pot of boiling water until just tender, about 11 minutes. Drain in a colander and cool immediately with cold running water. Drain thoroughly and place in a large bowl. Add the remaining salad ingredients and set aside.

**The dressing:** Whiz the garbanzo beans until smooth in a food processor or blender. Add the cottage cheese and continue processing until the mixture is very smooth. Add the rest of the dressing ingredients and pulse until mixed. Pour the dressing into the bowl with the salad ingredients, toss well, and let sit at room temperature for at least 30 minutes. (If it must sit for longer than 30 minutes, please put it into the refrigerator.) You might think there is too much dressing, but the pasta will soak it up as it sits.

**To serve:** Scatter the red and green lettuce leaves onto 4 serving plates and arrange the pasta salad on top. Dust with the Parmesan cheese and parsley, and enjoy.

Nutritional Profile per Serving: Calories—539; % calories from fat—12%; fat (gm)—7 or 11% daily value; saturated fat (gm)—3; sodium (mg)—496; cholesterol (mg)—14; carbohydrates (gm)—86; dietary fiber (gm)—13.

# CREAMY PASTA PRIMAVERA

*Whenever I'm asked to name my favorite dish, my mind turns to creamy white-sauced anything! The classic white sauces were loaded with fat to carry all the flavor. Here, I've used nonfat strained yogurt to create a velvety, flavorful sauce that enhances the fresh, steamed vegetables and is totally satisfying.*

*Time Estimate: Hands-on, 30 minutes*
Serves 4

PASTA AND VEGETABLES

8 ounces (225 gm) uncooked penne pasta
8 ounces (225 gm) cauliflower florets
8 ounces (225 gm) diagonally sliced carrots
8 ounces (225 gm) broccoli florets
4 ounces (115 gm) diagonally sliced zucchini

BASIC WHITE SAUCE

3 cups chicken stock (page 286)
3 tablespoons cornstarch mixed with 6 tablespoons de-alcoholized white wine (slurry)
1 cup strained yogurt (page 288), at room temperature
1 tablespoon finely chopped fresh parsley
1/8 teaspoon freshly grated nutmeg
1/8 teaspoon freshly ground sea salt
1/8 teaspoon freshly ground white pepper
1/4 cup chopped fresh basil
1/4 cup freshly grated Parmesan cheese

GARNISH

4 tablespoons freshly grated Parmesan cheese
Freshly ground black pepper to taste

**The pasta and vegetables:** Cook the penne according to the package directions, drain, and set aside. Keep warm.

Steam the cauliflower and carrots for 5 minutes; add the broccoli and zucchini to the same steamer and steam for an additional 5 minutes. Remove from the heat and set aside (but not for long).

**The sauce:** Pour the chicken stock into a medium saucepan over high heat, bring to a boil, and reduce by half, about 10 minutes. Remove from the heat, whisk in the cornstarch slurry, return to the heat, and boil for 30 seconds until clear and thick, stirring constantly. Remove from the heat and let the sauce cool.

Put the yogurt in a small bowl and stir gently until all the lumps are gone. Stir the yogurt into the cooled sauce. Reheat the sauce slowly over low heat and add the parsley, nutmeg, salt, white pepper, basil, and cheese. Remove 1 cup and set aside.

**To serve:** Put the penne in a large hot bowl, pour in the sauce from the saucepan, and toss the penne until well coated. (This is not globs and globs of sauce; each piece of penne is perfectly coated and glistens.) Divide the sauced pasta among individual dinner plates and surround with a colorful crescent of the vegetables. Drizzle with the reserved sauce and dust with the Parmesan cheese. A little coarsely ground black pepper adds visual interest and a zesty bite to each forkful.

Nutritional Profile per Serving: Calories—440; % calories from fat—12%; fat (gm)—6 or 9% daily value; saturated fat (gm)—3; sodium (mg)—498; cholesterol (mg)—12; carbohydrates (gm)—72; dietary fiber (gm)—6.

# GARDEN BURGERS

*The curry powder and raisins add a hard-to-describe spicy sweetness that I find irresistible.*

*Time Estimate: Hands-on, 15 minutes*
*Serves 4*

1/2 medium onion, peeled
2 teaspoons light olive oil with a dash of toasted sesame oil
1 tablespoon curry powder
1 (14½-ounce or 410-gm) can low-sodium red kidney beans, drained and rinsed
4 tablespoons dark raisins
1 tablespoon chopped fresh parsley
1 tablespoon freshly squeezed lemon juice
1 cup cooked long-grain brown rice
1/4 teaspoon freshly ground sea salt
4 whole-wheat buns
4 lettuce leaves
4 thick tomato slices

Process the onion, using the fast pulse, until it's in small but still discernible pieces.

Heat half of the oil in a medium skillet over high heat and cook the onion and curry powder for 3 minutes. Add the beans, raisins, parsley, lemon juice, and cooked onion to the processor and fast pulse 12 times. Transfer to a bowl, add the cooked rice and the salt, and mix well. Form into 2 patties.

Pour the remaining oil into a medium skillet over high heat and brown the patties on each side for 3 minutes.

**To serve:** Place a patty on each bun, top with the lettuce and tomato.

Nutritional Profile per Serving: Calories—371; % calories from fat—13%; fat (gm)—5 or 9% daily value; saturated fat (gm)—1; sodium (mg)—365; cholesterol (mg)—0; carbohydrates (gm)—70; dietary fiber (gm)—13.

# GHIVETCH

*In Romania, this meatless vegetable dish is often used to celebrate the arrival of the summer vegetables. I use it as a "vegetables only" dish to alternate with meat proteins. It keeps well in the refrigerator for four to five days. As a first course, Ghivetch can be served as a "terrine of vegetables" with whole-wheat toast and a little of Treena's vinaigrette on the side (page 276).*

*Time Estimate: Hands-on, 1 hour;*
*   unsupervised, 4 hours, 30 minutes*
*Serves 8*

1/4 teaspoon baking soda
2 cups boiling water
1 bunch spinach, washed and stemmed (winter "savoy" cabbage can be used in the fall season)
2 cups boiling low-sodium chicken stock (page 286)
1 cup bulgur wheat

FIRST LOT

1 tablespoon light olive oil with a dash of toasted sesame oil
1 clove garlic, bashed, peeled, and chopped
1 onion, peeled and chopped
1 large carrot, peeled and sliced on the diagonal, 1/8 inch thick
1 green bell pepper, seeded and chopped
1 tablespoon freshly squeezed lemon juice

SECOND LOT

2 tablespoons light olive oil with a dash of toasted sesame oil
1 large potato, peeled and cut into 1/2-inch (1.5-cm) cubes
1 pound (450 gm) eggplant, cut into 1/2-inch (1.5-cm) cubes
1 acorn squash, peeled and cut into 1/2-inch (1.5-cm) cubes
1 tablespoon chopped fresh dill
Juice of 1/2 lemon
1/2 teaspoon cracked black peppercorns

1/4 teaspoon freshly grated nutmeg
1 tablespoon chopped fresh chives
2 tablespoons chopped fresh parsley
3/4 cup green beans, topped and tailed
1 teaspoon freshly ground sea salt

THIRD LOT

1 ½ cups peas
1 pound (450 gm) tomatoes, seeded and diced
2 tablespoons chopped fresh basil
1 cup quartered mushrooms

SAUCE

1 cup low-sodium chicken stock (page 286)
Zest of 1 lemon, grated
2 tablespoons freshly squeezed lemon juice
1/4 teaspoon turmeric
1 tablespoon arrowroot mixed with 2 tablespoons
    water (slurry)
1 teaspoon chopped fresh dill

In a large saucepan, add the baking soda to the boiling water followed by the spinach leaves. Blanch for a moment then plunge the leaves immediately into iced water. When they are bright green, remove the leaves. Line a large serving bowl with them and set aside.

In a large saucepan, add the boiling chicken stock to the bulgur and let stand for 5 minutes.

**The first lot:** Heat the olive oil in a large, heavy frying pan over medium-high heat. Add the remaining "first lot" ingredients and cook about 2 minutes. Turn into a Dutch oven or pot large enough to hold all 3 lots of vegetables.

**The second lot:** In the same frying pan, heat half the olive oil over medium-high heat. Add the potato, eggplant, and acorn squash, and fry until brown on the edges, about 4 minutes. Add to the vegetables in the Dutch oven and stir together. Pour the remaining oil into the frying pan followed by the remaining "second lot" ingredients and the cooked bulgur. Cover and simmer for 35 minutes. Add more chicken stock as necessary to keep the mixture moist and avoid "catching" the wheat. Tip the contents into the Dutch oven.

**The third lot:** Add the "third lot" ingredients to the vegetables in the Dutch oven and mix. Fill the large, spinach leaf–lined bowl with the vegetable mixture. Press down firmly. Place a plate over the top and push down hard. Remove any extra liquid that collects in the plate. Chill the ghivetch.

**The sauce:** In a small saucepan, mix the chicken stock, lemon zest, lemon juice, turmeric, and arrowroot slurry. Heat to thicken and clear. Add the dill and set aside.

**To serve:** Unmold the vegetables onto a platter, slice into wedges, and serve the sauce on the side.

You can, by the way, serve it hot, as is, by the glorious spoonful, directly from the bowl.

Nutritional Profile per Serving: Calories—232; % calories from fat—11%; fat (gm)—3 or 4% daily value; saturated fat (gm)—.5; sodium (mg)—409; cholesterol (mg)—0; carbohydrates (gm)—47; dietary fiber (gm)—12.

# Green Pea Sauce for Pasta

*You'll love this fragrant, creamy sauce on your favorite pasta. Bread and salad on the side make a delicious meal.*

*Time Estimate: Hands-on, 20 minutes*
*Serves 4*

1 teaspoon light olive oil with a dash of toasted sesame oil
1 tablespoon very finely chopped fresh gingerroot
1 leek, thinly sliced
3 cups vegetable stock (page 288)
1/2 cup loosely packed fresh dill
3 cups frozen peas
2 tablespoons cornstarch mixed with 4 tablespoons water (slurry)
8 ounces uncooked pasta (your choice)
1/4 teaspoon freshly ground sea salt
1/8 teaspoon cayenne pepper

Pour the oil into a medium saucepan over medium-high heat and cook the gingerroot for 2 minutes. Add the leek and cook for 3 minutes. Stir in the stock and dill, and bring to a boil. Add the peas and bring back to a boil.

Remove from the heat. Pour into a blender and purée until smooth, about 5 minutes. Add the cornstarch slurry, return to the heat, and stir until thickened, about 1 minute.

Cook the pasta according to package directions, drain, and transfer to a large warm bowl.

**To serve:** Add the salt and cayenne, toss with the pasta, and enjoy.

Nutritional Profile per Serving: Calories—352; % calories from fat—8%; fat (gm)—3 or 5% daily value; saturated fat (gm)—1; sodium (mg)—262; cholesterol (mg)—0; carbohydrates (gm)—66; dietary fiber (gm)—8.

# Orange Butternut Sauce for Pasta

*Frankly, I'm fascinated by the almost universal popularity of smooth-sauced pastas. I fully appreciate the delight that comes from the "smooooooth mouthfeel" and set out to capture some of the texture while removing almost all the fat. By the way, this sauce also makes quite an appetizing first-course soup.*

*Time Estimate: Hands-on, 20 minutes;*
 *unsupervised, 15 minutes*
*Serves 7 to 8*

1/4 teaspoon light olive oil with a dash of toasted sesame oil
2 cloves garlic, bashed, peeled, and chopped
3 cups low-sodium chicken stock (page 286)
1 (2-pound or 900-gm) butternut squash, baked for 50 minutes at 350°F (180°C) to yield 3 cups of pulp
1 (6-inch or 15-cm) sprig rosemary
1 cup frozen corn
1/4 teaspoon freshly ground black pepper
1/8 teaspoon freshly ground sea salt
1/4 teaspoon ground cumin
2 tablespoons cornstarch mixed with 1/4 cup unsweetened orange juice (slurry)
14 ounces (400 gm) uncooked pasta (your choice)
1/4 cup strained yogurt (page 288)

Heat the oil in a large saucepan over medium heat and fry the garlic for 3 minutes. Stir in the stock, cooked butternut squash, and rosemary, and simmer for 15 minutes. Remove the rosemary and discard.

Stir in the corn, pepper, salt, cumin, and cornstarch slurry, and cook for 3 minutes. Pour into a blender and purée until very smooth, about 5 minutes.

Cook the pasta according to package directions, drain, and transfer to a large warm bowl.

**To serve:** Just before serving, whisk the yogurt into the sauce for a sense of added richness. Present immediately, tossed with the pasta, or refrigerate before adding the yogurt and reheat later.

Nutritional Profile per Serving: Calories—313; % calories from fat—7%; fat (gm)—2 or 4% daily value; saturated fat (gm)—5; sodium (mg)—81; cholesterol (mg)—.3; carbohydrates (gm)—63; dietary fiber (gm)—5.

# PASTA MARINARA

⌗

*There is so much truly excellent dried and freshly made pasta on the market that it might not seem necessary to make your own. However, for some wonderful reason, there are people who love to do it for themselves and who gain a great deal by converting their energy into a skilled gift of love. So for all you "make-it-from-scratch" people out there, here's a recipe for your very own Minimax pasta in a simple sauce.*

Time Estimate: Hands-on, 45 minutes;
   unsupervised, 30 minutes
Serves 4

PASTA

1½ cups all-purpose flour
1½ cups semolina flour
2 large eggs
1/4 teaspoon freshly ground sea salt
7 tablespoons water
1/2 cup loosely packed, fresh herbs (Use your favorite. I recommend oregano. Also, use more or less depending on your taste.)

MARINARA SAUCE

1 teaspoon light olive oil with a dash of toasted sesame oil
1 medium onion, peeled and finely sliced
1 clove garlic, bashed, peeled, and chopped
1 tablespoon fresh oregano leaves
1 (28-ounce or 800-gm) can whole plum tomatoes, seeded
1 tablespoon cornstarch mixed with 2 tablespoons water (slurry)

**The pasta:** In a food processor, combine both flours, the eggs, and salt. Process at high speed, gradually incorporating the water. When slightly tacky, remove the dough and put on a smooth surface.

Knead the dough until it becomes very smooth, about 2 to 3 minutes. Roll the dough into a 6-inch (15-cm) cylinder shape and let it rest for 30 minutes. Cut the dough into quarters and, using a rolling pin or pasta machine, roll each piece into a very thin sheet. You should be able to see the shadow of your hand through the thin dough. Cut sheets into manageable working pieces—about 12 to 15 inches (30 to 38 cm) long.

Fold the sheets of pasta in half lengthwise, creasing the folded edge to mark the center, then open the pasta sheet again. Line one side of the sheet with the herb leaves. Fold the pasta back along the crease, covering the herbs. Using the rolling pin or pasta machine, seal the two sides.

Cut the pasta into bite size pieces, incorporating an herb leaf in each piece. You could also leave them in sheets and use them for lasagna, ravioli, or tortellini!

**The marinara sauce:** In a medium saucepan over medium heat, cook the olive oil, onions, and garlic until the onions are translucent and they've released their volatile oils, about 5 minutes.

Add the oregano and cook for 1 minute to incorporate its flavor. Add the tomatoes and cook for 5 minutes more. Pour into a blender and whiz until mixture has reached a thick consistency.

Return the sauce to the saucepan and reheat. When it's hot, add the cornstarch slurry, bring to a boil, and stir constantly until thickened, about 30 seconds.

Cook the pasta in a large pot of boiling water for 2 to 3 minutes. Drain, toss with the sauce, and serve.

Nutritional Profile per Serving: Calories—447; % calories from fat—10%; fat (gm)—5 or 8% daily value; saturated fat (gm)—1; sodium (mg)—491; cholesterol (mg)—106; carbohydrates (gm)—85; dietary fiber (gm)—6.

# LENTIL, RICE, AND PINTO BEAN CASSEROLE

*I tested two methods for this simple and delicious recipe because I'd like you to consider the advantages of a pressure cooker. A pressure cooker will save you at least one hour over the standard oven bake.*

*This is an entire meal in one pot, featuring vegetables only—not even a meat stock! I thought that it lacked sufficient greenery and added the peas at the end of the cooking. The stored heat will warm them. As an alternative, you could add some finely sliced collard greens just before you serve it. The goat cheese–flavored bread is truly excellent as a side dish—please give it a go!*

*Time Estimate: Hands-on, 40 minutes*
*Serves 4*

BREAD SPREAD

4 tablespoons goat cheese
1 teaspoon chopped fresh basil
1 teaspoon chopped fresh thyme
1 teaspoon chopped fresh oregano
1/8 teaspoon freshly ground black pepper

1 French bread baguette

CASSEROLE

1/2 green bell pepper, seeded and finely diced
1/2 red bell pepper, seeded and finely diced
1 teaspoon light olive oil with a dash of toasted sesame oil
2/3 cup finely chopped onion
2 cloves garlic, bashed, peeled, and finely diced
1 cup dried pinto beans
2 teaspoons chopped fresh basil
2 teaspoons chopped fresh thyme
2 teaspoons chopped fresh oregano
2 bay leaves
1/4 teaspoon freshly ground sea salt
1/4 teaspoon freshly ground black pepper
3 cups water

3/4 cup dried lentils
1/2 cup uncooked brown rice
1/2 cup de-alcoholized white wine
1/4 teaspoon ground cayenne pepper
1 tablespoon freshly squeezed lemon juice

GARNISH

1/2 cup frozen green peas, thawed, or 2 cups finely sliced collard greens

**The bread spread:** In a small bowl, combine the cheese, basil, thyme, oregano, and pepper. Set aside.

**The casserole:** In another small bowl, mix the green and red peppers together. Set aside. In a pressure cooker, heat the oil and sauté the onion over medium-high heat until translucent, about 3 minutes. Add the garlic and cook 2 minutes. Add half of the bell pepper mixture, the pinto beans, 1 teaspoon of the basil, 1 teaspoon of the thyme, 1 teaspoon of the oregano, the bay leaves, salt, and pepper. Pour in the water, check to make sure the steam release holes are clear, put on the lid, and cook for 10 minutes from when the cooker starts hissing. Release the steam and uncover. Preheat the oven to 350°F (180°C).

Add the lentils and brown rice to the pressure cooker. Cover and cook 15 minutes more from when the cooker starts hissing. Release the steam cover, remove the bay leaves, and discard. Add the remaining 1 teaspoon each of basil, thyme, and oregano. Pour in the wine and add the remaining bell pepper mixture, the cayenne pepper, and lemon juice.

**The bread:** Cut the baguette in half and toast in the preheated oven until just brown around the edges, about 5 minutes. Apply the spread and cut into "fingers."

**To serve:** Spoon casserole into individual serving bowls and sprinkle with the green peas or collard greens. Serve with a finger of the toasted goat cheese bread.

Nutritional Profile per Serving: Calories—626; % calories from fat—12%; fat (gm)—8 or 12% daily value; saturated fat (gm)—3; sodium (mg)—531; cholesterol (mg)—14; carbohydrates (gm)—110; dietary fiber (gm)—19.

# Penne Primavera

*This hot pasta with vegetables owes its reputation to fresh herbs, a superb vegetable broth, and a colorful celebration of perfectly cooked vegetables.*

*Time Estimate: Hands-on, 45 minutes*
*Serves 6*

8 ounces uncooked penne pasta
1 teaspoon light olive oil with a dash of toasted sesame oil
1/2 red onion, peeled and sliced
2 cloves garlic, bashed, peeled, and chopped
1 medium red bell pepper, seeded and cut to the size of the pasta
1 cup sugar snap peas, cut in half on the diagonal, or 1 cup shelled fresh peas
3/4 pound (350 gm) asparagus, tough ends broken off and tender stems cut into 2-inch (5-cm) pieces
1 medium zucchini squash, cut into matchsticks
1 medium yellow summer squash, cut into matchsticks
4 plum tomatoes, cored and chopped
2 cups fresh or canned fava beans, skins removed
1/4 teaspoon freshly ground sea salt
1/4 teaspoon freshly ground black pepper
1 tablespoon arrowroot mixed with 1½ cups vegetable stock (page 288) (slurry)
2 tablespoons chopped fresh basil
1/4 teaspoon red pepper flakes
6 tablespoons freshly grated Parmesan cheese

Cook the pasta in a large pot of boiling water until just tender, about 11 minutes. Drain and set aside to add to the vegetables later.

In a large, high-sided skillet, heat the oil over medium-high heat. Add the onions and fry for 1 minute. Add the garlic and cook for 1 minute, being careful that the onions and garlic don't get brown and bitter. Toss in the peppers and peas, and cook for 2 to 3 minutes. Now add the asparagus, zucchini, summer squash, tomatoes, fava beans, salt, and pepper. Treat this like a stir-fry, tossing lightly and cooking the vegetables but keeping them crunchy, about 5 minutes.

Remove the skillet from the heat; stir in the arrowroot slurry, return to the heat, and bring to a boil over medium-high heat, stirring constantly. Add the cooked pasta, basil, and red pepper flakes, and toss gently to mix well.

**To serve:** Dish the pasta into large bowls and sprinkle with the Parmesan cheese. Serve with a lightly dressed green salad and hearty Italian bread.

Nutritional Profile per Serving: Calories—310; % calories from fat—13%; fat (gm)—4 or 6% daily value; saturated fat (gm)—2; sodium (mg)—263; cholesterol (mg)—5; carbohydrates (gm)—55; dietary fiber (gm)—8.

# TORTELLINI IN BUTTER BEAN SAUCE

*My favorite pasta suddenly got better! I'm really delighted with this recipe, which has only one real drawback: it takes time to make the tortellini. Use the packaged variety when you want to eat quickly.*

*This dish is wonderful with a colorful herbed salad in the summer, or perhaps freshly cooked green beans seasoned with a touch of fresh garlic and nutmeg.*

*Time Estimate: Hands-on, 3 hours*
*Serves 4 as a main course*

## TORTELLINI FILLING

8 ounces (225 gm) boneless, skinless turkey breasts, fat trimmed
1 ounce (30 gm) Canadian bacon
5 large sage leaves
1/4 teaspoon freshly ground black pepper
1/8 teaspoon freshly ground sea salt

## TORTELLINI PASTA

1½ cups all-purpose flour
1½ cups semolina flour
2 eggs
1/4 teaspoon freshly ground sea salt
4 quarts plus 7 tablespoons water

## SAUCE

3/4 cup whey from strained yogurt (page 288)
1½ cups butter beans, drained (from a 15-ounce or 425-gm can)
2 cups low-sodium chicken stock (page 286)
1/2 cup evaporated skim milk
1/2 teaspoon cayenne pepper
1/8 teaspoon freshly ground sea salt
1 teaspoon chopped fresh sage
1 teaspoon chopped fresh tarragon
1 tablespoon cornstarch mixed with 2 tablespoons evaporated skim milk (slurry)

**The tortellini filling:** In a meat grinder, coarsely grind the turkey breast and Canadian bacon, ending with 1 slice of whole-wheat bread. When you see the bread come through the grinder you know you've ground all the turkey (the bread is not part of the filling!). Spread the meat over a cutting board and sprinkle with the seasonings. Scrape together to combine all the ingredients and set aside.

**The tortellini pasta:** In a food processor, combine the flours, eggs, and salt. Process at high speed, gradually incorporating the 7 tablespoons of water. When slightly tacky, remove the dough and put it on a smooth surface.

Knead the dough until it becomes very smooth, about 2 to 3 minutes. Roll the dough into a 6-inch (15-cm) long cylinder shape and let rest for 30 minutes.

Cut the dough into quarters and, using a rolling pin or pasta machine, roll each piece into a very thin sheet. You should be able to see the shadow of your hand through the thin dough. Cut the sheets into manageable working pieces—about 12 to 15 inches (30 to 38 cm) long. Working with 1 sheet at a time, lay it on a cutting board. Cut out 2-inch (5-cm) diameter circles. You should have 48 circles from this recipe. Cover them with a damp cloth to prevent them from drying out before they are molded.

Using a small pastry brush, lightly brush the pasta circles with water. Put 1/4 teaspoon of the filling in the center of each circle—don't overfill. Fold the pasta in half, in the shape of a half moon. Crimp the folded-over edge tightly so it's completely sealed. Fold the half moon ends over toward each other, slightly twisting one end under the other in a graceful swirl (it's supposed to look like a belly-button!). Set aside on a plate with a little semolina flour underneath to keep them separate.

**The butter bean sauce:** In a food processor, purée the yogurt whey, butter beans, chicken stock, and skim milk until smooth. Pour into a large nonstick wok or high-sided frying pan. The pan needs to be large because you will be tossing the tortellini in the sauce. Add the cayenne pepper, salt, sage, and tarragon; bring to a boil and simmer for 5 minutes.

Just before adding the tortellini, stir in the cornstarch slurry, bring to a boil, and stir until thickened, about 30 seconds.

**Cooking the tortellini:** Put the water in a large pot and bring to a boil. Toss in the tortellini and boil until al dente, or just tender, about 3 minutes. Taste to see if the texture suits your palate.

Drain the cooked tortellini in a colander. Spoon them into the sauce and toss until well coated.

**To serve:** Bring to the table and dazzle your dinner guests!

Nutritional Profile per Serving: Calories—599; % calories from fat—12%; fat (gm)—8 or 12% daily value; saturated fat (gm)—2; sodium (mg)—534; cholesterol (mg)—146; carbohydrates (gm)—94; dietary fiber (gm)—9

# SUGAR 'N' SPICE BEANS 'N' RICE

*Beans and rice are always a satisfying and hearty combination, but the hint of orange juice imparts a delicious freshness. Accompany with a fresh steamed vegetable, like carrots or Swiss chard, on the side.*

*Time Estimate: Hands-on, 20 minutes; unsupervised, 35 minutes*

*Serves 6*

1 teaspoon light olive oil with a dash of toasted sesame oil
1/2 yellow onion, peeled and finely chopped
1½ teaspoons cumin seeds
1 tablespoon brown sugar
5 cups water
2 bay leaves
1 cup dried Great Northern beans
1 cup uncooked brown rice
Zest of 1 orange, finely chopped
8 green onions, white and pale green part, finely chopped
Juice of 1 orange
1/2 teaspoon freshly ground sea salt
1/4 teaspoon cayenne pepper

Pour the oil into a pressure cooker over medium-high heat and cook the onion, 1 teaspoon of the cumin seeds, and the sugar until the onion is translucent, about 5 minutes. Add the water and bay leaves, and bring to a boil. Stir in the beans, making sure none are sticking to the bottom of the pan, and fasten the lid. Wait until the cooker starts to hiss, reduce the heat, and simmer 10 minutes.

Remove from the heat, release the steam, and remove the lid. Remove the bay leaves and add the rice. Refasten the lid, return to the heat, and bring to a boil. When the cooker starts to hiss, reduce the heat and simmer 20 minutes. Remove from the heat, release the steam, and unfasten the lid. Stir in the orange zest and green onions. Season with the remaining cumin, the orange juice, salt, and cayenne.

**To serve:** Spoon onto plates with your favorite steamed vegetable on the side.

Nutritional Profile per Serving: Calories—254; % calories from fat—7%; fat (gm)—2 or 3% daily value; saturated fat (gm)—.4; sodium (mg)—192; cholesterol (mg)—0; carbohydrates (gm)—49; dietary fiber (gm)—7.

# VEGETABLE PAPOOSE

—— ✦ ——

*Part of the pleasure to be found in a Minimax change is the avalanche of fresh vegetables. This recipe suggests a novel method of presentation: the papoose! It's a colorful mix of root vegetables, well seasoned with a touch of Canadian bacon and horseradish, wrapped in red chard leaves and dusted with cheese. It's a terrific low-fat and low-calorie meal with tons of aromas, colors, and textures.*

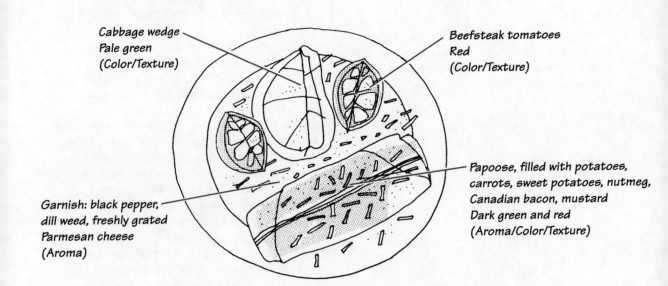

Cabbage wedge
Pale green
(Color/Texture)

Beefsteak tomatoes
Red
(Color/Texture)

Papoose, filled with potatoes,
carrots, sweet potatoes, nutmeg,
Canadian bacon, mustard
Dark green and red
(Aroma/Color/Texture)

Garnish: black pepper,
dill weed, freshly grated
Parmesan cheese
(Aroma)

*Time Estimate: Hands-on, 58 minutes; unsupervised, 27 minutes*
*Serves 4*

8 large red chard leaves, heavy bottom stalks removed
4 baking potatoes, preferably Yukon Gold, cut into
    1/2-inch (1.5-cm) dice
4 carrots, peeled and cut into 1/2-inch (1.5-cm) discs
2 large sweet potatoes, peeled and cut into 1/2-inch
    (1.5-cm) dice
1/4 teaspoon freshly grated nutmeg
1/8 teaspoon freshly ground sea salt
1/4 teaspoon freshly ground black pepper

3½ ounces (100 gm) Canadian bacon, coarsely
    chopped
1/4 cup freshly grated Parmesan cheese
4 teaspoons hearty mustard, preferably Grey Poupon
4 teaspoons prepared horseradish
1/2 medium head cabbage, cut into 4 wedges
4 very large beefsteak tomatoes, cut in half
2 tablespoons chopped fresh dill

Steam the chard leaves until just tender, about 3 minutes. Remove from the heat and transfer to a cold plate to stop further cooking. Carefully cut the bright red veins out of the leaves, leaving the leaves intact in a large piece. Chop the veins finely and set aside.

Start steaming the diced potatoes and cook for 2 minutes. Add the carrots and cook for 2 minutes. Add the sweet potatoes, nutmeg, salt, and pepper; toss well and continue steaming for 10 minutes, until just tender. Immediately transfer the steamed vegetables to a large bowl and toss with the Canadian bacon, half of the cheese, the mustard, horseradish, and reserved chopped chard veins.

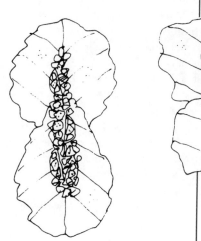

Place the cabbage wedges and tomatoes on a steamer rack. Sprinkle lightly with 1 tablespoon of the dill, cover, and steam for 5 minutes.

Preheat the oven to 350°F (180°C). On each of 4 individual ovenproof dinner dishes, place 2 of the cooked chard leaves. Cover with 1/4 of the seasoned vegetables in a long line down the middle of the leaf. Turn the edges of the chard leaves over the top and gently roll them over, tucking the edges under to form a neat cylinder (papoose). Repeat the process to form 3 more papooses. Gently push the chard papoose to one side of the plate. On the other side, place the cabbage wedge and flank it with the tomato halves. Place in the oven and reheat for 5 minutes.

**To serve:** Sprinkle each papoose with black pepper to taste, remaining dill, and the remaining Parmesan cheese.

| Nutritional Profile per Serving | | | |
|---|---|---|---|
| | **Classic** | **Minimax** | **Daily Value** |
| Calories | 1,360 | 374 | |
| Calories from fat | 57% | 11% | |
| Fat (gm) | 86 | 4 | 6% |
| Saturated fat (gm) | 29 | 2 | 10% |
| Sodium (mg) | 4,254 | 776 | 32% |
| Cholesterol (mg) | 360 | 16 | 0% |
| Carbohydrates (gm) | 118 | 72 | 24% |
| Dietary fiber (gm) | 118 | 12 | 48% |
| Classic compared: Corned Beef and Cabbage | | | |

# Puerto Rican Rice and Beans
## (Arroz con Habichuelas)

*One of the truly great dishes of the world, rice and beans is also one of those food combinations whose ingredients actually complement each other nutritionally. Rice and beans, when served together, provide more protein than when you eat them separately. Look at the numbers and you'll see the benefit. But the nutritional numbers are only half the battle! The real war is won with aroma, color, and texture—and this dish takes the prize for all three! Served in a bowl, it becomes a hearty meal with the addition of a colorful salad on the side.*

*Time Estimate: Hands-on, 30 minutes*
*Serves 4*

4 cups water
8 ounces (225 gm) smoked ham hock
1 cup dried pinto beans
1 cup uncooked long-grain rice
1 teaspoon light olive oil with a dash of toasted sesame oil
1/2 onion, peeled and diced
2 cloves garlic, bashed, peeled, and chopped
1 large red bell pepper, seeded and diced
2 jalapeño peppers, seeded and diced
1 tablespoon chopped fresh oregano
1 (15-ounce or 425-gm) can peeled plum tomatoes, drained and juice reserved
1/2 teaspoon freshly ground sea salt
1/2 teaspoon freshly ground black pepper
3 tablespoons chopped fresh cilantro
2 tablespoons capers

Place the water and ham hock in a pressure cooker, check to make sure the steam release holes are clear, and cook for 5 minutes. Add the pinto beans and cook 20 minutes more. Add the rice, and when the pressure cooker hisses, cook for another 5 minutes. (If you don't have a pressure cooker, put the water, ham hock, and beans in a soup pot and bring to a boil. Reduce the heat and simmer for 1½ hours. Add the rice and simmer for 20 minutes more, then continue with the recipe.)

While the rice and beans cook, heat the oil in a large skillet over medium-high heat and sauté the onion and garlic until the onion becomes translucent, about 2 minutes. Add the red pepper, jalapeño peppers, oregano, tomatoes, 1/4 cup of the reserved tomato juice, half of the salt, and half of the pepper. Lower the heat to simmer and cook for 15 minutes.

After the rice and beans have cooked, remove the ham hock, slice off 2 ounces (60 gm) of lean meat, and reserve. Add the cooked rice and beans to the pepper-tomato mixture in the skillet. Stir in the reserved ham hock meat, 2 tablespoons of the cilantro, the capers, and the remaining salt and pepper.

**To serve:** Spoon into bowls and garnish with the remaining cilantro.

Nutritional Profile per Serving: Calories—463; % calories from fat—12%; fat (gm)—6 or 9% daily value; saturated fat (gm)—2; sodium (mg)—642; cholesterol (mg)—10; carbohydrates (gm)—84; dietary fiber (gm)—12.

# 10% calories from fat

⌗

## Side Dishes
### &
## Vegetables

# BISTRO VEGETABLES WITH ROSEMARY

⌗

A wonderful medley of root vegetables, mushrooms, and butter beans infused with the earthy flavor of rosemary. Serve it as either a vegetable entrée or side dish.

Time Estimate: Hands-on, 32 minutes
Serves 4 as a main course

1 teaspoon light olive oil with a dash of toasted sesame oil
8 small onions, peeled and quartered
20 small carrots, cut in half lengthwise
6 small red new potatoes, quartered
2 cups vegetable stock (page 288)
1 (4-inch or 10-cm) sprig fresh rosemary
1/8 teaspoon freshly ground sea salt
8 ounces (225 gm) fresh mushrooms, halved
1 15-ounce (425-gm) can butter beans, rinsed
1 tablespoon arrowroot mixed with 2 tablespoons vegetable stock (slurry)
1 teaspoon chopped fresh thyme
1 tablespoon chopped fresh parsley

Put the oil in a large skillet, add the onions, and cook over medium heat until brown, about 5 minutes. Add the carrots, potatoes, vegetable stock, rosemary branch (making sure the rosemary is submerged in the liquid), and salt; cover and simmer 10 minutes. Add the mushrooms and simmer an additional 10 minutes.

Remove from the heat and take out the rosemary branch. Stir in the butter beans and arrowroot slurry, return to the heat, and stir until thickened. Sprinkle with the thyme and parsley and serve.

Nutritional Profile per Serving: Calories—415; % calories from fat—6%; fat (gm)—3 or 4% daily value; saturated fat (gm)—1; sodium (mg)—383; cholesterol (mg)—0; carbohydrates (gm)—85; dietary fiber (gm)—17.

# CHOU-CHOU SALAD

⌗

A substantial salad that could easily become a full meal with hearty whole-grain bread on the side.

Time Estimate: Hands-on, 18 minutes;
    unsupervised, 20 minutes
Serves 4

2 carrots, peeled and cut into matchsticks
1 cauliflower head, just the florets, each cut in half
1 cucumber, peeled, seeded, and sliced 1/4 inch (.75 cm) thick
2 large romaine lettuce leaves, finely sliced

DRESSING

1/4 teaspoon light olive oil with a dash of toasted sesame oil
1/4 teaspoon cayenne pepper
1 tablespoon mustard seeds
1 teaspoon cumin seeds
1 teaspoon turmeric
2 tablespoons brown sugar
1/4 cup rice wine vinegar
1/4 cup water
1 cup strained yogurt (page 288)
1 heaping tablespoon finely chopped fresh cilantro

GARNISH

2 tablespoons pine nuts
1/4 cup raisins

Steam the carrots and cauliflower until tender, about 10 minutes.

**The dressing:** To make a flavor base for the dressing, pour the oil into a small skillet over medium heat and sauté the cayenne, mustard seeds, cumin seeds, and turmeric for 3 minutes. Add the sugar and mix until well incorporated. Add the vinegar and water, reduce the heat, and simmer 30 minutes. Strain—you should have 3 tablespoons of highly concentrated flavor.

In a small bowl, gently stir the yogurt to remove the lumps. Add the spice flavor base and stir until it's the same consistency as a heavy mayonnaise. Fold in the cilantro until well incorporated.

**To assemble:** Put the steamed vegetables in a large bowl, add the cucumber, and toss well. Add the dressing and stir until the vegetables are well coated.

**To serve:** Place a mound of the vegetables, nestled in a wreath of the finely sliced lettuce leaves, on each plate. Garnish with the pine nuts and raisins.

Nutritional Profile per Serving: Calories—199; % calories from fat—15%; fat (gm)—3 or 5% daily value; saturated fat (gm)—1; sodium (mg)—149; cholesterol (mg)—2; carbohydrates (gm)—36; dietary fiber (gm)—4.

# CUCUMBER RAITA SALAD
❈

*This cooling salad is traditionally served with spicy Indian curries, but it could easily accompany hot dishes with Thai, Creole, or Cajun origins.*

*Time Estimate: Hands-on, 15 minutes;
   unsupervised, 10 minutes*
*Serves 4*

1 (1-pound or 450-gm) cucumber
3 large green onions, finely chopped
2 tablespoons chopped fresh cilantro
1 cup strained yogurt (page 288)
1 tablespoon freshly squeezed lime juice
1/2 teaspoon ground cumin
1/2 teaspoon ground coriander
1/4 teaspoon freshly ground white pepper
1/4 teaspoon freshly ground sea salt

Partially peel the cucumber in long strips, leaving alternating strips of green skin and white flesh. Cut into thin slices lengthwise and then crosswise to yield tiny matchstick pieces. Transfer to a large bowl and add the onions and cilantro.

In a small bowl, stir the remaining ingredients together until smooth. Pour into the vegetables, toss well, and let marinate for 10 minutes before serving.

Nutritional Profile per Serving: Calories—91; % calories from fat—0%; fat (gm)—0 or 0% daily value; saturated fat (gm)—0; sodium (mg)—235; cholesterol (mg)—2; carbohydrates (gm)—15; dietary fiber (gm)—1.

# GLAZED POTATOES
❈

*Nobody will miss gravy when you coat potatoes with this rosemary-infused glaze. I use the red-skinned new potatoes for both their color and firm flesh. Despite their hardy appearance, potatoes bruise easily. Store them, without washing, in a cool, dry, and well-ventilated area away from any kind of light. Both sunlight and artificial light cause green spots in the potato skin, which is an indication of a mild toxin that can give you mild intestinal discomfort.*

*Time Estimate: Hands-on, 10 minutes;
   unsupervised, 20 minutes*
*Serves 4*

2 cups low-sodium fish or chicken stock (page 287, 286)
1 (3-inch or 7.5-cm) sprig fresh rosemary
1 pound (450 gm) tiny red potatoes, cut into halves or quarters if large
1/8 teaspoon freshly ground sea salt
1/8 teaspoon freshly ground black pepper
1/2 teaspoon cornstarch mixed with 1 tablespoon cold stock or water (slurry)

Pour the fish or chicken stock into a 10-inch sauté pan; add the rosemary, bring to a boil, and reduce to 1/2 cup liquid. Remove the rosemary and discard.

Place the potatoes in a steamer tray. Season with the salt and pepper, and steam for 20 minutes.

Remove the potatoes from the steamer and "sauté" (stir-boil) in the reduced stock. Drizzle the cornstarch slurry into the stock and stir to form a glaze. Toss well to coat thoroughly.

Nutritional Profile per Serving: Calories—112; % calories from fat—8%; fat (gm)—1 or 2% daily value; saturated fat (gm)—0; sodium (mg)—0; cholesterol (mg)—105; carbohydrates (gm)—24; dietary fiber (gm)—2.

# MINIMAX SEED ROLLS

※

*This recipe has multiple uses. First, it can be used to make small dinner rolls that are obviously different and send a clear signal—homemade. The same recipe also can be used to make the savory, Slavic, meat-filled Pirogen (page 172). I serve my Minimax Seed Rolls with yogurt and herb spread on the side to prevent the temptation of slathering on loads of butter.*

Time Estimate: Hands-on, 45 minutes;
  unsupervised, 2 hours, 20 minutes
Makes 16 rolls

1 (.6-ounce or 18-gm) cake compressed yeast or
  1 package dry
1 cup lukewarm nonfat milk
3¾ cups all-purpose flour
3/4 cup liquid egg substitute
1/8 teaspoon freshly ground sea salt
1/8 teaspoon freshly ground black pepper
1 teaspoon sugar
1 tablespoon light olive oil with a dash of toasted sesame
  oil
1/4 cup plus 1½ teaspoons Minimax Seed Mix (page 195)
1 tablespoon nonfat milk

Crumble the cake of yeast into a small bowl and stir in 1/4 cup of the lukewarm milk until the yeast is dissolved. Slowly stir in the rest of the milk.

Sift 3 cups of the flour into a large bowl, pour in the yeast-milk mixture, and stir with a wooden spoon until the dough holds together. Knead the dough in the bowl with your hands until it no longer sticks to your fingers. Shape into a small bread loaf and set on a plate. Rinse out the bowl with warm water and dry. Lightly coat bowl with oil, return the dough to the bowl, cover with plastic wrap, and let stand in a warm place for 1 hour.

Uncover the dough and pierce deep holes into it with a knife. Pour the egg substitute into the holes. Sprinkle the loaf with 1/2 cup of the remaining flour, the salt, pepper, sugar, oil, and 1/4 cup of the Seed Mix. Mix together by cutting into the dough with a knife. When loosely combined, use your fingers to blend thoroughly.

Using part of the remaining 1/4 cup of flour, flour a board. Transfer the dough to the floured board and knead it until it no longer sticks to your hands. Put the dough back in the bowl, cover it, and let stand in a warm place for 30 minutes.

Place the dough back on the floured pastry board and cut it into quarters, then cut each quarter into quarters again, to give you 16 pieces. Fold each piece into a rough ball, put your hand down flat over the top, then roll the dough around until you form a smooth ball. Brush the tops with a little of the 1 tablespoon milk, dip each roll into the remaining Seed Mix, and place on a baking sheet. Cover and let stand until almost doubled, about 30 minutes.

Bake the rolls in a preheated 350°F (180°C) oven for 20 minutes.

Nutritional Profile per Serving: Calories—138; % calories from fat—15%; fat (gm)—2 or 4% daily value; saturated fat (gm)—.3; sodium (mg)—39; cholesterol (mg)—.3; carbohydrates (gm)—24; dietary fiber (gm)—1.

# POTATOES BAKED WITH APPLE AND ONION SAUCE

⌗

*Richly browned, caramelized onions are used here to create a glossy, aromatic sauce in which the potatoes are baked to become a heavenly side dish.*

*Time Estimate: Hands-on, 25 minutes;*
*  unsupervised, 60 minutes*
*Serves 4*

4 small russet potatoes, peeled and thinly sliced
1 sweet apple, peeled and thinly sliced
2 ounces (60 gm) Canadian bacon, finely chopped
1¼ teaspoons light olive oil with a dash of toasted
  sesame oil

SAUCE

1/4 teaspoon light olive oil with a dash of toasted
  sesame oil
2 large sweet onions, peeled and finely diced
1 teaspoon dill seeds
1 teaspoon caraway seeds
1 cup deeply colored, flavorful liquid*
1 cup de-alcoholized red wine
1 tablespoon arrowroot mixed with 2 tablespoons de-
  alcoholized red wine (slurry)

*Beef stock, tomato purée, red wine, ham hock stock, a deeply
colored vegetable stock, or any combination will provide depth
of color to the sauce.

**The sauce:** Heat the oil in a large skillet over medium heat and fry the onions, dill, and caraway for 5 minutes. Add the liquid and wine, scraping up all the pan residues into the liquid, and simmer for 5 minutes. Remove from the heat; stir in the arrowroot slurry, return to the heat, and stir until thickened and clear, about 30 seconds.

Preheat the oven to 350°F (180°C). Steam the potato slices for 5 minutes, remove from the heat, and cool under running water.

Layer half the potatoes in an oiled 9 X 9-inch

(23 X 23-cm) baking dish. Scatter the apple and Canadian bacon over the potatoes. Pour the sauce evenly on top. Arrange the rest of the potato slices in an overlapping pattern on the sauce and press down. Brush with the oil and bake, uncovered, for 1 hour.

Nutritional Profile per Serving: Calories—212; % calories from fat—13%; fat (gm)—3 or 5% daily value; saturated fat (gm)—1; sodium (mg)—195; cholesterol (mg)—7; carbohydrates (gm)—42; dietary fiber (gm)—5.

# SALSA DE QUESADILLA

⌗

*Salsas are winners in every food category: colorful, flavorful, bursting with texture, and extremely low in fat and calories. The addition of jicama in this combination provides an irresistible sweet crunch. You may substitute water chestnuts for the jicama if you can't find it in your grocery store.*

*Time Estimate: Hands-on, 10 minutes*
*Yields 2 cups*

1/2 large jicama, peeled and chopped into 1/4-inch (.75-
  cm) pieces
1 large tomato, peeled and chopped into 1/4-inch (.75-
  cm) pieces
1/2 green bell pepper, seeded and chopped into 1/4-inch
  (.75-cm) pieces
1/2 red bell pepper, seeded and chopped into 1/4-inch
  (.75-cm) pieces
2 tablespoons chopped green onions
1/4 cup chopped fresh cilantro
1 or more jalapeño peppers, seeded and finely chopped
Juice of 1 lime

Combine all the ingredients in a food processor and pulse until well blended but just coarsely chopped. Set aside for 30 minutes to let flavors blend.

Nutritional Profile per Serving: Calories—52; % calories from fat—7%; fat (gm)—0 or 0% daily value; saturated fat (gm)—.04; sodium (mg)—15; cholesterol (mg)—0; carbohydrates (gm)—12; dietary fiber (gm)—2.

# STEAMED LEEKS AND POTATOES

⚕

*Classic European style at its finest—a great winter weather first course! Do use the freshly grated nutmeg.*

*Time Estimate: Hands-on, 30 minutes*
*Serves 4 as a first course*

4 leeks, roots trimmed, dark green tops cut off and
    reserved, split open, and washed well
8 red new potatoes, 2 inches (5 cm) in diameter
I teaspoon chopped fresh thyme
2 teaspoons goat cheese

## SAUCE

I cup vegetable stock (page 288)
I tablespoon cornstarch mixed with 2 tablespoons
    water (slurry)
1/2 cup strained yogurt (page 288)
1/8 teaspoon freshly ground sea salt
1/8 teaspoon freshly ground white pepper
1/4 teaspoon freshly grated nutmeg

## GARNISH

Freshly ground black pepper
Finely chopped fresh parsley
Paprika
I lemon

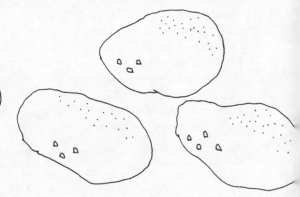

Pour about 1½ inches (4 cm) of water into a large pot, add the leek trimmings and dark green tops, and bring to a vigorous boil. Put the potatoes and leeks into a steamer tray. Sprinkle with the thyme, place over the pot, cover, and cook until tender, about 15 minutes. Remove the steamer tray and set aside.

**The sauce:** In a medium saucepan over medium heat, heat the stock through. Pour a small bit of hot stock into the cornstarch slurry, mix well, and pour back into the saucepan. Bring to a boil, stirring constantly until thickened, about 30 seconds. Remove from the heat, drop in a couple of ice cubes to cool the sauce quickly, and set aside. In a medium bowl,

stir the strained yogurt gently until smooth. When the sauce is cool, add it to the yogurt, stirring gently until well incorporated—don't overbeat! Fold in the salt, pepper, and nutmeg.

**To serve:** Coarsely chop the leeks and potatoes, and mix together. Make a small mound on each plate and sprinkle evenly with the goat cheese. Cover with the sauce. Sprinkle with the pepper, parsley, paprika, and a squeeze of lemon juice and enjoy.

Nutritional Profile per Serving: Calories—275; % calories from fat—%4; fat (gm)—I or 2% daily value; saturated fat (gm)—I; sodium (mg)—159; cholesterol (mg)—3; carbohydrates (gm)—58; dietary fiber (gm)—7.

# THANKSGIVING STUFFING LOAF

*Colorful layers of orange carrot and purple cranberry: one slice of this hearty loaf is a satisfying side dish for Thanksgiving turkey or any poultry.*

*Time Estimate: Hands-on, 20 minutes; unsupervised, 45 minutes*
*Serves 8*

1¼ teaspoons light olive oil with a dash of toasted sesame oil
5 large slices whole-wheat bread, crusts removed
1 teaspoon chopped fresh thyme
1 tablespoon chopped fresh sage
1 medium onion, peeled and coarsely chopped
2 medium parsnips (10 ounces or 300 gm), peeled and coarsely chopped
3 medium carrots (10 ounces or 300 gm), peeled and coarsely chopped
1/4 cup low-sodium turkey or chicken stock (page 286)
1/2 teaspoon freshly grated nutmeg
1/4 cup whole-berry cranberry sauce

Preheat the oven to 350°F (180°C).

Brush 1/4 teaspoon of the oil on the bottom and sides of an 8 X 4 X 2-inch (20 X 10 X 5-cm) loaf pan. Cut the bread slices into 24 (1-inch) strips. Lay 8 strips in the bottom of the pan and sprinkle 1 teaspoon of the chopped herbs over the top.

Heat the remaining teaspoon of oil in a skillet over medium-high heat and fry the onions for 2 minutes. Add the parsnips and carrots, and cook for 5 minutes. Add the stock and the remaining chopped herbs, and simmer, covered, until the vegetables are tender, about 20 minutes. Roughly mash the vegetables in the pan.

Spread half the mashed vegetables over the bottom layer of bread. Spread 2 tablespoons of the cranberry sauce on top and then add another layer of 8 bread strips. Repeat with another layer of vegetables and then more cranberry. Finish with the last 8 strips of bread to cover the top. Press down. Bake in the preheated oven for 40 minutes. Let cool for 5 minutes; loosen with a knife and then turn it out on a cutting board. Slice into 8 pieces and serve.

Nutritional Profile per Serving: Calories—107; % calories from fat—14%; fat (gm)—2 or 3% daily value; saturated fat (gm)—.3; sodium (mg)—129; cholesterol (mg)—0; carbohydrates (gm)—21; dietary fiber (gm)—3.

# STEAMED SWISS CHARD

*Swiss chard is actually the top of a variety of beet grown for its leaves rather than its root. It's valued for the texture of its leaves and stalks; indeed, in European countries, the stalks are considered chard's best part.*
*A good portion of the nutritional value in greens is released into their cooking liquid, so save it and whenever possible add it to soups, stews, casseroles, and sauces. Store Swiss chard, and all greens, unwashed, in damp paper towels, placed in plastic bags. They should last well in the refrigerator crisper for three to five days.*

*Time Estimate: Hands-on, 10 minutes*
*Serves 6*

3 pounds (1.4 kg) Swiss chard
1/8 teaspoon freshly ground sea salt
1/4 teaspoon freshly ground black pepper
1 tablespoon balsamic vinegar

Rinse the chard well. Trim off the red stems, finely chop, and place in a steamer tray. Add the whole chard leaves, salt, and pepper. Cover and steam for 4 minutes. Sprinkle with the balsamic vinegar and serve.

Nutritional Profile per Serving: Calories—57; % calories from fat—0%; fat (gm)—0 or 0% daily value; saturated fat (gm)—0; sodium (mg)—122; cholesterol (mg)—0; carbohydrates (gm)—12; dietary fiber (gm)—7

# 10% calories from fat

⁂

# Brunch
# &
# Breakfast Dishes

# Blueberry, Banana, and Bran Muffins

Reducing the effects of excess fat consumption means "fat down, fiber up," and originally the bran muffin promised both. Unfortunately, monster muffins slathered with butter are literally "muffins you could die for!" I set out to see if I could win back some popularity for the pioneer. This muffin should be served fresh from the oven or "warmed" for a few seconds in the microwave. No butter or fat spread, please. Instead, try the Blueberry, Banana, Yogurt Spread suggested in the recipe.

Time Estimate: Hands-on, 20 minutes;
  unsupervised, 25 minutes
Makes 12 muffins

2 tablespoons brown sugar
2 egg whites
1/2 cup nonfat milk
1/4 cup molasses
1/2 cup unsweetened applesauce
1 teaspoon vanilla extract
1 cup cake flour
1/2 cup whole-wheat flour
1 cup wheat bran
2 teaspoons baking powder
1/2 teaspoon baking soda
1 cup fresh or frozen (not thawed) blueberries
2 tablespoons sliced almonds
1 teaspoon cinnamon
1/2 ripe banana, sliced

BLUEBERRY, BANANA, YOGURT SPREAD
  (yields 1¼ cups)

1/2 cup mashed blueberries
1 medium ripe banana, mashed
1/4 cup plain nonfat yogurt

Preheat the oven to 400°F (205°C). In a large bowl, whisk the brown sugar and egg whites until frothy. Stir in the milk, molasses, applesauce, and vanilla.

In a medium bowl, combine the flours, bran, baking powder, and baking soda. Stir in the blueberries, almonds, and cinnamon. Add the banana slices, keeping them separated and making sure each slice is completely coated with the flour. Gently add the wet ingredients to the flour mixture. Don't overmix—it took me approximately 40 stirs to incorporate.

Line the muffin tins with foil muffin cups. Fill each cup two-thirds full and bake in the preheated oven for 25 minutes. The muffins really stick to paper cups. I believe this is due to the low-fat content of the batter.

**The yogurt spread:** While the muffins are baking, mix the blueberries, banana, and yogurt together until well incorporated.

**To serve:** Place each muffin on its own plate—remember: only one per serving—and spoon 1 tablespoon of the spread on the side.

Nutritional Profile per Serving: Calories—141; % calories from fat—7%; fat (gm)—1 or 2% daily value; saturated fat (gm)—.2; sodium (mg)—158; cholesterol (mg)—.3; carbohydrates (gm)—32; dietary fiber (gm)—4.

# Bran and Raspberry Muffins

The bright note of the raspberry is designed to startle your taste buds in mid-bite.

Time Estimate: Hands-on, 20 minutes;
  unsupervised, 30 minutes
Makes 6 large muffins

1 cup cake flour
1 cup wheat bran
2 teaspoons baking powder
1/2 teaspoon baking soda
2 egg whites
1/4 cup molasses
3/4 cup unsweetened applesauce
1/4 cup evaporated skim milk
1/2 cup frozen unsweetened raspberries, thawed but
  not mushy

Line a muffin tin with paper or foil muffin cups and preheat the oven to 350°F (180°C). In a large bowl, mix the flour, bran, baking powder, and baking soda until well incorporated.

In a medium bowl, whisk the egg whites and molasses until frothy. Whisk in the applesauce and milk.

Pour the liquids on top of the dry ingredients and stir until just incorporated—do not overstir. At this point you can cover the batter and leave in the refrigerator overnight. The fruit should be added just before baking.

Very gently fold in the raspberries, trying to prevent the fruit from breaking. Spoon a heaping 1/4 cup of the batter into each muffin cup, filling each completely; the muffins do rise, but not as much as their high-fat cousins. Bake for 25 minutes until golden brown. Remove the muffins from the tin and transfer to a wire rack to cool for 5 minutes.

**To serve:** Take them to the table while still warm. No need for added fat, preserves, or jelly. The muffin's complete in itself.

Nutritional Profile per Serving: Calories—162; % calories from fat—4%; fat (gm)—1 or 1% daily value; saturated fat (gm)—.1; sodium (mg)—304; cholesterol (mg)—.4; carbohydrates (gm)—38; dietary fiber (gm)—6.

# OPEN-FACED BAKED POTATO SANDWICH
## (WITH BASIC SAVORY TOPPING)

*On a night when you think you're too tired to cook, this simple baked-potato meal will revive your spirits. The savory topping is an excellent substitution for sour cream in all your dishes.*

*Time Estimate: Hands-on, 15 minutes; unsupervised, 1 hour*

*Serves 4*

4 medium russet potatoes

BASIC SAVORY TOPPING

3/4 cup strained yogurt (page 288)
1 tablespoon minced fresh parsley stalks
1 tablespoon minced fresh chives
1/2 teaspoon pure maple syrup
1/8 teaspoon coarsely ground black pepper
1 tablespoon de-alcoholized white wine

POTATO TOPPINGS

4 ounces (115 gm) diced smoked turkey or any lean meat
1/2 cup finely diced plum tomato

GARNISH

4 teaspoons freshly grated dry Monterey Jack cheese
Chopped fresh parsley
Freshly ground black pepper

Bake the potatoes at 375°F (190°C) for approximately 1 hour or until a fork inserts easily into the flesh.

While the potatoes are baking, gently stir the yogurt in a small bowl to remove the lumps. Stir in the parsley stalks, chives, maple syrup, and pepper. It's your choice whether or not to splash with the de-alcoholized wine. Be careful not to overstir the topping or it will lose its creamy mouthfeel and become thin.

**To serve:** Cut each baked potato in half lengthwise. Score the potato flesh with a knife and cover completely with a quarter of the topping. Sprinkle with the meat and tomato. Garnish each with 1 teaspoon of the cheese, chopped parsley, and black pepper to taste.

Nutritional Profile per Serving: Calories—238; % calories from fat—9%; fat (gm)—2 or 4% daily value; saturated fat (gm)—1; sodium (mg)—404; cholesterol (mg)—19; carbohydrates (gm)—40; dietary fiber (gm)—3.

# PIQUENIQUE PIE

X

*Layers of tender potatoes in a chewy, cheesey crust. Perfect fare for a brunch or a picnic—your choice!*

Time Estimate: Hands-on, 35 minutes;
  unsupervised, 55 minutes

Serves 6

BASIC RICE CRUST

2 cups cooked white rice
1/4 teaspoon grated Parmesan cheese
1/2 teaspoon freshly ground sea salt
1/4 teaspoon freshly ground black pepper
1 lightly beaten egg white

FILLING

1 teaspoon light olive oil with a dash of toasted sesame oil
1 large yellow onion, peeled and finely sliced
4 large red new potatoes (about 1¼ pounds or 560 gm),
  sliced paper thin
1½ teaspoons chopped fresh thyme
Freshly ground sea salt
Freshly ground black pepper
1 cup low-sodium beef stock (page 286)
1 cup liquid egg substitute

Freshly grated Parmesan cheese

**The rice crust:** Preheat the oven to 375°F (190°C). Pour about 1 inch (2.5 cm) of water into a medium saucepan and bring to a boil. Put the cooked rice in a sieve and place over the boiling water; cover and steam 5 minutes. This process gives you separate, fluffy grains—essential for the rice crust.

Transfer the warm rice to a medium bowl and work in the cheese until the grains are all a pale, uniform yellow. Add the salt and pepper, and stir well. Pour in the egg white and stir until the rice clumps together. Shape it into a large bowl and transfer to a 9-inch (23-cm) nonstick pie pan.

Keeping a bowl of ice water on the side to prevent your fingers from becoming too sticky, press the rice into a thin, uniform layer around the bottom and sides of the pie pan. Start on the bottom, moving to the sides and up to the rim. The crust should extend about 1/2 inch (1.5 cm) beyond the top of the pie pan. This crust shrinks a lot in the baking process. Bake in the preheated oven until just slightly brown, about 25 minutes. Remove and set aside.

**The filling:** Pour the oil into a large skillet over medium heat and cook the onion until just translucent, but not limp, about 5 minutes. Remove and set aside.

Set aside one-quarter of the potato slices for the top of the pie. In the same skillet, layer one-third of the remaining potatoes and sprinkle with 1/2 teaspoon of the thyme, a dusting of salt, and a dusting of pepper. Repeat the process with the remaining two-thirds of the potatoes and seasonings. Pour in the stock, cover, and simmer 10 minutes. Pour off any liquid that has not been absorbed.

**To assemble:** Layer one-third of the cooked potatoes and onion on the bottom of the prepared crust and pour in one-third of the egg substitute. Repeat the process until the crust is full. Decorate the top with a wreath of overlapping slices from the reserved raw potato. Liberally brush with the remaining skillet juices and bake for 35 minutes, until the top potatoes are translucent, the custard set, and the color golden. You might see little driblets of liquid in the center, but that's just the moisture from the stock and potatoes.

**To serve:** Serve at room temperature, sprinkled with the cheese.

Nutritional Profile per Serving: Calories—252; % calories from fat—10%; fat (gm)—3 or 4% daily value; saturated fat (gm)—1; sodium (mg)—391; cholesterol (mg)—4; carbohydrates (gm)—47; dietary fiber (gm)—3.

# Squash and Ginger Muffins

*Ginger is a fresh, lively addition to these muffins, but make sure you measure it absolutely flat and level so you don't overwhelm the muffins with its distinctive flavor. The baked squash should be somewhat crumbly, not completely smooth, so that it flecks throughout the batter. These muffins are also great for dinner with a pot of chili. Just before baking, grate a teaspoon of cheese on top.*

*Time Estimate: Hands-on, 15 minutes;*
  *unsupervised, 30 minutes*
*Makes 6 large muffins*

1¾ cups cake flour
2 teaspoons baking powder
1/2 teaspoon baking soda
1 teaspoon dried ginger
2 egg whites
1/4 cup brown sugar
3/4 cup unsweetened applesauce
1/4 cup evaporated skim milk
1 small butternut squash (about 1 pound or 450 gm),
  baked, to yield 3/4 cup mashed flesh

   Line a muffin tin with muffin cups and preheat the oven to 350°F (180°C). In a large bowl, whisk the flour, baking powder, baking soda, and ginger together until well incorporated.
   In a medium bowl, whisk the egg whites together with the brown sugar until frothy. Whisk in the applesauce and milk. Stir in the mashed squash until distributed evenly.
   Add the liquid mixture all at once over the top of the dry ingredients and stir until just combined—it's important not to overstir. Spoon a heaping 1/4 cup of the batter into each muffin cup; each should be full and well rounded. Bake in the preheated oven for 25 minutes or until golden brown. Turn the muffins out onto a wire rack to cool for 5 minutes.
   **To serve:** These muffins don't need butter or jams.

They also can be served as a biscuit alternative with casserole dishes.

Nutritional Profile per Serving: Calories—176; % calories from fat—2%; fat (gm)—.5 or .1% daily value; saturated fat (gm)—.1; sodium (mg)—302; cholesterol (mg)—.4; carbohydrates (gm)—38; dietary fiber (gm)—2.

# Sweet Potato and Raisin Muffins

⌘

*It's so vital to incorporate beta-carotene-rich vegetables into your life, and I can think of few more pleasant ways than with this colorful muffin.*

*Time Estimate: Hands-on, 15 minutes; unsupervised, 30 minutes*
*Makes 7 large muffins*

1¾ cups cake flour
2 teaspoons baking powder
1/2 teaspoon baking soda
1/2 teaspoon cinnamon
2 egg whites
2 tablespoons brown sugar
3/4 cup unsweetened applesauce
1/4 cup evaporated skim milk
2 medium sweet potatoes, baked, to yield 3/4 cup of mashed potato
1 tablespoon finely chopped lemon zest
2 tablespoons freshly squeezed lemon juice
1/2 cup dark raisins

Line muffin tins with paper or foil muffin cups and preheat the oven to 350°F (180°C). In a large bowl, whisk the flour, baking powder, baking soda, and cinnamon until well incorporated.

In a medium bowl, beat the egg whites with the sugar until just frothy. Stir in the applesauce and milk, then the mashed sweet potato, lemon zest, lemon juice, and raisins, stirring until well combined.

Add the liquid mixture all at once over the top of the dry ingredients and stir until *just* combined. Spoon a heaping 1/4 cup of the batter into each muffin cup; each should be full and well rounded. Bake for 25 minutes or until golden brown. Turn the muffins out onto a wire rack to cool for 5 minutes.

**To serve:** One per person, fresh from the oven.

Nutritional Profile per Serving: Calories—217; % calories from fat—2%; fat (gm)—.4 or .1% daily value; saturated fat (gm)—.1; sodium (mg)—258; cholesterol (mg)—.2; carbohydrates (gm)—50; dietary fiber (gm)— 3.

# Poipu Beach Breakfast

⌘

*I was quite content with my mornings until we spent some time on the Hawaiian Island of Kauai at Poipu Beach. One morning I raided the buffet, selecting yogurt, kiwi fruit, and strawberries. I topped it off with granola. A new recipe was born!*

*Time Estimate: Hands-on, 10 minutes*
*Serves 2*

1⅓ cups plain nonfat yogurt
4 teaspoons honey
1 cup Graham's Granola (see page 207)
2 kiwi fruit, peeled and thinly sliced
2 strawberries, stemmed and thinly sliced

GARNISH

1 kiwi fruit, peeled and thinly sliced
1 strawberry, stemmed and thinly sliced
2 small mint sprigs

In a small bowl, mix the yogurt and honey. For each serving, scoop 1/2 cup of the granola into a bowl. Spread slices of kiwi fruit and strawberry over the top. Spoon 2/3 cup of the yogurt mixture over the fruit. Garnish with 2 slices each of the kiwi fruit and the strawberry, and a mint sprig.

Nutritional Profile per Serving: Calories—334; % calories from fat—11%; fat (gm)—4 or 7% daily value; saturated fat (gm)—1; sodium (mg)—252; cholesterol (mg)—3; carbohydrates (gm)—67; dietary fiber (gm)—6.

# MEXICAN SCRAMBLED EGGS AND SALSA

*This classic Mexican egg dish is substantially changed with many complex tastes. I serve two tortillas for each adult, one per child. To keep the heat down, I suggest you add only half the habañero sauce and serve a small bottle on the side.*

Time Estimate: Hands-on, 35 minutes;
  unsupervised, 30 minutes
Serves 4

BLACK BEAN SALSA

1 (15-ounce or 425-gm) can black beans, drained and
  rinsed
1 cup unpeeled, finely chopped plum tomatoes
4 green onions, chopped in 1/4-inch (.75-cm) pieces
2 tablespoons chopped fresh cilantro
1/2 teaspoon green habañero chili sauce or Louisiana
  hot sauce
1/2 cup corn kernels, frozen or fresh
2 tablespoons freshly squeezed orange juice
1/8 teaspoon freshly ground sea salt
1/4 teaspoon ground cumin
1/2 teaspoon arrowroot mixed with 1 tablespoon water
  (slurry)

MEXICAN EGGS

1 cup chopped unpeeled plum tomatoes
1/2 teaspoon light olive oil mixed with a dash of toasted
  sesame oil
1 cup chopped onion
1/2 teaspoon seeded and chopped serrano or jalapeño
  chilies
1 tablespoon chopped fresh cilantro
1½ cups liquid egg substitute
1/4 cup chopped green onion tops, roughly chopped on
  the diagonal

8 soft corn tortillas, warmed
4 tablespoons strained yogurt (page 288)

**The salsa:** In a large bowl, combine the black beans, tomatoes, green onions, cilantro, habañero sauce, corn, and orange juice. Season with the salt and cumin, and let sit for 30 minutes. Strain, reserving both the vegetables and the liquid separately.

In a small saucepan, bring the reserved salsa liquid to a simmer over medium-high heat. Remove from the heat and add the arrowroot slurry. Return to the heat and stir until thickened.

In a small bowl, combine the reserved salsa solids and the thickened salsa liquid. The salsa now has a beautiful gloss and is ready to serve.

**The eggs:** Put the chopped tomatoes in a strainer and drain off any excess liquid. In a large sauté pan over medium-high heat, heat the oil and quickly sauté the onion and tomatoes until the onion is soft, about 5 minutes. Add the chilies, cilantro, egg substitute, and green onion tops. Cook the eggs, scrambling slowly and gently, until firm, about 4 minutes.

**To serve:** Spoon the Mexican eggs onto the warm tortillas, reserving 4 spoonfuls for garnish, and then roll the tortillas in order to enclose the egg mixture. Place 2 tortillas on each plate, with a spoonful of salsa on one side and a dollop of strained yogurt on the other. Finish with another spoonful of reserved eggs on top and . . . *olé!*

Nutritional Profile per Serving: Calories—381; % calories from fat—7%; fat (gm)—3 or 4% daily value; saturated fat (gm)—1; sodium (mg)—539; cholesterol (mg)—1; carbohydrates (gm)—71; dietary fiber (gm)—13.

# 10% calories from fat

⌘

# Desserts

# BLACKBERRY ZABAGLIONE

⌘

*Italian in origin, the first zabaglione is said to have been invented by accident in the seventeenth century by a chef who inadvertently poured wine into an egg custard. Well, in the twentieth century, chefs purposely pour enough liquors into this dessert to create about a 40 percent–alcohol content custard. But times have changed and now I've made a zabaglione that has a great new taste and color.*

*Time Estimate: Hands-on, 1 hour*
*Serves 6*

2½ cups frozen unsweetened blackberries, thawed
1½ cups de-alcoholized white wine
3 tablespoons maple syrup
1/4 teaspoon almond extract
1/4 teaspoon vanilla extract
2 tablespoons cornstarch mixed with 1/4 cup de-alcoholized white wine (slurry)
1 cup water
1 cup liquid egg substitute
1/2 cup superfine sugar

Spoon 1½ cups of the blackberries into 6 (6-ounce or 170-gm) wine glasses. They should each be half full.

Push the remaining blackberries through a sieve to yield 8 tablespoons of purée.

In a saucepan, bring the de-alcoholized white wine to a boil. Add the maple syrup, almond extract, and vanilla. Stir in the cornstarch slurry, bring to a boil, and stir. Set aside.

In a medium saucepan, bring the water to a boil. Set a round copper bowl in the saucepan to create a double-boiler effect and reduce the heat to a simmer. Now combine the egg substitute and sugar in the bowl and beat until the consistency is thick and creamy, like a frothy pudding.

Slowly whisk the syrup mixture into the sweetened egg substitute. Add 6 tablespoons of the blackberry purée and beat well over heat to combine.

Pour the custard over the blackberries in the wine glasses. Top with the remaining blackberry purée. Present warm (cookies on the side are entirely optional).

Nutritional Profile per Serving: Calories—149; % calories from fat—2%; fat (gm)—.3 or 0% daily value; saturated fat (gm)—0; sodium (mg)—43; cholesterol (mg)—0; carbohydrates (gm)—35; dietary fiber (gm)—2.

## THE COPPER EFFECT

I feel that a good 10-inch (25-cm) copper bowl is an essential Minimax kitchen tool, because I use egg whites so often to give added volume and texture—without a gram of fat!

The reason why copper works so well with liquid egg substitutes is that they are made predominantly of egg white. In this recipe I used a copper bowl over hot water as a double boiler; I had the space to use a wisk, and it worked wonderfully.

Try to use Fleischmann's Egg Beaters. We did some comparative tests with other yolkless products and didn't think they were nearly as good.

# BREAD AND BUTTER PUDDING

Nutritional Profile per Serving: Calories—325; % calories from fat—7%; fat (gm)—3 or 4% daily value; saturated fat (gm)—1; sodium (mg)—299; cholesterol (mg)—7; carbohydrates (gm)—66; dietary fiber (gm)—3.

*Bread and Butter Pudding is a British standard, and many farmers have family recipes. These recipes are usually drowned in cream and eggs. I've tried hard to keep the "feelings" alive but reduce the fat. See what you think for yourself!*

*Time Estimate: Hands-on, 20 minutes;*
  *unsupervised, 35 minutes*
*Serves 6*

1½ cups 2%-fat milk
1½ cups evaporated skim milk
Zest of 1 orange in long strips
2 teaspoons dried rosemary
1/4 cup sugar
1 teaspoon vanilla extract
1/4 teaspoon cardamom
1½ cups liquid egg substitute
6 slices whole-wheat bread
1 orange, cut into sections, sections halved
1/2 cup dried cranberries
6 tablespoons pure maple syrup

## CRUSTS ON OR OFF

The British traditionally cut the crusts off their bread. This might have started as a means of cutting away mold or removing travel soil. Whatever the reason, it doesn't make good sense to throw out such good food, especially since it provides added texture. So I left the crusts on. I hope you enjoy their textural pleasure.

Preheat the oven to 350°F (180°C). Heat both milks with the rosemary and orange zest in a large saucepan. When it is hot but not boiling, strain it into a bowl. Stir in the sugar, vanilla, and cardamom, and whisk until the sugar dissolves. Now pour in the egg substitute and stir to combine.

Cut the bread slices into triangles and layer them in an 8 X 8-inch (20 X 20-cm) baking dish. Scatter the orange sections and cranberries around the bread pieces. Pour the custard mixture over the bread and set the baking dish in a larger baking dish. Pour hot water into the larger baking dish so the water comes at least halfway up the sides of the smaller dish. Bake in the preheated oven for 1 hour or until puffed and set.

**To serve:** Spoon into dessert bowls and splash each with a tablespoon of maple syrup.

# Bumbleberry Strudel

※

*One of our most favorite places to eat when we're in Victoria, British Columbia, is about seven miles from the city in a village called Oak Bay. There you will find the Blethering Place, an English tea shop owned by New Zealander Ken Agate, which serves a great "cuppa" (tea) and a wonderful mixed-fruit pie. I've kept the berries and changed the crust—grounds for diplomatic conflict?*

Time Estimate: Hands-on, 50 minutes;
  unsupervised, 30 minutes

Serves 6

## SAUCE

1 tablespoon local, fresh honey (I use fireweed when I
  can get it)
1 cup strained yogurt (page 288)

## STRUDEL

1 large Granny Smith apple, peeled, cored, and chopped
  into 1/4-inch (.75-cm) dice
1 cup finely sliced rhubarb
1 cup unsweetened apple juice
1/4 teaspoon ground cloves
1/4 cup brown sugar
1 tablespoon freshly grated lemon zest
1 cup frozen unsweetened blackberries
1 cup frozen unsweetened raspberries
2 teaspoons cornstarch mixed with 1/4 cup water (slurry)
8 sheets phyllo dough
Olive oil cooking spray
1/2 cup dried bread crumbs
2 tablespoons fresh, local honey

## GARNISH

6 fresh mint sprigs

**The filling:** In a high-sided casserole or heavy saucepan, heat the apple, rhubarb, apple juice, and cloves. Stir in the sugar and bring to a rolling boil for about 2 minutes. Stir in the lemon rind, blackberries, and raspberries. Remove from the heat and stir in the cornstarch. Return to the heat and bring to a boil, stirring constantly until thickened. Remove from the heat and set aside.

**The Sauce:** Mix the honey and the strained yogurt until smooth and reserve.

**The strudel:** On a flat surface, stretch out a slightly damp dish towel. Lay a sheet of the phyllo dough on top of the towel running lengthwise. Spray lightly with the olive oil and repeat with 3 more sheets of the phyllo.

Sprinkle 1/4 cup of the bread crumbs in a strip 3 inches (8 cm) wide across the length of the phyllo, leaving 2 inches (5 cm) at either end. Now take half of the fruit mixture and carefully spoon it along the bread-crumb strip.

With the long side of the dough and fruit filling in front of you, lift the edge of the damp cloth nearest you and roll slowly away from you, as you would a jelly roll. Repeat for the remaining dough and fruit mixture.

Preheat the oven to 350°F (180°C). Spray a cookie sheet lightly with the oil and place the strudel seam side down. Lightly brush each roll with the honey. Bake for 30 minutes. When done, place the cookie sheet on a wire rack and let the strudel cool for 15 minutes before slicing. Slice each roll into thirds and serve with a dollop of the honey-sweetened yogurt. Garnish with a sprig of the mint.

Nutritional Profile per Serving: Calories—298; % calories from fat—4%; fat (gm)—1 or 2% daily value; saturated fat (gm)—.2; sodium (mg)—185; cholesterol (mg)—2; carbohydrates (gm)—66; dietary fiber (gm)—4.

# Turos Palascinta

※

*Turos are Hungarian sweet pancakes, smothered in cottage cheese and sugar. After being reheated in the oven, they are topped with fruit jam and dollops of sour cream. My Minimax turos recipe uses red raspberries, blueberries, and white cottage cheese for a remarkably patriotic dessert—depending, of course, on your nationality!*

*Time Estimate: Hands-on, 30 minutes;
   unsupervised, 30 minutes*
*Serves 4 (yields 8 crêpes)*

## CRÊPE BATTER

I whole egg
I egg yolk
I teaspoon grated lemon zest
I cup nonfat milk
1/2 cup all-purpose flour
I teaspoon light oil with a dash of toasted sesame oil

## FILLING

1/2 cup 1%-fat cottage cheese
1/2 cup fresh or frozen blueberries
I tablespoon fresh local honey
1/2 teaspoon vanilla extract

## SAUCE

3 cups raspberries
1/4 cup de-alcoholized white wine
I tablespoon cornstarch mixed with 2 tablespoons
   water (slurry)
1/4 cup strained yogurt (page 288)
1/2 teaspoon vanilla extract
2 tablespoons fresh local honey

## GARNISH

Jar of honey (preferably fireweed) kept warm in a
   saucepan of hot water
1/4 cup raspberries
1/4 cup blueberries
I teaspoon confectioners' sugar

**The crêpe batter:** In a medium bowl, beat the whole egg, egg yolk, lemon zest, and milk. Sift the flour into another bowl, make a well in the center of the flour, and stir in the liquid mixture. Cover and let rest for 30 minutes.

**The crêpes:** In a crêpe pan, heat the oil, then tip the excess into the batter and stir thoroughly to create self-releasing batter. Pour 1/4 cup of the batter into the pan and swirl to make a round crêpe. Cook until slightly brown, then flip and brown the other side, approximately 1 minute on each side. Set aside, then cook the other 3 crêpes. Cook any batter that is left and freeze the extra crêpes to use another time.

**The filling:** In a medium bowl, mix the cottage cheese, blueberries, honey, and vanilla. Set aside.

**The sauce:** Push the raspberries through a sieve into a medium bowl. You should have approximately 2/3 cup of raspberry purée. Transfer the purée to a saucepan, stir in the wine, and bring to a boil. Remove from the heat and add the cornstarch slurry. Bring back to a boil for 30 seconds to thicken the purée, stirring constantly. Remove from the heat and let cool.

Smooth out any small lumps in the strained yogurt and stir it gently into the sauce until it is just incorporated. Add the vanilla and honey. Return to low heat to keep warm until serving.

**To serve:** Spread each crêpe with 2 tablespoons of filling, roll into a cylinder, and place on a serving plate. Brush the crêpes with warm honey to make them glisten. Spoon the raspberry sauce delicately over the top. Garnish with a few raspberries and blueberries on each side and dust lightly with confectioners' sugar.

Turos can be served hot on a cold winter's night by baking the filled pancake at 325°F (165°C) for 10 minutes, then coating with the sauce and adding the garnish. We also like them cold on a warm summer's night—your choice!

Nutritional Profile per Serving: Calories—223; % calories from fat—12%; fat (gm)—3 or 5% daily value; saturated fat (gm)—1; sodium (mg)—165; cholesterol (mg)—55; carbohydrates (gm)—42; dietary fiber (gm)—3.

# BUTTERNUT SQUASH GINGER CHEESECAKE

—— ⌗ ——

*Try this instead of pumpkin pie for a holiday dessert.*
*It has some of the same spicy qualities but much lower fat content.*

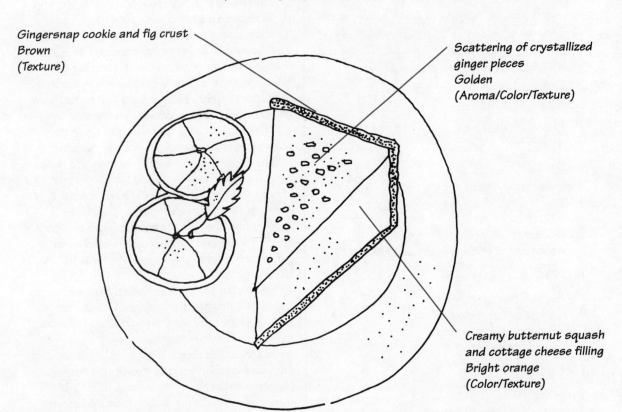

**Gingersnap cookie and fig crust**
**Brown**
**(Texture)**

**Scattering of crystallized**
**ginger pieces**
**Golden**
**(Aroma/Color/Texture)**

**Creamy butternut squash**
**and cottage cheese filling**
**Bright orange**
**(Color/Texture)**

*Time Estimate: Hands-on, 30 minutes;*
   *unsupervised, 3 hours 40 minutes*
*Serves 12*

FIG CRUST

18 dried figs, stalk ends removed
1 cup broken ginger snap cookies

FILLING

1 small butternut squash, cut in half and seeded
2 packets unflavored gelatin
1/2 cup water

3/4 cup brown sugar
1½ cups 2%-fat cottage cheese
1/2 teaspoon cinnamon
1/2 teaspoon ground ginger
1/4 teaspoon ground cloves
3/4 cup strained yogurt (page 288)

GARNISH

1 tablespoon finely chopped crystallized ginger

**Start the filling:** Preheat the oven to 350°F (180°C). Place the squash halves facedown on a baking sheet and bake in the preheated oven for 40 minutes. Remove and let cool. Scoop out 2 cups of the flesh for this recipe and freeze the rest for future use.

**For the crust:** Process the figs in a food processor for a few seconds, add the broken ginger snaps, and continue processing until they clump together in a sticky ball. Don't process too long or the cookies will lose their texture. Press the crust mixture into the bottom and up the sides of a lightly greased, high-sided, 7-inch (18-cm) springform pan. Dip your fingers into a bowl of cold water to alleviate any stickiness.

**For the filling:** Sprinkle the gelatin over the water in a small saucepan and allow to soften for 1 minute. Warm over low heat, stirring, until the gelatin is completely dissolved, about 3 minutes. Place the squash, softened gelatin, and the remaining filling ingredients in the processor and whiz until smooth, about 2 minutes. Pour the filling into the prepared crust, pop into the refrigerator, and chill until set, about 3 hours.

**To serve:** Unmold, slice with a warm knife, and garnish each piece with the crystallized ginger.

| Nutritional Profile per Serving | | | |
|---|---|---|---|
| | **Classic** | **Minimax** | **Daily Value** |
| Calories | 410 | 203 | |
| Calories from fat | 62% | 9% | |
| Fat (gm) | 28 | 2 | 3% |
| Saturated fat (gm) | 17 | 1 | 7% |
| Sodium (mg) | 271 | 154 | 6% |
| Cholesterol (mg) | 123 | 3 | 1% |
| Carbohydrates (gm) | 34 | 42 | 14% |
| Dietary fiber (gm) | 1 | 4 | 15% |
| Classic compared: Best Cheese Pie | | | |

# CARROT CAKE

⚙

*This recipe is a perfect example of springboarding. It comes from an in-flight meal experience had by Chef David Burke of The River Café in New York City. He made changes to suit his special needs by making a hot, cream-cheese soufflé topping. I subsequently made my own changes and added a spiced, creamy, apple-butter topping. I like to split the dish and serve half the cake with the topping and leave the rest of the cake for simple snacking. If you have twelve people to serve, just double the topping.*

*Time Estimate: Hands-on, 45 minutes;
    unsupervised, 40 minutes*

*Serves 12*

## CAKE

1/2 cup raisins, preferably seedless flame variety
1¾ cups all-purpose flour
2/3 cup whole-wheat flour
2 teaspoons baking soda
1½ teaspoons cinnamon
1 tablespoon allspice
1/2 teaspoon freshly grated nutmeg
1/8 teaspoon freshly ground sea salt
3/4 cup firmly packed brown sugar
3 tablespoons light olive oil with a dash of toasted
    sesame oil
2 eggs
2/3 cup buttermilk
2 teaspoons vanilla extract
1½ cups coarsely shredded carrot
1 (8-ounce or 225-gm) can crushed, unsweetened
    pineapple

## TOPPING

1/2 cup apple butter
1/2 cup strained yogurt (page 288)
2 tablespoons pure maple syrup

## GARNISH

12 sprigs fresh mint

**The cake:** Put the raisins in a small bowl, cover with hot water, and soak until soft and plump, about 10 to 15 minutes. Drain.

Preheat the oven to 350°F (180°C). In a large bowl, combine the flours, baking soda, cinnamon, allspice, nutmeg, and salt. Stir well and set aside.

In a large bowl, combine the brown sugar and oil. Add the eggs, one at a time, beating well with a wire whisk after each addition. Stir in the buttermilk and the vanilla. Stir in the flour mixture. Add the carrots, raisins, and pineapple.

Lightly grease an ovenproof skillet or round cake pan 11 inches (28 cm) in diameter. Pour in the batter and shake to distribute evenly. Place the skillet on the middle rack of the preheated oven and bake for 40 minutes. Turn cake out on a wire rack to cool.

**The topping:** In a small bowl, mix the apple butter, strained yogurt, and maple syrup.

**To serve:** Place a wedge of the hot carrot cake on a serving dish, spoon 3 tablespoons of the topping over the top, and garnish with a sprig of the fresh mint.

Nutritional Profile per Serving: Calories—283; % calories from fat—15%; fat (gm)—5 or 8% daily value; saturated fat (gm)—1; sodium (mg)—293; cholesterol (mg)—36; carbohydrates (gm)—56; dietary fiber (gm)—3.

# CHEESECAKE WITH MIXED BERRY TOPPING

When it comes right down to it, cheesecake is the number one temptation. We all know it's loaded with calories and fat, but what to do about it? I replaced cream cheese with cottage cheese and strained yogurt, and held the crust together with sweet, chewy figs instead of butter. Give it a try and let me know what you think.

Time Estimate: Hands-on, 20 minutes;
  unsupervised, 2 hours
Serves 12

## CRUST

1 cup dried white figs
1 cup broken graham crackers (6 rectangles)

## FILLING

1 packet unflavored gelatin
1/4 cup cold water
1 cup 2%-fat cottage cheese
1/3 cup brown sugar
1 teaspoon vanilla extract
1 cup strained yogurt (page 288)
2 tablespoons freshly squeezed lemon juice
1 teaspoon freshly grated lemon zest
1/2 cup evaporated skim milk

## TOPPING

1 (10-ounce or 285-gm) package sweetened, frozen
  strawberries
1/2 cup unsweetened frozen blueberries
1/2 cup unsweetened frozen raspberries
1½ tablespoons cornstarch

**The crust:** Drop the figs in a food processor and whiz about 30 seconds. Add the graham crackers and pulse just until they are combined. Press the mixture into the bottom and a little way up the sides of a 9-inch (23-cm) springform pan. Dip your fingers into a bowl of cold water to alleviate any stickiness.

**The filling:** Sprinkle the gelatin onto the water in a small saucepan and allow to soften for 1 minute. Cook over low heat, stirring, until completely dissolved.

Put the cottage cheese, brown sugar, and vanilla in a processor or blender and whiz for 10 seconds. Add the yogurt, lemon juice, lemon zest, evaporated skim milk, and the dissolved gelatin. Pulse a few times, just to mix. Pour into the crust and chill 1 hour before topping.

**The topping:** Combine all the topping ingredients in a saucepan and cook over medium-high heat until thickened and glossy, about 2 minutes. Allow to cool while the cheesecake is chilling. Spread cooled berry mixture over the top of the cheesecake and chill for 1 more hour. This cheesecake is best eaten the same day.

Nutritional Profile per Serving: Calories—176; % calories from fat—7%; fat (gm)—1 or 2% daily value; saturated fat (gm)—1; sodium (mg)—169; cholesterol (mg)—3; carbohydrates (gm)—35; dietary fiber (gm)—2.

White figs are sometimes hard to find. In this recipe I use them to keep the color of the crust light, but that isn't absolutely necessary. Use black ones if that's all you can find; they'll taste just as good.

# Champorodi Guava

This is a triumph of mind over coconut matter, possibly the most delicious milk pudding in the entire world. I invented it as a creative alternative to the classic coconut and chocolate chip rice dish that is a breakfast favorite in the Philippines.

Time Estimate: Hands-on, 15 minutes;
  unsupervised, 1 hour
Serves 6

2½ cups nonfat milk
1 teaspoon coconut essence
1 cup uncooked short-grain pearl rice
1 tablespoon brown sugar

## SAUCE

1 (12-ounce or 350-gm) can guava nectar
1 tablespoon arrowroot mixed with 2 tablespoons
  water (slurry)

Preheat the oven to 400°F (205°C). Combine the milk, coconut essence, rice, and brown sugar in an ovenproof saucepan and bring to a boil. Cover and bake in the preheated oven for 1 hour.

**For the sauce:** In a saucepan, bring the guava nectar to a boil and reduce by half. Remove the saucepan from the heat, stir in the arrowroot slurry, return to the heat, and stir until thickened. Set aside.

**To serve:** Champorodi Guava can be served hot from the oven or chilled in small molds. To chill, fill 6 small molds or timbales with the baked rice and set in the refrigerator to cool and set. Hot or cold, coat the servings with pink guava sauce—it is wonderfully delicious.

Nutritional Profile per Serving: Calories—232; % calories from fat—2%; fat (gm)—1 or 1% daily value; saturated fat (gm)—0; sodium (mg)—86; cholesterol (mg)—3; carbohydrates (gm)—48; dietary fiber (gm)—1.

# Chocolate and Strawberry Angel Food Cake

Less well known than its almost white (more angelic?) cousin, this chocolate angel food cake is filled with creamy topping and fresh strawberries. It delivers a delicious treat with only 1 gram of fat per serving.

Time Estimate: Hands-on, 90 minutes;
  unsupervised, 80 minutes
Serves 12

## CAKE

3/4 cup sifted cake flour
1/4 teaspoon baking soda
1/4 cup unsweetened cocoa powder
1 cup granulated sugar
11 egg whites, at room temperature
1 teaspoon water
1½ teaspoons cream of tartar
1/4 teaspoon freshly ground sea salt
1½ teaspoons vanilla extract

## FILLING

9 tablespoons nonfat dried milk powder
1/2 cup ice water
3 tablespoons superfine sugar
1 teaspoon safflower oil
1/4 teaspoon vanilla extract
1 envelope unflavored gelatin
3 tablespoons cold water
3 tablespoons boiling water
1 cup strained yogurt (page 288)
3/4 pound (350 gm) strawberries, stemmed and
  washed

## GARNISH

6 strawberries with leaves, cut in half

**The cake:** Preheat the oven to 350°F (180°C). Sift the flour, baking soda, cocoa, and 1/3 cup of the granulated sugar together 3 times into a large bowl and set aside.

In a large bowl, beat the egg whites with an electric mixer at high speed until foamy. Add the water, cream of tartar, salt, and vanilla, and beat until soft peaks form. Gradually beat in the remaining 2/3 cup sugar until stiff peaks form. Fold in the flour mixture, 1/4 cup at a time.

Pour the batter into an ungreased 10-inch (25-cm) angel food cake pan, spreading evenly. Bake for 35 to 40 minutes or until the cake springs back when lightly touched. Invert the pan and let the cake cool, about 40 minutes. Using a narrow metal spatula, loosen the cake from the sides of the pan and remove from the pan.

Cut a 1-inch (2.5-cm) layer off the top of the cake. Place the lower cake layer on a serving dish. Scoop out a 2 X 2-inch (5 X 5-cm) trench around the inside of this layer.

**The filling:** In a small metal bowl, beat the dried milk and ice water with a wire whisk for 6 to 7 minutes. Gradually beat in the sugar and oil. Add the vanilla and continue beating for 1 minute more.

In another small bowl, mix the gelatin with the cold water and let sit 3 minutes to soften. Stir in the boiling water to dissolve the gelatin. In a large bowl, combine the milk mixture with the gelatin and strained yogurt.

**To assemble:** Place the strawberries in the hollowed-out section of the cake. Spoon 1 cup of the filling over the strawberries. Now place the top layer of the cake back in its original position, over the strawberries, and top with the remaining filling. As the filling drips down the sides of the cake, use a spatula to smooth and even the frosting, being sure to cover the entire cake. Garnish with the 12 strawberry halves, one for each slice.

**To serve:** This cake looks superb presented whole and sliced at the table, or presliced and served on individual plates. When the filling is added and the top and sides "frosted," it takes an hour in the refrigerator to completely set, although it can also be served moist immediately. Either way, have fun!

Nutritional Profile per Serving: Calories—173; % calories from fat—5%; fat (gm)—1 or 1% daily value; saturated fat (gm)—3; sodium (mg)—172; cholesterol (mg)—1; carbohydrates (gm)—34; dietary fiber (gm)—1.

## CREAM OF TARTAR

Some people enjoy the science of cooking. In the case of angel food cake, science can explain the way cream of tartar reacts with albumen, or egg white. Cream of tartar is solid salt or tartaric acid. By adding acidic cream of tartar, one lowers the pH value of the egg white, and that, in turn, stabilizes the foam to prevent it from overcoagulating.

# CHOCOLATE CHEESECAKE WITH FIG CRUST

——— ⌗ ———

*This recipe is great news for self-confessed chocolate addicts like me. Creamy chocolate filling in a dark chocolate crust
satisfies our desire for chocolate without loading us up with fat.*

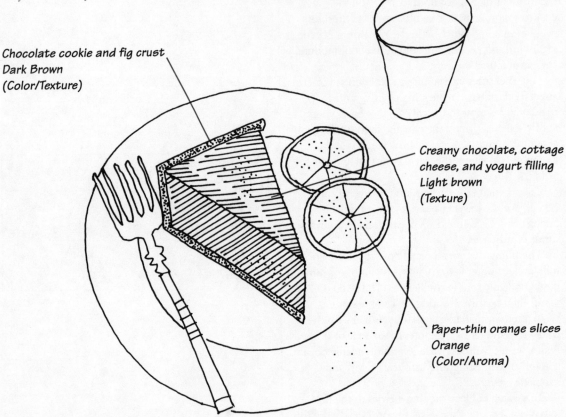

**Chocolate cookie and fig crust
Dark Brown
(Color/Texture)**

**Creamy chocolate, cottage
cheese, and yogurt filling
Light brown
(Texture)**

**Paper-thin orange slices
Orange
(Color/Aroma)**

Time Estimate: Hands-on, 20 minutes;
  unsupervised, 3 hours
Serves 12

CRUST

18 dried figs, stalk ends removed
1 cup crushed chocolate wafers

FILLING

2 packets unflavored gelatin
1 cup evaporated skim milk
4 tablespoons unsweetened cocoa powder, preferably
  Dutch-processed

2 teaspoons vanilla extract
2 cups 2%-fat cottage cheese
3/4 cup brown sugar
1 cup strained yogurt (page 288)

GARNISH

Paper-thin orange slices or blanched orange zest strips

**The crust:** In a food processor, process the figs for a few seconds, add the broken cookies, and continue processing until they clump together in a sticky ball. Don't process too long or the cookies will lose their texture. Press the crust mixture into the bottom and up the sides of a lightly greased, high-sided, 9-inch (23-cm) springform pan. Dip your fingers into a bowl of cold water to alleviate any stickiness.

**The filling:** Sprinkle the gelatin over the evaporated milk in a small saucepan and allow to soften for 1 minute. Warm over low heat, stirring, until the gelatin is completely dissolved, about 3 minutes. In a food processor, whiz the cocoa powder, vanilla, cottage cheese, brown sugar, and strained yogurt until smooth. Add the milk and gelatin mixture, and pulse until well mixed. Pour into the prepared crust and pop into the refrigerator until set, about 3 hours.

**To serve:** Unmold, slice with a warm knife, and garnish each piece with a paper-thin orange slice or blanched orange zest.

I prefer European-style or Dutch-process cocoa for my cooking. Cocoa has natural acids, which can pose some taste problems. "Dutched" cocoa has had an alkali added to it and thus has a mellower flavor.

| Nutritional Profile per Serving | | | |
|---|---|---|---|
| | Classic | Minimax | Daily Value |
| Calories | 444 | 190 | |
| Calories from fat | 61% | 10% | |
| Fat (gm) | 30 | 2 | 3% |
| Saturated fat (gm) | 17 | 1 | 5% |
| Sodium (mg) | 241 | 248 | 10% |
| Cholesterol (mg) | 120 | 5 | 2% |
| Carbohydrates (gm) | 40 | 2 | 1% |
| Dietary fiber (gm) | 2 | 2 | 8% |
| Classic compared: Chocolate Cheesecake | | | |

# CRANBERRY-RASPBERRY ICE

⁂

*This dessert is so simple, all you have to do is start it two days before serving.*

Time Estimate: Hands-on, 27 minutes;
  unsupervised, 16 hours
Serves 8 to 16

1 (1½-quart or 1.4-l) bottle of cranberry-raspberry juice
2 packets gelatin
1½ cups whole raspberries, fresh or frozen, unthawed to
  maintain their shape

GARNISH

4 teaspoons finely chopped fresh mint leaves (optional)
Freshly ground black pepper (optional)


Two days before serving, heat 1 cup of the cranberry-raspberry juice in a small saucepan and stir in the gelatin until completley dissolved. Add to the rest of the juice and mix well. Pour the juice into a large (15 X 10-inch or 38 X 25-cm) roasting pan to a depth of 1 inch (2.5 cm) and freeze overnight until solid.

The day before serving, take the fruit ice out and let it soften for 15 minutes. Cut it into pieces. In small batches, transfer the ice to a large electric mixer bowl and beat until smooth. Continue beating until all the ice is frothy and light but *not* melted. Use a rubber spatula to work the mixture through the beater blades. The final product should have enough body to hold together on a spoon, like wet beaten egg whites.

Cover the bottom of a 2-quart rectangular plastic container with a single layer of raspberries. Spoon the beaten ice on top, slicing through occasionally with your spatula to get out any major air bubbles. When the pan is filled to the top, drop it several times on the counter to pop any remaining air bubbles. Cover with plastic wrap and freeze overnight until solid enough to slice.

**To serve:** This is great stuff for kids, sliced from the loaf or scooped into little paper cones. The adults might enjoy a version mixed with 1/2 teaspoon of the finely chopped mint per serving and seasoned with the freshly ground black pepper.

Nutritional Profile per Serving: Calories—124; % calories from fat—2%; fat (gm)—0 or 0% daily value; saturated fat (gm)—0; sodium (mg)—7; cholesterol (mg)—0; carbohydrates (gm)—31; dietary fiber (gm)—1.

# CRÈME CARAMEL

*Crème Caramel is a great favorite in many restaurants. It is basically a super-rich baked egg custard made with added heavy cream. It looks small and innocent, but packs a devastating amount of "shadow energy" (many calories with few nutrients). Our substitutions are indeed radical . . . but they are delicious, and reduce the fat significantly.*

*Time Estimate: Hands-on, 15 minutes; unsupervised, 2 hours*

*Serves 6*

1½ cups (1 can) evaporated skim milk
1½ cups 2%-fat milk
Zest of 1 orange, in strips
2 (4-inch or 10-cm) sprigs fresh rosemary
1/4 cup sugar
1 teaspoon vanilla extract
1 cup liquid egg substitute

GARNISH

6 teaspoons maple syrup
6 sprigs fresh rosemary

Nutritional Profile per Serving: Calories—143; % calories from fat—8%; fat (gm)—1 or 2% daily value; saturated fat (gm)—1; sodium (mg)—146; cholesterol (mg)—7; carbohydrates (gm)—24; dietary fiber (gm)—0.

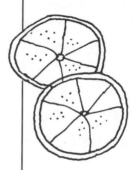

Preheat the oven to 325°F (165°C). In a large saucepan, heat the two kinds of milk, orange zest, and rosemary until just about to boil. Place the sugar and vanilla in a large bowl and strain the hot milk into it. Whisk in the egg substitute.

Set 6 small custard cups in a 9 X 13-inch (23 X 33-cm) baking pan. Pour the custard into the cups and place it in the oven. Pour hot water into the baking pan, filling until the cups are three-quarters submerged. Bake in the preheated oven for 1 hour or until a knife inserted into the center comes out clean. Take the cups out of the water and let them cool a bit, about 1 hour.

**To serve:** Loosen the custard from the dish with a knife. Invert the dish over an individual serving plate and shake out the custard. Spoon 1 teaspoon of the maple syrup over the top and garnish with a sprig of fresh rosemary on the side. You can serve Crème Caramel at room temperature or chilled.

# CREMPOG
## (WELSH PANCAKES)
※

*In Wales there is a charming seasonal custom of cooking Crempog for the children, who go from house to house in search of the best buttered, best sugared, softest fudge-syruped . . . well . . . it's charming! My changes have kept the Welsh-styled soft pancake and used the seasonal apples and plums of the area to make a most unusual dessert. No cream needed—this is full of its own flavors.*

*Time Estimate: Hands-on, 60 minutes;*
  *unsupervised, 75 minutes*

*Serves 4*

### PANCAKE BATTER

1½ cups all-purpose flour
1 egg, lightly beaten
3/4 cup nonfat plain yogurt
1 cup nonfat milk
1 large Granny Smith apple, peeled and cored, but left
  whole
3 large red plums
1 teaspoon baking soda
1 teaspoon cider vinegar
1 teaspoon light olive oil with a dash of toasted sesame oil

### SYRUP

1 cup water
1 cup cranberry juice
2 tablespoons brown sugar
1 (3-inch or 8-cm) cinnamon stick
8 whole cloves
1/8 teaspoon freshly grated nutmeg
4 allspice berries
2 tablespoons arrowroot mixed with 4 tablespoons
  water (slurry)

**The pancake batter:** Sift the flour into a bowl, make a well in the center, and pour in the lightly beaten egg, yogurt, and 3/4 cup of the milk. Beat until smooth. The batter should be thick. Cover and let rest for 1 hour.

Cut the apple into 4 thick slices. The slices should look like flat donuts. Cut one plum in half and remove the stone.

**The syrup:** Combine the water, cranberry juice, brown sugar, cinnamon stick, cloves, nutmeg, and all-spice berries in a saucepan and bring to a boil. Add the apple slices, the whole plums, and the plum halves, and poach for 2 minutes or until the fruit is soft. Remove the apple slices and whole plums, leaving the 2 plum halves. Remove the skins from the whole plums and cut them in half.

Reduce the syrup to 1 cup. Strain and transfer to a clean saucepan. Stir in the arrowroot paste and heat over medium-high, stirring, until thickened and clear.

**The pancakes:** Mix the baking soda and vinegar together and stir into the batter. Before you cook the pancakes, adjust the batter's consistency by adding the remaining milk (up to 1/4 cup) until the batter runs smoothly off the ladle.

Heat an 8-inch (20-cm) sauté pan and brush with oil. Ladle 1/4 cup of the batter into the prepared pan and cook until bubbles appear and burst on the surface, about 1 minute. Turn the pancake over and cook another minute. Remove and cool on a wire rack. Repeat with the remaining batter. You need 8 pancakes for this recipe.

**To assemble:** Trim the pancakes into even circles (a cookie cutter works very well for doing this). Place one pancake on a serving plate and set a poached apple slice on top. Top with a second pancake, so that you have an apple sandwich. Top with a plum half and drizzle with the syrup.

Nutritional Profile per Serving: Calories—379; % calories from fat—8%; fat (gm)—4 or 5% daily value; saturated fat (gm)—1; sodium (mg)—402; cholesterol (mg)—55; carbo-hydrates (gm)—76; dietary fiber (gm)—4.

# GINGER PUMPKIN CUPS

*This delicious dessert is the perfect accompaniment to a Thanksgiving dinner, but don't be restricted to enjoying Ginger Pumpkin Cups just one day a year—they're great anytime!*

*Note: If you are at risk for serious side effects from sal-monella, you might want to replace the uncooked egg whites with meringue powder.*

*Time Estimate: Hands-on, 90 minutes;*
  *unsupervised, 60 minutes*
*Serves 12*

4 sheets phyllo dough
Light olive oil with a dash of toasted sesame oil
1/4 cup brown sugar
1 cup nonfat milk
1 envelope unflavored gelatin
1 teaspoon ground ginger
1 large egg yolk
1 (1-pound or 450-gm) can solid-pack pumpkin
1/2 teaspoon freshly ground cinnamon
1/2 teaspoon freshly grated nutmeg
3 large egg whites
1/4 cup granulated sugar

Preheat the oven to 400°F (250°C). Lay out 1 sheet of the phyllo dough on a cutting board and brush with the oil. Cover with a second, third, and fourth sheet, brushing each layer with oil. Cut the layered dough into 12 (4-inch [10-cm]) circles. Gently brush the top layer with oil. Fit the layered circles, oiled side down, into muffin tins to form cups. Gently brush again with oil. Bake in the preheated oven until brown, about 10 minutes. Remove from the tins and cool on a wire rack. These should be baked as close as possible to the serving time, as phyllo has a tendency to soften with time.

In a small saucepan, combine the brown sugar and 1/4 cup of the milk. Sprinkle the gelatin and ginger evenly over the surface and let soften for 5 minutes.

Put the saucepan on low heat and cook, stirring con-stantly, for 5 to 6 minutes or until the gelatin and sugar dissolve. Remove from the heat.

In a small bowl, beat the egg yolk and remaining 3/4 cup milk together. Slowly whisk in the hot gelatin mixture, then pour it back into the saucepan. Stir over low heat for 2 to 3 minutes or until slightly thick-ened. Be careful not to let the mixture boil or it will curdle. Transfer to a large bowl. Blend in the pump-kin, cinnamon, and nutmeg. Cover and refrigerate for 20 to 30 minutes, stirring occasionally, until the mix-ture mounds slightly when dropped from a spoon.

In a large bowl, beat the egg whites at moderate speed until they begin to hold a shape. Add the sugar gradually and beat at a moderately high speed until the whites hold soft peaks. Fold the egg whites into the pumpkin mixture and refrigerate for 30 minutes. If you are using meringue powder, follow the package directions for 3 eggs and fold into the pumpkin mix-ture. If yours is a sweetened meringue powder, leave out the 1/4 cup sugar.

**To assemble:** Not more than 1 hour ahead of serv-ing time (because of the pastry's tendency to soften), spoon the pumpkin filling into the phyllo cups. Refrigerate until ready to serve.

Nutritional Profile per Serving: Calories—89; % calories from fat—10%; fat (gm)—1 or 2% daily value; saturated fat (gm)—.3; sodium (mg)—54; cholesterol (mg)—18; carbo-hydrates (gm)—17; dietary fiber (gm)—1.

# Honey and Apple Flan Soufflé

The Spanish people have a wonderful way with flan, their word for egg custard. My version is real comfort food: very sweet and creamy.

Time Estimate: Hands-on, 20 minutes
Serves 6

## FLAN

1 cup water
1 cup liquid egg substitute
1/2 cup superfine sugar
1½ cups de-alcoholized white wine
3 tablespoons local, fresh honey (I prefer fireweed when I can find it.)
1/4 teaspoon almond extract
1/4 teaspoon vanilla extract
2 tablespoons cornstarch mixed with 1/4 cup de-alcoholized white wine (slurry)
1 cup cored and finely diced Granny Smith apple
3 tablespoons sliced almonds

## PAPUFA TOPPING

9 tablespoons nonfat dried milk powder
1/2 cup ice water
3 tablespoons superfine sugar
1/8 teaspoon orange flower water
1/4 teaspoon vanilla extract
1 teaspoon safflower oil

## GARNISH

12 thin apple slices sprinkled with 2 tablespoons fresh lemon juice

**The flan:** In a medium saucepan, bring the water to a boil. Set a copper bowl in the saucepan, creating a double-boiler effect. Beat the egg substitute and sugar in the bowl until creamy.

In a small saucepan, bring the wine to a boil.

Remove from the heat and add the honey, almond extract, vanilla, and cornstarch slurry. Return to a boil and stir until thickened, about 30 seconds.

Slowly whisk the wine-syrup mixture into the egg substitute and sugar. Stir in the apple and almonds and set aside.

**Papufa topping:** In a small metal bowl, beat the dried milk and ice water with a wire whisk for 6 to 7 minutes, then gradually beat in the sugar, orange flower water, vanilla, and oil. Be sure to chill the water until nearly iced and do not give up beating too early. The whole adventure is great aerobic exercise when you do it by hand.

**To serve:** Spoon the flan into wine glasses and dollop with 2 spoonfuls of the topping. Garnish with lemon juice–dipped apple slices, overlapping them to form a heart shape. This dessert can be served hot or cold.

Nutritional Profile per Serving: Calories—210; % calories from fat—11%; fat (gm)—2 or 4% daily value; saturated fat (gm)—3; sodium (mg)—79; cholesterol (mg)—1; carbohydrates (gm)—43; dietary fiber (gm)—1.

Papufa is my invention to replace whipped cream. The name is an acronym for "physiologically active polyunsaturated fatty acid." It is totally saturated-fat free and cholesterol free.

# Lemon Cream Fruit Tart

*A beautiful, bright, summer fruit tart with a rich, creamy custard. No one will ever know it has only 3 grams of fat.*

Time Estimate: Hands-on, 35 minutes;
  unsupervised, 8 hours or overnight
Serves 8

## FILLING

1 quart 2%-fat vanilla yogurt
1 teaspoon finely grated lemon zest
2 cups strawberries, stemmed and halved
2 kiwi fruit, peeled and sliced
1 cup fresh or frozen blueberries (do not thaw)
1/3 cup apricot preserves

## CRUST

1/4 teaspoon light olive oil
8 whole low-fat graham crackers
1/2 cup dried apricots
2 tablespoons apricot preserves

**The night before serving, start the filling:** Strain the yogurt using a yogurt strainer or a paper towel–lined sieve. Cover and leave in the refrigerator overnight or until you are ready to use it. You can't overstrain it; it just keeps getting thicker and yummier.

**The day of serving start the crust:** Brush a 9-inch (23-cm) removable-bottom tart pan or pie plate with the oil. Whiz the graham crackers and apricots in a food processor until there are no discernible apricot chunks. This might take as long as 2 minutes or more. Add the apricot preserves and whiz until it starts to clump. Tip this crumbly mixture into the prepared pan and press over the bottom and up the sides with wet fingers. Set aside.

**The filling:** Combine the strained yogurt and lemon zest gently in a medium mixing bowl. Spread the filling over the bottom of the prepared crust. Lay the strawberry halves around the outside edge with the pointed ends touching the rim of the pan. Moving toward the center, make another row of strawber-

ries slightly overlapping the first. Now make a row of all the kiwi slices, overlapping them as much as you need to to make them fit. Fill the center with blueberries and set blueberries around the edge where there is any white filling showing.

To finish this masterpiece, melt the apricot preserves in a small saucepan set over medium heat or in the microwave and strain into a small bowl. Gently brush the fruit with the strained preserves. This will hold the blueberries in place and give the fruit a glorious shine. The tart is ready to eat immediately or can be chilled for several hours, but it will look best if eaten the same day you make it.

Nutritional Profile per Serving: Calories—282; % calories from fat—10%; fat (gm)—3 or 5% daily value; saturated fat (gm)—1; sodium (mg)—167; cholesterol (mg)—6; carbohydrates (gm)—59; dietary fiber (gm)—2.

# Long White Cloud
## (New Zealand Christmas Pudding)

⋇

*Christmas day in New Zealand occurs in their summer and can be really hot, with a temperature of 90°F (32°C) on occasions. When Treena and I lived there (from 1958 to 1966), we had midwinter traditions in a summer climate. So we changed our Christmas Pudding to Long White Cloud, which is part of the English translation of the native Maori word for New Zealand, Aotearoa—the land of the long white cloud!*

*This recipe is a very lean edition of the British classic, which combines dried fruit with beef suet (the creamy fat that surrounds the kidney), brandy, heavy beer, and eggs.*

*Time Estimate: Hands-on, 1 hour, 30 minutes; unsupervised, 10 hours*

*Serves 12*

### PUDDING

1/2 cup minced dried apricots
1/2 cup minced dried peaches
1/2 cup minced raisins, preferably the seedless flame variety
1/2 cup minced dried figs
1/3 cup sliced almonds
1 (16-ounce or 450-gm) can syrup-packed plums, drained, syrup reserved separately
1 large Granny Smith apple, peeled, cored, and finely chopped
2 tablespoons molasses
1/2 teaspoon freshly ground cloves
1/2 teaspoon freshly ground mace
1/2 teaspoon freshly ground cinnamon
2 teaspoons baking powder
1/2 cup all-purpose flour
1/8 teaspoon light olive oil with a dash of toasted sesame oil

### TOPPING

1 pint frozen nonfat vanilla yogurt

2 (16-ounce or 450-gm) cans apricot halves, drained and juices reserved
1/4 teaspoon freshly grated nutmeg
1 teaspoon arrowroot

### GARNISH

Small holly sprigs

**The day before serving:** Combine the apricots, peaches, raisins, and figs and mix well. Add the almonds, drained plums, apple, molasses, and the spices, and mix well. Shape into a ball and put the mixture on a board.

In a small bowl, sift the baking powder and flour together, then sift again over the fruit mixture. Chop it all together with a broad knife or scraper until it's thoroughly combined. Now drizzle in the reserved plum syrup, chopping as you go.

Scoop the pudding mixture into a lightly oiled bowl that will fit into a large pot or Dutch oven that you can use for steaming. Press down gently, allowing some room for the baking powder to expand. Place wax paper and a light cotton towel over the top of the bowl. Tie this down with string. Now tie the tails of the cotton material over the top of the bowl to give you a nice handle.

Place the bowl in a large pot or Dutch oven and add enough water to reach halfway up the sides of the bowl. Drop a dozen marbles in the water and put the lid on. Turn the heat to high and cook for 2 hours. If the water boils away, the marbles will start to clatter, giving you a noisy reminder to add more water!

Spoon the hot, cooked pudding mixture into a lightly oiled 9½ X 5-inch (24 X 13-cm) loaf pan. Press the mixture down into the pan, cover with plastic wrap, and refrigerate overnight.

In another loaf pan of the same size, pack the frozen yogurt until it's a layer 1 inch (2.5 cm) thick. Put the pan in the freezer. The pudding and its topping are now the same size.

**The day of serving, make the sauce:** Purée the apricots in a food processor or blender, reserving 5 halves for garnish. Pour the purée and syrup into a medium saucepan set over medium heat. Stir in the nutmeg.

Make a paste of the arrowroot with 2 teaspoons of the apricot syrup and stir into the sauce. Bring to a boil, stirring until the sauce thickens. Remove from the heat.

**To assemble:** The pudding must be warm before serving. Heat an ovenproof serving platter in a 500°F (260°C) oven for 10 minutes. Remove and put on a baking rack on top of the stove burner on medium heat.

Unmold the pudding onto the hot serving platter. Unmold the frozen yogurt and place it on top of the pudding. Garnish or decorate with the reserved apricot halves.

**To serve:** Place a 1/2-inch (1.5-cm) slice of the Long White Cloud on a plate. Drizzle 2 tablespoons of warm sauce on the side. Garnish with a small branch of holly (just don't eat the berries!).

Nutritional Profile per Serving: Calories—245; % calories from fat—7%; fat (gm)—2 or 3% daily value; saturated fat (gm)—.2; sodium (mg)—112; cholesterol (mg)—.4; carbohydrates (gm)—58; dietary fiber (gm)—4.

# HOT FUDGE SUNDAE
※

*Here's a dessert the whole family will love. I bet nobody will guess that the Hot Fudge Sauce is such a substantial change from the classic. Try it and see for yourself!*

*Time Estimate: Hands-on, 20 minutes*
*Serves 4*

BASIC HOT FUDGE SAUCE
*Makes 12 tablespoons*

5 tablespoons warm water
3 tablespoons unsweetened Dutch-process cocoa
    powder
4 tablespoons brown sugar
1 tablespoon arrowroot mixed with 2 tablespoons
    water (slurry)

SUNDAE

16 ounces (450 gm) nonfat vanilla frozen yogurt
1 cup frozen cherries

**The hot fudge sauce:** Pour the water, cocoa, and sugar into a small saucepan and stir over low heat until dissolved. Remove from the heat, stir in the arrowroot slurry, return to the heat, and whisk until thickened. Remove from the heat and whisk until smooth.

**To serve:** Scoop 4 ounces (115 gm) of the yogurt into a parfait glass. Top with 3 tablespoons of the Basic Hot Fudge Sauce and garnish with a few of the cherries.

Nutritional Profile per Serving of Sauce: Calories—75; % calories from fat—15%; fat (gm)—1 or 2% daily value; saturated fat (gm)—1; sodium (mg)—5; cholesterol (mg)—0; carbohydrates (gm)—17; dietary fiber (gm)—2.

Nutritional Profile per Serving of Sundae: Calories—214; % calories from fat—5%; fat (gm)—1 or 2% daily value; saturated fat (gm)—1; sodium (mg)—65; cholesterol (mg)—2; carbohydrates (gm)—51; dietary fiber (gm)—2.

# MAPLE MERINGUE

※

*It's hard to imagine a more dramatic dessert. It also has a sweetness that only pure maple syrup can achieve: lots of flavor without a cloying aftertaste.*

*Time Estimate: Hands-on, 50 minutes;*
  *unsupervised, 30 minutes*

*Serves 4*

2 medium Granny Smith apples, peeled and cored
4 egg whites
1/8 cup cold water
1/8 teaspoon freshly ground sea salt
1/2 cup confectioners' sugar
1/4 cup pure maple syrup
6 ounces (175 gm) frozen unsweetened raspberries,
  thawed, no syrup
1/4 cup strained yogurt (page 288)

Cut pieces of parchment paper, brown paper, or aluminum foil long enough to tie around small individual soufflé dishes and high enough to come 1 inch (2.5 cm) above the rim. Wrap the paper around each soufflé dish and secure in place with a rubber band. This creates a collar that prevents the meringue from puffing over the sides while baking.

Cut the apples in half. You will now have 4 halves, each with a flat side and a rounded side. Cut enough off the rounded side to leave a 1-inch (2.5-cm) thick slice of apple.

Preheat the oven to 350°F (180°C). In a 9-inch (23-cm) skillet, add enough water to fill to 1/4 inch (.75 cm) in depth. Over medium-high heat, bring the water to a simmer and poach the apple slices 5 minutes on each side. The apple should not be mushy, but just cooked through. Remove to a plate with a slotted spoon to cool.

In a large bowl, with an electric mixer at medium speed, beat the egg whites with the cold water and the salt, gradually increasing the speed to high, until the mixture forms soft peaks. Beat in the confectioners' sugar until a spoonful of meringue held upside down holds a 3-inch (8-cm) drip.

In a small saucepan, heat the maple syrup. Then very gradually, drizzle the heated syrup into the meringue, stirring to incorporate. The meringue will be ready when a spoonful turned upsidedown holds a 1-inch (2.5-cm) drip. It will be glossy, creamy-beige in color.

Place the apple slices in the soufflé dishes. Add 1 tablespoon of the raspberries and 5 tablespoons of the meringue. Just drop in the spoonfuls. Do not stir them! Try not to get the meringue on the parchment paper.

Put the filled soufflé dishes in a baking pan, place in the preheated oven, and pour boiling water into the pan to about 1/2 inch (1.5 cm) up the sides of the soufflé dishes. Bake for 30 minutes or until the meringue has puffed up and looks a toasty light brown.

While the meringues bake, make a raspberry-yogurt sauce. Over a small bowl, push the remaining raspberries through a sieve. Don't push too hard—you just want the juice, not the fiber. You should have 1/4 cup of the sieved raspberry juice. Stir in the strained yogurt and put in the refrigerator to set.

**To serve:** The meringues should be served as soon as possible after baking or they will start deflating. Remove the parchment paper and put each soufflé dish on an individual serving plate. Serve the raspberry-yogurt sauce on the side and offer a spoonful to each guest at the table. This sauce offsets the sweetness of the meringue and provides multiple counterpoints—cold to hot, sour to sweet, red to fawn.

Nutritional Profile per Serving: Calories—201; % calories from fat—2%; fat (gm)—1 or 1% daily value; saturated fat (gm)—.1; sodium (mg)—149; cholesterol (mg)—1; carbohydrates (gm)—45; dietary fiber (gm)—2.

# PEAR AND RASPBERRY COBBLER

*I have turned the cobbler upside down, in order to feature the fruit. The colors are great, and when served really hot from the skillet, the scent of wine and cinnamon fills the air.*

Time Estimate: Hands-on, 30 minutes;
   unsupervised, 30 minutes
Serves 12

RASPBERRY SYRUP

1/2 cup de-alcoholized dry white wine
1/4 cup brown sugar
1 (12-ounce or 350-gm) bag unsweetened frozen raspberries
2 tablespoons cornstarch

PEAR SYRUP

1/4 cup de-alcoholized dry white wine
2 tablespoons granulated sugar
3 large Bosc pears, peeled, cored, and cut in half

BATTER

2 cups all-purpose flour
2½ teaspoons baking powder
1/4 teaspoon freshly ground sea salt
3/4 cup brown sugar
1/2 cup regular rolled oats
1/4 cup sliced almonds
2 teaspoons cinnamon
2 tablespoons light olive oil with a dash of toasted sesame oil
1¾ cups nonfat milk

**The raspberry syrup:** In a small saucepan, combine the wine and brown sugar and cook over medium-high heat, stirring, until the sugar dissolves. Pour over the raspberries in a medium bowl and let sit for 10 minutes.

Remove 1/4 cup of the raspberry syrup and place in a small bowl. Stir in the cornstarch to form a paste and then stir it into the raspberries.

**The pear syrup:** Pour the wine into a 10-inch (25-cm) ovenproof skillet. Over low heat, stir in the sugar until dissolved. Bring just to a boil over medium-high heat.

Put the pear halves into the syrup, round side up, and with the stem ends pointing toward the center. The position is important because this determines how the finished cobbler will look. Let the pear halves steam in the syrup for 5 minutes, then turn them over and steam 5 minutes more. Turn the heat down if syrup starts to boil. Watch the syrup carefully; don't let it turn brown.

**The batter:** Sift the flour, baking powder, salt, and sugar together into a large bowl. Add the oats, almonds, and cinnamon. Pour in the oil and milk, and stir until smooth.

**To assemble:** Preheat the oven to 375°F (190°C). (Note: If you don't have a large ovenproof skillet, you can transfer the pears and their syrup to a 10-inch [25-cm] round, straight-sided baking pan at this point.) Pour the raspberries in the thickened raspberry syrup over the pears in the skillet, making sure that the raspberries get into the spaces between the pears and cover the bottom of the skillet.

Pour the batter slowly and carefully to cover the pears and raspberries completely. Don't worry if the batter is thinner in some places than others. Put a baking sheet on a lower rack in the oven to catch the drips. Place the skillet on the middle rack of the preheated oven and bake the cobbler for 45 minutes.

**To serve:** Don't leave the cobbler in its baking pan too long or it will overcook. To remove it from the skillet, put a serving plate on top and flip the skillet over. Voilà! Gorgeous plump pears, nestled in pink raspberries. Slice the cobbler so each person gets a quarter of a pear.

Nutritional Profile per Serving: Calories—266; % calories from fat—14%; fat (gm)—4 or 6% daily value; saturated fat (gm)—1; sodium (mg)—172; cholesterol (mg)—1; carbohydrates (gm)—54; dietary fiber (gm)—4.

# Pear Compote with Basic Sweet Topping

*Strained yogurt, that versatile Minimax ingredient, again comes to the rescue, providing a smooth, sweet dipping sauce for the beautifully spiced pear compote. Use the basic sweet topping over all your favorite fruit for a great dessert.*

*Time Estimate: Hands-on, 35 minutes; unsupervised, 65 minutes*

*Serves 4*

## PEARS

4 (8-ounce or 225-gm) fresh pears (Comice or Bartletts are good)
Juice of 1/2 lemon
1½ quarts water
2 whole cloves
1 (1-inch or 2.5-cm) piece of cinnamon stick
1/4 cup brown sugar
1 tablespoon cornstarch mixed with 2 tablespoons water (slurry)

## BASIC SWEET TOPPING

1 cup frozen unsweetened raspberries, thawed
2 tablespoons fresh local honey (I use fireweed when I can get it.)
1/4 teaspoon vanilla extract
3/4 cup strained yogurt (page 288)

**The pears:** Peel, core, and quarter the pears, reserving the peels and cores separately. Submerge the pears in cool water, to which you've added the lemon juice, to prevent browning, until ready to use.

In a large saucepan, cover the reserved pear peels and cores with the water, add the cloves and cinnamon stick, and bring to a boil; simmer for 30 minutes. Strain and return the liquid to the same saucepan. Add the brown sugar, bring to a boil, and remove from the heat. Add the pears, return to the

heat, and simmer until tender, about 25 minutes. Remove from the heat and drain, reserving both the pears and liquid.

Pour 2 cups of the reserved pear-poaching liquid back into the same saucepan and reduce by half. Pour the remaining liquid and the poached pears into a bowl and put in the refrigerator to cool.

Remove the reduced pear liquid from the heat and stir in the cornstarch slurry. Return to the heat, bring to a boil, and stir until thickened, about 30 seconds. Remove from the heat and put in the refrigerator to cool.

When both the pears and syrup are cold, remove the pears and chop into neat squares. Add the syrup and toss until well coated.

**The basic sweet topping:** Push the raspberries through a fine sieve into a small bowl to make 1/4 cup of purée. Stir in the honey and vanilla. In another bowl, stir the strained yogurt gently with a spoon to flatten the small lumps. Combine with the sweetened raspberry purée and you've made a great topping.

**To serve:** Spoon the pears into 4 serving bowls. *Your choice:* Serve the sweet topping in the middle of the table and dip the poached pear pieces like fondue or give each person their own individual dipping bowl of dessert topping.

Nutritional Profile per Serving: Calories—242; % calories from fat—4%; fat (gm)—1 or 2% daily value; saturated fat (gm)—.2; sodium (mg)—79; cholesterol (mg)—2; carbohydrates (gm)—56; dietary fiber (gm)—6

# PEAR ICE IN A BLACKBERRY PUDDLE

※

*A rich ice cream is maxing-out on temptation: it promises, it delivers, and it is immediately available! I decided to look at the fruit ice as a creative alternative. I chose pear as the base for this ice because it, too, has that dense, smooth . . . even rich . . . mouthfeel of ice cream. As always, I've matched it to some bright notes: ginger, blackberry, and lemon.*

Time Estimate: Hands-on, 25 minutes;
   unsupervised, 35 minutes
Serves 6, generously (yields 5 cups)

1½ pounds (750 gm) Bartlett or Comice pears (2 or 3 pears)
5 quarter-size slices unpeeled fresh gingerroot
1 cup water
2/3 cup granulated sugar
6 fresh mint leaves, torn into small pieces and bruised
1 tablespoon freshly squeezed lemon juice
1 teaspoon loosely packed finely chopped fresh gingerroot
1 pound (450 gm) fresh or thawed frozen blackberries

GARNISH

5 large fresh mint leaves
1½ fresh pears

Peel the pears, keeping the flesh and peels separate. Submerge the pears in a bowl of water with a squeeze of lemon juice to keep the flesh from browning. Quarter the pears, slice out the seeds, and return them to the acidulated water. You should have approximately 1 pound (450 gm) of pear flesh. Put the pear trimmings, pits, and peels in a saucepan.

Add the slices of ginger, water, sugar, and mint to the pear peels, and simmer 5 minutes over medium heat, crushing the fruit and spices with a wooden spoon or potato masher to squeeze out all their flavor. Pour through a fine mesh into a small bowl, pressing

gently on the residue, without pushing any solids through. Return the liquid to the saucepan, bring to a boil, and reduce to 2/3 cup, about 10 minutes. Remove from the heat and let cool.

Drain the pears, transfer to a food processor, add the lemon juice and chopped ginger, and pulse to a semi-smooth purée, about 30 seconds. You want to be careful to retain some of the pears' texture for the final dish.

Pour the blackberries into a small, fine sieve and push the berries through into a bowl. You should have 1 cup of blackberry purée. Stir in the pear purée and mix well. Transfer 4 tablespoons of the mixed purées to a small bowl and set aside. Whisk the pear reduction into the pear-blackberry purée.

Ready your ice-cream maker according to the manufacturer's directions. Pour in the pear-blackberry purée and freeze until solid.

**To serve:** Cut the pears into quarters. Place each pear slice lengthwise on a cutting board and cut small layers like a fan. Place a large mint leaf on a small dessert plate and cover the stem end with 4 small scoops of the ice. Dollop the reserved blackberry-pear purée to one side and place the pear garnish on top of the "puddle."

Nutritional Profile per Serving: Calories—211; % calories from fat—4%; fat (gm)—1 or 2% daily value; saturated fat (gm)—0; sodium (mg)—1; cholesterol (mg)—0; carbohydrates (gm)—54; dietary fiber (gm)—8.

> Good ices depend on the right blend of sugar to the acid of the fruit and the volume of water. The more sugar, the easier it is to spoon. Leave the sugar out, and the ice crystals set up in icy layers without enough *cling* to bind into a scooped ball, almost like solid ice when drawn straight from the deep freeze. In the Cranberry-Raspberry Ice (page 112), the gelatin step allows for texture without added sugar.

# PEARS ROVER

※

*My good friend Chef de Cuisine Thierry Rautureau, chef/owner of Rovers in Seattle, Washington, worked with me to develop this idea. We springboarded off the classic French Bavorois dessert: a rich, egg yolk, heavy-cream custard with a wonderful texture and taste. Our dish begins by using strained yogurt in place of the cream! It's a good dessert for a hot summer evening.*

*Time Estimate: Hands-on, 60 minutes;
  unsupervised, 7 hours*

*Serves 4*

4 sweet pears, preferably D'Anjou
1¼ cups plus 1/4 teaspoon water
1½ cups de-alcoholized white wine
2 egg whites
Dash of salt
1 envelope unflavored gelatin
1¼ cups strained yogurt (page 288)
1 tablespoon honey, preferably fireweed

Lightly grease 4 individual dessert molds with oil.

Peel and core the pears, but leave them whole. Save the peels and cores. Cover the pears with water into which a few drops of lemon juice have been squeezed, to prevent browning.

In a medium saucepan, cover the pear peels and cores with 1 cup of the water, bring to a boil, and reduce to 1/2 cup. Mash and strain, saving the pear juice and discarding the peels.

In a large saucepan, cook the wine, whole pears, and the strained pear juice until the pears are tender, about 20 to 30 minutes.

In a large bowl, beat the egg whites with 1/4 teaspoon water and a dash of salt, until just firm.

Sprinkle the gelatin on top of 1/4 cup of water and let sit for 3 minutes. Stir the softened gelatin into the yogurt and honey.

Remove the pears from the cooking liquid and chop into small pieces. Cook the juice down to 1/4 cup pear "nectar." Stir the nectar into the strained yogurt mixture. Fold the whipped egg whites gently into the yogurt mixture.

**To assemble:** Spoon 1 tablespoon of the yogurt mixture into each dessert mold. Top with a layer of diced pears, followed by a last layer of the yogurt mixture. Put in the refrigerator to chill.

**To serve:** Unmold the chilled desserts on a serving plate by submerging the mold in boiling water for a few seconds and then inverting onto serving plates.

Nutritional Profile per Serving: Calories—192; % calories from fat—3%; fat (gm)—1 or 1% daily value; saturated fat (gm)—.2; sodium (mg)—218; cholesterol (mg)—3; carbohydrates (gm)—36; dietary fiber (gm)—4.

---

You can serve Pears Rover encircled in a ring of bright, red hearts. Simply beat some strained yogurt until thin. Pour a small amount in a ring around each individual serving. With an eye dropper, squeeze raspberry purée in small drops, evenly spaced, on top of the yogurt. Drag a toothpick or knife tip lightly through the center of the raspberry dots to create small heart shapes: a good-hearted garnish!

# PEPPERED STRAWBERRIES WITH MINT SORBET

※

*You must try this one: the warm pepper is a great heat sensation for strawberries.*

Time Estimate: Hands-on, 15 minutes;
   unsupervised, 1 hour
Serves 4

4 cups fresh strawberries, tops trimmed
3 tablespoons sugar
1 cup plain nonfat yogurt
1 tablespoon fresh local honey
1 tablespoon chopped fresh mint leaves
1/4 teaspoon freshly ground black pepper

GARNISH

4 sprigs fresh mint
4 to 8 whole strawberries (optional)

   Purée the berries in a blender or food processor, gradually adding the sugar, yogurt, honey, chopped mint, and pepper. Scoop the mixture into an ice cream maker and process according to the manufacturer's directions.
   Transfer the sorbet to a bowl with a tight-fitting lid and put in the freezer for at least 1 hour.
   **To serve:** An ice cream scoop will help serve the sorbet in glistening globes. Garnish with the fresh mint and perhaps a whole strawberry or two.

Nutritional Profile per Serving: Calories—142; % calories from fat—5%; fat (gm)—1 or 1% daily value; saturated fat (gm)—.1; sodium (mg)—49; cholesterol (mg)—1; carbohydrates (gm)—32; dietary fiber (gm)—3.

# POACHED APPLE CUSTARD

—— ❊ ——

*I can imagine this dish with an infinitely varied (and infinitely pleasing) variety of fruits and spices—mangoes with a gingery spice blend, for instance. Use your imagination.*

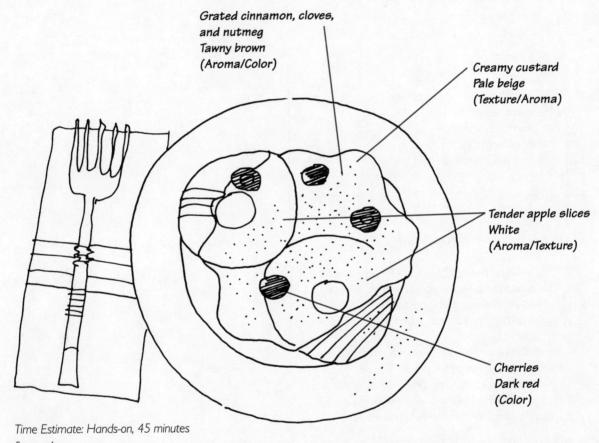

Grated cinnamon, cloves, and nutmeg
Tawny brown
(Aroma/Color)

Creamy custard
Pale beige
(Texture/Aroma)

Tender apple slices
White
(Aroma/Texture)

Cherries
Dark red
(Color)

*Time Estimate: Hands-on, 45 minutes*
*Serves 4*

SPICE BLEND

1 (1/2-inch or 1.5-cm) piece of cinnamon stick
3 whole cloves
1/4 teaspoon freshly grated nutmeg

APPLE CUSTARD

2 large Granny Smith apples, peeled, cored, and sliced into thick rings

2 cups unsweetened apple juice
1 cup water
16 canned or fresh black cherries
1½ cups 2%-fat milk
1 teaspoon vanilla extract
2 tablespoons cornstarch mixed with 1/4 cup 2%-fat milk (slurry)
1 cup liquid egg substitute
1/2 cup brown sugar

**The spice blend:** Put the cinnamon, cloves, and nutmeg in a small coffee mill or blender and grind to a fine powder.

**The apple custard:** Place the apple rings in a medium saucepan, pour in the apple juice and water, and cover. Bring to a boil, reduce the heat, and simmer until the apples are tender, about 5 minutes. A knife inserted into an apple ring should go in and come out easily. Transfer the apple rings to a small bowl, reserving the poaching liquid in the pan over very low heat. Add the cherries to the saucepan and let them heat through. Remove from heat, drain, and set aside.

Pour the milk into another medium saucepan and bring to a point just before the boil. Check frequently, stirring to prevent scorching. Just before the milk boils, remove from the heat and stir in the vanilla and the cornstarch slurry. Return to the heat and boil until thickened, stirring constantly, about 30 seconds. Remove from the heat and set aside.

Pour about 1 inch (2.5 cm) of water into a medium saucepan, cover, and bring to a point where the water is hot, but not at a breaking boil. There should be literally hundreds of little bubbles on the bottom of the pan. Pour the egg substitute and sugar into a medium copper bowl, set the bowl over the nearly boiling water, and whisk the egg substitute until thick and frothy, about 5 minutes. If the liquid should begin to boil, just pull the pan off the heat until it settles down, otherwise the egg will curdle.

Pour the milk mixture in a thin stream into the frothy egg mixture and whisk until well incorporated—it should increase in volume dramatically. Remove from the heat and set aside.

**To serve:** Place 2 apple rings on a dessert plate, cover with the thickened custard, and garnish with 4 artfully placed cherries. Put a small amount of the spice blend in a small, fine-meshed sieve and push gently through, covering the custard with an even dusting.

| Nutritional Profile per Serving | | | |
|---|---|---|---|
| | **Classic** | **Minimax** | **Daily Value** |
| Calories | 350 | 326 | |
| Calories from fat | 77% | 8% | |
| Fat (gm) | 30 | 3 | 5% |
| Saturated fat (gm) | 19 | 1 | 5% |
| Sodium (mg) | 43 | 130 | 5% |
| Cholesterol (mg) | 104 | 8 | 3% |
| Carbohydrates (gm) | 20 | 70 | 23% |
| Dietary fiber (gm) | 1 | 3 | 12% |
| Classic compared: Apple Custard | | | |

# Tadmill Almond Roll

The original dessert from the Frogmill Inn was truly a luxurious-tasting confection: heaped full of whipped French custard and drenched in crème de cacao liqueur. Just as truly, this version has its own luxury: the sponge cake soaked in chocolate syrup, a tart yogurt filling, and a sweet almond meringue topped with toasted almond flakes. Just a "tadpole" though in comparison to the "frog" classic's calories and fat.

Time Estimate: Hands-on, 45 minutes;
  unsupervised, overnight plus 10 minutes

Serves 10

## SPONGE CAKE

1/3 cup sifted cake flour
3 tablespoons cornstarch
3 large eggs, at room temperature
3 large egg whites
1 teaspoon light olive oil
1/2 cup plus 1 tablespoon sugar
1 teaspoon vanilla extract
1/2 teaspoon cream of tartar

## CHOCOLATE SYRUP

2 tablespoons unsweetened Dutch-process cocoa
  powder
2 tablespoons sugar
1/4 cup water
1/4 teaspoon vanilla extract

## PASTRY CREAM

1/2 teaspoon almond extract
2 cups strained low-fat yogurt (page 288)

## MERINGUE

4 egg whites
1/2 teaspoon cream of tartar
1/2 cup superfine sugar
1/4 teaspoon almond extract
1 tablespoon sliced almonds

Preheat the oven to 450°F (232°C). Grease the bottom, but not the sides, of an 11 X 17-inch (28 X 43-cm) cookie sheet. Cut a piece of parchment paper or wax paper to fit the bottom of the pan, then grease and flour the paper.

**The sponge cake:** Combine the flour and cornstarch in a medium bowl and set aside. Break 2 of the eggs into a large mixing bowl. Separate the third egg, placing the white in a small mixing bowl with the other 3 whites, and the yolk in the larger bowl with the whole eggs. Add the oil and 1/2 cup of the sugar to the bowl with the yolks and beat for a full 5 minutes, until the mixture is thick and creamy. Add the vanilla. Fold the flour mixture into the eggs and sugar one-half at a time.

Beat the egg whites in the small mixing bowl. Add the cream of tartar when they're foamy and continue beating. Add the remaining tablespoon sugar when soft peaks form and then continue beating until stiff and shiny. Fold the beaten whites into the batter. Pour into the prepared pan and smooth evenly. Bake for 6 minutes in the preheated oven. The cake will be golden in color and springy to the touch. Loosen the cake from the sides of the pan with a knife, place a clean dish towel over the top, and flip it over. Peel the parchment from the bottom and roll the cake in the dish towel. Start rolling from one of the short ends and roll tightly. Set on a rack to cool.

**The chocolate syrup:** Combine the cocoa and sugar in a small saucepan. Now add the water and vanilla, and stir, over medium heat, until smooth. Set aside to cool.

**The pastry cream:** Stir the almond extract into the strained yogurt.

**To assemble:** Unroll the cooled cake, sprinkle with the chocolate syrup, and spread the filling over all but 2 inches (5 cm) on one end of the cake. Roll the cake up like a jelly roll and set it on an ovenproof plate, seam down. Set in the refrigerator until you are ready to put the meringue on it. It can even be made a day ahead up to this point and kept in the refrigerator overnight.

**The meringue:** Preheat the oven to 500°F (260°C). Wash the beaters carefully so there's not a whisper of grease on them. Beat the egg whites in a small mixing bowl with an electric mixer, starting slowly, and gradually increasing the speed. When foamy, add the cream of tartar and continue beating. As soft peaks form, sprinkle with the sugar, increase the speed of the mixer, and beat until stiff peaks form (10 plus minutes). Add the almond extract at the very end. Cover the whole roll with the meringue, smoothing it attractively, and sprinkle the almonds over the top. Pop it into the preheated oven for 3 minutes or until it is golden in color.

**To serve:** You may serve it right out of the oven or wait a few hours. Bring the whole dessert to the table to show off just a little. Slice it into 10 pieces and serve. It helps to wet the knife when you cut through the meringue.

Nutritional Profile per Serving: Calories—260; % calories from fat—12%; fat (gm)—4 or 5% daily value; saturated fat (gm)—1; sodium (mg)—115; cholesterol (mg)—68; carbohydrates (gm)—49; dietary fiber (gm)—1.

# TRADITIONAL SUMMER PUDDING

⌗

*It's a summer rite of passage in Britain: when the berries are ripe, the puddings begin. I have used frozen berries in this recipe so you can make it year-round. It's light and refreshing—just what a dessert should be.*

Time Estimate: Hands-on, 30 minutes;
  unsupervised, 3 hours
Serves 8

1½ cups frozen unsweetened raspberries
1½ cups frozen unsweetened blackberries
1½ cups frozen unsweetened strawberries
1½ cups frozen unsweetened blueberries
1/2 cup sugar
1/4 cup water
1 packet unflavored gelatin
8 thin slices hearty white bread, crusts removed

GARNISH

1 cup vanilla 2%-fat yogurt (page 288)
8 sprigs fresh mint

Put all the berries and the sugar in a medium saucepan and heat over low heat until they are just thawed and the sugar is dissolved, about 10 minutes. As soon as they are thawed, take them off the heat so they won't cook.

Pour the water into a small saucepan, sprinkle with the gelatin, and let sit for 1 minute. Cook on low heat until the gelatin is completely dissolved and then stir into the berries.

Cut a circle from one of the slices of bread to fit into the bottom of a 6-cup bowl. Fit 6 bread slices around the sides of the bowl, overlapping them 1/4 inch (.75 cm). If the bottom of the bowl is smaller than the top, cut the bottom of the slices a little narrower than the top so the bread will fit in smoothly. Pour in the berries and cover the top with the remaining bread. Cover the top of the pudding with a saucer or small plate just smaller than the top of the bowl and weight it down with a heavy can. This will force the berry juice to soak into the bread. Let it set in the refrigerator for at least 3 hours, or longer for better flavor saturation. You can even make this delicious dessert the day before you want to serve it and let it set overnight.

Just before serving, run a rubber spatula around the edge of the pudding all the way down into the bowl. Cover the top with a plate and turn it over gently, easing the pudding out of the bowl onto the plate.

**To serve:** Cut the pudding into 8 wedges and garnish with a dollop of the strained vanilla yogurt and a sprig of the fresh mint.

Nutritional Profile per Serving: Calories—227; % calories from fat—7%; fat (gm)—2 or 3% daily value; saturated fat (gm)—1; sodium (mg)—121; cholesterol (mg)—3; carbohydrates (gm)—49; dietary fiber (gm)—4.

If you are fortunate enough to have fresh berries, combine them with the frozen berries. If using fresh strawberries, slice them first. Add the sugar and stir until it's completely dissolved. Let them sit for an hour to extract the juice and then treat the same way you would the frozen berries.

# TRIFLE WITH CRYSTALLIZED VIOLETS

*This is no "mere trifle": it is actually one of the best known of English desserts. Even the Italians call it* Zuppa Inglese, *or English Soup.*

*Your guests will never miss the traditional whipped cream when you dazzle them with crystallized violets scattered enchantingly over the top. You can find these in many cooking stores, or make your own!*

Time Estimate: Hands-on, 45 minutes;
    unsupervised, 2 hours

Serves 6

SPONGE CAKE

4 eggs, separated
3/4 cup sugar
1 teaspoon vanilla extract
1 cup cake flour

JELLY

4 cups fresh raspberries, or frozen berries with no
    added sugar or syrup
3 cups cold water
2 tablespoons brown sugar
2 packages unflavored gelatin softened in 1/2 cup water
    for 5 minutes

CUSTARD

2 cups nonfat milk
1 vanilla bean, or 1 teaspoon vanilla extract
2 tablespoons liquid egg substitute
3 tablespoons honey, preferably fireweed
2 talespoons cornstarch
2 packages unflavored gelatin, softened in 1/2 cup water
    for 5 minutes

GARNISH

Crystallized violets (optional)

**The sponge cake:** Preheat the oven to 370°F (190°C). Lightly oil and flour a 9-inch (23-cm) cake pan. Beat the egg yolks and sugar together in a large bowl over hot, but not boiling, water until the volume has doubled, about 5 minutes. Be sure the water doesn't touch the bottom of the bowl. Stir in the vanilla. Fold in the flour until fully incorporated.

Beat the egg whites until stiff, but not dry. Stir one-third of the egg whites into the flour mixture to lighten it. Fold in the remaining egg whites, one-half at a time. Pour into the prepared cake pan and tap the pan on the counter to release any trapped bubbles. Bake in the preheated oven for 30 minutes or until the top springs back when you touch it. Turn out to cool on a rack, then cut into 1-inch (2.5-cm) cubes.

**The jelly:** In a medium saucepan, combine 3 cups of the raspberries with the water and brown sugar, and bring to a boil. Pour the contents through a sieve, catching the raspberry liquid in a bowl. Now capture the last essence of raspberry flavor by gently pressing the raspberries in the sieve to extract the juice. BE GENTLE. You don't want seeds in the raspberry juice. While the sieved juice is still warm, stir in the softened gelatin mixture.

Put the sponge cake pieces and the remaining cup of raspberries into your best clear bowl and cover with the warm raspberry juice. Press the sponge cake into the juice so that each piece is soaked. Put a plate on top to keep the cake submerged in the juice. Pop this into the refrigerator to cool and set.

**The custard:** In a large saucepan, heat the nonfat milk and vanilla bean pod (or vanilla extract) over medium-high heat for about 5 minutes, until the milk is scalded but does not actually boil.

In a small bowl, whisk together the egg substitute, honey, and cornstarch. Tip this mixture into the scalded milk, bring just to a boil, and stir until thickened. Remove from the heat and stir in the softened gelatin. This gives it more "holding power." Let it cool.

**To assemble:** Take the cooled sponge cake out of the refrigerator. Pour the custard on top. Cover with plastic wrap and pop back into the refrigerator until set, approximately 30 minutes.

I made this dessert as one large bowlful for at least 6 people. You may wish to assemble it and fill several small dessert cups.

**To serve:** Spoon the chilled trifle into individual serving bowls and garnish with crystallized violets.

Nutritional Profile per Serving: Calories—368; % calories from fat—10%; fat (gm)—4 or 6% daily value; saturated fat (gm)—1; sodium (mg)—101; cholesterol (mg)—143; carbohydrates (gm)—70; dietary fiber (gm)—3.

---

## CRYSTALLIZED VIOLETS

1/2 cup superfine sugar
4 drops peppermint extract
2 egg whites
20 large fresh violet blossoms
Very small clean paintbrush

Preheat the oven to 180°F (82°C). Line a baking sheet with foil. In a small bowl, rub the sugar and peppermint together with your thumb and forefinger. Whip the egg whites to stiff peaks. Paint each violet on both sides with a thin layer of egg white.

Dip the painted violets into the bowl of sugar and place them carefully on the foil-lined baking sheet. When all the violets are painted, place them in the preheated oven for 1 hour. Leave the door slightly ajar to prevent any accumulation of moisture. Remove carefully and cool completely before using. Store the crystallized violets in an airtight jar in a cool, dry place.

---

# TROPICAL RICE PUDDING

*Cultures comingling in comfort—no, not the United Nations, but a dessert that combines the delights of a creamy Italian risotto with sweet English rice pudding and the fruits of the tropics.*

Time Estimate: Hands-on, 1 hour
Serves 8

## PUDDING

1½ cups evaporated skim milk
2 cups unsweetened pineapple juice
1 cup water
1/4 cup brown sugar
1⅓ cups uncooked short-grain white rice
3/4 teaspoon freshly grated nutmeg

## SAUCE

1 cup unsweetened pineapple juice
1/8 teaspoon cloves
1 mango, peeled and coarsely chopped
1 papaya, peeled and coarsely chopped
1/2 pineapple, peeled, cored, and coarsely chopped
1/2 cup dried cranberries
1 tablespoon cornstarch mixed with 2 tablespoons pineapple juice (slurry)

**The pudding:** Pour the milk, juice, and water into a saucepan over low heat and stir until the sugar is dissolved. Keep over very low heat just to keep warm.

Put the rice in a large saucepan with one quarter of the milk mixture, stirring occasionally over medium heat until the liquid is absorbed. Repeat the process, adding a small portion of the milk mixture each time and cooking until all the milk is absorbed and the rice is tender. The entire process takes about 30 to 40 minutes. Remove from the heat and stir in 1/2 teaspoon of the nutmeg.

**The sauce:** Pour the pineapple juice into a saucepan and bring to a boil. Add the remaining nutmeg, cloves, the fresh fruit, and the dried cranberries, and heat through. Remove from the heat and stir in the cornstarch slurry. Return to the heat, bring to a boil, and stir until thickened, about 30 seconds.

**To serve:** Divide the rice between 8 serving dishes and top with the fruit sauce. This sauce is also delicious by itself or as a sauce for nonfat frozen yogurt.

Nutritional Profile per Serving: Calories—338; % calories from fat—3%; fat (gm)—1 or 1% daily value; saturated fat (gm)—0; sodium (mg)—64; cholesterol (mg)—2; carbohydrates (gm)—77; dietary fiber (gm)—3.

# TROPICAL SORBET

⌘

*An assortment of tropical fruits combine in a flavorful,
light dessert.*

*Time Estimate: Hands-on, 20 minutes;
  unsupervised, 1 1/2 hours*
*Serves 8*

1 pineapple
2 mangoes, peeled and diced
1 banana, peeled and sliced
1 teaspoon finely grated lime zest
3 tablespoons freshly squeezed lime juice
1 cup plain nonfat yogurt
3 tablespoons sugar

Cut the pineapple, including the leafy top, in half lengthwise. Cut out the tough core and discard. Cut out the pulp, leaving a 1/4-inch (.75-cm) wall. Place the pulp and any juice into a food processor along with the mangoes and banana, and process until smooth. Add the lime zest, lime juice, yogurt, and sugar, and whiz until mixed.

Transfer the mixture to an ice cream maker and follow the manufacturer's directions. When it's frozen, scoop into the pineapple halves and place in the freezer for at least an hour.

**To serve:** Just before serving, cut each pineapple half lengthwise into 4 wedges. Place 1 wedge on each plate and celebrate a taste of the tropics. The sorbet may also be simply served in small dishes and garnished with a sprig of mint.

Nutritional Profile per Serving: Calories—112; % calories from fat—8%; fat (gm)—1 or 1% daily value; saturated fat (gm)—0; sodium (mg)—27; cholesterol (mg)—1; carbohydrates (gm)—27; dietary fiber (gm)—2.

# 20% calories from fat

⌗

## Appetizers
## &
## Soups

# Black Bean Soup

*A Brazilian favorite, this fusion of African and South American cuisines brings to mind Rio, Ipanema, and the bossa nova. I love it with corn bread and fruit salad. Samba in good health!*

Time Estimate: Hands-on, 30 minutes;
  unsupervised, 8 hours soaking plus 1½ hours cooking
Serves 6

1 pound (450 mg) dried black turtle beans
1½ teaspoons light olive oil with a dash of toasted
    sesame oil
2 yellow onions, diced
4 cloves garlic, bashed, peeled, and chopped
2 quarts ham hock stock (page 287)
2 quarts water
1/2 teaspoon freshly ground black pepper
2 teaspoons cumin seeds
4 (3-inch or 8-cm) oregano sprigs or 1 teaspoon dried
2 bay leaves
1 cup coarsely chopped celery
1 large red bell pepper, seeded and chopped
3 tablespoons chopped fresh parsley
2 teaspoons ground cumin
2 tablespoons freshly squeezed lemon juice
Grated zest and juice of 1 orange
1/2 teaspoon crushed red pepper flakes (more or less
    to taste)
3/4 cup reserved ham hock meat, trimmed of all fat
    (from cooking the ham hock above)
1/4 teaspoon freshly ground sea salt

GARNISH

6 tablespoons nonfat yogurt
1 tablespoon chopped fresh cilantro

The night before making this splendid soup, place the black beans in a bowl of water to soak overnight. Rinse and drain thoroughly.

In a large Dutch oven, heat 1 teaspoon of the oil over medium-high heat and fry the onions and garlic until soft, about 2 minutes. Add the beans, stock, water, pepper, cumin seeds, oregano, and bay leaves, and bring to a boil; simmer for 1½ hours. Remove the bay leaves and discard. When the beans have cooled just a little, scoop out 1½ cups and purée in a blender. Return the purée to the pot.

Heat the remaining 1/2 teaspoon oil in a small skillet over medium-high heat. Fry the celery, red pepper, parsley, and ground cumin for about 3 minutes. Mix in the lemon juice, orange zest and juice, and crushed red pepper. Pour into the soup along with the ham hock meat and salt.

**To serve:** Serve in soup bowls with a dollop of yogurt and a sprinkling of cilantro.

Nutritional Profile per Serving: Calories—407; % calories from fat—18%; fat (gm)—8 or 12% daily value; saturated fat (gm)—2; sodium (mg)—383; cholesterol (mg)—12; carbohydrates (gm)—61; dietary fiber (gm)—15.

# THAI SHRIMP SOUP

*Fragrant with ginger and garlic, this flavorful soup is also incredibly fast to make.*

*Time Estimate: Hands-on, 27 minutes*
*Serves 4*

FLAVOR BASE

1/4 teaspoon light olive oil with a dash of toasted sesame oil
1/4 teaspoon toasted sesame oil
1 clove garlic, bashed, peeled, and chopped
8 quarter-size slices fresh peeled gingerroot
4 green onions, white and green parts separated, finely chopped
1 cup low-sodium chicken stock (page 286)

SOUP

1/4 teaspoon toasted sesame oil
12 ounces (350 gm) shrimp (41/50 count per pound), peeled and deveined
8 ounces (225 gm) fresh mushrooms, quartered
1 tablespoon fish sauce
4 cups low-sodium chicken stock (page 286)

**The flavor base:** Pour the oils into a large skillet over medium heat, add the garlic, ginger, and the white parts of the green onions, and cook 3 minutes. Pour in the chicken stock and bring to a boil for 3 minutes. Strain into a small bowl, pressing firmly on the solids until they squeeze through the sieve in the form of a flavor-packed pulp. Set aside.

**The soup:** Pour the sesame oil into a large wok over medium heat, add the shrimp all at once, and cook until they turn pink, stirring constantly for 1 minute. Stir in the mushrooms and cook 1 minute. Add the fish sauce and 1/4 cup of the reserved flavor base, and cook for 3 minutes, stirring constantly.

Pour in the chicken stock and the remaining flavor base, and bring *just* to a boil—if it gets to a rolling-boil stage, the shrimp will become very tough. Remove from the heat and skim the foam that rises to the surface.

**To serve:** Ladle into bowls and sprinkle each with 1 tablespoon of the reserved dark green parts of the onions.

Nutritional Profile per Serving: Calories—102; % calories from fat—24%; fat (gm)—3 or 4% daily value; saturated fat (gm)—1; sodium (mg)—336; cholesterol (mg)—80; carbohydrates (gm)—6; dietary fiber (gm)—1.

# MULLIGATAWNY SOUP

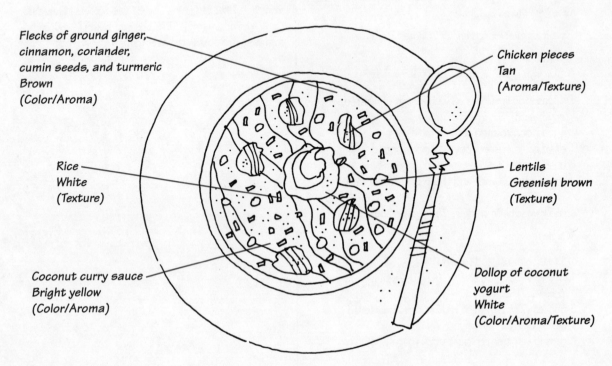

**Flecks of ground ginger, cinnamon, coriander, cumin seeds, and turmeric Brown (Color/Aroma)**

**Chicken pieces Tan (Aroma/Texture)**

**Rice White (Texture)**

**Lentils Greenish brown (Texture)**

**Coconut curry sauce Bright yellow (Color/Aroma)**

**Dollop of coconut yogurt White (Color/Aroma/Texture)**

*Time Estimate: Hands-on, 35 minutes;
  unsupervised, 55 minutes*
*Serves 4*

SPICE MIX

1 teaspoon coriander
1/2 teaspoon cumin seeds
1/2 teaspoon ground ginger
1/8 teaspoon cinnamon
1/2 teaspoon turmeric

SOUP

4 cups low-sodium chicken stock (page 286)
4 (4-ounce or 115-gm) chicken thighs, trimmed of all
  visible fat and skin
1 teaspoon light olive oil with a dash of toasted sesame oil
1 large yellow onion, peeled and thinly sliced

2 cloves garlic, bashed, peeled, and finely chopped
4 teaspoons curry powder
1/2 cup dried lentils
1 bay leaf
1 cup cooked white rice
1 teaspoon coconut essence
1/2 cup strained yogurt (page 288)
Juice of 1 lemon
1/4 teaspoon freshly ground sea salt

GARNISH

1/4 cup strained yogurt (page 288) mixed with
  1/4 teaspoon coconut essence

**The spice mix:** Spoon the coriander, cumin seeds, ginger, cinnamon, and turmeric into a small coffee mill and grind to a fine powder. Set aside.

**The soup:** Bring the chicken stock to a slow boil, add the chicken, and cook for 25 minutes or until the internal temperature of the chicken reads 165°F (75°C) on a kitchen thermometer. Remove the chicken, let it cool enough to handle, then pull the meat away from the bone. Separate the chunks of meat into smaller pieces and set aside. Strain and reserve the chicken stock.

Pour the oil into a large stockpot over medium heat, add the onion and garlic, and cook 2 minutes. Stir in the curry powder until the onion and garlic are well coated and the curry powder is warmed. Add the lentils, bay leaf, and reserved chicken stock. Bring to a boil, reduce the heat, and simmer 30 minutes.

Remove the bay leaf, add the chicken meat and rice, and warm through. Push 1 teaspoon of the Spice Mix through a fine sieve into the soup, add the coconut essence, and mix well.

Just before serving, remove the soup from the heat and stir in the yogurt until well incorporated. The soup cannot be too hot for this step or the yogurt will curdle. Add lemon juice to taste and the salt, and mix well.

**To serve:** Ladle the soup into individual serving bowls and garnish with a dollop of the yogurt-coconut mixture. Push 1/4 teaspoon of the Spice Mix through a fine sieve over the top of each serving.

I've used a coconut essence to replace the classic coconut cream, which is high in saturated fat. This is a departure for me, but it does seem to deliver the aroma, and the strained yogurt helps to bring in some of the mouthfeel. Good supermarkets and specialty foods stores stock the essence in the herb and spice section, alongside vanilla.

| Nutritional Profile per Serving | | | |
|---|---|---|---|
| | **Classic** | **Minimax** | **Daily Value** |
| Calories | 250 | 355 | |
| Calories from fat | 52% | 20% | |
| Fat (gm) | 15 | 8 | 12% |
| Saturated fat (gm) | 8 | 2 | 10% |
| Sodium (mg) | 953 | 315 | 13% |
| Cholesterol (mg) | 57 | 52 | 17% |
| Carbohydrates (gm) | 17 | 40 | 13% |
| Dietary fiber (gm) | 2 | 5 | 22% |
| Classic compared: Mulligatawny Soup | | | |

# 20% calories from fat

⌘

## Entrées

# Fish 'n' Chips 'n' Peas

⌗

*Without doubt, this is England's most famous dish. Always deep fried, the fish is mostly cod, and the batter made with eggs, milk, and flour. Liberally salted, the fish and chips are traditionally doused with malt vinegar and wrapped in newspaper, so that everything goes limp. My recipe is designed not to flaunt tradition, but to make the taste available to those who count fat grams for good reason.*

*Time Estimate: Hands-on, 45 minutes*
*Serves 4*

## CHIPS

2 tablespoons light olive oil with a dash of sesame oil
2 large russet potatoes, each sliced lengthwise into 9
    even "sticks"
1/2 teaspoon freshly ground sea salt

## FISH

1/2 cup cornmeal
1/2 cup bread crumbs
1/2 teaspoon cayenne pepper
1/2 teaspoon freshly ground sea salt
1 tablespoon finely chopped fresh parsley
1 tablespoon finely chopped fresh dill
1/2 cup 2%-fat milk
1/4 cup sifted all-purpose flour
1 tablespoon light olive oil with a dash of toasted sesame
    oil
4 (4-ounce or 115-gm) cod fillets, skin removed

## MINTY PEAS

1/4 cup water
2 cups frozen peas
1/8 teaspoon freshly ground sea salt
1 small sprig fresh mint
1 teaspoon sugar

## GARNISH

4 sprays watercress, washed and dried well
1 lemon, cut into wedges

**The chips:** Preheat the oven to 500°F (260°C). In a large frying pan, heat the oil over medium-high heat and fry the potato sticks until brown on all sides, about 13 minutes. Transfer the potatoes to a roaster pan and bake for 10 minutes. Remove from the oven and sprinkle with the salt.

**The fish:** In a small bowl, combine the cornmeal, bread crumbs, cayenne, salt, parsley, and dill. Spread the mixture out on a large plate.

Pour the milk, flour, and oil onto large individual plates. Set all 4 plates side by side.

Dip the fillets into the milk and then into the flour, turning until completely covered. Next dip the fish back into the milk, then into the bread crumb mixture and through the oil. Place the breaded cod on a baking sheet and bake in the preheated oven for 8 minutes (you can time the fish to cook for the last 8 minutes with the chips).

**The peas:** In a medium saucepan, bring the water to a boil and simmer the peas, salt, mint, and sugar until the peas are tender, about 3 minutes.

**To serve:** Divide the fish and chips among 4 dinner plates. I serve this classic with a "handy" wedge of lemon (easy to squeeze), the peas, and if available, a good spray of the watercress. It's the combination of golden browns, vivid greens, and lemon yellow that makes such a great picture.

Nutritional Profile per Serving: Calories—484; % calories from fat—24%; fat (gm)—13 or 20% daily value; saturated fat (gm)—2; sodium (mg)—775; cholesterol (mg)—55; carbohydrates (gm)—63; dietary fiber (gm)—7. ⬆

# Salmon China Moon

*Barbara Tropp, one of my favorite cookbook writers and owner/chef of the China Moon restaurant in San Francisco, suggested this simple yet elegant salmon dish for our collaboration. It took only very minor changes to meet the low-fat nutrition profile.*

*This dish is very elegant, especially if it's served on one of those glossy black plates. The sauce is brushed on the fish but can also be strained into small pots for dipping.*

Time Estimate: Hands-on, 55 minutes
Serves 4

4 (5- to 6-ounce or 150- to 175-gm) fresh salmon steaks, cut 3/4 inch (2 cm) thick
2 cups water
1 cup uncooked long-grain white rice
1/4 red bell pepper, thinly sliced, 1½ inches (4 cm) long
4 green onions, green part only, finely sliced
1 teaspoon light olive oil with a dash of toasted sesame oil
2 cloves garlic, bashed, peeled, and finely minced
2 tablespoons finely sliced threads of fresh gingerroot
1 tablespoon fermented black beans
1 teaspoon dried red pepper flakes
1 tablespoon rice vinegar
1/2 cup de-alcoholized white wine

Remove the salmon's free bones (see sidebar).

Put the water in a medium saucepan and bring to a boil. Add the rice and simmer 15 minutes. The rice should have a firm texture, without sticking together. Add the peppers and half of the sliced green onions, stir well, and set aside.

In a large sauté pan, heat the olive oil over medium-high heat and sauté the minced garlic, half the ginger, the beans, and red pepper flakes, stirring to blend, for 5 minutes. Add the rice vinegar and half of the de-alcoholized white wine and set aside.

On an ovenproof plate or Pyrex pie pan at least 1 inch (2.5 cm) smaller in diameter than your steamer, lay the fish steaks back to belly for a pretty fit. Sprinkle with the remaining green onions and ginger, then pour the black bean mixture evenly on top. Use only a bare sprinkling of ginger if it is the stronger, thick-skinned variety. You can be more liberal with the subtle, young type.

Pour water into your steamer pot to a depth of 4 inches (10 cm) and bring to a full boil. Put the plate of prepared salmon in the steamer, cover tightly, and steam over medium-high heat for 8 minutes. While steaming, do not lift the lid to peek at the fish, lest you dissipate the heat. When properly steamed, the fish will still look moist and red, but will not be fleshy or raw.

Remove the plate from the steamer. Pour the steaming liquid through a strainer into a small saucepan. Stir in the remaining de-alcoholized white wine.

**To serve:** Serve the hot fish immediately. You can also serve this dish at room temperature: just remove the salmon from the steamer when it is about 1 minute underdone and let it cook to completion from its own inner heat.

Just before serving, remove the rib and backbones and pull off the skin in a neat ribbon with the aid of a small knife. Discard most of the green onion, leaving a few nuggets on top for color, or garnish the salmon with one of the prettier whole green onion stalks. Serve the fish in the steamer basket, or transfer it carefully to heated serving plates with a spatula.

Spoon the rice into small, individual molds and flip onto each serving plate. Glaze the salmon and rice with the salmon steaming liquid. Leftovers keep 1 to 2 days in the refrigerator and are very good cold. The salmon juices gel into a delicious aspic.

Nutritional Profile per Serving: Calories—420; % calories from fat—21%; fat (gm)—10 or 15% daily value; saturated fat (gm)—3; sodium (mg)—348; cholesterol (mg)—95; carbohydrates (gm)—44; dietary fiber (gm)—1.

## To Debone Salmon Steaks

Before you steam the salmon, remove the "free" bones. They fan out on either side of the backbones in a "V" shape. Press down either side of the bone ends as this will make them protrude. Using a pair of fine needle-nosed pliers, pull out the bones and discard. After the fish is cooked, strip off the outer skin and carefully remove the rib and backbones.

# THE PEACEMAKER
## (OYSTER AND BACON LOAF)

——— ⊗ ———

*When Lorraine Haley sent me her Peacemaker recipe to "fix," I was already familiar with the recipe, as I had used it when I had a television cooking series in New Zealand in 1969. Lorraine reports that this lightened version is "delicious—even better than the original." I hope you agree.*

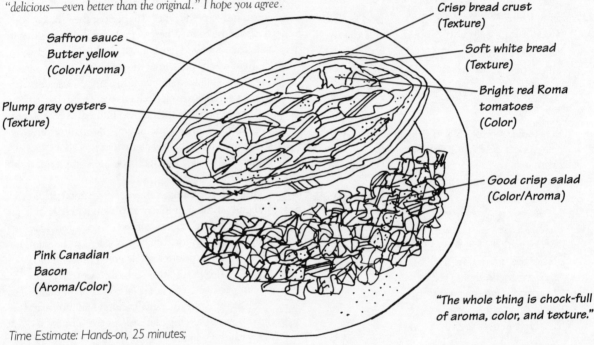

Saffron sauce
Butter yellow
(Color/Aroma)

Plump gray oysters
(Texture)

Pink Canadian
Bacon
(Aroma/Color)

Crisp bread crust
(Texture)

Soft white bread
(Texture)

Bright red Roma
tomatoes
(Color)

Good crisp salad
(Color/Aroma)

*"The whole thing is chock-full of aroma, color, and texture."*

*Time Estimate: Hands-on, 25 minutes; unsupervised, 10 minutes*
*Serves 6*

1 (12 × 6-inch or 30 × 15-cm) French bread loaf

FILLING

2 teaspoons light olive oil with a dash of toasted sesame oil
1 clove garlic, bashed, peeled, and finely chopped
3 ounces (90 gm) Canadian bacon, very thinly sliced and cut into matchsticks
1 teaspoon chopped fresh tarragon
1/2 cup all-purpose flour
1/8 teaspoon freshly ground sea salt
1/8 teaspoon freshly ground black pepper plus additional pepper to taste

15 ounces (425 gm) small fresh shucked oysters from a jar, strained, liquid reserved
1 tablespoon chopped fresh parsley
2 tablespoons freshly squeezed lemon juice
3 plum tomatoes, halved lengthwise

SAUCE

1/2 cup strained yogurt (page 288)
1 teaspoon prepared horseradish
Pinch of ground saffron
1 tablespoon chopped fresh parsley

Slice open the French bread loaf down one side, leaving a hinge on the least cracked side of the bread. Scoop out the softer center, leaving 1/2 inch (1.5 cm) of bread all around. (You should have about 6 ounces (175 gm) of good bread crumb material that you can dry out, freeze, and use later.)

**The filling:** Pour the oil into a large skillet and fry the garlic over medium heat for 30 seconds. Add the bacon and fry for 1 minute. Stir in the tarragon and remove from the heat.

Preheat the oven to 450°F (230°C). Measure the flour, salt, and pepper into a plastic resealable bag and shake to mix well. Put about 3 oysters into the bag at a time and shake until well coated, then lay on top of the cooked bacon mixture. When all the oysters are coated and in the skillet, return to the heat and fry for 3 minutes on each side. Sprinkle with the parsley, lemon juice, and a small amount of pepper. Spoon into one side of the hollowed-out bread loaf.

In the same skillet, fry the tomatoes for 1 minute on each side—just to soak up the pan juices. Place the tomatoes, cut side down, on top of the oysters. Top the filled loaf with its lid and wrap with aluminum foil quite tightly, making sure it's covered well. Place on a baking sheet and bake in the preheated oven for 10 minutes. Open the foil and bake for 5 minutes to crisp the bread.

**The sauce:** While the loaf is baking, deglaze the skillet with the reserved oyster juices, making sure to scrape up any bits from the bottom and sides of the pan. Strain this into a small bowl and mix together with the strained yogurt, horseradish, and saffron. It should be the same color as mayonnaise.

**To serve:** Remove the loaf from the oven and place on a carving board. Open the bread lid, pour in the sauce, and close. Cut into 6 slices and serve on individual plates, garnished with the parsley. It can be served warm or cold.

## EXTRA MEAL

When you make The Peacemaker, prepare two, leaving out the tomatoes and the sauce in the second one. Slice the one you are going to freeze into 6 pieces, cutting not quite through the bottom. Place a piece of waxed paper between each slice, wrap tightly in plastic, and place in a resealable freezer bag. The frozen Peacemaker should be used within 2 months. When you are ready to use it, let it thaw in the refrigerator. Wrap the thawed Peacemaker in foil and bake at 300°F (150°C) for 1 hour. If you are using just one serving slice, bake it for 15 minutes.

| Nutritional Profile per Serving | | | |
|---|---|---|---|
| | Classic | Minimax | Daily Value |
| Calories | 600 | 315 | |
| Calories from fat | 50% | 17% | |
| Fat (gm) | 33 | 6 | 9% |
| Saturated fat (gm) | 11 | 2 | 10% |
| Sodium (mg) | 1,055 | 774 | 32% |
| Cholesterol (mg) | 152 | 27 | 22% |
| Carbohydrates (gm) | 49 | 45 | 15% |
| Dietary fiber (gm) | 3 | 2 | 8% |
| Classic compared: The Peacemaker, Oyster and Bacon Loaf | | | |

# SMOKED CHILEAN SEA BASS
# WITH THAI VINAIGRETTE

⌘

*If you have a taste for the exotic, you'll love this smoky seafood supper or luncheon dish.*

**Garnish
Gingerroot finely sliced horizontally
Pale golden cream
(Color)**

**Garnish
Cucumber, carrot, red
peppers cut in fine
shreds**

**Couscous
aromatically seasoned
fine-grain pasta
Pale green
(Aroma/Texture)**

**Vinaigrette slightly bound with
arrowroot
Pale green, glistening
(Texture/Aroma/Color)**

**Chilean sea bass smoked over
Earl Grey tea
Golden brown
(Texture/Color/Aroma)**

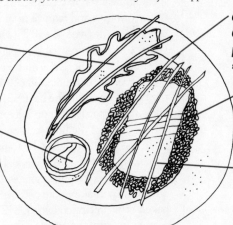

*Time Estimate: Hands-on, 45 minutes*
*Serves 4*

## SEA BASS AND TEA SMOKE

4 (4-ounce or 100-gm) Chilean sea bass fillets, skin
  removed
2 tablespoons uncooked rice
4 whole cloves
Tea leaves from 2 Earl Grey tea bags, removed from
  packets
1/4 teaspoon light olive oil with a dash of toasted
  sesame oil

## COUSCOUS

1/2 teaspoon light olive oil with a dash of toasted
  sesame oil
1/4 cup roughly chopped fresh lemon grass
2 tablespoons finely chopped fresh gingerroot
1/4 cup chopped green onion, white bulb only
Zest of 1/2 lime, grated
3¾ cups fish stock (page 287)
1/8 teaspoon freshly ground sea salt
1 (10-ounce or 300-gm) box instant couscous

## VINAIGRETTE

1 cup reserved seasoned fish stock (see directions below)
1 tablespoon thinly sliced gingerroot
1/4 cup thinly sliced lemon grass
3 tablespoons freshly squeezed lime juice
1 tablespoon low-sodium soy sauce
2 tablespoons light olive oil
1/4 teaspoon toasted sesame oil
2 tablespoons fresh cilantro leaves
12 fresh mint leaves
2 teaspoons arrowroot mixed with 4 teaspoons
  reserved vinaigrette (slurry) (see directions below)

## RAW VEGETABLE GARNISH

1 (5- to 6-inch or 13- to 15-cm) piece of fresh gingerroot, sliced lengthwise into 4 flat pieces
2 green onions, sliced lengthwise into whisper-thin pieces
1 red bell pepper, seeded and cut into long, toothpick-
  size pieces
1/2 English cucumber, cut into long, thin strips
1 carrot, cut into long, thin strips
Thinly sliced mint leaves

**The sea bass and tea smoke:** Rinse and pat dry the fish fillets with a paper towel. Cut 3 sheets of heavy-duty aluminum foil into 15-inch (38-cm) squares. Roll the edges under to form a three-ply saucer that fits in the bottom of a Dutch oven. The pot should *not* be made of a light alloy or alloy bonded to other metals. Cast iron or cast aluminum pans work fine. You should have a foil "saucer" approximately 5 inches (13 cm) in diameter. When the edge is rolled to about 1 inch (2.5 cm) high, stop and flatten the foil. Depress the center to hold the smoke ingredients.

In the depression of the aluminum foil saucer, sprinkle the rice on the bottom, the cloves, and then the contents of the tea bags. Place the foil dish in the bottom of the Dutch oven, cover tightly, and cook over high heat until the ingredients in the foil start smoking, about 5 minutes.

Brush a long-legged steamer basket with the olive oil. Place the sea bass on the steamer platform. Put into the Dutch oven over the smoke ingredients, cover, and continue smoking over high heat until cooked through, about 8 minutes. Remove from the heat and let cool.

**The couscous:** Pour the oil into a medium saucepan and fry the lemon grass, ginger, green onion, and lime zest over medium-high heat for 2 minutes. Add the stock and bring to a boil. Turn the heat down and simmer for 10 minutes to allow for infusion and reduction. Strain into a large measuring cup—you want to have 3 cups of liquid. Reserve 1 cup for the vinaigrette. Pour the remaining 2 cups back into the saucepan and bring back to a boil. Stir in the salt and couscous. Cover, remove from the heat, and let stand for 5 minutes.

**The vinaigrette:** In a medium saucepan, combine the reserved 1 cup stock, ginger, and lemon grass, and boil until reduced to 1/2 cup, about 10 minutes. Strain into a blender jar. Add the lime juice, soy sauce, olive oil, sesame oil, cilantro, and mint leaves and whiz for 2 minutes to emulsify or hold together. Reserve 1½ tablespoons. Pour the rest into a small saucepan and bring to a boil. Remove from the heat. Stir in the arrowroot slurry, return to the heat, and bring to a boil to thicken and clear, about 30 seconds.

**To serve:** Make a mound of couscous on each plate and place a smoked fillet on top. Arrange the raw vegetable garnish (except the mint) around the plate. Ladle the vinaigrette over the sea bass and garnish it with slivers of the mint.

## Extra Meal

The vinaigrette in this recipe is great to have standing by as a light sauce for salmon, shrimp, and other seafood. Double the vinaigrette portion of the recipe. Pour the extra into ice cube trays and freeze. When it's frozen solid, pop the cubes out of the trays and store them in resealable freezer bags. Expel as much air as possible, label, and date. They will last for 6 months.

| Nutritional Profile per Serving: | | | |
|---|---|---|---|
| | **Classic** | **Minimax** | **Daily Value** |
| Calories | 867 | 499 | |
| Calories from fat | 56% | 20% | |
| Fat (gm) | 54 | 11 | 17% |
| Saturated fat (gm) | 8 | 2 | 10% |
| Sodium (mg) | 1,008 | 395 | 16% |
| Cholesterol (mg) | 120 | 60 | 20% |
| Carbohydrates (gm) | 54 | 63 | 21% |
| Dietary fiber (gm) | 8 | 4 | 16% |

Classic compared: Seafood Salad with Blue Lake Beans and Sweet Corn in Saffron Vinaigrette

# SALMON MUMMIES

※

*Catch 35 is a wonderful, mainly seafood restaurant in downtown Chicago. Here you can eat very fresh fish in an upbeat environment and enjoy simple elegance. Chef/owner Eak Prukpitikul is a trained architect who sketches out his dish before he cooks. This recipe is basically his idea, with some considerable Minimaxing from our kitchen. The major change is in the use of bok choy in place of hard-to-find banana leaves.*

*Time Estimate: Hands-on, 60 minutes*

*Serves 4*

## MARINATED VEGETABLES

1 red bell pepper, seeded and cut into matchsticks
2 stalks bok choy, cut into matchsticks
12 cilantro leaves, finely chopped
4 tablespoons rice wine vinegar
1/4 teaspoon toasted sesame oil

## RICE

5 green onions
1/2 teaspoon toasted sesame oil
1 (2-inch or 5-cm) piece gingerroot, peeled and bruised
4 tablespoons chopped fresh cilantro sprigs
Zest of 1 lemon, cut in strips and bruised
1/4 teaspoon freshly ground sea salt
1/8 teaspoon cayenne pepper
2 cups water
1 cup uncooked long-grain white rice

## SALMON

12 large bok choy leaves, stems removed (or Savoy cabbage)
1¼ pounds (575 gm) salmon fillet, skin and bones removed, cut into 4 equal pieces
4 slivers gingerroot

**The marinated vegetables:** In a large bowl, combine the sliced red pepper, bok choy stalks, and cilantro leaves with the vinegar and sesame oil and set aside.

**The rice:** Cut 1-inch (2.5-cm) pieces off the green ends of the onions and set aside. Cut the rest of the green onions in thin diagonal slices.

In a large saucepan, heat the sesame oil over medium-high heat and quickly sauté the green ends of the onion, the ginger, cilantro stalks, and lemon zest for 2 minutes. Add the salt, cayenne, and water, and simmer 10 minutes. Strain into a bowl. Return the liquid to the saucepan and bring to a boil. Add the rice, cover, and simmer for 12 minutes. Take out 1/2 cup of the cooked rice and reserve. Stir the rest of the rice into the marinating vegetables.

**The salmon:** Steam the bok choy leaves until just limp—about 30 seconds.

Spread the reserved rice on a large plate. Roll one of the salmon pieces in the rice, giving it a light rice crust. Then wrap it in the steamed bok choy leaves in the following manner: Spread 2 steamed bok choy leaves on a cutting board, stems overlapping about 2 inches (5 cm). Place the salmon in the center with a ginger sliver on top. Fold the ends of the leaves over the salmon. Roll the Salmon Mummies like a burrito. Repeat for the remaining 3 salmon pieces. Steam the Salmon Mummies for 8 minutes.

**To serve:** Place one of the remaining steamed bok choy leaves on each dinner plate and make a mound of one-quarter of the marinated rice and vegetables on the stem end. Cut the Salmon Mummies in half and nestle 2 halves, cut side up, in the rice on each plate to reveal the moist salmon interior to your dinner guests.

Nutritional Profile per Serving: Calories—382; % calories from fat—19%; fat (gm)—8 or 13% daily value; saturated fat (gm)—2; sodium (mg)—228; cholesterol (mg)—79; carbohydrates (gm)—44; dietary fiber (gm)—2.

# Braised Turkey and Celery

*I have made several dishes from turkey breast, which has caused some to ask, "What about the leftover thighs?" Not wishing to have a segregated kitchen or a fridge full of hindquarters, I have made this dish out of fresh thighs, which, when braised with celery hearts, rosemary, and sage, are delicious. It's full of flavor, easy to prepare, and lets me cook the breast separately without guilt.*

*Time Estimate: Hands-on, 75 minutes;
    unsupervised, 20 minutes*

*Serves 4*

2 (13-ounce or 375-gm) whole turkey legs, yielding 12
    ounces (350 gm) of thigh meat
1 teaspoon light olive oil with a dash of toasted sesame oil
1 large onion, peeled and diced
2/3 cup de-alcoholized red wine
2 celery hearts, trimmed to 4 inches (10 cm) and cut in
    half lengthwise
1 sprig rosemary
1 fresh sage leaf
3 cups turkey broth (page 286)
3 tablespoons arrowroot mixed with 1/4 cup de-
    alcoholized red wine (slurry)

SIDE DISH: STEAMED VEGETABLES

8 red new potatoes
12 baby carrots
1/4 teaspoon freshly grated nutmeg
1 turnip, peeled and finely sliced
1/4 teaspoon freshly ground black pepper
1/8 teaspoon freshly ground sea salt

To separate the turkey thigh from the drumstick: Feel on the inside of the turkey leg. Run your finger down from the exposed ball-and-socket joint at the top of the thigh and you will find a joint about 4 inches (10 cm) away, depending on the size of the turkey. Press the knife down through the joint, separating the thigh from the drumstick. Repeat with the other whole leg and set aside. Freeze the turkey drumsticks for later use.

Preheat the oven to 350°F (180°C). In a Dutch oven set on medium-high heat, heat the oil and sauté the onion until slightly soft, about 3 minutes. Remove the onion and set aside.

Place the turkey thighs, cut side down (the cut side is the side opposite the skin side), in the same pan. Brown well on each side for 2 minutes. Remove the browned thighs, remove the skin, and discard. Put the thighs back in the pot and lightly brown the area from which the skin was removed, about 1 minute. Remove the thighs and set aside.

Wipe a paper towel around the pot to blot up the excess grease, then deglaze the pot with 1/3 cup of the wine and add the cooked onion, the celery hearts, rosemary, and sage. Lay the browned thighs, cut side up, on top. Pour in the turkey broth and the remaining 1/3 cup wine and bring to a boil. Remove from the heat, cover, and bake in the preheated oven for 40 minutes.

About 20 minutes before the turkey is done, cook the side vegetables: Place the potatoes in a steamer tray and steam, covered, for 15 minutes total. After 6 minutes, place the carrots in the center of another steamer tray, sprinkle with the nutmeg, and stack on the first steamer. After 4 minutes, spread the turnip slices around the carrots, sprinkle with the pepper and salt, and steam for 5 minutes.

Remove the Dutch oven from the oven. Spoon out the celery hearts and the turkey. Cut the turkey thighs into 4 pieces. Strain the remaining pan juices into a fat-separator cup and wait for the fat to rise to the top. Pour the separated juices back into the stewpot, keeping the fat in the separator.

In the stewpot, bring the pan juices to a boil. Remove from the heat. Add the arrowroot slurry, return to the heat, and stir until thickened. Add the braised celery hearts and turkey pieces and warm through.

**To serve:** Place a quarter of the turkey pieces, 1 piece of the celery, 2 potatoes, 3 carrots, and several slices of the turnip on each plate. Drizzle with the thickened pan juices.

Nutritional Profile per Serving: Calories—425; % calories from fat—16%; fat (gm)—7 or 11% daily value; saturated fat (gm)—2; sodium (mg)—313; cholesterol (mg)—53; carbohydrates (gm)—66; dietary fiber (gm)—8.

# Chicken and Red Bell Pepper Pasta

*I think I'm genuinely embarrassed—sometimes I find it hard to judge! When Treena and I visit the Beach Café at Yarrow Bay on Lake Washington, near Seattle, I almost always order the same dish, yet I keep on proposing "variety, variety." My only defense is that this is one of the best pasta dishes I've ever eaten! So, embarrassed or not, I keep going back to the same thing. Now you can, too!*

Time Estimate: Hands-on, 45 minutes

Serves 6

13 dry-pack sun-dried tomato halves
1 (3-pound or 1.4-kg) chicken, quartered, or 1 whole breast, split, and 2 whole legs
1/2 teaspoon black peppercorns
1/2 teaspoon allspice berries
4 whole cloves
1 tablespoon chopped fresh thyme or 1 teaspoon dried
1/8 teaspoon freshly ground sea salt
4 cups loosely packed spinach leaves, sliced into thin strips
1 teaspoon light olive oil with a dash of toasted sesame oil
1 (14½-ounce or 435-ml) can low-sodium chicken stock
1 bouquet garni (page 289)
1 cup roasted sweet red bell peppers (page 41)
2 tablespoons chopped fresh parsley
1 tablespoon arrowroot mixed with 2 tablespoons de-alcoholized white wine (slurry)
12 ounces (350 gm) uncooked fettuccine
1 tablespoon balsamic vinegar

Cut 5 of the sun-dried tomato halves in half and reserve. Put the remaining sun-dried tomatoes in a small saucepan and cover with water. Bring to a boil, then take off the heat and let soak 30 minutes. Drain and cut each tomato in half. Set aside.

Remove the bones from the chicken pieces, keeping the skin on. Use the leftover bones for chicken stock.

Put the black peppercorns, allspice berries, cloves, thyme, salt, and the reserved sun-dried tomatoes in a small grinder and whiz. Sprinkle the ground spices liberally over both sides of the chicken and evenly pack the spices under the skin.

In a large skillet, heat the oil and brown the chicken pieces over medium-high heat for 5 minutes on both sides. Remove from the pan and discard the skin. Slice the chicken meat into bite-size pieces and set aside. Drain the fat from the skillet.

In a saucepan, bring the chicken stock to a boil, add the bouquet garni, and simmer for 5 minutes. Remove the bouquet garni. Pour the stock into the skillet used to brown the chicken. Stir in the reconstituted sun-dried tomatoes, red peppers, and parsley, and cook over medium heat for 5 minutes. Stir in the chicken and remove the skillet from the heat. Stir in the arrowroot slurry, return to the heat, and stir until thickened.

Drop the fettuccine into a large pot of boiling water and cook for 8 minutes. Drain over a large bowl. Discard the water and now you have a beautifully warmed bowl ready to serve your pasta! Put the fettuccine in the bowl.

Toss the fettuccine with the sliced raw spinach. Pour in the red pepper sauce and balsamic vinegar, toss well, and serve.

Nutritional Profile per Serving: Calories—408; % calories from fat—16%; fat (gm)—7 or 11% daily value; saturated fat (gm)—2; sodium (mg)—234; cholesterol (mg)—66; carbohydrates (gm)—51; dietary fiber (gm)—3.

# CHICKEN ENGLISH MEHSON

*This dish was created for a viewer whom we met in the streets of New York. Gary Mehson just happened to be English, but that didn't stop him from raving on about chicken in a rich sauce with mushrooms . . . on pasta . . . with LOTS of sauce. So I created Chicken English Mehson just for him. In the end, he flew in from London to Seattle to put it to the ultimate personal test. He liked it, so it carries his name.*

*A crisp salad to follow wouldn't hurt!*

Time Estimate: Hands-on, 35 minutes;
  unsupervised, 20 minutes
Serves 2

3 teaspoons light olive oil with a dash of toasted sesame oil
1 medium onion, peeled and thinly sliced
2 teaspoons shallots, thinly sliced
1 ounce (30 gm) Canadian bacon, cut into matchsticks
1 teaspoon fresh thyme
1 tablespoon chopped fresh parsley
2 (6-ounce or 175-gm) chicken breasts, with skin
1 tablespoon low-sodium tomato paste
2 ounces (60 gm) pimiento, cut into matchsticks
1/2 cup de-alcoholized white wine
24 button mushrooms, quartered
14 pitted black olives, halved
5 teaspoons capers
2 cups low-sodium beef stock (page 286)
2 tablespoons arrowroot mixed with 1/4 cup de-alcoholized white wine (slurry)
4 ounces (115 gm) spaghetti
3 quarts water
1 cup collard greens, thinly sliced

GARNISH

Chopped fresh parsley

In a large skillet, heat 1 teaspoon of the olive oil and sauté the onion and shallots over medium-high heat until translucent. Add the Canadian bacon, thyme, and parsley and cook for 2 to 3 minutes. Turn the contents of the pan out onto a plate and set aside.

Heat 1 more teaspoon of the olive oil and brown the chicken breasts on medium heat for 4 minutes on each side. Add the tomato paste and pimiento, and cook until lightly browned. Remove the chicken and place it on a dish. Deglaze the pan with the de-alcoholized white wine. Remove the skin from the chicken.

Return the cooked onion mixture and chicken breasts to the skillet. Add the mushrooms, olives, and 4 teaspoons of the capers. Pour in the beef stock and remove the pan from the heat. Stir in the arrowroot slurry, return to the heat, and cook, stirring, until thickened.

Cook the pasta in 3 quarts of boiling water for 10 minutes. Pour the pasta into a strainer set over a serving bowl. Pour the hot water out and place the noodles in the heated bowl. Toss with the collard greens and the remaining capers.

**To serve:** Make a bed of the pasta and place the chicken breasts in the center. Spoon the sauce over the chicken and garnish with the chopped parsley.

Nutritional Profile per Serving: Calories—548; % calories from fat—24%; fat (gm)—14 or 22% daily value; saturated fat (gm)—3; sodium (mg)—652; cholesterol (mg)—69; carbohydrates (gm)—64; dietary fiber (gm)—7.

# CHICKEN STIR-BOIL

*You've heard of "stir-frying," now try "stir-boiling." The result is a quick, flavorful chicken-vegetable soup that the whole family will love.*

*Time Estimate: Hands-on, 45 minutes*
Serves 4

2 cups low-sodium chicken stock (page 286)
1/4 teaspoon light olive oil with a dash of toasted sesame oil
4 (6-ounce or 175-gm) boneless chicken breasts, with skin
1/4 cup water
8 ounces (225 gm) fresh mushrooms, quartered
8 ounces (225 gm) frozen lima beans
1 (8-ounce or 225-gm) can whole water chestnuts, drained
1 tablespoon chopped fresh dill
1 tablespoon freshly squeezed lemon juice
1/4 teaspoon freshly ground sea salt
1/4 teaspoon freshly ground black pepper
1/4 teaspoon cayenne pepper
2 teaspoons arrowroot mixed with 1 teaspoon water (slurry)

Pour the chicken stock into a large skillet and boil until reduced to 1/2 cup, about 15 minutes.

While the stock is reducing, brush a large skillet over medium-high heat with the oil and place the chicken breasts skin side down in the skillet to brown, turning them every 2 minutes, for a total of 10 minutes. In cooking the chicken with the skin on, less moisture is lost, resulting in a plumper, juicier chicken breast. Remove from the heat, transfer chicken to a plate, and pull off the skin and discard. Slice the chicken into 2 X 1/2-inch (5 X 1.5-cm) strips. If you see a little pink color, don't worry, the chicken will cook a bit more in the next step. Blot the skillet with a paper towel to absorb the excess fat.

Pour the water into the skillet and deglaze over high heat, scraping all the residues up into the liquid, then pour in the reduced chicken broth. Bring to a boil. Add the mushrooms, lima beans, and water chestnuts, and "stir-boil" until just tender, about 5 minutes. Stir in the cooked chicken and just heat through. Sprinkle with the dill, lemon juice, salt, black pepper, and cayenne pepper, and stir well.

Remove from the heat and tip the pan so that the juices collect in a clear space. Add the arrowroot slurry, return to the heat, and stir until thickened.

**To serve:** Ladle into bowls and don't miss a single drop!

Nutritional Profile per Serving: Calories—320; % calories from fat—16%; fat (gm)—6 or 9% daily value; saturated fat (gm)—2; sodium (mg)—289; cholesterol (mg)—94; carbohydrates (gm)—23; dietary fiber (gm)—5.

# Coq au Vin

*My version of this classic dish can be prepared ahead of time and easily reheated for your family and guests. A special aspect of this Coq au Vin is that you strip the hens of their fatty skin and small bones. Since you win from both presentation and fat viewpoints, I call this a "double benefit."*

*Time Estimate: Hands-on, 30 minutes; unsupervised, 35 minutes*
Serves 4

1 teaspoon light olive oil with a dash of toasted sesame oil
2 Cornish game hens, cut in half
4 small yellow onions, peeled and ends trimmed
1 pound (450 gm) small, whole red new potatoes
2 medium turnips, peeled and cut into eighths
8 medium mushrooms
1/2 teaspoon thyme
2 cups ham hock stock (page 287), meat reserved
2 cups de-alcoholized red wine
1 bay leaf
3 tablespoons arrowroot mixed with 6 tablespoons de-alcoholized red wine (slurry)

GARNISH

2 tablespoons chopped fresh parsley
1/4 teaspoon freshly ground sea salt
1/4 teaspoon freshly ground black pepper

Heat 1/2 teaspoon of the oil in a large, high-sided skillet over medium heat and brown the hens, skin side down. When the skin is nice and brown, about 3 minutes, remove from the pan and set aside. Pour the remaining oil into the pan over medium-high heat, add the onions, and cook to release the volatile oils, about 5 minutes. Stir in the remaining vegetables and the thyme, and cook 2 minutes. Pour in the ham hock stock, reserved ham, de-alcoholized wine, and bay leaf. Now add the game hen halves, cover, and cook over medium heat until tender, about 30 minutes.

Transfer the cooked hens to a plate and the veg-etables and ham to a bowl with a slotted spoon. Strain the cooking liquid into a fat strainer; you should have about 4 cups. If not, make up the difference with more stock or wine. Rinse the pan and return to the heat. Pour in the cooking liquid without the fat, bring to a boil, and reduce to 3 cups, which will take about 5 minutes.

While the cooking liquid is reducing, you may start removing the skin and small bones from the cooked hens. Remove the skin and discard. Take the meat from the wings and breast and leave the legs and thighs whole.

Remove the reduced cooking liquid from the heat. Stir in the arrowroot slurry, return to the heat, and stir until thickened. Add the prepared hen pieces, the vegetables, and ham to the sauce; stir gently and heat through.

**To serve:** Spoon the Coq au Vin onto dinner plates, coat with additional sauce, and dust with the parsley, salt, and pepper.

Nutritional Profile per Serving: Calories—418; % calories from fat—21%; fat (gm)—10 or 15% daily value; saturated fat (gm)—3; sodium (mg)—292; cholesterol (mg)—103; carbohydrates (gm)—41; dietary fiber (gm)—5.

# Crêpes Antonin Carême

*In contrast to Antonin Carême's original complex recipes, today's approach is to simplify and to reduce risk while at the same time enhancing aroma, color, and texture.*

*Time Estimate: Hands-on, 1 hour*
*Serves 4*

CRÊPE BATTER (Makes 10 crêpes)

1 whole large egg
1 large egg yolk
1 cup nonfat milk
1/2 cup all-purpose flour
1/8 teaspoon freshly ground white pepper
1/2 teaspoon dried tarragon
1 teaspoon light olive oil with a dash of toasted sesame oil

FILLING

2 cups low-sodium chicken stock (page 286)
2 (6-ounce or 175-gm) boneless, skinless chicken breasts
1/2 cup finely chopped celery
1/4 cup finely chopped onion
1 cup sliced mushrooms
1/2 teaspoon dried tarragon

SAUCE

2/3 cup evaporated skim milk
1 cup low-sodium chicken stock (page 286)
3 tablespoons cornstarch mixed with 1/2 cup de-alcoholized white wine (slurry)
1/4 teaspoon freshly ground sea salt
1/8 teaspoon freshly ground white pepper
1/8 teaspoon freshly grated nutmeg

GARNISH

2 tablespoons freshly grated Parmesan cheese
1 tablespoon chopped fresh parsley

**The crêpes:** In a large bowl, beat together the egg, egg yolk, and milk. Beat in the flour, pepper, and tarragon until fully incorporated. Set aside to rest for 30 minutes.

Heat the oil in the bottom of a nonstick 8-inch (20-cm) omelet pan, swirling it around to cover the entire bottom. Turn the pan upside down over the batter bowl to drain the excess oil. Whisk it into the batter to help make the crêpes self-releasing and eliminate the need to re-oil the pan.

Pour a scant 1/4 cup of the batter into the hot pan over medium-high heat. Roll the pan quickly to distribute the batter over the entire bottom surface. Wait until the top turns waxy and dull, about 1 to 2 minutes, then turn the crêpe and cook 1 more minute. You should have 9 crêpes, giving you 1 extra in case of mistakes.

**The filling:** Gently simmer the chicken breasts in the stock with the celery, onions, and mushrooms for 10 minutes. Strain the stock into a bowl and set aside to use in the sauce. Cool the chicken breasts, then dice and combine with the poached vegetables and tarragon.

**The sauce:** In a small saucepan over medium heat, mix the milk and stock. (Some of the stock from the filling may have evaporated, so combine the strained stock from the filling with 1 cup of new stock and add enough to make 2 cups.) Remove the saucepan from the heat and stir in the cornstarch slurry. Return to the heat and stir until thickened. Season with the salt, pepper, and nutmeg. Add 1 cup of the sauce to the chicken filling. Set the rest aside.

**To assemble:** Preheat the oven to 400°F (205°C). Pour a little of the sauce over the bottom of a large ovenproof serving dish. Lay a crêpe on a cutting board, spoon about 1/3 cup of filling in a line down the center and roll up. Lay the filled crêpe, seam side down, in the prepared serving dish. Proceed to fill 8 of the crêpes in this manner. Pour the remaining sauce over the crêpes, sprinkle each one lengthwise with a line of Parmesan cheese, and pop them into the preheated oven to heat through for 10 minutes. Turn the oven to broil to lightly brown the tops. Scatter the parsley on top and serve.

Nutritional Profile per Serving: Calories—323; % calories from fat—22%; fat (gm)—8 or 12% daily value; saturated fat (gm)—3; sodium (mg)—375; cholesterol (mg)—158; carbohydrates (gm)—30; dietary fiber (gm)—2.

# PIZZA POLESE

## ✳

*Incredibly popular, the classic pizza has an almost no-fault crust, especially when compared to the rich, fatty, pie crust used for quiche and some fruit pies. Instead, it's the pizza toppings that can go overboard—our version tries to keep you in the boat!*

Time Estimate: Hands-on, 45 minutes;
    unsupervised, 60 minutes
Serves 6

PIZZA CRUST

1 clove garlic
2 loosely packed tablespoons oregano leaves
1 tablespoon packed fresh rosemary leaves
1½ cups all-purpose flour
1/4 cup liquid egg substitute
1/4 cup water
1 tablespoon light olive oil with a dash of toasted sesame
    oil
1/4 teaspoon freshly ground sea salt
1/2 ounce compressed yeast
1 tablespoon hot water to blend yeast

TOPPING

2 (4-ounce or 115-gm) skinless and boneless chicken
    breasts
1 red bell pepper, seeded and finely diced
1½ cups seeded and diced plum tomatoes
1 tablespoon chopped fresh oregano
1 tablespoon chopped fresh parsley
1/2 teaspoon freshly ground black pepper
4 teaspoons capers
6 thin slices part-skim mozzarella cheese
4 good-quality anchovy fillets, soaked in a little milk to
    remove the saltiness, drained, and quartered length-
    wise, soaking milk reserved

   **The pizza crust:** Put the garlic, oregano, and rose-mary into a small food grinder or pepper mill and process to a fine, moist "dust."
   Preheat the oven to 500°F (260°C). Put the flour

in a large bowl. Make a well in the center and pour in the egg substitute, water, oil, salt, and ground herb mixture. In another small bowl, break the compressed yeast into small pieces, add the hot water, and stir until completely dissolved. Pour into the flour well.
   Gradually start incorporating the flour and egg mixture together. Stir gently up against the sides of the well, mixing in a little flour at a time. The dough will be fairly stiff. When it's hard to stir, use your hands to form the dough into a ball. Turn it out onto a board and continue kneading until the dough feels springy. It will be slightly tacky but should come off your hands after you press into it. Form it into a ball, put it back in the bowl, cover it with a towel, and leave it in a warm place for 30 minutes, or until doubled in size.
   Turn the proofed dough out onto a board. Knead it just a couple more times then roll it out to fit a 14-inch (35cm) pizza pan. The dough should be fairly thin, about 1/8-inch (.5cm) thick.
   Prepare the pizza pan with a light dusting of semolina flour. Press the dough to fit the shape of the pan and let it sit for 15 minutes before baking. Bake in the preheated oven for 8 minutes or until light brown.
   **The topping:** On the coarsest setting, grind the chicken. In a small bowl, mix the ground chicken, red pepper, tomatoes, oregano, parsley, black pepper, and 3 teaspoons of the capers.
   **To assemble:** Flip your cooked pizza crust over so that the browned, crisp side is now on the bottom. Spread the topping over the crust, leaving a 1/2-inch (1.5-cm) crust edge. Place the mozzarella slices around the edge of the filling. Sprinkle the remaining capers on top and decorate with a crisscross of anchovy fillets.
   Bake in the preheated oven for 8 more minutes. When the pizza comes out of the oven, brush the exposed crust very lightly with the reserved anchovy soaking milk. Cut into 6 slices and serve.

Nutritional Profile per Serving: Calories—244; % calories from fat—24%; fat (gm)—7 or 10% daily value; saturated fat (gm)—2; sodium (mg)—322; cholesterol (mg)—31; carbo-hydrates (gm)—28; dietary fiber (gm)—2.

# PHEASANT & CHESTNUTS

Pheasant is now raised commercially on special farms. It is larger and less "gamey" in taste than its wild cousin. This dish is quite expensive but good results can also be achieved using a fresh, 3-pound (1.4-kg) chicken. Couple this with steamed broccoli and some long, thin, whole, steamed and glazed carrots and you have a fabulous special dinner dish.

*Time Estimate: Hands-on, 40 minutes; unsupervised, 60 minutes*
*Serves 2*

## HERB STUFFING

1/2 tablespoon chopped fresh parsley
1 teaspoon chopped fresh thyme
1 teaspoon chopped fresh sage
1/4 teaspoon chopped fresh tarragon
1/4 teaspoon cracked black pepper
1/8 teaspoon freshly ground sea salt
2 tablespoons chopped onion

## PHEASANT

1 (2-pound or 900-gm) pheasant
Rice Pilaf (Follow instructions on pages 51. Use chicken stock instead of turkey stock and leave out the shrimps.)

## CHESTNUT SAUCE

1 teaspoon light olive oil with a dash of toasted sesame oil
1 onion, peeled and sliced
1 clove garlic, bashed, peeled, and finely chopped
1 stalk celery, sliced
1 medium carrot, peeled and sliced
Bouquet garni (see below)
Reserved pheasant bones
4 cups water
2 cups de-alcoholized red wine
2 tablespoons arrowroot mixed with 2 tablespoon de-alcoholized red wine (slurry)
4 ounces (115 gm) peeled chestnuts

1/4 teaspoon chopped fresh tarragon
1/4 teaspoon chopped fresh thyme
1/2 teaspoon chopped fresh parsley

## BOUQUET GARNI

2 bay leaves
6 parsley stalks
4 sprigs thyme

**The herb stuffing:** Combine all the ingredients in a small bowl and mix well.

**The pheasant:** Preheat the oven to 375°F (190°C). Wash the pheasant and dry with absorbent paper. To remove the leg and thigh portion from the bird, cut down between the breast and thigh joint. Carefully bone the breast meat off the pheasant. Make sure to cut away any visible fat. Reserve the legs, thighs, and the bones.

Cut the breast in half. Coat the inner surface of the breast halves with the herb stuffing. Place one breast half on top of the other and squash together so that all the stuffing is on the inside.

Place the stuffed pheasant breast on a rack in a baking pan and roast in the preheated oven for 35 minutes, or until the internal temperature reaches 165°F (75°C) on a meat thermometer. Remove from the oven and keep warm. The rice pilaf can be baked at the same time as the pheasant, for 30 minutes.

**The chestnut sauce:** Heat the olive oil in a large Dutch oven. Add the onion, garlic, celery, carrot, bouquet garni, and the pheasant bones, and cook for 5 minutes. Pour in the water and de-alcoholized wine, and simmer gently until reduced to 4 cups. Add the reserved pheasant legs and thighs, and cook for 35 minutes more. Remove and strip the meat from the bones, and save for another recipe. Strain the stock into a fat-strainer cup and let sit until the fat has risen to the top. Pour the stock into a saucepan, leaving the fat behind. Boil until reduced to 1½ cups.

Remove the pan from the heat and mix in the arrowroot slurry. Return to the heat and stir until thickened. Add the chestnuts, tarragon, thyme, and parsley.

**To serve:** Transfer the cooked pheasant breast from the oven to a cutting board. Slice off the skin and carve the breast vertically into thick slices. Serve on a bed of the rice pilaf with the chestnut sauce.

Nutritional Profile per Serving: Calories—619; % calories from fat—18%; fat (gm)—12 or 19% daily value; saturated fat (gm)—3; sodium (mg)—377; cholesterol (mg)—51; carbohydrates (gm)—98; dietary fiber (gm)—8.

# EVIL JUNGLE PRINCESS
## (THAI CHICKEN AND VEGETABLES)
※

*An exotic name for a dish that bursts with tropical flavors. Serve it with rice on the side.*

Time Estimate: Hands-on, 35 minutes
Serves 2

2 tablespoons strained yogurt (page 288)
2 tablespoons evaporated skim milk
1/4 cup low-sodium chicken stock (page 286)
1/4 teaspoon coconut extract
1/2 teaspoon cornstarch
1/2 teaspoon chili powder
1 teaspoon peanut oil
2 cloves garlic, bashed, peeled, and chopped
2 tablespoons finely chopped lemon grass*
2 Kaffir lime leaves*, softened in a little warm water and finely chopped
8 ounces (225 gm) chicken breast, skinned and sliced into 2 X 1/4-inch (5 X .75-cm) strips
1 teaspoon sugar
7 fresh mint leaves, finely chopped
1 tablespoon fish sauce*
1/2 teaspoon cayenne pepper, or to taste
1 tablespoon freshly squeezed lime juice, or to taste
2 cups finely sliced chinese cabbage
2 cups finely sliced red cabbage
1⅔ cup enoki mushrooms*

*Available at Asian markets.

Combine the yogurt, milk, chicken stock, coconut extract, cornstarch, and chili powder in a small bowl. Stir until smooth with a wire whisk and set aside.

Heat the peanut oil in a large skillet and cook the garlic over medium heat until the oil has been infused with the garlic, about 1 minute, then remove and discard the garlic. Add the lemon grass, lime leaves, and chicken, and stir-fry until the chicken turns white and just loses its raw look. Add the yogurt mixture and stir-fry until the chicken turns completely white and the sauce has cooked down into a coating, not floating, cream.

Stir in the sugar, mint leaves, and fish sauce. You also need to add the cayenne pepper at this time, but remember: the amount of cayenne pepper you add will determine a 1- to 5-star heat factor. I can't go past a ** but my wife, Treena, can manage at least a *****, or 1 full teaspoonful! Pour in the lime juice to suit your taste. Remove from the heat and keep warm.

Turn the sliced cabbages and mushrooms into a hot skillet with just enough chicken stock or water to create a little steam. Toss until heated through, about 2 minutes.

**To serve:** Lay the cabbage on warm dinner plates and spoon the sauced chicken on top. Serve with a small bowl of steaming short-grain white rice on the side.

Nutritional Profile per Serving: Calories—231; % calories from fat—23%; fat (gm)—6 or 9% daily value; saturated fat (gm)—1; sodium (mg)—470; cholesterol (mg)—46; carbohydrates (gm)—21; dietary fiber (gm)—6.

# POLLO DI PRINCE

*The tang of a small amount of creamy goat cheese makes this a very special treat. I suggest you serve it with a good salad.*

*Time Estimate: Hands-on, 1 hour*
*Serves 4*

## BREAD

4 teaspoons goat cheese
1 teaspoon chopped fresh basil
1/8 teaspoon cayenne pepper
4 slices Italian bread (1/2 inch or 1.25 cm thick)

## TOMATO SAUCE

1 teaspoon light olive oil with a dash of toasted sesame oil
1 cup chopped onion
1 clove garlic, bashed, peeled, and chopped
2 medium carrots, peeled and diced
2 tablespoons low-sodium tomato paste
1 (28-ounce or 800-gm) can plum tomatoes, diced, juice reserved
2 teaspoons dried basil
1/8 teaspoon freshly ground sea salt
1/4 teaspoon freshly ground black pepper
1 tablespoon arrowroot mixed with 2 tablespoons de-alcoholized white wine (slurry)
2 tablespoons chopped fresh parsley

## CHICKEN

4 (4-ounce or 115-gm) boneless chicken breasts with skin
1/8 teaspoon freshly ground sea salt
1/4 teaspoon freshly ground black pepper
1 teaspoon light olive oil with a dash of toasted sesame oil
8 ounces (225 gm) fresh mushrooms
1 teaspoon dried sage
1 tablespoon freshly squeezed lemon juice
1/8 teaspoon cayenne pepper
1/2 cup de-alcoholized white wine

## GARNISH

1/2 cup chopped fresh parsley

**For the bread:** In a small bowl, mix the goat cheese with the basil and cayenne pepper. Spread one-quarter of the goat cheese mixture on each bread slice. Just before serving, set under the preheated broiler for 2 minutes.

**For the sauce:** Heat the oil in a large skillet and fry the onions, garlic, and carrots over medium-high heat for 2 minutes. Add the tomato paste and cook until it darkens somewhat. Stir in the tomatoes, basil, salt, and pepper, and bring to a vigorous boil. Reduce the heat, cover, and simmer for 10 minutes or until the carrots are tender. Remove from heat and stir in the arrowroot slurry. Return to the heat and stir until thickened. Add the parsley and keep warm.

**For the chicken:** Sprinkle the breasts with the salt and pepper. Heat the oil in a medium frying pan and cook the chicken breasts 4 minutes on each side. Add the mushrooms and sage, cover and cook 2 more minutes. Transfer the chicken breasts to a warm plate and remove and discard the skin. Transfer the mushrooms to a small bowl and sprinkle them with the lemon juice and cayenne pepper. Tip the fat out of the frying pan and discard. Place the pan back on the burner and deglaze with the wine. Add the warmed wine from the pan to the tomato sauce.

**To serve:** Spread the garnish parsley out on a flat plate. Pour a bed of the tomato sauce on each warm dinner plate. Take a slice of the bread and press the toasted cheese side into the tomato sauce and then into the parsley and set in the center of the plate in the tomato sauce. Place a chicken breast on the bread and spoon the reserved mushrooms over the top. Garnish with a sprinkle of parsley and serve.

Nutritional Profile per Serving: Calories—350; % calories from fat—19%; fat (gm)—7 or 11% daily value; saturated fat (gm)—2; sodium (mg)—515; cholesterol (mg)—67; carbohydrates (gm)—40; dietary fiber (gm)—7.

# POULET BASQUAISE

*I've often used this recipe as an example of how fresh foods in season were simply assembled in a geographically isolated area between France and Italy to become a significant flavor combination that identified this region. This is a "food-of-the-people" dish—nothing* haute cuisine *about it. There's no need for other vegetables . . . it's complete as is.*

*Time Estimate: Hands-on, 50 minutes;
   unsupervised, 50 minutes*
*Serves 4*

1 (3 ½-pound or 1.6-kg) whole chicken
2 teaspoons light olive oil with a dash of toasted sesame
   oil
2 cloves garlic, bashed, peeled, and chopped
2/3 cup finely diced mushrooms
1 (6-ounce or 175-gm) can low-sodium tomato paste
2 green bell peppers, seeded and diced
1 red bell pepper, seeded and diced
3/4 cup de-alcoholized dry white wine
4 large tomatoes, seeded and diced
Freshly ground black pepper to taste
8 cups water
1¼ cups uncooked long-grain white rice
3 sliced mushrooms
1 tablespoon sliced fresh basil leaves
2 tablespoons chopped fresh parsley
1 teaspoon baking powder

Cut the chicken into 3 pieces: the whole breast and two legs and thighs. Remove all the skin. In a large, low-sided casserole, heat half of the oil and sauté the garlic and mushrooms over medium-high heat for 2 minutes. Turn out onto a side dish and reserve.

Pour the remaining oil into the casserole, turn the heat up high, and brown the chicken pieces, turning often. Stir in the tomato paste, making sure the chicken gets coated. The tomato paste caramelizes and turns brown: the Maillard reaction. Add the diced peppers. Make sure you dredge up any brown residue off the bottom of the pot. This provides a smokiness that gives depth of taste without fat.

Pour in the wine, the reserved mushrooms, and the tomatoes. Grind the fresh black pepper to taste. Make sure the chicken breast is turned meat side down into the pot to ensure thorough cooking. Cover the pot and simmer over medium heat for 35 minutes.

While the Poulet Basquaise is simmering, bring the water to a boil in a medium saucepan. Add the rice, return to a boil, cover, and simmer for 10 minutes. Drain the rice through a metal strainer or colander. To keep the rice hot, add 2 inches (5 cm) of hot water to the pan. Put the strainer full of cooked rice on top, cover with a small lid, and keep on medium heat for up to 15 minutes. The rice will continue to cook in a gentle steam and will be perfectly fluffy without becoming overcooked.

After the chicken is done, transfer it from the pot to a cutting board and carve it into nice chunks. By cooking the chicken in large pieces you get a much more attractive and succulent piece of meat. Drop the chicken pieces back into the sauce. Stir in the sliced mushrooms, chopped basil, and parsley—a fresh, fieldlike touch to your finished dish! And now an ingredient that will make an astonishing taste difference: stir in the baking powder. This smooths out the flavor, canceling any acidity and allowing the sweetness to come through.

**To serve:** Put the cooked rice on a large serving platter, make a well in the middle, and fill with the chicken.

Nutritional Profile per Serving: Calories—523; % calories from fat—17%; fat (gm)—10 or 15% daily value; saturated fat (gm)—2; sodium (mg)—244; cholesterol (mg)—75; carbohydrates (gm)—74; dietary fiber (gm)—7.

# ROAST CHICKEN AND VEGETABLES

*I often forget how satisfying this very simple meal is. Try it soon!*

**Creamy gravy**
**Pale yellow**
**(Color/Aroma/Texture)**

**Potatoes**
**White**
**(Texture)**

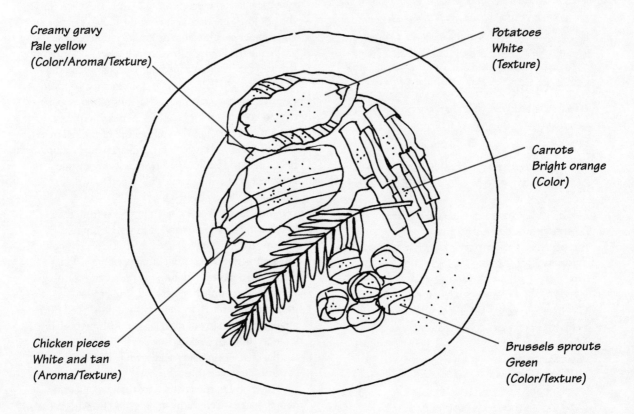

**Carrots**
**Bright orange**
**(Color)**

**Chicken pieces**
**White and tan**
**(Aroma/Texture)**

**Brussels sprouts**
**Green**
**(Color/Texture)**

*Time Estimate: Hands-on, 30 minutes;*
  *unsupervised, 90 minutes*
*Serves 4*

1 (3-pound or 1.4-kg) whole chicken
4 large russet potatoes, scrubbed
8 ounces (225 gm) Brussels sprouts
8 ounces (225 gm) carrots, peeled and cut in 1-inch
   (2.5-cm) pieces

1 cup low-sodium chicken stock (page 286)
1 tablespoon arrowroot mixed with 2 tablespoons de-
   alcoholized white wine (slurry)
1 tablespoon chopped fresh parsley

Preheat the oven to 350°F (180°C). Put the chicken on a rack in a roasting pan and roast until the internal temperature reaches 165°F (75°C), about 90 minutes. Put the potatoes in the oven to bake while the chicken is roasting.

Just before the chicken is done, put 1 inch (2.5 cm) of water in a steamer and steam the Brussels sprouts and carrots until tender, about 10 minutes. They should be perfectly cooked when the chicken is ready to serve.

Remove the chicken from the oven, transfer to a plate, and keep warm. Put the roasting pan on a stovetop burner. Pour in the chicken stock, scrape up the pan residues completely, and pour through a sieve into a fat strainer. Pour the juices into a medium saucepan and bring to a boil. Take the saucepan off the heat. Add the arrowroot slurry, return to the heat, and stir until the gravy thickens. Strain out any meat scraps and pour into a serving bowl or gravy boat.

Just before serving, slice the potatoes in half lengthwise, put on a baking sheet, and pop under the broiler until just golden brown, about 4 minutes.

**To serve:** Put the chicken on a flat surface, remove the skin, and separate the chicken into pieces. Trim the leg ends with poultry scissors. Divide the meat, potatoes, and vegetables among the 4 plates and spoon on the gravy. Don't forget to sprinkle with the parsley; it distracts attention from the skinless meat. A branch of rosemary adds a wonderful fresh aroma and drama!

| Nutritional Profile per Serving | | | |
|---|---|---|---|
| | **Classic** | **Minimax** | **Daily Value** |
| Calories | 757 | 471 | |
| Calories from fat | 41% | 16% | |
| Fat (gm) | 34 | 8 | 3% |
| Saturated fat (gm) | 11 | 2 | 12% |
| Sodium (mg) | 349 | 164 | 7% |
| Cholesterol (mg) | 148 | 98 | 33% |
| Carbohydrates (gm) | 63 | 58 | 19% |
| Dietary fiber (gm) | 8 | 7 | 30% |
| Classic compared: Roasted Chicken with Vegetables and Creamy Gravy | | | |

# Roast Turkey with Apple-Orange Gravy, Swiss Chard, and Sweet Potatoes

—— ⌘ ——

*A revolutionary roast turkey: bread-and-sausage–based stuffing is replaced by aromatic spices and fruits that infuse the turkey meat with flavor. The traditional pan-drippings gravy becomes a turkey-meat broth spiked with citrus. And the pièce de résistance? A cranberry relish studded with crisp red chard and the deep tang of balsamic vinegar. I hope you'll celebrate this recipe with me: a feast fit for kings and queens and one of the healthiest meals you'll ever celebrate.*

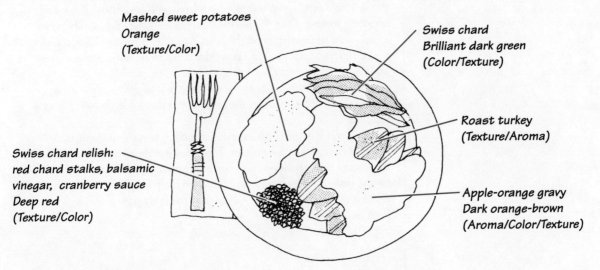

Mashed sweet potatoes
Orange
(Texture/Color)

Swiss chard
Brilliant dark green
(Color/Texture)

Roast turkey
(Texture/Aroma)

Swiss chard relish:
red chard stalks, balsamic
vinegar, cranberry sauce
Deep red
(Texture/Color)

Apple-orange gravy
Dark orange-brown
(Aroma/Color/Texture)

*Time Estimate: Hands-on, 1 hour;
    unsupervised, 2 hours*
*Serves 6 with ample leftover turkey*

SIDE DISHES

3 pounds Swiss chard
3 tablespoons balsamic vinegar
6 medium yams
1/2 cup jellied cranberry sauce

TURKEY

1 teaspoon light olive oil with a dash of toasted sesame
    oil
1/2 cup coarsely chopped onion
1 (10-pound or 4.5-kg) turkey, wings and liver removed,
    and neck, gizzard, and heart reserved

2 cups unsweetened, unfiltered apple juice
2 cups unsweetened orange juice
1 tablespoon all-purpose flour
1 onion, peeled and stuck with 6 whole cloves
1 orange, slashed with a small knife several times
1/2 cup fresh thyme leaves
1/2 cup fresh sage leaves
1/2 cup water
2 tablespoons arrowroot mixed with 2 tablespoons
    water (slurry)

Cut the red stems off the chard leaves. Finely chop the stems, mix them in a small bowl with the vinegar, and marinate for 2 hours. Reserve the leaves separately.

To make turkey stock for the gravy: Heat the oil in a large skillet over low heat and fry the chopped onion until soft, about 10 minutes. Add the turkey wings, neck, gizzard, and heart, and the apple and orange juice. Bring to a boil, reduce the heat, and simmer, uncovered, for 1 hour. This should yield 2 cups stock. Strain and set aside.

Preheat the oven to 325°F (165°C). Rinse the turkey and its cavity thoroughly. Dust the top of the bird with flour. Stuff the cavity with the clove-studded onion, orange, and fresh herbs. Tuck the drumsticks back into the metal clip (often provided with the bird), or tie the legs together with string. Put on a rack in a roasting pan, add the water, and roast for 2½ hours, or until the internal temperature of the thigh is 175° F (77°C). Check every half hour, and if the pan is dry, add another 1/2 cup of water. Remove from the oven and let stand about 20 minutes before carving.

After the turkey has been cooking for 1½ hours, place the yams in the oven with the turkey and bake for 40 minutes. Remove and peel off the skin. Mash them in a small bowl and keep warm until ready to serve, or simply cut in half.

Pour the chopped chard stalks and vinegar into a small pan. Over low heat, stir in the cranberry sauce until completely incorporated and just heat through, about 5 minutes. Don't cook the sauce until it becomes syrupy. Remove from the heat and transfer to a small bowl.

To complete the gravy: Put the roasting pan full of turkey cooking juices on a stovetop burner on medium heat. Pour in the turkey-apple-orange stock, scraping the pan until you have stirred in all the flavor-filled pan residue. Strain in a fat-separator cup, allowing the fat to rise to the top, about 5 minutes.

Pour the separated turkey juice from the strainer cup into a medium saucepan, making sure not to include any of the separated fat, and heat to a boil. Remove from the heat. Stir in the arrowroot slurry, return to the heat, and stir until thickened. Remove from the heat and set aside.

Place the reserved chard leaves in a steamer, cover, and cook for 4 minutes. Remove from the heat and set aside.

**To serve:** Carve the turkey into thin slices, put 3 on each dinner plate, and ladle with the gravy. Spoon a mound of the yams and chard on the side and garnish with the chard relish.

| Nutritional Profile per Serving | | | |
|---|---|---|---|
| | Classic | Minimax | Daily Value |
| Calories | 1,173 | 600 | |
| Calories from fat | 42% | 18% | |
| Fat (gm) | 55 | 12 | 18% |
| Saturated fat (gm) | 20 | 3 | 15% |
| Sodium (mg) | 1,594 | 496 | 21% |
| Cholesterol (mg) | 336 | 141 | 47% |
| Carbohydrates (gm) | 91 | 68 | 23% |
| Dietary fiber (gm) | 9 | 8 | 32% |
| Classic compared: Roast Turkey with Pan Gravy and Candied Yams | | | |

# SLOPPY JOES

*Everyone raised in North America seems to have a Sloppy Joe in his gastronomic experience, and every recipe has its own secret ingredient. I've got several in this recipe and they all add up to Minimax flavor with much less fat and refined carbohydrate. It's also a lot of fun and easy to fix! A crispy coleslaw dressed with strained yogurt goes nicely with this.*

Time Estimate: Hands-on, 20 minutes;
  unsupervised, 20 minutes
Serves 4

1 teaspoon light olive oil with a dash of toasted sesame oil
1 cup chopped onion
2 cloves garlic, bashed, peeled, and chopped
1/4 cup chopped carrot
1/4 cup chopped celery
1/2 cup green bell pepper, seeded and finely chopped
8 ounces (225 gm) mushrooms, chopped
6 ounces (175 gm) leanest ground turkey breast
6 ounces (175 gm) leanest ground beef
1 tablespoon chopped fresh oregano or 1 teaspoon dried
1/8 teaspoon freshly ground sea salt
1/4 teaspoon freshly ground black pepper
1 tablespoon Worcestershire sauce
1 tablespoon red wine vinegar
1/4 cup low-sodium ketchup
1 cup low-sodium tomato sauce
4 whole-wheat hamburger buns

Heat the oil in a large skillet and fry the onions over medium-high heat for 1 minute. Add the garlic and the rest of the vegetables, and cook until just tender, about 5 minutes. Tip the vegetables into a bowl and set aside.

Combine the turkey and beef, and brown in the same skillet. Sprinkle in the oregano and return the cooked vegetables to the pan. Season with the salt and pepper. Add the Worcestershire, vinegar, ketchup, and tomato sauce. Cover and simmer for 20 minutes. Put the hamburger buns into a low-heat oven to toast for the last few minutes of cooking.

**To serve:** Place the bottom half of a toasted bun on a plate and spoon the Sloppy Joe mixture over the top. Set the top just slightly over to one side to expose the filling.

Nutritional Profile per Serving: Calories—349; % calories from fat—21%; fat (gm)—8 or 12% daily value; saturated fat (gm)—2; sodium (mg)—586; cholesterol (mg)—49; carbohydrates (gm)—45; dietary fiber (gm)—7.

## GROUND TURKEY

All you have to do is look: it's there in its little plastic packet waiting for you to buy it. Leaner (especially in the saturated fat department) and less expensive than ground beef, turkey is a good substitute in many dishes. Don't wait until next Thanksgiving! My personal choice (that means you are not under any pressure to agree) is to buy turkey breast or thigh, according to the recipe, and then grind it when I need it.

## WHOLE-WHEAT BUNS

Every bit of fiber helps! When you look for whole-grain buns, don't just grab the first brown-colored bread you see. Brown color might just indicate that there's a lot of molasses in the recipe. let me suggest that you read the label. You'll get the most nutrients if one of the first ingredients listed is 100% stone-ground whole-wheat flour. The next-best thing is whole-wheat or other whole-grain flour (not stone-ground).

# FILLET OF BEEF MEURICE

*Treena and I first ate this dish at the famous Hotel Meurice in Paris, France. It was in the days when cream, butter, eggs, beef, and pâté de foie gras were "just part of my job." Now things have changed, and so have we! Accompany with lightly steamed fresh spinach and sliced red tomatoes on the side.*

*Time Estimate: Hands-on, 25 minutes; unsupervised, 1 hour*
Serves 2

## RICE PILAF

1½ cups low-sodium beef stock (page 286)
1/8 cup uncooked wild rice
1/4 cup uncooked long-grain white rice
1/8 cup uncooked pearl barley
1 bay leaf
1 (4-inch or 10-cm) sprig tarragon
1 (4-inch or 10-cm) sprig parsley
1 tablespoon Dijon mustard
1 teaspoon chopped fresh tarragon

## FILLET AND SAUCE

1/8 teaspoon freshly ground sea salt
1/4 teaspoon freshly ground black pepper or more to taste
8 ounces (225 gm) beef tenderloin fillet
1/2 teaspoon light olive oil with a dash of toasted sesame oil
1 tablespoon chopped shallots
1 teaspoon dried tarragon
1/4 cup de-alcoholized white wine
1/4 cup wine vinegar
1/2 cup low-sodium beef stock (page 286)
2 teaspoons cornstarch mixed with 2 tablespoons de-alcoholized white wine (slurry)
1/3 cup strained yogurt (page 288)

## GARNISH

1 teaspoon chopped fresh tarragon

**The pilaf:** Preheat the oven to 375°F (190°C). In a medium, ovenproof saucepan, bring the beef stock to a boil. Add the wild rice, cover, and cook over low heat for 15 minutes. Stir in the long-grain rice and pearl barley. Lay the bay leaf, tarragon, and parsley on top, and bake, uncovered, in the preheated oven for about 45 minutes. When done, remove the herbs and stir in the mustard and chopped tarragon.

**The fillet and sauce:** Sprinkle the salt and pepper on the fillets. Heat a medium nonstick frying pan over high heat until it's nice and hot. Pour the oil into the pan and cook the fillets for 2 to 4 minutes on each side or until done to your taste. Remove the meat and keep warm. Add the shallots and tarragon to the same pan and fry for 2 minutes over medium heat. Pour in the de-alcoholized wine and wine vinegar to deglaze the pan. Now add the beef stock, bring to a boil, and reduce by half, about 5 minutes. Pour in the cornstarch slurry, off the heat, then return to the heat to thicken, about 30 seconds. Remove from the heat, add two ice cubes to cool slightly, then stir into the strained yogurt.

**To serve:** Place the rice and meat on warm plates, coat with the sauce, and sprinkle with fresh tarragon.

Nutritional Profile per Serving: Calories—457; % calories from fat—22%; fat (gm)—11 or 17% daily value; saturated fat (gm)—4; sodium (mg)—412; cholesterol (mg)—66; carbohydrates (gm)—51; dietary fiber (gm)—3.

# BROILED HAMBURGERS

⁘

*A Minimax breakthrough: the combination of the bright notes of raisins, lemon juice, curry powder, and garlic with the leanest ground beef is the beginning of a beautiful hamburger for your low fat life-style. Of course, once my broiled burgers are ensconced in family dining rooms across the United States, can the fast-food purveyor be far behind? I hope not!*

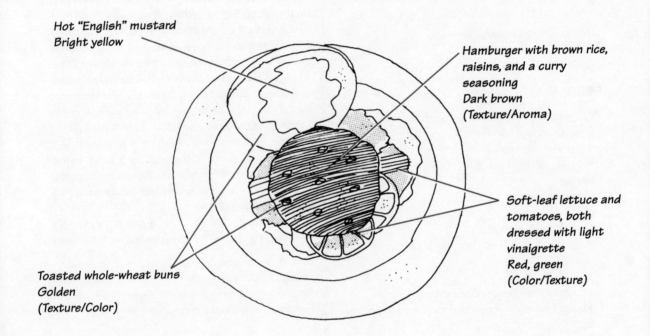

Hot "English" mustard
Bright yellow

Hamburger with brown rice, raisins, and a curry seasoning
Dark brown
(Texture/Aroma)

Soft-leaf lettuce and tomatoes, both dressed with light vinaigrette
Red, green
(Color/Texture)

Toasted whole-wheat buns
Golden
(Texture/Color)

*Time Estimate: Hands-on, 30 minutes*
*Serves 4*

1/2 teaspoon light olive oil with a dash of toasted sesame oil
1½ cups chopped onion
2 cloves garlic, bashed, peeled, and chopped
1 tablespoon curry powder
1/4 cup dark raisins
1 tablespoon freshly squeezed lemon juice
2 tablespoons chopped fresh parsley
1 tablespoon water

1 cup cooked brown rice
8 ounces (225 gm) ground beef, the leanest possible—freshly ground at home is the best
1 teaspoon light olive oil
4 teaspoons hot English mustard
4 whole-wheat hamburger buns
1 large tomato
4 lettuce leaves
2 teaspoons Vinaigrette Salad Dressing (page 276)

Heat the 1/2 teaspoon oil in a large skillet over high heat and cook the onions until just translucent, about 5 minutes. Stir in the garlic and curry powder, and cook 1 minute. Add the raisins, lemon juice, and parsley; mix well and transfer to a large bowl. Pour the water into the hot pan, scrape up the pan residues, and add this liquid to the cooked seasonings.

Stir the cooked rice into the seasonings. Transfer the mixture to a food processor and purée for 1 minute until well blended, but not a paste. Return the mixture to the bowl, add the freshly ground beef, and mix thoroughly.

Shape the hamburgers into 4 patties and lightly brush with the 1 teaspoon olive oil. Heat a large nonstick skillet and, without adding any oil, cook the burgers on medium-high for about 4 minutes on each side.

**To serve:** Spread mustard on each bun, slide in the cooked burgers, and garnish with the tomato and lettuce. Drizzle with the vinaigrette for extra zest.

| Nutritional Profile per Serving | | | |
|---|---|---|---|
| | Classic | Minimax | Daily Value |
| Calories | 604 | 354 | |
| Calories from fat | 51% | 23% | |
| Fat (gm) | 34 | 9 | 14% |
| Saturated fat (gm) | 10 | 2 | 10% |
| Sodium (mg) | 1,109 | 310 | 13% |
| Cholesterol (mg) | 86 | 32 | 11% |
| Carbohydrates (gm) | 45 | 53 | 18% |
| Dietary fiber (gm) | 53 | 6 | 24% |
| Classic compared: Hamburger | | | |

# Hard-Hat Pizza

※

*This hearty crustless pizza was inspired by the food preferences of Scott Keck, a construction worker whom we met in our travels. Beef, tomato, sweet potato, and crisp greens are put together to make a satisfying, low-fat, and unique all-in-one meal.*

*Time Estimate: Hands-on, 30 minutes;*
  *unsupervised, 90 minutes*
*Serves 4*

8 ounces (225 gm) beef bottom round
1½ large yams, preferably garnet
10 large Savoy cabbage leaves, cores removed
1/4 teaspoon freshly grated nutmeg
1/4 teaspoon freshly ground black pepper
4 plum tomatoes, sliced lengthwise
4 basil leaves, thinly sliced
Freshly ground sea salt
Freshly ground black pepper

## SAUCE

1 teaspoon light olive oil with a dash of toasted sesame oil
1 clove garlic, bashed, peeled, and chopped
8 ounces (225 gm) low-sodium tomato sauce
1 tablespoon chopped fresh basil leaves
1 tablespoon chopped fresh parsley stalks
1/8 teaspoon freshly grated nutmeg
1/4 teaspoon freshly ground black pepper
1/2 cup de-alcoholized white wine
1 tablespoon arrowroot mixed with 2 tablespoons de-alcoholized white wine (slurry)
1 plum tomato, finely diced
1/2 teaspoon baking powder
1 tablespoon chopped fresh parsley
1/2 teaspoon horseradish

Roast the beef at 350°F (180°C) for 25 minutes. The meat thermometer should measure 140°F (60°C). Remove the roast from the oven, let it cool for 15 minutes, and then slice it into thin strips.

Bake the yams for 1 hour at 350°F (180°C).

Remove from the oven, allow to cool, peel, and slice 1 inch (2.5 cm) thick.

Place the cabbage leaves in a steamer and steam for 2 to 3 minutes. Make a bed of 5 leaves on a large ovenproof plate or pizza pan. The leaves should fully cover the base of the plate and have a slight overhang. Lay the yam slices over the leaves, sprinkle with the nutmeg and pepper, and cover with 2 cabbage leaves.

Layer tomato slices on top of the cabbage and sprinkle with the basil, salt, and pepper. Cover with the remaining cabbage leaves. Trim the overhanging leaves and place an inverted ovenproof plate on top. Your pizza is now ready to go into the oven!

Place the covered pizza in the oven and bake at 350°F (180°C) for 20 minutes.

**The sauce:** Heat the oil in a large saucepan and cook the garlic, tomato sauce, basil, parsley stalks, nutmeg, and pepper over medium-high heat for 2 minutes. Add the wine and cook for 15 minutes over medium heat. Remove from the heat and add the diced tomato and strips of beef. Stir in the baking powder, parsley, and horseradish and keep warm.

**To serve:** Slice the pizza into quarters and serve on individual plates. Spoon a quarter of the sauce onto each serving.

Nutritional Profile per Serving: Calories—213; % calories from fat—16%; fat (gm)—4 or 6% daily value; saturated fat (gm)—1; sodium (mg)—125; cholesterol (mg)—30; carbohydrates (gm)—32; dietary fiber (gm)—5. ⬇

# KAREWAI STEAK PISCATELLA

*Can this steak compete with the American favorite: prime rib with baked potato and Hollandaise sauce? Joe Piscatella, bestselling author of* Don't Eat Your Heart Out, *answers with a resounding "yes!"*

Time Estimate: Hands-on, 20 minutes
Serves 4

1½ cups uncooked orzo pasta
1 pound (450 gm) flank steak
1 tablespoon very coarsely ground black pepper
1 teaspoon light olive oil with a dash of toasted sesame oil
1 cup chopped onion
3 cloves garlic, bashed, peeled, and chopped
1 cup no-salt tomato sauce
1/2 cup de-alcoholized red wine
1 tablespoon balsamic vinegar
1/4 teaspoon freshly ground sea salt
5 tablespoons chopped fresh basil

Cook the orzo in a large pot of boiling water for 9 minutes, drain, and set aside. Time the cooking to coincide with the steak's completion.

Trim any fat or "silver" off the flank steak. Spread the coarsely ground pepper on a large cutting board. Press the flank steak on top of the pepper, on both sides, so that the pepper adheres to the meat. Heat a large skillet over high heat until it smokes. Brush with 1/4 teaspoon of the oil and brown the prepared steak for about 1 minute on each side. Remove from the heat and set aside.

In the same pan, pour in the rest of the oil and fry the onions for 1 minute. Add the garlic and cook over medium heat until the onions are translucent, about 4 minutes. Add the tomato sauce, wine, and vinegar to the pan, scraping up any brown bits, and bring to a boil. Add 2 tablespoons of the fresh basil. Lay the steak in the sauce and cook for 2 or 3 minutes per side, depending on how done you like your beef. It will remain more tender if you don't cook it too long. Remove the steak from the tomato-onion sauce and place on a cutting board with a gutter to catch the juices. Carve the steak across the grain in thin diagonal slices.

Add the cooked orzo, 2 more tablespoons of the basil, and any juice from the cutting board to the sauce and heat through.

**To serve:** Divide the pasta and sauce between 4 warm plates. Lay the meat slices on top of the pasta and sprinkle with the remaining basil.

Nutritional Profile per Serving: Calories—422; % calories from fat—22%; fat (gm)—10 or 16% daily value; saturated fat (gm)—3; sodium (mg)—213; cholesterol (mg)—65; carbohydrates (gm)—49; dietary fiber (gm)—3.

# Meat Loaf
# with Mushroom Sauce

*Adding flavor is a basic tenet of Minimax cooking. This meat loaf is a veritable sampler of added flavor: flavorful vegetables, herbs, spices, and yes—cocoa!*

*Time Estimate: Hands-on, 1 hour;
   unsupervised, 1 hour, 10 minutes*
*Serves 10*

## MEAT LOAF

1/2 cup nonfat milk
1½ cups torn pieces whole-wheat bread
1 teaspoon light olive oil with a dash of toasted sesame oil
1 cup chopped onion
3 cloves garlic, bashed, peeled, and chopped
1/2 cup finely chopped red bell pepper
1/2 cup finely chopped carrot
1/4 cup finely chopped celery
3 tablespoons low-sodium tomato paste
1 pound (450 gm) leanest ground beef (9% fat)
1 pound (450 gm) leanest ground turkey breast
1 medium russet potato, peeled, boiled, and roughly
   mashed
2 egg whites
1 teaspoon dried thyme
1 teaspoon dried oregano
1 teaspoon ground cumin
1/4 teaspoon allspice
1 tablespoon chili powder
1 tablespoon unsweetened Dutch-process cocoa powder
1 teaspoon freshly ground sea salt

## SIDE DISHES

2 large butternut squash, cut in half and seeded
1 tablespoon tarragon
1/2 teaspoon freshly ground black pepper
1/4 teaspoon freshly ground sea salt
5 cups broccoli florets
5 cups cauliflower florets

## SAUCE

1 teaspoon light olive oil with a dash of toasted sesame oil
1/4 cup finely chopped onion
1 clove garlic, bashed, peeled, and chopped
2 cups sliced mushrooms
1 tablespoon low-sodium tomato paste
1/4 teaspoon dried thyme
1/4 teaspoon dried oregano
1/4 teaspoon ground cumin
1 teaspoon unsweetened Dutch-process cocoa powder
1 teaspoon chili powder
1/4 teaspoon salt
2 cups low-sodium beef broth (page 286)
1 tablespoon arrowroot mixed with 2 tablespoons
   water (slurry)

**The meat loaf:** Preheat the oven to 375°F (190°C). Pour the milk over the bread and set aside to soak. Heat the oil in a medium frying pan over medium heat and fry the onions until they are wilted, about 2 minutes. Add the garlic and cook for 1 more minute. Add the peppers, carrots, and celery, and cook for 5 minutes or until the vegetables are tender. Turn the heat to medium-high and add the tomato paste, stirring until it begins to darken. Remove from the heat and set aside to cool slightly.

Combine the ground beef, ground turkey, mashed potato, softened bread, and egg whites in a large mixing bowl. Add the herbs, spices, cocoa, salt, and cooked vegetables, and mix thoroughly. Shape into a loaf and set into a nonstick 9 X 5 X 2-inch (23 X 13 X 5-cm) loaf pan. Bake in the preheated oven for 65 minutes. Remove and let the meat loaf cool for 10 minutes.

**The side dishes:** Place the squash, cut side down, on a baking sheet. Bake alongside the meat loaf until it's very soft, about 1 hour. Spoon the pulp out into a bowl and mash well. Stir in the tarragon, pepper, and 1/8 teaspoon of the salt, and keep warm until you are ready to serve.

Microwave the cauliflower with 1/4 cup water for 4 minutes in a waxed-paper-covered glass dish. Add the broccoli, sprinkle with the remaining salt, and microwave another 3 minutes. (Or steam the cauliflower for 3 minutes, add the broccoli, sprinkle with the remaining salt, and steam for 3 more minutes.)

**The sauce:** Heat the oil in a medium saucepan over medium-high heat and fry the onion until it wilts. Add the garlic and mushrooms, and cook for 2 minutes. Stir in the tomato paste and keep stirring until it darkens, about 2 more minutes. Add the herbs, cumin, cocoa, chili powder, and salt, and cook for 1 minute. Deglaze the pan with the beef broth and allow to simmer very gently until just before you are ready to serve dinner. Remove from the heat and stir in the arrowroot slurry. Return to the stove and stir until the sauce clears and thickens, which will happen almost instantly. You can add any juices that have accumulated under the meat loaf, but be sure you skim off any fat.

**To serve:** Place a generous 1/2-inch (1.25-cm) slice of meat loaf on each warm plate, giving each person about 5 ounces (140 gm) of meat. Spoon the sauce over the meat and arrange the squash and vegetables on the side. The extra sauce can be presented at the table in a sauceboat.

Nutritional Profile per Serving: Calories—339; % calories from fat—22%; fat (gm)—8 or 13% daily value; saturated fat (gm)—2; sodium (mg)—477; cholesterol (mg)—53; carbohydrates (gm)—42; dietary fiber (gm)—13.

# STEAK DIANE
✤

*In the 1960s and 1970s, when most "gourmet" restaurants had table-side cooking with flames, Steak Diane was an all-time favorite. In this version, I've doused the conflagration, lessened the portion size, and reduced the fat, so that the classic's 1,036 calories and 74 grams of fat per serving are now a mere 551 calories and 11 grams of fat.*

*Time Estimate: Hands-on, 60 minutes*
*Serves 2*

8 ounces (225 gm) beef tenderloin or eye of round
1/8 teaspoon freshly ground sea salt
1/4 teaspoon freshly ground black pepper
4 ounces (115 gm) red new potatoes, quartered

8 ounces (225 gm) fresh green beans, topped and tailed
Freshly grated nutmeg to taste
1/4 teaspoon freshly squeezed lemon juice
1 teaspoon light olive oil with a dash of toasted sesame oil
1 clove garlic, bashed, peeled, and finely chopped
2 shallots, peeled and finely chopped
1/2 cup chopped fresh parsley
2 small plum tomatoes, sliced
2 tablespoons Worcestershire sauce
2/3 cup low-sodium beef stock (page 286)

Tenderize the beef by pounding it with your fist or a mallet. The thickness should be less than 1/4inch (.75 cm). Sprinkle with the salt and pepper.

Place the potatoes in a steamer tray and steam, covered, over boiling water for 14 minutes. Add the green beans to the steamer, sprinkle with nutmeg to taste, and steam, covered, for 6 minutes. Separate the potatoes and the beans, sprinkle the beans with the lemon juice, and set aside.

Heat half the oil in a large skillet over medium-high heat and drag both sides of the tenderloin through the oil. Then brown it quickly, not more than 30 seconds on each side, and transfer to a plate. Keep warm.

In the same skillet over medium-high heat, cook the garlic and shallots in the remaining oil for 2 minutes. Add half of the parsley and the tomato slices, and turn the tomato slices to heat through. Transfer the tomatoes to a plate and set aside. Pour the Worcestershire sauce and beef stock into the same skillet and boil until reduced by a third. Add the browned tenderloin, the remaining parsley, and the steamed potatoes, and make sure they are all coated with the sauce.

**To serve:** Cut the beef into two pieces. Place one piece on each warm dinner plate and put potatoes, tomatoes, and green beans on the side. Pour the pan juices over the top and serve.

Nutritional Profile per Serving: Calories—551; % calories from fat—19%; fat (gm)—11 or 18% daily value; saturated fat (gm)—4; sodium (mg)—413; cholesterol (mg)—65; carbohydrates (gm)—80; dietary fiber (gm)—11.

# Scottish Beef Collops

※

*This is real home-style cooking: thin slices of potato, beef, and mushrooms in a rich sauce. So satisfying and comfortable, with only 280 calories and 5 grams of fat per serving, compared to the classic's 730 calories and 41 grams of fat. Cook it in a pretty serving dish that you can bring directly to the table. Tiny green peas sprinkled with mint or finely shredded steamed carrot are great color contrasts on the side. Incidentally, the word* collops *comes from the French word* escallop, *meaning thin slices.*

Time Estimate: Hands-on, 50 minutes;
    unsupervised, 65 minutes
Serves 6

1¼ pounds (565 gm) beef bottom round steak
2 teaspoons light olive oil with a dash of toasted sesame
    oil
3 cups chopped onions
4 ounces (115 gm) mushrooms, finely chopped
2 tablespoons all-purpose flour
2 pickled walnuts, finely chopped
2 tablespoons chopped fresh thyme
1¼ cups low-sodium beef stock (page 286)
4 ounces (115 gm) mushrooms, thinly sliced
1½ pounds (680 gm) potatoes, peeled and cut into
    1/4-inch (.75-cm) slices

GARNISH

1 tablespoon chopped fresh parsley
Carrot shavings

Preheat the oven to 350°F (180°C). Cut the beef into 1/4-inch slices, across the grain, at a slight diagonal. You should have about 48 slices.

In a low-sided casserole dish, heat half of the oil over medium-high heat and cook the onions until they're soft and slightly brown, about 10 minutes. Transfer the onions to a plate and set aside. Pour the remaining oil into the same casserole over medium-high heat and cover the bottom with half of the beef slices, letting them brown on both sides. Transfer the cooked beef to a plate. Add the rest of the beef and brown it on both sides. Transfer all the cooked beef, the cooked onions, the chopped mushrooms, flour, walnuts, and thyme to a bowl and mix well. Rinse the sides and bottom of the casserole with the beef stock, scraping up any brown residue. Pour into a bowl and reserve.

Spread half of the beef mixture over the bottom of the casserole. Cover with half of the sliced mushrooms and half of the sliced potatoes. Repeat with layers of the remaining beef mixture and sliced mushrooms, and top with the remaining potatoes. Pour the reserved beef stock over the top, cover, and bake in the oven for 40 minutes.

**To serve:** Sprinkle with the parsley and carrot shavings and bring the casserole to the table to spoon onto the plates.

Nutritional Profile per Serving: Calories—280; % calories from fat—18%; fat (gm)—5 or 8% daily value; saturated fat (gm)—1; sodium (mg)—57; cholesterol (mg)—50; carbohydrates (gm)—35; dietary fiber (gm)—4. ⬇

## Pickled Walnuts Substitute

If you can't find this ingredient, you can use 6 medium, pitted black olives marinated in 1/4 cup of cider vinegar and 1 tablespoon of molasses for 3 hours. The marinated olives have a slightly different texture but very similar flavor.

# KARE POAKA

⌘

*I created this sweet and spicy pork curry in honor of the Queen Mother of England, who visited my National Food and Wine Center in New Zealand in 1963. The name is taken from the native Maori words for "curried pork." Royalty are not permitted to taste things in passing, but she said she loved the aroma!*

Time Estimate: Hands-on, 35 minutes;
    unsupervised, 30 minutes
Serves 4

## COCONUT CREAM

2/3 cup strained yogurt (page 288)
1/4 teaspoon coconut extract
1 teaspoon pure maple syrup

## PORK CURRY

1 teaspoon light olive oil with a dash of toasted sesame oil
12 ounces (350 gm) pork shoulder, trimmed of all fat
    and cut into 1-inch (2.5-cm) cubes
1 medium onion, peeled and finely diced
1 clove garlic, bashed, peeled, and chopped
1 green bell pepper, seeded and cut into 1-inch (2.5-cm)
    dice
1 red bell pepper, seeded and cut into 1-inch (2.5-cm) dice
2 medium sweet potatoes, peeled and cut into 1-inch
    (2.5-cm) dice
1 tablespoon curry powder
1½ cups low-sodium chicken stock (page 286)
1/4 teaspoon coconut extract
1/4 cup low-sodium tomato sauce
1 bay leaf
1 teaspoon garam masala (page 2)
1/4 teaspoon cayenne pepper
1 tablespoon freshly squeezed lemon juice
1/4 teaspoon freshly ground sea salt
1 tablespoon cornstarch mixed with 2 tablespoons
    water (slurry)
4 cups cooked long-grain white rice

## GARNISH

1 tablespoon chopped fresh parsley

**The coconut cream:** Combine all the ingredients with a wire whisk until smooth. Set aside.

**The pork curry:** Preheat the oven to 350°F (180°C). Brush 1/4 teaspoon of the oil in a large, high-sided, nonstick ovenproof skillet. Heat the pan over high heat and brown the pork on one side only. This will leave the other side unsealed to absorb sauce flavors. Remove the browned pork and set aside.

In the same pan heat the remaining oil and fry the onion over medium-high heat for 2 minutes before adding the garlic, peppers, and sweet potatoes. Sprinkle on the curry powder and cook for 3 more minutes, until the onion is translucent and the vegetables are coated with curry. Pour in the chicken stock, coconut extract, and tomato sauce, and stir to deglaze the pan. Add the pork and the bay leaf, and bring to a boil. Cover and bake in the preheated oven for 30 minutes.

Remove from the oven and stir in the garam masala, cayenne pepper, lemon juice, salt, and cornstarch slurry. Bring to a boil to thicken, about 30 seconds. Gently whisk in the coconut cream.

**To serve:** Spoon into a deep bowl with steamed rice on the side or into a nest of rice with the pork curry on top. In both cases, sprinkle with the chopped fresh parsley for garnish.

Nutritional Profile per Serving: Calories—492; % calories from fat—18%; fat (gm)—10 or 15% daily value; saturated fat (gm)—3; sodium (mg)—254; cholesterol (mg)—39; carbohydrates (gm)—76; dietary fiber (gm)—4.

# Pirogen with Beet Salad

*In many Slavic nations there is a common way of encasing meat or vegetable filling with an egg-enriched bread dough, either baking or deep-frying the package and serving instantly. I have, as usual, made some major changes, and the result is a bread crust spiked with seeds and a filling sparked by Worcestershire sauce. It has a very different taste, but the concept is intact.*

Time Estimate: Hands-on, 90 minutes;
  unsupervised, 1 hour, 45 minutes
Serves 6

## DOUGH

1 (.6-ounce or 18-gm) cake compressed yeast or
  1 package dry
1 cup lukewarm nonfat milk
1 teaspoon sugar
3/4 cup liquid egg substitute
3¾ cups all-purpose flour
1/8 teaspoon freshly ground sea salt
1/8 teaspoon freshly ground black pepper
1/4 cup plus 1½ teaspoons Seed Mix (page 195)
1 tablespoon light olive oil with a dash of toasted sesame
  oil
1 tablespoon nonfat milk

## SIDE DISH: BEET SALAD

1 (16-ounce or 450-gm) can beets, drained
1/3 cup cider vinegar
1 teaspoon fresh chives
1/2 cup strained yogurt (page 288)
1 tablespoon chopped fresh parsley

## FILLING

1/2 teaspoon light olive oil with a dash of toasted
  sesame oil
1 medium onion, peeled and minced
8 ounces (225 gm) cooked pork loin
2 tablespoons dried mushrooms, soaked in 1/2 cup
  boiling water for 30 minutes
3 tablespoons Worcestershire sauce

1 teaspoon dried dill weed
1/8 teaspoon freshly ground sea salt
1/4 teaspoon freshly ground black pepper
1 cup shredded green cabbage

**The dough:** Crumble the cake of yeast into a small bowl and stir in 1/4 cup of the lukewarm milk and the sugar until the yeast is dissolved. Slowly add the liquid egg substitute and the remaining milk.

Sift 3½ cups of the flour into a large bowl with the salt, pepper, and 1/4 cup of the seed mix. Pour in the yeast mixture and oil, and stir with a wooden spoon until the dough holds together. Turn the dough out onto a floured board and lightly knead until it no longer sticks to your fingers.

Put the dough back into the bowl, cover it, and let stand until almost doubled, about 1 hour.

**The beet salad:** In a large bowl, mix the beets, vinegar, and chives, and marinate for 30 minutes. Strain, discarding the marinade. Place the beets back into the bowl and stir in the yogurt and parsley.

**The filling:** Heat the oil in a medium sauté pan and cook the onion over medium-high heat until soft and slightly translucent, about 5 minutes. Remove and set aside.

Mince the pork and cooked onion through a meat grinder and into a large bowl. Stir in the mushrooms, Worcestershire sauce, dill weed, salt, pepper, and cabbage, and mix well.

**To assemble:** Lightly knead the dough on a lightly floured board, cut into 6 equal pieces, and shape into balls. Roll each dough piece into a short, thin oval, about 5 inches (13 cm) long and 1/8 inch (.5 cm) thick. Spoon 3 tablespoons of the filling on one half of each oval. Fold the other half over and crimp the edges. Turn the half oval onto its side on a baking sheet, crimped edge facing up. Cover and let stand 30 minutes.

Preheat the oven to 450°F (230°C). Brush the tops of the pirogen with the milk. Scatter the remaining seed mix evenly over the pirogen, pressing the seeds gently into the surface of the dough. Bake in the preheated oven for 15 minutes.

**To serve:** Serve the pirogen hot out of the oven with the beet salad on the side.

Nutritional Profile per Serving: Calories—550; % calories from fat—22%; fat (gm)—14 or 21% daily value; saturated fat (gm)—3; sodium (mg)—370; cholesterol (mg)—33; carbohydrates (gm)—78; dietary fiber (gm)—7. ⬆

# LOBSCOUSE

*"Lob" means a piece of meat and "scouse" has come to mean an inhabitant of the city of Liverpool, England, where lobscouse is a well-known meat and vegetable stew. This recipe is based on old clipper ship recipes of pickled pork and navy beans served with hardtack biscuits. (You may skip the hardtack biscuits in this version.)*

*Time Estimate: Hands-on, 45 minutes; unsupervised, 50 minutes*

*Serves 6*

1 teaspoon light olive oil with a dash of toasted sesame oil
12 ounces (350 gm) lean pork shoulder, cut into
   1/2-inch (1.5-cm) cubes
1 large onion, peeled and diced
2 carrots, sliced
1½ pounds (680 gm) potatoes, peeled and diced into
   1-inch (2.5-cm) cubes
1 tablespoon chopped fresh mint
1 tablespoon chopped fresh thyme
1/2 teaspoon freshly ground sea salt
1/2 cup yellow split peas
1/2 cup green split peas
3 cups low-sodium chicken stock (page 286)
3 bay leaves
1/2 teaspoon freshly ground black pepper
1 cup celery leaves

In an ovenproof casserole pot, heat the oil and fry the pork over medium-high heat until browned. Scatter the onions over the pork; do not stir. This allows the pork to continue to brown on the bottom of the pot and the onions to steam. Add the carrots and potatoes on top of the onions. Sprinkle in the mint, thyme, and salt. Add the yellow and green peas, and mix thoroughly, scraping the residue from the bottom of the pan.

Pour in the stock, push the bay leaves under the surface, and add the pepper to taste. Bring to a boil, cover, and simmer for 90 minutes. Garnish with the celery leaves before serving.

**To serve:** Ladle into bowls and enjoy.

Nutritional Profile per Serving: Calories—351; % calories from fat—22%; fat (gm)—9 or 13% daily value; saturated fat (gm)—3; sodium (mg)—249; cholesterol (mg)—36; carbohydrates (gm)—46; dietary fiber (gm)—6.

# Stuffed Pork Chops

⚜

I created the original dish, Pork Chops Ngauruhoe, for New Zealand Television in 1963 and over the years have had rave notices about it. The percentage of calories from fat for the Minimax version is really good for such a large meat serving. Oh yes, in case you're wondering, Ngauruhoe is one of New Zealand's largest mountains on the North Island.

Time Estimate: Hands-on, 60 minutes
Serves 4

SIDE DISHES: MASHED YAMS AND POTATOES;
   STEAMED BROCCOLI

1½ pounds (680 gm) yams
1½ pounds (680 gm) russet potatoes
1/4 cup finely chopped green onions, white part only
1 orange, peeled and chopped, peel reserved
1/8 teaspoon ground cloves
1/8 teaspoon freshly ground black pepper
1/2 pound (225 gm) steamed broccoli florets

STUFFING

1 tablespoon very fine orange zest threads
1½ teaspoons very fine gingerroot threads
1/4 apple, peeled, cored, and finely diced, preferably
   Granny Smith
2 tablespoons dark raisins
1/16 teaspoon ground cloves
1/8 teaspoon freshly ground sea salt
1/8 teaspoon freshly ground white peppercorns
3 fresh sage leaves, finely chopped
2 tablespoons finely chopped green onions, green part
   only

PORK CHOPS

4 pork rib chops, 1½ inches (4 cm) thick
1 teaspoon light olive oil with a dash of toasted sesame oil
1/8 teaspoon freshly ground sea salt
1/4 teaspoon freshly ground white peppercorns

SAUCE

1 cup freshly squeezed orange juice
1 cup de-alcoholized white wine
2 tablespoons arrowroot mixed with 2 tablespoons de-
   alcoholized white wine (slurry)

GARNISH

Finely sliced green onion tops

**The mashed yams and potatoes:** Preheat the oven to 350°F (180°C). Wash the yams and potatoes well and prick each one several times with a fork. Bake in the preheated oven for 1 hour. Remove from the oven and let cool. When cool, peel off the skins and discard. In a large bowl, mash the yam and potato meat, then stir in the green onion bulbs, orange, cloves, and pepper, or more to taste. Set aside and keep warm.

**The stuffing:** In a small bowl, combine the orange zest, ginger, apple, raisins, cloves, salt, pepper, sage, and green onion tops.

**The pork chops:** Make a pocket for the stuffing by plunging a thin-bladed knife through the side of each pork chop, creating a horizontal incision through the fat to the bone. Without enlarging the initial cut, fan the knife blade back and forth along the bone side to create a large, triangle-shaped pocket. Stuff each prepared pork chop with 2 tablespoons of the stuffing. Fasten the opening shut with a toothpick.

Pour the oil on a plate and sprinkle with the salt and pepper. Using a pastry brush, brush the oil mixture around the plate, then moisten both sides of each pork chop by rubbing them on the plate. Place the pork chops in a large skillet over medium heat. Brown each side, then cook for 15 minutes, turning to prevent excessive browning. Remove and set aside.

**The sauce:** In a small saucepan, mix the orange juice and wine. Deglaze the pork-browning skillet with 1/2 cup of the orange-wine mixture. Strain the liquid back into the saucepan with the rest of the orange-wine mixture and warm through over medium heat. Remove from the heat and stir in the arrowroot slurry. Return to the heat and stir until thickened.

Just before serving, put the mashed potatoes in a

small saucepan over low heat and heat through. Briefly steam the broccoli florets to warm.

**To serve:** Remove the toothpicks from the cooked pork chops. Place 1 chop on each dinner plate, accompanied by a heaping spoonful of the mashed yams and potatoes and a few bright green florets of the steamed broccoli. Make a deep depression in the mashed potatoes and yams and fill it with the sauce. Brush extra sauce over the pork chop to make it glisten and dust the whole dish with the sliced green onion tops.

Nutritional Profile per Serving: Calories—528; % calories from fat—17%; fat (gm)—10 or 16% daily value; saturated fat (gm)—3; sodium (mg)—211; cholesterol (mg)—70; carbohydrates (gm)—80; dietary fiber (gm)—8.

# PORK TENDERLOIN WITH GLAZED PEARS

⌘

*Another dish from my "galloping" days, and, remarkably, it wasn't too bad! I've tweaked it a bit in order to further reduce the fat, and I'm delighted at having found a new technique that gives fresh fruit a light pickled spice. The colors of the dish are really wonderful with the plump, pale, saffron-tinted pears. So, I'd recommend just adding some fresh steamed French green beans with a hint of nutmeg.*

*Time Estimate: Hands-on, 50 minutes*
*Serves 4*

2 (8-ounce or 225-gm) butterflied pork tenderloins
1/8 teaspoon freshly ground sea salt
1/4 teaspoon freshly ground black pepper
7 tablespoons brown sugar
2 cups water
1/8 teaspoon saffron threads
1/2 teaspoon allspice berries
1/2 teaspoon cloves

1/4 cup cider vinegar
2 pears, preferably Comice, peeled, halved lengthwise, and cored
2 tablespoons light olive oil with a dash of toasted sesame oil
1 ounce (30 gm) Canadian bacon (about 2 slices), diced
1 tablespoon honey, preferably fireweed

Pound the butterflied pork tenderloins until they are 1/2 inch (1.5 cm) thick. Season with the salt and pepper.

In a medium saucepan over medium heat, dissolve 4 tablespoons of the brown sugar in the water. Add the saffron, allspice berries, cloves, and vinegar, and bring to a simmer. Poach the pears in this syrup, turning them so that the "cup side" is uppermost. This is done so that if there is oxidation, it occurs on the side not seen in the final dish! The poaching process should take about 15 minutes. Transfer the pears to a small bowl. Reserve the poaching liquid separately.

Heat the olive oil in a small saucepan over medium-high heat and fry the Canadian bacon for 5 minutes. Brush the oil from the pan over the pork tenderloins and on the base of the broiler pan. Sprinkle half of the Canadian bacon bits on top of the tenderloins. Place under the broiler for 6 minutes. Turn the pork, brush with more oil, and sprinkle with the remaining Canadian bacon bits. Place under the broiler 4 minutes longer.

In a skillet over medium heat, mix the honey and the remaining 3 tablespoons brown sugar. Add 1/4 cup of the reserved pear poaching liquid. Bring to a boil, then simmer until reduced to a thin glaze. Add the pears and coat with the glaze.

**To serve:** Cut each tenderloin into 1/2-inch (1.5-cm) slices. Fan a quarter of the tenderloin on a plate and place a glazed pear half in the middle. Brush with the remaining glaze.

Nutritional Profile per Serving: Calories—347; % calories from fat—22%; fat (gm)—9 or 13% daily value; saturated fat (gm)—2; sodium (mg)—220; cholesterol (mg)—75; carbohydrates (gm)—41; dietary fiber (gm)—3.

# VEAL BUCO WITH SAFFRON RISOTTO

✳

*Here is one of my all-time favorites! A wonderful risk-reduced version of the rich classic Osso Buco.*

*Time Estimate: Hands-on, 30 minutes; unsupervised, 90 minutes*
Serves 4

1 teaspoon light olive oil with a dash of toasted sesame oil
1 cup diced celery
1 cup diced carrot
2 cloves garlic, bashed and peeled
1 pound (450 gm) veal shank, trimmed of all fat and cut into 1-inch (2.5-cm) pieces
1¼ cups low-sodium tomato purée
Bouquet garni (see below)
1/4 teaspoon freshly ground black pepper
1/4 cup de-alcoholized chardonnay wine
1 cup low-sodium veal stock (page 286)
8 ounces (225 gm) mushrooms, quartered
1/2 teaspoon grated lemon zest
1 tablespoon chopped fresh parsley
1 tablespoon capers
1 tablespoon arrowroot mixed with 2 tablespoons water (slurry)

## BOUQUET GARNI

4 sprigs thyme
2 bay leaves
6 parsley stalks

## SAFFRON RISOTTO

1 teaspoon light olive oil with a dash of toasted sesame oil
1 medium onion, peeled and very finely diced
1 cup uncooked arborio rice
1 pinch powdered saffron
2 cups low-sodium chicken stock (page 286)
1/2 cup de-alcoholized chardonnay wine
1/8 teaspoon freshly ground sea salt
Freshly ground black pepper to taste
2 tablespoons finely chopped fresh parsley
1 ounce (30 gm) finely grated Parmesan cheese

In an ovenproof casserole, heat the olive oil and sauté the celery, carrot, and garlic over medium-high heat for 5 minutes. Remove the cooked vegetables and set aside. In the same casserole, increase the heat to high and add the veal, one piece at a time. If you put all the meat in at once, liquid is released and the meat simmers instead of browns. Keep turning the meat until all the surfaces are lightly browned. Browning adds more depth of flavor.

Return the cooked vegetables to the casserole and stir in the tomato purée. Add the bouquet garni, black pepper, wine, and the veal stock, and bring to a boil. Cover, reduce the heat, and simmer gently for about 70 minutes.

**The saffron risotto:** In a large saucepan, heat the oil and sauté the onion over medium-high heat for 2 minutes. Add the rice, stirring until it's well coated. Scatter the saffron evenly over the rice and stir. In a small bowl, mix the chicken stock and wine. Pour in enough to just cover the rice and stir, over low heat, until it is absorbed. Continue to add the rest of the liquid, stirring until all of it has been absorbed. Remember, to achieve the proper consistency, the rice must be stirred. Finally, fold in the salt, pepper, parsley, and cheese. Keep warm.

After the veal is cooked, remove the bouquet garni, stir in the mushroom quarters, and simmer, uncovered, for 5 minutes.

Just before serving, stir in the lemon zest, chopped parsley, and capers. Remove the casserole from the heat and add the arrowroot slurry. Return to the heat and stir until thickened.

**To serve:** Ladle the Veal Buco onto warm dinner plates with the saffron risotto on the side.

Nutritional Profile per Serving: Calories—485; % calories from fat—21%; fat (gm)—11 or 17% daily value; saturated fat (gm)—4; sodium (mg)—718; cholesterol (mg)—101; carbohydrates (gm)—61; dietary fiber (gm)—5.

# VEAL PIZZAIOLA WITH FENNEL RISOTTO

*I use sun-dried tomatoes and sliced fennel to substitute for the flavor of the enormous amount of butter and cheese normally added to the classic risotto made in Milan.*

*Time Estimate: Hands-on, 60 minutes; unsupervised, 30 minutes*
Serves 2

## RISOTTO

1/4 cup sun-dried tomatoes
1/2 teaspoon light olive oil with a dash of toasted sesame oil
1/2 cup finely diced onion
1/2 cup finely chopped fennel bulb
1/2 cup uncooked arborio rice
1½ cups low-sodium chicken stock (page 286)
1 cup de-alcoholized white wine
1/4 cup *very* finely chopped fennel bulb
1 tablespoon freshly grated Parmesan cheese
1 teaspoon finely chopped fresh fennel fronds
1/2 teaspoon chopped fresh parsley

## VEAL

6 ounces (175 gm) veal bottom round (have your butcher slice it very thin)
1½ teaspoons light olive oil with a dash of toasted sesame oil
1/8 teaspoon freshly ground sea salt
1/4 teaspoon freshly ground black pepper
1/2 cup finely diced onion
3 cloves garlic, bashed, peeled, and finely chopped
1/4 cup finely chopped fennel bulb
1 fennel bulb, quartered
3 cups peeled, seeded, and chopped plum tomatoes
1 tablespoon chopped fresh oregano
1 tablespoon Worcestershire sauce
1 ounce (30 gm) mozzarella cheese, julienned
1½ teaspoons chopped fresh parsley
1 teaspoon chopped fresh fennel fronds

## GARNISH

Chopped fresh parsley

**The risotto:** To reconstitute the risotto's sun-dried tomatoes, put them in a small saucepan, cover with water, bring to a boil, then take off the heat and let soak 30 minutes. Drain and chop.

In a small Dutch oven, heat the oil and quickly sauté the onion and 1/2 cup finely chopped fennel bulb over medium-high heat until translucent, about 5 minutes. Add the rice and stir until well coated.

In a small bowl, mix the chicken stock and wine, and pour in enough to just cover the rice. Cook and stir over medium heat until the liquid is absorbed. Continue pouring and stirring until all of the stock and wine are absorbed. Stir in the sun-dried tomatoes and cook over medium heat for 35 minutes. Fold in the 1/4 cup of very finely chopped fennel bulb, the Parmesan cheese, chopped fennel fronds, and parsley, and keep warm.

**The veal:** Pound the veal slices until very thin. Pour 1 teaspoon of the oil on a plate and sprinkle with the salt and pepper. Dredge each slice through the seasoned oil on both sides.

In a large saucepan over medium heat, lightly brown the prepared veal slices on both sides. Remove the veal to a plate. Heat the remaining oil in the same saucepan and cook the onion, garlic, the 1/4 cup finely chopped fennel bulb, and fennel bulb quarters until translucent, about 2 minutes. Stir in the tomatoes and oregano, and cook for 10 minutes. Add the Worcestershire sauce and cook 5 minutes more.

Stir the browned veal into the vegetable mixture. Lay the mozzarella strips on top and sprinkle with the chopped parsley and fennel fronds. Cover and heat through, letting the cheese melt.

**To serve:** Place half the veal on each dinner plate, spoon half the vegetable mixture on top, and serve with 1/4 cup of the risotto. Garnish with an emerald dusting of the chopped fresh parsley.

Nutritional Profile per Serving: Calories—599; % calories from fat—22%; fat (gm)—15 or 22% daily value; saturated fat (gm)—5; sodium (mg)—700; cholesterol (mg)—83; carbohydrates (gm)—85; dietary fiber (gm)—12.

# VEAL RISOTTO

————— ❖ —————

*This is a dish that works very well when you want to reduce the quantity of meat in your meals. In this recipe, you'll see that it's entirely possible to enjoy a low-fat risotto when the recipe takes full advantage of some of the aroma, color, and texture concepts of fat replacement.*

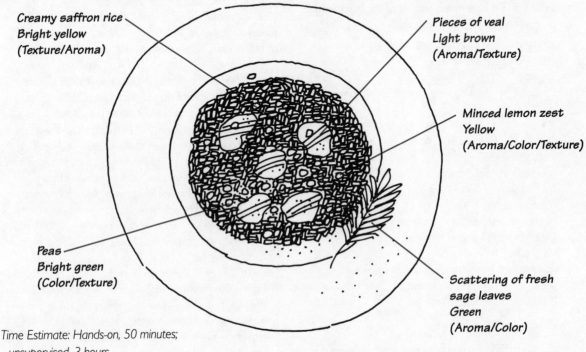

Creamy saffron rice
Bright yellow
(Texture/Aroma)

Pieces of veal
Light brown
(Aroma/Texture)

Minced lemon zest
Yellow
(Aroma/Color/Texture)

Peas
Bright green
(Color/Texture)

Scattering of fresh
sage leaves
Green
(Aroma/Color)

*Time Estimate: Hands-on, 50 minutes;
   unsupervised, 3 hours*
*Serves 4*

STOCK

1/4 teaspoon light olive oil with a dash of toasted
   sesame oil
1 onion, peeled and finely chopped
1/2 cup celery tops
1 cup chopped carrots
1 (1½-pound or 680-gm) veal shank
1 bay leaf
2 cloves
6 black peppercorns
2 quarts water

RISOTTO

1/2 teaspoon light olive oil with a dash of toasted
   sesame oil

1/2 onion, peeled and finely chopped
1 cup uncooked arborio rice
1 cup de-alcoholized white wine
1/16 teaspoon powdered saffron
1 quart veal stock (see left column)
1/2 cup freshly grated Parmesan cheese
1/4 teaspoon freshly ground sea salt
1/4 teaspoon freshly ground black pepper
1 cup frozen peas, thawed

GARNISH

2 teaspoons minced lemon zest
4 fresh sage leaves, minced

**The veal stock:** Pour the oil into a large stockpot over medium heat and sauté the onion, celery, and carrots for 3 minutes. Add the veal shank, bay leaf, cloves, and peppercorns, and cover with the water. Bring to a boil, reduce the heat, and simmer 2 hours. Skim off any foam that rises to the surface. After 1 hour, add enough water to bring the liquid up to the original level, about 1 cup. Remove the veal shank, pull off the meat, and set aside—you should have 8 ounces (225 gm) of meat. Strain the broth and remove the surface fat. Pour the stock into a fat strainer—you should have about 1 quart of stock. Pour it back into the stockpot and keep warm.

**The risotto:** Pour the oil into a large heavy saucepan over medium heat and sauté the onion for 2 minutes. Add the rice and stir until well coated. Pour in the wine and saffron, stir well, then let the wine be absorbed into the rice, stirring occasionally, for about 5 minutes. When the rice seems "dry," add enough hot stock to cover the rice—about 1 cup—stirring and cooking until it's absorbed into the rice. Continue the process of adding stock and stirring until all of it is absorbed, about 30 minutes.

Add the cheese, salt, and pepper, and stir well. Fold in the reserved veal. Just before serving, stir in the peas and heat through.

**To serve:** Divide among 4 dinner plates and sprinkle with the lemon zest and sage.

| Nutritional Profile per Serving | | | |
|---|---|---|---|
| | **Classic** | **Minimax** | **Daily Value** |
| Calories | 832 | 401 | |
| Calories from fat | 38% | 21% | |
| Fat (gm) | 35 | 9 | 14% |
| Saturated fat (gm) | 13 | 4 | 21% |
| Sodium (mg) | 1,072 | 503 | 21% |
| Cholesterol (mg) | 350 | 72 | 24% |
| Carbohydrates (gm) | 28 | 49 | 16% |
| Dietary fiber (gm) | 3 | 3 | 12% |
| Classic compared: Veal Osso Buco | | | |

# VEAL SUTTON

*This is a simple dish with tropical flavors served in a nest of rice. The papaya and avocado balls glisten under the slightly spicy curry sauce, their delicate flavors blending with the veal. Bright, tart pomegranate seeds provide highlights.*

*Time Estimate: Hands-on, 40 minutes*
Serves 4

## RICE

2½ cups low-sodium beef stock (page 286)
2 tablespoons garam masala (page 3)
1/4 teaspoon freshly ground sea salt
1/4 cup uncooked wild rice
1 cup uncooked long-grain white rice

## MEAT AND SAUCE

1 papaya, halved lengthwise and seeded
1 avocado, halved and pitted
1/2 cup pomegranate seeds
2 tablespoons fresh lime juice
1 tablespoon chopped fresh cilantro
12 ounces (350 gm) bottom round veal, trimmed of all
     visible fat
1/4 teaspoon freshly ground sea salt
1/4 teaspoon freshly ground black pepper
1¼ teaspoons light olive oil with a dash of toasted
     sesame oil
2 shallots, peeled and finely chopped
2 teaspoons curry powder
1⅓ cups canned papaya nectar
1 tablespoon arrowroot mixed with 2 tablespoons
     papaya nectar (slurry)

## GARNISH

4 sprigs fresh cilantro

**The rice:** Pour the beef stock into a large saucepan, stir in the garam masala and salt, and bring to a boil. Add the wild rice and cook, covered, on low heat for 25 minutes. Add the white rice, turn the heat

to the lowest possible point, and cook, covered, for 20 more minutes. Remove from the heat and set aside.

Scoop the papaya and avocado into small balls using a melon baller. Place in a bowl and stir in the pomegranate seeds, lime juice, and cilantro and set aside.

**The meat and sauce:** At a 45-degree angle, cut the veal across the grain into 1/4-inch (.75-cm) slices. Pound each slice to tenderize and increase the size by about one-third. Salt and pepper each slice.

Heat a large skillet over high heat, brush 1/4 teaspoon of the oil to thoroughly cover the pan, and brown as many of the veal slices as will fit without overlapping. This will take about 30 seconds per side. Remove, set aside, and repeat with the rest of the veal slices, using up to 1 teaspoon of oil.

Into the same pan, which will now be covered with a flavorful brown crust, pour the remaining 1 teaspoon of oil, shallots, and curry powder. Stir and cook over medium-high heat for about 1 minute. Pour in the papaya nectar and deglaze the pan. Remove from the heat, add the arrowroot slurry, and return to the heat to thicken. As soon as the sauce clears, add the browned veal slices and fruit to just heat through.

**To serve:** Divide the rice among 4 warm plates, place the veal slices beside it, and spoon the fruit and sauce over all. Garnish with sprigs of the cilantro.

Nutritional Profile per Serving: Calories—553; % calories from fat—23%; fat (gm)—14 or 22% daily value; saturated fat (gm)—3; sodium (mg)—381; cholesterol (mg)—73; carbohydrates (gm)—81; dietary fiber (gm)—7.

The pomegranate is an ancient fruit that figures prominently in the world's mythologies. My use of pomegranates is definitely modern as their seeds are lovely brighteners in low-fat cooking. The pomegranate has a leathery skin which you must cut through to get to the seeds within. Cut from the top to the stem end, just through the skin, and peel back. Remove the seeds into a bowl with your fingers so as not to lose any more juice than necessary. Discard the pulp surrounding the seeds.

# VEAL WEYERHAEUSER

⌘

*This is an elegant dish that is cooked just before serving.*
*Dijon mustard and fresh basil give it a sophisticated finish.*
Time Estimate: Hands-on, 30 minutes;
   unsupervised, 30 minutes
Serves 4

## RICE PILAF

1 teaspoon light olive oil with a dash of toasted sesame oil
1 cup finely chopped onion
1 clove garlic, bashed, peeled, and chopped
1 cup uncooked white rice
2 cups low-sodium veal or chicken stock (page 286)
2 bay leaves
1 sprig fresh parsley
1 sprig fresh thyme
1 cup small fresh or frozen green peas
1 cup sliced fresh mushrooms

## VEAL AND SAUCE

12 ounces (350 gm) boneless veal loin, trimmed of all
   visible fat
2 teaspoons light olive oil with a dash of toasted sesame
   oil
1 green pepper, seeded and cut into 1-inch (2.5-cm)
   strips
1 red bell pepper, seeded and cut into 1-inch (2.5-cm)
   strips
1 yellow bell pepper, seeded and cut into 1-inch (2.5-cm)
   strips
1 cup low-sodium veal or chicken stock (page 286)
1½ tablespoons cornstarch
1/4 cup de-alcoholized dry white wine
1/4 cup evaporated skim milk
1 tablespoon Dijon mustard
1/4 teaspoon freshly ground sea salt
1/4 teaspoon freshly ground black pepper
3 tablespoons chopped fresh basil

**The rice:** Preheat the oven to 375°F (190°C). Heat the oil in an ovenproof skillet and fry the onions and garlic over medium-high heat until the onions are translucent, 2 minutes. Add the rice and stir until well coated. Add the stock and lay the herbs on top. Bake, uncovered, in the preheated oven for 30 minutes. When it's done, remove the herbs, stir in the peas and the mushrooms, and return to the oven to heat through, about 5 minutes.

**The veal and sauce:** Cut the veal across the grain into 20 evenly sized pieces, just over 1/4 inch (.75 cm) thick. Heat 1/2 teaspoon of the oil in a large nonstick skillet over medium-high heat and fry as many veal pieces as will cover the bottom of the pan for about 30 seconds on each side. Place the cooked veal on a plate and keep warm while cooking the remaining pieces. Use 1/2 teaspoon of the oil each time you start to brown more veal. You will be able to do 6 or 7 pieces each time.

Put the last 1/2 teaspoon of the oil into the same skillet and fry the peppers for 1 minute. Add the veal stock and bring to a boil, scraping the meat residues off the bottom of the pan in order to blend all the flavors. Remove the pan from the heat.

Combine the cornstarch, wine, evaporated milk, and Dijon mustard in a small bowl. Add to the pan with the peppers and stock, and bring to a boil, stirring, to thicken. Add the browned meat and any accumulated juices, and heat through. Season with the salt, pepper, and 2 tablespoons of the basil.

**To serve:** Put 5 slices of the veal on each dinner plate with the sauce ladled over the top. Sprinkle with the remaining chopped basil.

Nutritional Profile per Serving: Calories—447; % calories from fat—18%; fat (gm)—9 or 14% daily value; saturated fat (gm)—2; sodium (mg)—335; cholesterol (mg)—75; carbohydrates (gm)—62; dietary fiber (gm)—6.

In the old days, we looked for the whitest veal. Now we know that the price of white veal is great suffering for the animals. The veal that is a reddish-pink color is from animals that have received most of their nourishment from their mothers. They may have had a little grass or hay, and if they were confined at all, there was still enough room to romp and play. This darker veal is high quality and definitely the one I choose. If you have any doubts about how the calf was raised, talk to your butcher. The darker color is also a good clue.

# Venison with Spiced Pears

*Venison is extra tasty and extra lean meat whether it comes from the hunter's bag or a properly regulated game farm. This recipe can also be made using well-trimmed pork loin.*

Time Estimate: Hands-on, 45 minutes;
  unsupervised, 30 minutes
Serves 6

## MARINADE

1/2 cup de-alcoholized red wine
1/2 cup cider vinegar
4 sprigs fresh rosemary

## VENISON

1¼ pounds (565 gm) venison or pork loin
1 teaspoon light olive oil with a dash of toasted sesame oil
3 tablespoons low-sodium tomato paste
2 large carrots, cleaned and chopped into 1-inch (2.5-cm) chunks
2 medium leeks, cleaned and chopped into 1-inch (2.5-cm) chunks
1 tablespoon chopped fresh thyme
1 cup de-alcoholized red wine
1 sprig fresh rosemary
8 juniper berries
1 tablespoon arrowroot mixed with 2 tablespoons water (slurry)

## SPICED PEARS

1/2 cup de-alcoholized red wine
1/2 cup cider vinegar
6 whole cloves, freshly ground
6 allspice berries
1 (3-inch or 8-cm) cinnamon stick
2 pears, peeled, halved, and cored
1 cup water or amount needed to cover

## GARNISH

Sprigs fresh rosemary

**The day before serving:** Mix the marinade ingredients together in a glass or ceramic bowl. Trim away the excess fat and silver skin from the venison, place in the marinade, and refrigerate overnight.

**The day of serving:** Remove the venison from the marinade and blot dry with paper towels. Reserve the marinade. Roll the venison loin and tie with kitchen twine or wrap in butcher's net.

Preheat the oven to 375°F (190°C). Pour the reserved marinade into a small saucepan, bring to a boil, and set aside.

Heat the oil in a low-sided casserole over medium-high heat and fry the tomato paste, carrots, and leeks until the tomato paste darkens in color, about 5 minutes. Put the wrapped venison into the pan and brown, rolling it to brown the entire outer surface. Add the thyme, wine, boiled marinade, rosemary sprig, and juniper berries. Cover and put in the preheated oven to braise for 40 minutes.

**The pears:** In a medium saucepan, heat the wine and vinegar. Mix in the cloves, allspice berries, and the cinnamon stick. Add the pear halves, cover with the water, and poach for approximately 30 minutes.

**Finish the venison:** Transfer the cooked venison to a cutting board. Pour the casserole juices through a strainer into a small heated saucepan. Remove the saucepan from the heat. Add the arrowroot paste, return to the heat, and stir until thickened.

Cut the twine or butcher's net away from the venison and discard. Cut the meat into 1/4-inch (.75-cm) slices.

**To serve:** Arrange the venison slices in the center of a serving tray and surround with the pear halves. Pour the thickened sauce over the venison and garnish with the rosemary sprigs.

Nutritional Profile per Serving: Calories—168; % calories from fat—18%; fat (gm)—3 or 5% daily value; saturated fat (gm)—1; sodium (mg)—44; cholesterol (mg)—78; carbohydrates (gm)—13; dietary fiber (gm)—2. ⬇

# GOLD MEDAL BEANS AND RICE

*I'm convinced that eating more peas, beans, lentils, and whole grains will make a tremendous difference to our health, especially when used to replace meats and fried foods high in saturated fat. This hearty, spicy bean dish always wins a gold medal from me!*

Time Estimate: Hands-on, 25 minutes;
  unsupervised, 25 minutes
Serves 4

6 cups ham hock stock (page 287), finely chopped meat
  reserved
1 cup dried pinto beans
1 cup uncooked brown rice
2 tablespoons freshly squeezed lemon juice
1 (16-ounce or 450-gm) bunch of collard greens, stems
  trimmed and very finely diced
1/4 teaspoon freshly ground black pepper
1/4 teaspoon freshly ground sea salt
1/2 teaspoon cumin seeds
1/4 teaspoon cayenne pepper
2 whole cloves
1/4 teaspoon dried thyme

Pour 5 cups of the stock into a pressure cooker and bring to a boil. Add the beans, fasten the lid, and let the pressure build up inside. When the cooker starts to hiss, turn the heat down to medium-low—the cooker should be just hissing—and cook 10 minutes.

Remove from the heat and release the steam. Unfasten the lid, add the rice, refasten the lid, and bring the liquid to a boil. When the cooker starts to hiss, turn the heat down to medium-low and simmer 15 minutes more. Remove from the heat and release the steam. Spoon the cooked beans and rice into a large serving dish and keep warm.

Put the remaining 1 cup of the stock into the pressure cooker, add the lemon juice, and bring to a boil. Add the ham hock meat and reduce the liquid by half, about 2 minutes. Drop in the collard greens, season with the black pepper and salt, stir well, and simmer 2 minutes.

**To serve:** Make a hollow in the middle of the rice and beans and spoon in the cooked collards and ham, pouring in any excess juices. Place the cumin seeds, cayenne, cloves, and thyme in a small coffee mill and grind to a fine powder. Sprinkle 1 teaspoon of the spice mixture over the finished beans and rice.

Nutritional Profile per Serving: Calories— 352; % calories from fat—20%; fat (gm)—8 or 12% daily value; saturated fat (gm)—2; sodium (mg)—436; cholesterol (mg)—13; carbohydrates (gm)—55; dietary fiber (gm)—8.

# CHRISTMAS RISOTTO

— ✕ —

*A gorgeous red and green—perfect for Christmas or any time of the year. The butternut squash gives this a marvelous texture without the fat so typical of classic Italian risotto.*

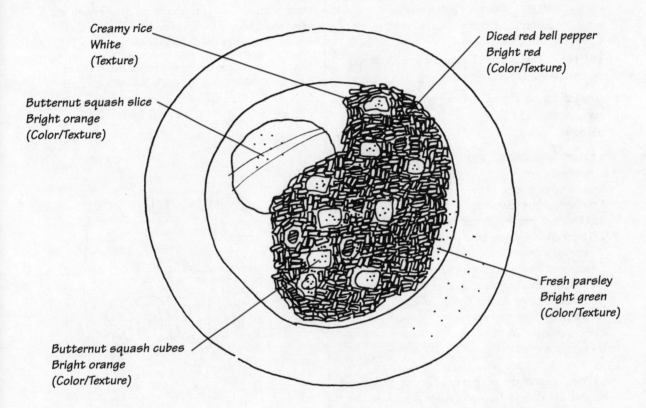

Creamy rice
White
(Texture)

Diced red bell pepper
Bright red
(Color/Texture)

Butternut squash slice
Bright orange
(Color/Texture)

Fresh parsley
Bright green
(Color/Texture)

Butternut squash cubes
Bright orange
(Color/Texture)

Time Estimate: Hands-on, 50 minutes
Serves 4

1 (2½-pound or 1.1-kg) butternut squash
4 cups vegetable stock (page 288)
1/2 teaspoon ground cumin
1/4 teaspoon cayenne pepper
1/4 teaspoon ground allspice
1 teaspoon light olive oil with a dash of toasted sesame oil
1/2 onion, peeled and finely chopped

1 clove garlic, bashed, peeled, and chopped
1 cup uncooked arborio rice
1 cup de-alcoholized white wine
1/2 cup freshly grated Parmesan cheese
1/4 teaspoon freshly ground sea salt
1/4 teaspoon freshly ground black pepper
1 sweet red bell pepper, seeded and finely diced
1 tablespoon finely chopped parsley stalks

Preheat the oven to 350°F (180°C). Cut off the neck part of the squash. Trim off the stem and then cut the neck into 4 slices 1 inch (2.5 cm) thick. Place on a lightly greased baking sheet and bake in the preheated oven for 20 minutes; turn and bake 5 more minutes. Remove from the oven. Set aside and keep warm. The rest of the squash is cut in half, peeled, seeded, and diced small, yielding about 1 pound (450 gm) of diced squash.

Heat the vegetable stock in a medium saucepan over medium heat and keep warm. In a small bowl, mix together the cumin, cayenne, and allspice. Pour the oil into a large saucepan over medium heat and cook the onion and garlic for 3 minutes. Add 1/2 teaspoon of the spice mixture and stir well. Add the diced squash, stir well, cover, and cook 5 minutes. Pour in 1/2 cup of the warm stock and cook 5 more minutes. Remove from the heat and strain the squash juices through a sieve into the saucepan with the vegetable stock. Return the vegetables to their original saucepan.

Add the rice to the squash and shake together, to avoid stirring and breaking the squash pieces. Pour in the wine and 1 cup of the warm stock. Stir carefully and cook over medium heat until the liquid is absorbed. Continue adding the stock, cooking and stirring until you've used all the stock, about 30 minutes.

Stir in the remaining spice mixture, the cheese, salt, and pepper. Fold in the red pepper and parsley stalks.

**To serve:** Peel the skin from the baked squash neck slices. Place 1 slice on each plate and partially cover with the risotto, leaving half the slice exposed.

| Nutritional Profile per Serving | | | |
|---|---|---|---|
| | **Classic** | **Minimax** | **Daily Value** |
| Calories | 323 | 374 | |
| Calories from fat | 32% | 18% | |
| Fat (gm) | 12 | 8 | 12% |
| Saturated fat (gm) | 5 | 3 | 13% |
| Sodium (mg) | 776 | 427 | 18% |
| Cholesterol (mg) | 18 | 10 | 3% |
| Carbohydrates (gm) | 44 | 64 | 21% |
| Dietary fiber (gm) | 1 | 8 | 30% |
| Classic compared: Risotto con Due Formaggi | | | |

# Orzo Pasta with Chicken and Red Peppers

⁙

*Orzo is pasta shaped into small ricelike pieces. (Orzo is actually Italian for "barley.") I've added chicken for garnish and a substantial amount of rosemary to make the dish really come alive. You could serve it with a garnish of freshly cooked peas or a salad on the side.*

Time Estimate: Hands-on, 40 minutes
Serves 4

ENHANCED CHICKEN STOCK

2 (14-ounce or 400-gm) cans low-sodium chicken broth
3 large stalks fresh parsley
3 sprigs fresh rosemary
1 clove garlic, bashed and peeled
3 whole cloves
2 bay leaves
3/4 cup water
1 cup de-alcoholized white wine

ORZO

2 teaspoons light olive oil with a dash of toasted sesame oil
1/2 yellow onion, peeled and sliced
2 cloves garlic, bashed, peeled, and finely diced
1 tablespoon finely chopped fresh rosemary
1 tablespoon finely chopped fresh basil
2 tablespoons finely chopped fresh parsley
1½ cups uncooked orzo pasta

CHICKEN

3 (5-ounce or 150-gm) boneless chicken breasts, skin removed, cut into 2 X 1/2-inch (5 X 1.5-cm) strips
1 red bell pepper, seeded and thinly sliced

GARNISH

4 tablespoons freshly grated Parmesan cheese
4 sprigs fresh basil
Chopped fresh parsley to taste
Freshly ground black pepper to taste

**The enhanced chicken stock:** In a saucepan, combine the chicken broth, parsley, rosemary, garlic, cloves, bay leaves, and water, and bring to a boil. Reduce the heat, cover, and simmer 10 minutes. Remove from the heat and strain into a large bowl. Stir in the wine and set aside.

**The orzo:** In a large saucepan, heat 1 teaspoon of the oil and sauté the onion and garlic over high heat for 3 minutes. Stir in half of the herbs, the orzo, and the chicken stock, and cook over medium heat for 25 minutes, stirring occasionally.

**The chicken:** While the orzo is cooking, heat the remaining oil in a large skillet and sauté the chicken pieces, red pepper, and the remaining herbs over medium-high heat for 3 minutes. Stir into the cooked orzo.

**To serve:** Spoon onto individual dinner plates and garnish each serving with a tablespoon of the Parmesan cheese, a sprig of the basil, a sprinkling of parsley, and black pepper to taste.

Nutritional Profile per Serving: Calories—363; % calories from fat—20%; fat (gm)—8 or 12% daily value; saturated fat (gm)—2; sodium (mg)—204; cholesterol (mg)—47; carbohydrates (gm)—43; dietary fiber (gm)—2.

# SWEET STUFF PASTA

*Pasta sauced with a velvety stock reduction, sweet parsnips, and ham—what could be better!*

Time Estimate: Hands-on, 30 minutes;
   unsupervised, 15 minutes

Serves 4

20 ounces (570 gm) parsnips, trimmed, peeled, and
   finely chopped
1 quart ham stock (page 287)
8 ounces (225 gm) ham hock meat (from the stock
   recipe), diced the same size as the parsnips
8 ounces (225 gm) dried angel hair pasta
2 tablespoons arrowroot mixed with 4 tablespoons
   water (slurry)
2 tablespoons chopped fresh parsley

GARNISH

Freshly ground black pepper
4 tablespoons freshly grated dry Monterey Jack cheese
   (optional)

Put the parsnips in a large saucepan, cover with 1 quart water, and bring to a boil. Reduce the heat and simmer 15 minutes. Drain and set aside, reserving both the liquid and the parsnips.

Pour the ham hock stock into a saucepan, bring to a boil, and reduce by half to 2 cups, about 15 minutes. Add the ham hock meat and parsnips, stir until completely incorporated, then simmer for 4 minutes.

At the same time that you add the parsnips and ham to the stock, bring the reserved parsnip water to a boil, add the pasta, and cook until just tender, 4 minutes. Stir it well so it doesn't stick to the bottom of the pan. Drain through a colander into a large serving bowl. Pour out the water in the warmed serving bowl and put the cooked pasta into the heated bowl.

Remove the ham hock–parsnip mixture from the heat, add the arrowroot slurry, return to the heat, and stir until thickened. Stir in the parsley.

**To serve:** Pour the sauce over the pasta, toss, and garnish with pepper and a whisper of the cheese, if you wish. A whisper for me is 1 level tablespoon. (It all depends on whether you are hard of hearing or not.) A whisper will increase your fat by 1.5 grams per serving. If you leave it out, the calories from fat are reduced to 12 percent.

Nutritional Profile per Serving: Calories—453; % calories from fat—18%; fat (gm)—9 or 14% daily value; saturated fat (gm)—3; sodium (mg)—380; cholesterol (mg)—18; carbohydrates (gm)—75; dietary fiber (gm)—7.

# Vegetable Lasagne Roll-ups

Lasagne is definitely a comfort-food-of-the-people and has earned its place as a favorite of millions. This recipe drains the fat from the classic dish, adds a huge amount of fiber, and allows for an unusual presentation that is much easier to serve. It becomes a complete meal when you serve it with a good, crisp, colorful salad and lots of crusty bread.

Time Estimate: Hands-on, 1 hour;
   unsupervised, 40 minutes

Serves 8

8 ounces uncooked lasagne noodles

FILLING

1 cup part-skim ricotta cheese
1/4 cup part-skim mozzarella cheese
1/4 cup freshly grated Parmesan cheese
8 ounces (225 gm) fresh spinach, washed, stemmed, and
   coarsely chopped
1 (15-ounce or 425-gm) can low-sodium white kidney
   beans, drained and rinsed
2 tablespoons chopped fresh oregano
2 tablespoons chopped fresh basil
1½ teaspoons light olive oil with a dash of toasted
   sesame oil
2 cups chopped onions
2 cloves garlic, bashed, peeled, and chopped
2 cups finely diced eggplant
1 large red bell pepper, seeded and finely diced

SAUCE

2 tablespoons low-sodium tomato paste
1/4 teaspoon red pepper flakes
1 cup de-alcoholized red wine
1 (16 ounce or 450-gm) can whole tomatoes, with liquid
1 tablespoon freshly squeezed lemon juice
1/2 teaspoon freshly ground sea salt
1/2 teaspoon freshly ground black pepper
2 tablespoons freshly grated Parmesan cheese

**The lasagne noodles:** Cook the pasta according to the package directions for just tender (al dente) texture. Drain and run under cold water. Keep the cooled noodles in a bowl of cold water until ready to use.

**The filling:** In a large mixing bowl, combine the three cheeses, the spinach, half the beans, half the oregano, and half the basil, and set aside.

Preheat the oven to 350°F (180°C). Pour 1/2 teaspoon of the oil into a large skillet over medium-high heat and fry the onions and garlic for 5 minutes, stirring often. Transfer half to the spinach and cheese filling and set the other half aside to be used in the sauce. Wipe the pan clean.

Add 1/2 teaspoon of the oil to the same pan and, over medium heat, cook the eggplant for 8 minutes, stirring often. It's important that the bottom of the pan does not scorch. Spoon the cooked eggplant into the filling mixture and stir well. Wipe the pan clean.

Add the remaining oil to the same pan and, over medium heat, cook the red bell pepper for 3 minutes. Spoon the cooked pepper into the filling mixture. Wipe the pan clean.

**The sauce:** Add the tomato paste to the same pan and, over medium heat, cook until it turns brown, about 5 minutes. It is very important that it doesn't burn but just browns. Stir in the red pepper flakes and the wine. Bring to a boil, lower the heat to a simmer, and reduce the liquid by about one-fourth, about 15 minutes. Add the canned tomatoes and their liquid, stirring until the tomatoes break into pieces.

Add the remaining beans, oregano, basil, and reserved cooked onions and garlic, and cook for 5 minutes at a very low simmer. Stir in the lemon juice, salt, and black pepper, and mix well.

**To assemble:** Lay a cooked lasagne noodle flat on a cutting board. Form 1/2 cup of the filling into a rough ball, lay on one end of the lasagne, and roll it up end-to-end. Repeat with the remaining noodles.

Pour the sauce into a 9 X 13-inch (23 X 33-cm) baking pan. Place the lasagne rolls on top, seam side down, and spoon some of the sauce over them. Cover with aluminum foil and bake for 40 minutes. Remove the foil, sprinkle with the Parmesan cheese, and bake for another 5 minutes.

**To serve:** Each dinner guest gets 1 roll-up ladled with some of the delicious sauce.

Nutritional Profile per Serving: Calories—315; % calories from fat—19%; fat (gm)—6 or 10% daily value; saturated fat (gm)—3; sodium (mg)—394; cholesterol (mg)—15; carbohydrates (gm)—49; dietary fiber (gm)—8.

# RADIATORE

⌗

*Most people think a radiatore is the "thing-am-a-jig" between the headlights of their car! But it's actually an unusual, spiral pasta, cooked here in a remarkable way. Instead of hurling it into massive amounts of water, the pasta is cooked from its raw state in its finishing sauce—a most extraordinary taste and texture.*

*Time Estimate: Hands-on, 45 minutes*
*Serves 4*

10 plum tomatoes
1 cup water
1 tablespoon light olive oil with a dash of toasted sesame oil
1 red bell pepper, seeded and chopped
2 cloves garlic, bashed, peeled, and chopped
1 cup de-alcoholized white wine
1 branch of fresh basil (at least 6 leaves)
8 ounces (225 gm) uncooked radiatore
1 tablespoon chopped fresh oregano
1 tablespoon chopped fresh parsley
4 tablespoons grated dry Monterey Jack cheese
4 teaspoons pine nuts

Use one of the following methods to make a tomato purée: Using the traditional method, remove the stalk ends and then drop the tomatoes into a pot of boiling water. In a few moments, you'll see the skins start to peel back. Drain the tomatoes and plunge them into cold water. You should be able to pick them up quite easily. Peel off the skin and cut out the seeds, reserving the seeds and skins. Take the tomato meat and put it into the work bowl of your food processor. Use the pulse switch and process into a smooth purée.

A faster and simpler way involves a new machine, called a "tomato press." Simply quarter the tomatoes and hurl them into a saucepan on medium heat until they're just heated through—just a few minutes. Then pour them into the top of the press. When you turn the handle, the tomatoes will be processed so that the skin and seeds come out one end and the tomato purée comes out the other! Not only is this method much less time consuming than the old-fashioned way, it is also a good aerobic activity!

In a small saucepan, add the water to the reserved tomato skins and seeds, and bring to a boil. Drain the tomato skins and seeds into a small strainer. Press out all the juice you can. This gives you an extra taste of the tomatoes. Set the liquid aside. And don't throw those skins out yet! Pour them into your potted plants (not over them, that would look sordid, but under) to enrich the soil.

In a large saucepan, heat the olive oil with the chopped pepper and garlic over medium-high heat. Add the tomato purée, tomato-skin water, de-alcoholized wine, and the branch of fresh basil. Stir in the radiatore. Turn the heat to low and put the lid on the saucepan. Cook for 4 minutes if you have fresh pasta, 8 minutes for dried pasta. This will cook the pasta *verde verde*, or just a little bit less than al dente. You'll see that most of the sauce is absorbed into the radiatore. Remove the basil branch. Add the oregano and parsley, and stir.

**To serve:** Place in serving bowls and sprinkle with the grated cheese and pine nuts.

Nutritional Profile per Serving: Calories—365; % calories from fat—22%; fat (gm)—9 or 13% daily value; saturated fat (gm)—2; sodium (mg)—144; cholesterol (mg)—5; carbohydrates (gm)—61; dietary fiber (gm)—6.

# SPAGHETTI SALMONARA

*Treena and I have sampled Italian restaurants from Naples to Venice, indeed, all over the world. To these I must now add Babbo Ganza, in Santa Fe, where the pasta was cooked better than at any other restaurant in my lifetime of experience. Congratulations to owner/chef Giovanni Scorzo on his commitment to excellence, and my thanks to him for letting me Minimax off several of the key ideas he uses to make his seafood pastas.*

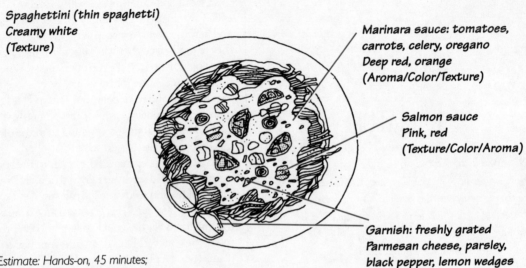

**Spaghettini (thin spaghetti)**
**Creamy white**
**(Texture)**

**Marinara sauce: tomatoes,**
**carrots, celery, oregano**
**Deep red, orange**
**(Aroma/Color/Texture)**

**Salmon sauce**
**Pink, red**
**(Texture/Color/Aroma)**

**Garnish: freshly grated**
**Parmesan cheese, parsley,**
**black pepper, lemon wedges**

*Time Estimate: Hands-on, 45 minutes;*
*   unsupervised, 30 minutes*
Serves 6

MARINARA SAUCE (This recipe allows for 1 extra
   cup of marinara to be used for another dish.)

1 teaspoon light olive oil with a dash of toasted sesame oil
1/3 cup diced onion
1/3 cup diced carrots
1/3 cup diced celery
2 pounds (900 gm) plum tomatoes
1/4 teaspoon freshly ground sea salt
1/4 teaspoon freshly ground black pepper
3 (3-inch or 8-cm) sprigs fresh oregano

SALMON SAUCE

1/2 teaspoon light oil with a dash of toasted sesame oil
2 ounces (60 gm) shallots, peeled and chopped
2 cups fish stock (page 287)
2 (6-ounce or 175-gm) salmon steaks
4 large beefsteak tomatoes, quartered and seeded,

seeds and pulp reserved
1/4 teaspoon freshly ground sea salt
2 tablespoons arrowroot mixed with 2 tablespoons
   water (slurry)
2 tablespoons fresh oregano

PASTA

1 pound (450 gm) uncooked spaghettini or thin
   spaghetti
1/2 cup freshly grated Parmesan cheese
1/4 cup chopped fresh parsley
1/4 teaspoon freshly ground black pepper

GARNISH

1 lemon, cut in wedges

**The marinara sauce:** Heat the oil in a medium saucepan over medium-high heat. Fry the diced vegetables for 15 minutes.

Put the tomatoes in a plastic bag and press down gently until they are somewhat squashed; do not mash completely. Transfer them to the saucepan and stir in the salt, pepper, and oregano; cover and cook for 15 minutes. Remove from the heat and strain, to yield 2 cups of sauce. Reserve 1 cup for another use.

**The salmon sauce:** Heat the oil in a large skillet over medium-high heat and shallow-fry the shallots until just translucent, about 5 minutes. Add the fish stock, bring to a boil, then reduce the heat until just simmering. Add the salmon, cover, and cook for 8 minutes, or until the salmon flakes easily.

Leaving the stock simmering, transfer the salmon to a plate and carefully remove the skin and bones. Add the skin and bones with the reserved tomato seeds and pulp to the simmering stock to reinforce its flavor. Break the salmon meat into bite-sized pieces and set aside.

Remove the stock from the heat and strain to yield 1½ cups. If you don't have 1 ½ cups, add enough fish stock, water, or wine to come to that level. Return to the saucepan and add 1 cup of the marinara sauce, the quartered beefsteak tomatoes, salt, and the arrowroot slurry.

Return to medium-high heat and stir until thickened. Gently stir in the oregano and cooked salmon meat, and keep warm until ready to serve.

Cook the pasta in a large pot of boiling water until just tender, about 5 minutes, depending on the pasta. Strain in a metal colander, letting the cooking water pour into a serving bowl. Pour out the water when the bowl is heated through.

**To serve:** Pour the salmon sauce into the hot serving bowl. Add the hot, drained pasta, Parmesan cheese, parsley, and black pepper, and toss well. Bring to the table to serve. Offer the lemon wedges on the side.

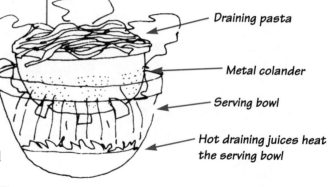

Draining pasta

Metal colander

Serving bowl

Hot draining juices heat the serving bowl

| Nutritional Profile per Serving: | | | |
|---|---|---|---|
| | Classic | Minimax | Daily Value |
| Calories | 958 | 497 | |
| Calories from fat | 60% | 18% | |
| Fat (gm) | 64 | 10 | 15% |
| Saturated fat (gm) | 25 | 3 | 15% |
| Sodium (mg) | 548 | 375 | 16% |
| Cholesterol (mg) | 273 | 39 | 13% |
| Carbohydrates (gm) | 43 | 75 | 25% |
| Dietary fiber (gm) | 43 | 6 | 24% |
| Classic compared: King Salmon with Pesto | | | |

# 20% calories from fat

⌗

# Side Dishes
# &
# Vegetables

# Glazed Green Beans

The flavorful glaze on these green beans is particularly glossy from the addition of the arrowroot slurry. When choosing fresh green beans, look for thin beans about the width of a pencil. They should be a vivid green color, without limpness or brown spots. If possible, use green beans the day they are purchased; otherwise refrigerate them, unwashed, in plastic bags, for a maximum of 4 days. Want a color variation? Try the yellow variety.

*Time Estimate: Hands-on, 30 minutes*
*Serves 4*

2 cups low-sodium stock (choose your favorite, pages 286–288)
4 sprigs fresh dill
1 pound (450 gm) fresh green beans, topped and tailed
1/8 teaspoon freshly grated nutmeg
1/8 teaspoon freshly ground sea salt
1/8 teaspoon freshly ground black pepper
1 teaspoon arrowroot mixed with 1 tablespoon cold stock or water (slurry)
1 teaspoon finely chopped fresh dill

Pour the stock into a large skillet; add the dill, bring to a boil, and reduce to 1/2 cup liquid, about 10 minutes. Remove the dill sprigs and discard.

Place the green beans in a steamer tray. Sprinkle with the nutmeg, salt, and pepper, and steam for 4 minutes.

Bring the reduced stock in the large skillet back to a boil. Add the steamed green beans and "stir-boil" for 1 minute. Drizzle the arrowroot slurry over the top to form a glaze and toss well, until thoroughly coated. To serve, dust with the chopped dill.

Nutritional Profile per Serving: Calories—39; % calories from fat—23%; fat (gm)—1 or 2% daily value; saturated fat (gm)—0; sodium (mg)—108; cholesterol (mg)—0; carbohydrates (gm)—7; dietary fiber (gm)—3.

# Minimax Seed Bread

This is a robust bread: full of flavor, texture, and good nutrient density. It toasts beautifully and if that isn't enough, it only needs one proofing!

*Time Estimate: Hands-on, 30 minutes;*
*  unsupervised, 2 hours*
*Makes one 18-slice loaf*

3/4 cup Minimax Seed Mix (see below)
1/4 teaspoon light olive oil with a dash of toasted sesame oil
1 tablespoon honey
2 cups warm (105°F; 40°C) water
1 package active dry yeast
2 cups stone-ground whole-wheat flour
2 cups all-purpose flour
1 teaspoon freshly ground sea salt

Preheat the oven to 300°F (150°C). Scatter the seed mix onto a cookie sheet and toast the seeds for 15 minutes.

Grease a large 9 X 5 X 3-inch (23 X 13 X 8-cm) loaf pan with the olive oil. In a small bowl, mix the honey, warm water, and yeast, and let sit for 10 minutes, until it gets frothy.

In a large bowl, combine the whole-wheat flour, 1 cup of the white flour, the salt, and the toasted seed mix. Pour in the liquid and mix well. The dough will be very sticky. Knead as much of the white flour into the sticky batter as you need to make a springy dough. Continue kneading for 10 minutes. Form into a loaf and set in the prepared loaf pan. Cover with a cloth and set in a warm place to rise for about 1 hour.

Preheat the oven to 350°F (180°C). When the dough has risen to about twice its size, or it looks as if it might spill out of the loaf pan, bake it for 50 minutes or until the interior temperature reaches 190°F (90°C). Just insert an instant-read thermometer in the center of the loaf to check the temperature. If you don't like the idea of a small hole in the top of your bread, just tip the loaf out of the pan and go in from the bottom. (According to Betsy Openeer, a truly gifted bread maker and teacher, this is the only really accurate way to find out if bread is done.) Let the bread cool before slicing.

**To serve:** Slice and serve it with your favorite homemade jam. This bread makes glorious toast.

Nutritional Profile per Serving: Calories—133; % calories from fat—22%; fat (gm)—3 or 5% daily value; saturated fat (gm)—0; sodium (mg)—121; cholesterol (mg)— 0; carbohydrates (gm)—22; dietary fiber (gm)—3. ⬇

> Minimax Seed Mix is a very nutritious way of adding crunch to a meal. It's quite tasty and high in protein. Combine equal measures of sunflower seeds, unhulled sesame seeds, green pumpkin seeds, sliced almonds, and a half measure of flax seeds. These unroasted seeds and nuts can be found packaged in your grocery store or in bulk at a food cooperative or health-food store. Make a big batch and keep it tightly covered in the refrigerator for handy use. I sprinkle some on my cereal every morning.

# GREEN RISOTTO

*This has to be my favorite course or the very best accompaniment you could serve with a plain, broiled chicken breast or fish steak. It can also become a "vegetables-only" main dish. Even if you double the serving size it still has less than 10 grams of fat and only 500 calories per serving.*

Time Estimate: Hands-on, 45 minutes;
  unsupervised, 20 minutes
Serves 4

RISOTTO

1 teaspoon light olive oil with a dash of toasted sesame oil
1/2 cup chopped onion
1/2 cup chopped fennel bulb
3/4 cup uncooked arborio rice

3 cups strained vegetable stock (page 288)
1/2 cup de-alcoholized white wine
1/4 cup freshly grated Parmesan cheese

PEA MIXTURE

1 cup frozen green peas
1/4 cup strained vegetable stock (page 288)
1 tablespoon chopped fresh basil
1 tablespoon chopped fresh parsley
7 large green butter lettuce leaves
1/4 cup de-alcoholized white wine

GARNISH

Freshly grated Parmesan cheese
Freshly ground black pepper
Sliced fennel bulb
Chopped fresh parsley

**The risotto:** In a large saucepan, heat the oil and sauté the onion over medium-high heat for 3 minutes. Add the fennel and rice, and cook for 2 minutes, stirring until the rice is well coated. Add 1 cup of the vegetable stock and the wine, and bring to a vigorous boil, stirring until the liquid is absorbed. Add another cup of the strained vegetable stock, bring back to a boil, and cook and stir until the stock is absorbed; repeat with the remaining cup of stock. This process should take about 25 minutes. Stir in the cheese and set aside.

**The pea mixture:** Pour the frozen peas into a large sauté pan over medium heat. Add the vegetable stock, basil, parsley, and lettuce leaves; cover and cook 5 minutes. Turn the pea mixture into a food processor or blender, add the wine, and purée until smooth. Pour the puréed peas into the risotto and stir thoroughly.

**To serve:** Garnish each serving with a sprinkle of the Parmesan cheese, black pepper, fennel bulb slices, and chopped parsley.

Nutritional Profile per Serving: Calories—250; % calories from fat—17%; fat (gm)—5 or 7% daily value; saturated fat (gm)—2; sodium (mg)—229; cholesterol (mg)—6; carbohydrates (gm)—41; dietary fiber (gm)—3.

# PANJABI KALI DAL
## (LENTIL STEW)

*Treena and I have never had such delicious dal (lentil stew) as at the New Delhi Restaurant in San Francisco, and we've eaten Indian food on four continents.*
*Dal is usually served as a side dish with either poultry or meat and sometimes as an appetizer. Not only is it full of flavor, it is extremely nutritious and quite satisfying eaten with whole-grain pita bread.*

*Time Estimate: Hands-on, 30 minutes;*
  *unsupervised, 20 hours*

*Serves 6*

1/4 cup dried kidney beans (rajmah)
1/4 cup yellow split peas (split bengal gram or chana dal)
1/2 cup dried garbanzo beans (black gram)
1 tablespoon light olive oil with a dash of toasted sesame oil
1 teaspoon garam masala (page 3)
1/2 teaspoon cayenne pepper
1 teaspoon paprika
1/2 teaspoon turmeric
1 teaspoon coriander
Bouquet garni (see below)
1 teaspoon freshly grated gingerroot
2 cloves garlic, bashed, peeled, and finely diced
1 tablespoon chopped fresh cilantro
1/4 cup strained yogurt (page 288)
1 tablespoon freshly squeezed lemon juice

### BOUQUET GARNI

4 bay leaves
4 pieces whole green cardamom
2 pieces whole black cardamom
4 whole cloves
1 teaspoon whole cumin seeds

### GARNISH

6 sprigs fresh cilantro

Pour the kidney beans, yellow split peas, and garbanzo beans into a large stockpot. Add just enough water to cover, bring to a boil, and simmer for 2 minutes. Remove from the heat, cover, and let stand 1 hour. Drain and rinse well.

In a small high-sided casserole, heat half the olive oil. Add the garam masala, cayenne, paprika, turmeric, and coriander. Mix to make a curry paste. Stir the strained beans and lentils into the curry paste. Add 3 cups of water and the bouquet garni. Bring to a boil, cover, and simmer for 1 hour. Remove the bouquet garni.

In a small sauté pan, heat the remaining olive oil and sauté the ginger and garlic over medium-high heat for 1 minute. Combine with the cooked beans and stir in the cilantro. Take out a third of the beans and set aside. Scoop the rest into a food processor, purée, and return to the pot. Stir in the reserved whole beans, the strained yogurt, and lemon juice.

**To serve:** Ladle into bowls and garnish with a sprig of the fresh cilantro.

Nutritional Profile per Serving: Calories—147; % calories from fat—21%; fat (gm)—3 or 5% daily value; saturated fat (gm)—.5; sodium (mg)—19; cholesterol (mg)—.4; carbohydrates (gm)—22; dietary fiber (gm)—4. ⬇

# Steamed Vegetable Medley

*Stacking vegetable steamers allow you to cook each vegetable in this dish to perfection, at the same time.*

*Time Estimate: Hands-on, 25 minutes*
*Serves 4 as a side dish*

2 yams, cut into 1/2-inch (1.5-cm) slices
2 tablespoons chopped fresh thyme
1/4 teaspoon freshly ground black pepper
2 tomatoes, halved and cored
6 ounces (175 gm) spinach, well rinsed and stems trimmed
4 tablespoons freshly grated Parmesan cheese

Put a small amount of water in a steamer pot and bring it to a boil. Put the yams on a steamer tray and sprinkle with a bit of the thyme and pepper. Put the tray in the steamer pot, cover, and begin steaming.

After 16 minutes, put the tomatoes in another steamer tray and sprinkle with thyme and pepper. Stack on top of the yams, cover, and continue steaming for 3 minutes.

Now put the spinach in a third steamer tray and sprinkle with thyme and pepper. Stack on top of the tomatoes, cover, and steam 3 more minutes. At 22 minutes total, voilà—perfectly steamed vegetables ready for your meal.

**To serve:** Arrange the vegetables on a serving platter: bright orange yams, scarlet tomatoes, and deep-green spinach. Sprinkle with the remaining thyme and pepper, and the Parmesan cheese.

Nutritional Profile per Serving: Calories—106; % calories from fat—16%; fat (gm)—2 or 3% daily value; saturated fat (gm)—1; sodium (mg)—131; cholesterol (mg)—4; carbohydrates (gm)—18; dietary fiber (gm)—3. ⊘

# 20% calories from fat

※

# Brunch
## &
# Breakfast Dishes

# BRITISH BACON AND TOMATO SANDWICH

All the world loves a sandwich and some of them have become quite famous. My contribution to the world of sandwiches features a zesty Garlic and Herb Yogurt Spread with a low fat and calorie count.

Time Estimate: Hands-on, 15 minutes;
  unsupervised, 35 minutes
Serves 4

## GARLIC AND HERB YOGURT SPREAD

1 large head garlic
2 teaspoons fresh rosemary leaves
12 juniper berries
12 black peppercorns
1/2 cup strained yogurt (page 288)
6 sun-dried tomatoes, soaked in hot water for 30 minutes, drained, and finely chopped

## SANDWICH CONDIMENT

1/4 cup balsamic vinegar
1 tablespoon light olive oil with a dash of toasted sesame oil
4 plum tomatoes
1/2 cup radish or alfalfa sprouts
1/4 teaspoon freshly ground black peppercorns
8 slices whole-wheat bread
4 ounces (115 gm) Canadian bacon, thinly sliced

**The yogurt spread:** Roast the garlic by slicing about 1/2 inch (1.5 cm) off the top of the garlic head. Wrap the garlic head in aluminum foil and bake at 375°F (190°C) for 35 minutes.

While the garlic is roasting, whiz the rosemary, juniper berries, and black peppercorns in a small coffee grinder. When the garlic is done, squeeze the soft flesh out of the roasted skin and mash. Mix with the strained yogurt, sun-dried tomatoes, and 4 teaspoons of the "whizzed" herb mixture. Reserve the excess herb mixture for later use.

**The sandwich condiment:** Combine the vinegar and oil, and shake well. Slice the tomatoes and place on a dinner plate. Sprinkle with the sprouts, pepper, and the oil and vinegar, and let marinate for at least 15 minutes. Place another serving plate on top of the tomatoes and, holding the plates vertically, squeeze them together, allowing the excess juices to drain into a small bowl. (These juices can be added to any salad dressing.)

**To assemble:** Spread one side of the bread slices with the Garlic and Herb Yogurt Spread. Layer one bread slice with the Canadian bacon, the marinated sprouts, and tomato slices. Place another slice of bread on top and press down hard.

**To serve:** Slice off the crusts and cut the sandwiches into quarters. Serve with extra sprouts on the side, if you like. (Of course, slicing off the crusts is just a habit from my British heritage. Keep them on if you prefer.)

Nutritional Profile per Serving: Calories—249; % calories from fat—18%; fat (gm)—5 or 7% daily value; saturated fat (gm)—1; sodium (mg)—767; cholesterol (mg)—15; carbohydrates (gm)—39; dietary fiber (gm)—4. ⬇

# Chocolate Waffles with Basic Cocoa Sauce

*My best defense against my weakness for chocolate has been unsweetened Dutch-process cocoa powder. The flavor and color of chocolate are very much alive in cocoa powder, but with substantially less fat. This luscious breakfast treat is a great example. If you prefer, the Basic Cool Cocoa Sauce can be served warm on the waffles—it's your choice.*

Time Estimate: Hands-on, 45 minutes
Serves 5

1¾ cups all-purpose flour
2 teaspoons baking powder
1/8 teaspoon salt
3 tablespoons sugar
1/2 cup unsweetened Dutch-process cocoa powder
2 cups nonfat milk
1 egg
2 tablespoons light olive oil
3 egg whites
4 teaspoons chocolate morsels
1 recipe Basic Cool Cocoa Sauce (see below)

In a large bowl, stir together the flour, baking powder, salt, sugar, and cocoa powder until well mixed. In another bowl, beat the milk, whole egg, and the oil until well mixed. Stir the wet ingredients into the dry mix and beat until smooth and creamy.

Preheat a waffle iron according to the manufacturer's directions, or until a drop of water sizzles and bounces.

Just before cooking, beat the egg whites in a copper bowl until they form soft peaks. Gently fold the meringue into the waffle batter, one-third at a time, until just mixed.

Brush the waffle iron squares lightly with olive oil then pour approximately 1/2 cup of the batter per waffle square, or enough to fill the entire iron. This will depend on the type of waffle iron you're using. Sprinkle with 1/2 teaspoon of the chocolate morsels and cook for 3 minutes. If the waffles are not crisp enough for your taste, put them on a wire rack and toast for a minute under a hot oven broiler. If you can't serve the waffles immediately, lay them out on oven racks to keep crisp at 250°F (120°C). Please never stack them, as they'll all go limp.

**To serve:** Present the waffles "hot from the iron" with the Basic Cool Cocoa Sauce on the side.

Nutritional Profile per Serving: Calories—423; % calories from fat—20%; fat (gm)—10 or 15% daily value; saturated fat (gm)—3; sodium (mg)—376; cholesterol (mg)—46; carbohydrates (gm)—70; dietary fiber (gm)—5.

## BASIC COOL COCOA SAUCE
*Makes 12 tablespoons*

2 tablespoons unsweetened Dutch-process cocoa powder
3 tablespoons brown sugar
2 tablespoons nonfat milk
1 teaspoon vanilla extract
1 cup strained yogurt (page 288), stirred until smooth

In a small bowl, mix together the cocoa and sugar. Stir in the milk until completely dissolved, then the vanilla. Gently stir the cocoa mixture into the strained yogurt until well incorporated, but not too thin.

Nutritional Profile per Serving: Calories—87; % calories from fat—10%; fat (gm)—1 or 2% daily value; saturated fat (gm)—1; sodium (mg)—54; cholesterol (mg)—1; carbohydrates (gm)—22; dietary fiber (gm)—1

# Dutch Pancakes

※

*This is basically a pancake and ham sandwich with glazed apples on top and a maple-flavored custard sauce. I serve it as an unusual breakfast for a crowd. Everyone seems to have a good time!*

Time Estimate: Hands-on, 40 minutes;
  unsupervised, 30 minutes
Serves 2

PANCAKE BATTER

1 whole egg
1 egg yolk
1¼ cups 2%-fat milk
1 cup all-purpose flour
1/4 teaspoon freshly ground sea salt
1/4 teaspoon freshly ground white pepper
1 teaspoon light olive oil with a dash of toasted sesame oil

SAUCE

1/4 cup unsweetened evaporated skim milk
1/4 cup pure maple syrup
1 tablespoon cornstarch mixed with 2 tablespoons
   water (slurry)
1/2 cup strained yogurt (page 288)

FILLING

4 slices (2 ounces or 60 gm) Canadian bacon
1 Granny Smith apple, peeled, cored, and sliced
1 teaspoon brown sugar
1/4 teaspoon ground cinnamon

**The pancakes:** In a small bowl, mix the egg, egg yolk, and milk. Sift the flour, salt, and pepper into a medium bowl and make a well in the center. Pour the egg mixture into the well and gradually stir it together with the flour until fully incorporated with no lumps. Set the batter aside in a cool place to rest for 30 minutes. The resting will relax the starch cells and provide a more delicately finished pancake.

Heat a 10-inch (25-cm) nonstick frying pan over medium heat. Pour the olive oil into the pan, coat well, then pour the excess oil into the pancake batter. Mix thoroughly. This will help make the pancake self-releasing.

Pour one ladle (1/2 cup) of the pancake batter into the heated frying pan. Rotate the pan until the entire surface is covered. When the edges of the pancake start curling up and the top looks waxy, flip the pancake over. Cook the other side until it's light brown—just a minute or two—and turn out onto a dish. Finish cooking the other pancakes. Overlap, not stack, finished pancakes.

**The sauce:** In a small saucepan over medium heat, combine the evaporated skim milk and maple syrup. Cook until hot but not boiling. Stir the cornstarch slurry into the milk mixture, bring to a boil, and stir until thickened, about 30 seconds. It will have the consistency of whipped honey. Remove from the heat and let cool.

To finish the sauce, stir in the strained yogurt and return to lowest heat, stirring occasionally to keep the sauce from sticking.

**To assemble:** Put 1 pancake on an individual, ovenproof serving plate. Place the Canadian bacon on top of the pancake. Arrange the oven rack 3 inches (8 cm) from the broiler element and broil the pancake until brown, approximately 2½ minutes. Remove from the broiler, cover with another pancake, and arrange the apple slices around the edge in two concentric circles: one circle around the outside edge and one in the middle. Extend the slices just over the edge of the pancake so the delicate edge doesn't burn.

Dust with a scattering of the brown sugar and cinnamon, and pop under the broiler until the apples are just brown on the edges and glazed.

**To serve:** Present one per customer, warm from the oven, and the sauce on the side.

Nutritional Profile per Serving: Calories—542; % calories from fat—22%; fat (gm)—13 or 21% daily value; saturated fat (gm)—3; sodium (mg)—691; cholesterol (mg)—119; carbohydrates (gm)—83; dietary fiber (gm)—2.

# French Rarebit

⋇

*Cheese on toast? Well, not really! The Welsh make fine cheese, and like every cheese-producing area, they developed their own bread-and-cheese idea (Welsh Rarebit): a little beer, some mustard, a slice of toast. I've minimaxed on this classic to produce my own recipe.*

*This is really a snack food for fall or winter weather: a firm "welcome home" when it's raw outside and the family has been burning energy. I've dropped the calories from 529 to 311 with only 7 grams of fat . . . so it's within the limit.*

Time Estimate: Hands-on, 20 minutes;
  unsupervised, 60 minutes

Serves 6

1½ pounds (680 gm) yellow new potatoes (preferably
  Yukon Gold variety)
1/4 cup nonfat milk
1/4 teaspoon freshly ground white pepper
1/4 teaspoon freshly grated nutmeg
2 tablespoons white wine Worcestershire sauce
1/2 cup de-alcoholized beer
1 teaspoon dry mustard
1 cup grated dry Monterey Jack cheese (or another
  good grating cheese)
1 French baguette loaf (about 15 inches [38 cm] long),
  sliced in half horizontally, doughy center scooped out
Paprika
Fresh chopped parsley

Bake the potatoes at 375°F (190°C) for 1 hour. Wrap them in a towel and gently squeeze from all sides to break up the flesh, taking care not to rupture the skin. Spoon the potato out of the skins and into a medium mixing bowl, and mash well. Save the skins for use in Cynthia's Skins (see sidebar).

Return the hot potato to a warm saucepan over medium heat. Add the milk, white pepper, and nutmeg, and beat well until smooth and creamy. Now stir in the Worcestershire sauce, beer, dry mustard, and finally 3/4 cup of the cheese—mix well and taste

it! Pour the cheese mixture into the hollowed-out baguette. Dust with the remaining cheese and a little of the paprika. Broil until dappled brown.

**To serve:** Dust with the parsley and serve piping hot from the oven.

Nutritional Profile per Serving: Calories—311; % calories from fat—21%; fat (gm)—7 or 11% daily value; saturated fat (gm)—4; sodium (mg)—702; cholesterol (mg)—13; carbohydrates (gm)—48; dietary fiber (gm)—3.

During the testing of this recipe, my food assistant, Cynthia, suggested an idea for the leftover skins. We tried it, and it worked so well we named it after her! The recipe is as follows: Brush the leftover potato skins with a little beaten egg white and put them on a baking sheet. Sprinkle them with cayenne pepper to taste and about 2 tablespoons of your favorite grated or crumbled cheese. Pop them under the broiler for 4 minutes and serve.

# Egg Foo Yung Scramble

*So easy and simple, perfect to end a day when you have no time to cook. This version also manages to reduce the classic recipe's fat from 18 to 8 grams.*

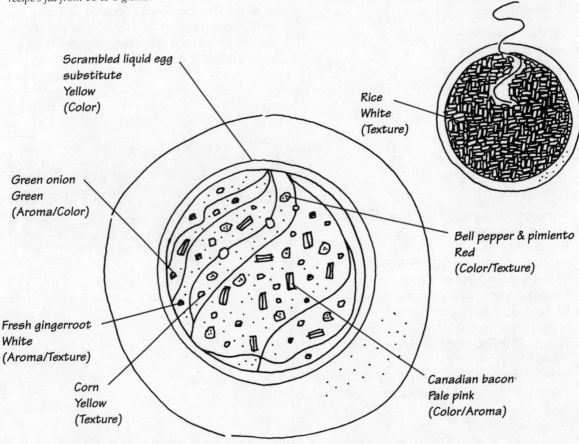

Scrambled liquid egg
substitute
Yellow
(Color)

Rice
White
(Texture)

Green onion
Green
(Aroma/Color)

Bell pepper & pimiento
Red
(Color/Texture)

Fresh gingerroot
White
(Aroma/Texture)

Corn
Yellow
(Texture)

Canadian bacon
Pale pink
(Color/Aroma)

*Time Estimate: Hands-on, 25 minutes*
*Serves 2*

1 teaspoon light olive oil with a dash of toasted sesame
   oil
1 clove garlic, bashed, peeled, and finely chopped
10 dime-size slices of peeled gingerroot, finely chopped
2 green onions, separated into white and green parts,
   cut into 1/8-inch (3-mm) pieces
1 cup frozen corn

2 ounces finely chopped pimiento
1/4 cup finely diced sweet red bell pepper
2 ounces (60 gm) finely diced extra-firm tofu
1/4 cup finely diced Canadian bacon
1 cup liquid egg substitute
2 cups hot cooked white rice

Brush half of the oil over the bottom of a small skillet over medium heat and cook the garlic, ginger, and the white parts of the green onions, stirring, until their fragrance is released, about 30 seconds. Add the remaining oil, the corn, pimiento, red pepper, tofu, Canadian bacon, and dark green onion tops, and stir-fry for 1 minute. Transfer the vegetables to a bowl.

Pour the egg substitute into the same skillet and cook until firm, about 3 minutes. Keep the eggs pushed into the center of the pan. When they're almost completely set, spoon the vegetables on top and very gently lift and turn together, until completely combined.

**To serve:** Spoon the eggs and vegetables into bowls and serve with the steamed rice in separate bowls.

| Nutritional Profile per Serving | | | |
|---|---|---|---|
| | Classic | Minimax | Daily Value |
| Calories | 453 | 443 | |
| Calories from fat | 36% | 16% | |
| Fat (gm) | 18 | 8 | 12% |
| Saturated fat (gm) | 4 | 2 | 8% |
| Sodium (mg) | 737 | 497 | 21% |
| Cholesterol (mg) | 329 | 13 | 4% |
| Carbohydrates (gm) | 6 | 70 | 23% |
| Dietary fiber (gm) | 1 | 7 | 28% |
| Classic compared: Egg Foo Yung | | | |

# FU YUNG GAI
## (CHINESE CHICKEN OMELET)

⌗

*Are you a tofu fan yet? When I made this dish for the television program, most of the people in our studio audience were quite hesitant! But once they had dabbed a bit of fresh ginger and oyster sauce behind their ears, they were ready for anything! Maybe all you'll need to do is taste this dish's unique combination of textures and flavors to become a true tofu connoisseur!*

*Time Estimate: Hands-on, 45 minutes*
*Serves 4*

OMELET

6 ounces (175 gm) skinless, boneless chicken breast, finely diced
4 teaspoons freshly squeezed lemon juice
4 teaspoons rice wine vinegar
2 green onions, chopped
1/2 teaspoon freshly grated gingerroot
1/2 teaspoon freshly ground white pepper
3 ounces (90 gm) tofu, finely diced
1 teaspoon light olive oil with a dash of toasted sesame oil
1/2 ounce (15 gm) butter
3 large eggs, beaten
1 tablespoon chopped fresh cilantro
4 cups cooked rice

SAUCE

1/2 cup low-sodium chicken stock (page 286)
2 tablespoons oyster sauce
2 teaspoons freshly squeezed lemon juice
1 teaspoon arrowroot mixed with 1 teaspoon water (slurry)

Marinate the diced chicken in 3 teaspoons of the lemon juice, 3 teaspoons of the rice wine vinegar, the green onions, ginger, and freshly ground white pepper for 20 minutes. Strain out the chicken and set aside.

Marinate the tofu for 30 minutes in the remaining lemon juice and rice wine vinegar. Strain out the tofu and set aside.

**The sauce:** Heat the chicken stock, oyster sauce, and lemon juice in a small pan over high heat. Remove the pan from the heat, add the arrowroot slurry, return to the heat, and stir until thickened. Set aside and keep warm.

**The omelet:** Heat the olive oil in a nonstick pan over medium-high heat and quickly fry the marinated chicken until white, about 1 to 2 minutes. Add the tofu pieces so the flavors can mingle. Because the pieces are the same size, the tofu will give you the feeling of a lot more chicken. Cook for 1 minute, then remove the pan from the heat and turn the chicken and tofu out onto a plate.

Wipe the pan, add the butter, and heat until it just begins to turn brown—this is the correct time to add the eggs! Pour the beaten eggs into the pan and stir quickly, spreading the eggs to cover the entire pan (stirring will bring the butter taste into the omelet).

When the eggs look fairly set, sprinkle the chicken and tofu on top in a vertical line down the center of the pan. Fold over each side as for a regular omelet.

**To serve:** Gently shake the omelet out of the pan onto the warmed plate so that the fold is on the bottom and the egg completely covers it. Pour your warm coating sauce over the top and sprinkle with fresh cilantro. What color! What aroma! The cooked rice is the perfect accompaniment to sop up every drop!

Nutritional Profile per Serving: Calories—383; % calories from fat—25%; fat (gm)—11 or 16% daily value; saturated fat (gm)—4; sodium (mg)—441; cholesterol (mg)—190; carbohydrates (gm)—49; dietary fiber (gm)—1.

# GRAHAM'S GRANOLA

*Crunchy, nutty, and a little bit sweet—what a way to start the day!*

*Time Estimate: Hands-on, 10 minutes;*
*unsupervised, 15 minutes*
*Serves 12 (1/2-cup servings)*

1/2 cup raw sunflower seeds
1/4 cup sliced almonds
1 cup Grape-Nuts cereal
2 cups oat flakes
1 cup bran flakes
1 cup apple chips (baked, not fried), broken up
1/4 cup raisins
1/4 cup crystallized mango or papaya
1/4 cup dried cranberries

Roast the sunflower seeds and almonds together for 15 minutes at 350°F (180°C). Combine with the remaining ingredients and store in an airtight container.

Nutritional Profile per Serving: Calories—140; % calories from fat—21%; fat (gm)—3 or 5% daily value; saturated fat (gm)—0; sodium (mg)—146; cholesterol (mg)—0; carbohydrates (gm)—28; dietary fiber (gm)—4.

---

## ROLLED OATS

These oat groats have been heated to soften, then rolled or literally flattened. Rolled oats will cook more quickly than oat groats, which can take up to 2 hours.

---

# MUESLI

*Since 1978, I have alternated between the Kerrmush (page 208) and the muesli cereals each morning, according to either the weather or boredom! One of my "dinner" guests on television was terrorized by porridge as a child—this recipe helped to change his mind. If it changes yours, you will have taken the largest single step toward a more creative food-style. Most breakfasts are either smothered in fat or don't exist at all. Kerrmush and muesli are low in fat and provide lots of good energy all morning.*

*Time Estimate: Hands-on, 15 minutes*
*Serves 1*

2 tablespoons rolled oats
1 tablespoon dark raisins
1/2 Granny Smith apple, unpeeled and grated
1 tablespoon freshly squeezed lemon juice
1 tablespoon honey, preferably fireweed
2 tablespoons plain nonfat yogurt
1 tablespoon Minimax Seed Mix (page 195), ground
    until just broken
Fruit of choice

Soak the oats and raisins in water overnight. Drain the oats and raisins and stir in the grated apple and lemon juice.

Mix together the honey and yogurt and stir into the oat mixture. Sprinkle with the Seed Mix, garnish with small pieces of bright fruit, and serve.

Nutritional Profile per Serving: Calories—285; % calories from fat—18%; fat (gm)—6 or 9% daily value; saturated fat (gm)—1; sodium (mg)—29; cholesterol (mg)—1; carbohydrates (gm)—58; dietary fiber (gm)—5.

# Leek and Mushroom Quiche

*This recipe eliminates the fat reservoirs found in classic pastry crusts by using steamed rice seasoned with just a hint of cheese and molded into a "dough" with egg white. It does need a short time to precook before adding the filling. I've created an egg-substitute filling in order to provide a flavor very much like custardy quiche. I think a fresh green salad is the perfect complement.*

*Time Estimate: Hands-on, 45 minutes; unsupervised, 40 minutes*

Serves 6

1 Rice Crust, baked (page 29)

FILLING

2 pounds (900 gm) leeks to yield 1 pound (450 gm)
   white bulbs only, greens discarded
1 teaspoon light olive oil with a dash of toasted sesame oil
1 tablespoon chopped fresh thyme
8 ounces (225 gm) sliced fresh mushrooms
1/4 teaspoon freshly ground sea salt
1/4 teaspoon freshly ground black pepper
1 cup liquid egg substitute
1/2 cup 2%-fat milk
1 tablespoon freshly grated Parmesan cheese

**The filling:** Cut the white bulbs of the leeks in half lengthwise, rinse well, then slice thinly.

Into a large casserole over medium heat, pour half of the oil. Add the leeks, stir until well coated, and cook 10 minutes, stirring occasionally. Add the thyme and cook an additional 5 minutes. The leeks should be just turning brown. Remove the leeks from the pan.

Preheat the oven to 375°F (190°C). Pour the remaining oil into the same pan, add the mushrooms, and cook over low heat for 8 minutes, stirring occasionally. Stir in the cooked leeks, salt, and pepper. Increase the heat to medium and cook for 2 minutes. Remove from the heat and turn into the prepared crust.

In a bowl, mix together the egg substitute and milk, and pour gently over the cooked vegetables. Bake for 30 to 35 minutes until the custard is just set. Remove from the oven and let stand 10 minutes before slicing.

**To serve:** Sprinkle the pie with the Parmesan cheese.

Nutritional Profile per Serving: Calories—150; % calories from fat—18%; fat (gm)—3 or 5% daily value; saturated fat (gm)—1; sodium (mg)—428; cholesterol (mg)—6 carbo-hydrates (gm)—22; dietary fiber (gm)—3.

# Kerrmush

*Everyone should have a mush named after them—I mean it! Please take this recipe and make it your own with your favorite nuts and fruit. And then you can start each day brightly with "marvelous mush o'mine."*

*Time Estimate: Hands-on, 10 minutes*

Serves 4

1 cup rolled oats
4 tablespoons dark raisins
2⅔ cups nonfat milk
4 tablespoons Minimax Seed Mix (page 195)
4 teaspoons fresh local honey

Simmer the oats, raisins, and milk until just cooked, about 10 minutes. Stir and remove from the heat. Sprinkle with the Seed Mix, either whole or partly or fully ground. I use a small electric coffee bean grinder to do this fresh each day. Drizzle the honey on top and serve hot.

Nutritional Profile per Serving: Calories—255; % calories from fat—22% fat (gm)—6 or 9% daily value; saturated fat (gm)—1; sodium (mg)—87; cholesterol (mg)—3; carbo-hydrates (gm)—42; dietary fiber (gm)—3.

# SALMON HASH

*Hash has a great history in America. It's a food of working people, made famous by thrifty housewives and cooks in diners across our land. My version is a hearty yet low-fat dish that will please your hard-working, hard-playing family. Add slices of fresh, sweet cantaloupe and pear for a complete meal.*

*Time Estimate: Hands-on, 35 minutes*
*Serves 4*

1½ pounds (680 gm) Yukon Gold or russet potatoes, peeled and cut into eighths
1/4 teaspoon freshly ground sea salt
8 ounces (225 gm) fresh salmon fillet
2 tablespoons freshly squeezed lemon juice
1/4 teaspoon freshly ground black pepper
2 teaspoons light olive oil with a dash of toasted sesame oil
1/2 cup green onion pieces, 1/4 inch (.75 cm) long, diagonally cut
1/2 red bell pepper, cut into 1-inch (2.5-cm) matchsticks
1 teaspoon dried tarragon
1 tablespoon Worcestershire sauce
1/4 teaspoon cayenne pepper
1/2 cup peeled and diced cucumber
1¼ cups liquid egg substitute
1/4 teaspoon freshly ground black pepper
1/3 cup freshly grated Parmesan cheese
3 tablespoons chopped fresh parsley

Steam or boil the potatoes with the salt until tender, about 20 minutes. Place in cold water until cool enough to chop coarsely. Set aside. Remove the skin and bones from the salmon and cut into 1-inch (2.5-cm) chunks. Place in a bowl with the lemon juice and pepper.

Heat the oil in a large skillet, preferably nonstick, over medium-high heat. Toss in the onion and red bell pepper, and cook, stirring, for 1 minute. Add the potatoes, tarragon, Worcestershire sauce, and cayenne pepper, and cook for about 5 minutes, until the potatoes are hot and nicely browned. Make sure you scrape up the flavorful brown bits on the bottom of the pan. Add the cucumber and salmon; stir gently to mix, cover, and cook for 4 minutes.

Combine the egg substitute, pepper, Parmesan cheese, and 1 tablespoon of the chopped parsley. Pour into a hot, medium nonstick skillet and cook, stirring and scraping the bottom, until just firm, about 4 minutes. Remove from the heat and set aside.

**To serve:** Divide the hash between 4 warm plates. Place one-quarter of the eggs on each and sprinkle with the remaining chopped parsley.

Nutritional Profile per Serving: Calories—316; % calories from fat—24%; fat (gm)—8 or 13% daily value; saturated fat (gm)—3; sodium (mg)—450; cholesterol (mg)—44; carbohydrates (gm)—37; dietary fiber (gm)—4.

# Waffles with Apple Butter

*Minimax Waffles with Apple Butter are a crisp, crunchy wholesome food for a special breakfast. A variation on the apple butter can be made by combining it with a little strained yogurt. You'll be delighted with the resulting whipped cream–like mixture. And never forget the sweet pleasures of ripe, sliced fruit on a steaming waffle!*

*Time Estimate: Hands-on, 1 hour*
*Serves 5*

### APPLE BUTTER

3 sweet cooking apples, washed, cored, and sliced
1/4 cup clear, unsweetened apple juice
1/4 cup water
1/8 cup dark raisins (without sulfites)
1/4 cup brown sugar
1/8 teaspoon cinnamon
Dash of ground cloves
Dash of ground allspice
1/4 teaspoon freshly grated nutmeg
1 teaspoon grated lemon zest

### WAFFLES

1¾ cups all-purpose flour
2 teaspoons baking powder
Pinch of salt
1 tablespoon sugar
2 cups nonfat milk
1 egg
2 tablespoons light olive oil with a dash of toasted
    sesame oil
3 egg whites
Canola oil

**The apple butter:** Put the apples, apple juice, water, and raisins in a saucepan and bring to a boil. Cover, reduce the heat, and simmer until the apples are soft, about 20 minutes.

Press the fruit through a sieve, or whiz at high speed in a food processor until smooth, then return to the saucepan. Continue to simmer, uncovered, on very low heat, or in a preheated 300°F (150°C) oven. Add the brown sugar, spices, and lemon zest. Cook for another 30 minutes until very thick and a lovely dark brown.

**The waffles:** In a medium mixing bowl, stir together the flour, baking powder, salt, and sugar. In another bowl combine the milk, whole egg, and oil. Stir the wet ingredients into the dry ones and blend until smooth and creamy.

Just before cooking the waffles, in a copper bowl, beat the egg whites until they form soft peaks. Gently fold the beaten egg whites into the waffle batter, one-third at a time.

Preheat the waffle iron according to the manufacturer's directions, or until a drop of water sizzles and bounces when dropped onto the hot iron.

Brush the waffle iron lightly with the canola oil, then pour approximately 1/2 cup batter per waffle square or enough to fill the entire waffle iron. Cook for 3 minutes.

**To serve:** Present immediately on plates with the apple butter on the side.

Nutritional Profile per Serving: Calories—380; % calories from fat—17%; fat (gm)—7 or 11% daily value; saturated fat (gm)—1; sodium (mg)—353; cholesterol (mg)—44; carbohydrates (gm)—68; dietary fiber (gm)—3.

> If you can't eat your waffles immediately, never stack them. Stacking causes waffles to go limp! Instead, preheat the oven to 300°F (150°C) and slip them onto the oven racks, leaving the door slightly open. They will stay crisp for at least 30 minutes.

# *20% calories from fat*

# *Desserts*

# ALMOST HEAVEN BROWNIES

Nutritional Profile per Serving: Calories—81; % calories from fat—23%; fat (gm)—2 or 3% daily value; saturated fat (gm)—0; sodium (mg)—102; cholesterol (mg)—0; carbohydrates (gm)—15; dietary fiber (gm)—1.

*I went back to the drawing board on these and used my newest findings on low-fat baking: fruit purées to provide moisture; cocoa powder for chocolate taste; cake flour for its texture; and crispy rice cereal instead of high-fat nuts for texture. You might want to try Grape-Nuts cereal for a more noticeable crunch. I think you'll find these brownies delicious.*

*Time Estimate: Hands-on, 20 minutes;*
  *unsupervised, 25 minutes*
*Serves 16*

1/4 cup dried, pitted prunes
1/4 cup hot water
1/2 cup cocoa powder (American-style)
1 teaspoon vanilla extract
3 tablespoons light olive oil
1/2 cup buttermilk
4 large egg whites
1 cup sugar
1 cup cake flour
1/4 teaspoon freshly ground sea salt
1 teaspoon baking soda
1 cup crisp rice cereal

> I use American-style cocoa instead of the Dutch-processed in this recipe because its higher acid content adds to the acid in the buttermilk, which activates the soda to act as the leavening agent.

Preheat the oven to 350°F (177°C). Spray a 9 X 13-inch (23 X 33-cm) baking dish with pan spray. Cut a piece of waxed paper to fit the bottom of the pan, lay it in, and spray over the whole bottom.

Soak the prunes in hot water for 15 minutes to soften. Purée in a food processor or blender. Combine puréed prunes, cocoa, vanilla, and oil in a medium bowl and mix well. Add the buttermilk and whisk until the mixture is smooth, with no lumps of cocoa. Whisk in the egg whites until light.

Mix the sugar, flour, salt, and soda in a large mixing bowl. Fold in the chocolate mixture and then stir in the rice cereal. Pour into the prepared pan and bake for 25 minutes or until a toothpick inserted in the middle comes out clean. Cool and cut into 24 pieces.

# CAPIROTADA

*It's hard to believe that green peppers and onions can be part of a dessert, but here is a classic—this time served up without its incredibly high sugar content. This Mexican dish is often served during Lent, but frankly it doesn't seem to represent sacrifice! It has a wonderfully complex taste that doesn't need any whipped cream or ice cream or custard. I've added a very sharp nonfat yogurt sauce that balances well with the sweet bread pudding—you'll only need a wee drop!*

*Time Estimate: Hands-on, 30 minutes; unsupervised, 1 hour*

Serves 8

## SYRUP

1/4 cup chopped green pepper
1/4 cup chopped onion
1/2 cup chopped fresh cilantro
1/2 teaspoon grated orange zest
1/2 teaspoon grated cinnamon stick
4 cups water
1 cup brown sugar
3 whole cloves

## BREAD PUDDING

1 cup low-fat cottage cheese (use lowest fat content available, but do not use "no-fat" cottage cheese)
3/4 cup Minimax Seed Mixture (page 195), coarsely cracked in an electric coffee grinder
1 cup raisins
2 apples, preferably Rome, cored and thinly sliced
2 lemon wedges
1 small uncut loaf of whole-wheat bread
1 medium tomato, sliced

## LEMON YOGURT SAUCE

Juice and grated zest of 1 lemon
2 cups nonfat plain yogurt
Honey to taste

**The syrup:** Combine all the ingredients for the syrup in a saucepan over medium heat and cook for 30 minutes. Strain.

**The bread pudding:** Preheat the oven to 350°F (180°C). Mix the cottage cheese, 1/2 cup of the seed mixture, and raisins. Set aside. Put the apples and the lemon wedges in a bowl with enough cold water to cover to prevent browning. Cut the bread into 1/2-inch (1.5-cm) cubes and toast 10 minutes in the preheated oven.

**To assemble:** Layer half the bread cubes, cottage cheese mixture, and apples in an 8-cup baking dish, finishing with a layer of bread. Arrange the tomato and remaining seed mix on top. Carefully pour the syrup on top, letting the bread cubes soak up the syrup from underneath. Don't drown them from the top. Bake in the preheated oven for 1 hour. The Capirotada should be crisp on top, bubbling around the edges.

**The sauce:** Combine all the ingredients and set aside.

**To serve:** Bring warm to the table, with the lemon yogurt sauce on the side. Wait until your taste buds have a go at it! It's a marvelous thing when a nuance of green pepper comes through.

Nutritional Profile per Serving: Calories—537; % calories from fat—17%; fat (gm)—10 or 16% daily value; saturated fat (gm)—2; sodium (mg)—480; cholesterol (mg)—3; carbohydrates (gm)—103; dietary fiber (gm)—6.

# Banana Spice Bread

⣿

*A single serving of the classic recipe for Banana Bread could have as much as 25 grams of fat. This version keeps the delight of a dense, spicy snack, with only 5 grams of fat per serving. Check the dried fruit section of your grocery store for the sun-dried bananas. The sweet banana essence is incredibly concentrated through the drying process. Remember, the dried bananas are not the common banana chips, which are fried in oil.*

Time Estimate: Hands-on, 30 minutes;
  unsupervised, 60 minutes.

Serves 12

1/4 cup plus 1/8 teaspoon margarine
1 cup plus 1 teaspoon all-purpose flour, sifted
1 cup whole-wheat flour
2 teaspoons baking soda
2 ounces (60 gm) sun-dried whole bananas or sun-dried
  papaya chunks
5 tablespoons light brown sugar
1 egg
1/2 cup 1%-fat buttermilk
3 ripe bananas, mashed
1 teaspoon vanilla extract
1 teaspoon cinnamon
1 teaspoon allspice
2 tablespoons sliced almonds

Preheat the oven to 350°F (180°C). Grease a 9 X 5 X 3-inch (23 X 13 X 8-cm) loaf pan with 1/8 teaspoon of the margarine. Dust with 1 teaspoon of the flour and shake out the surplus.

Sift 1 cup of the all-purpose flour, all of the whole-wheat flour, and the baking soda into a bowl. Cut the bananas or papayas into 1/4-inch (.75-cm) chunks and toss them in the flour mixture, making sure all the chunks are well coated and separated.

In a large bowl, cream the remaining 1/4 cup margarine and the brown sugar until creamy. Beat in the egg and buttermilk. Add the mashed bananas, vanilla, cinnamon, and allspice, and beat with an electric mixer on low speed until all the ingredients are well combined. Gradually beat in the flour mixture and sun-dried fruit until just combined. Pour the batter into the prepared loaf pan and lightly tap the pan on a hard surface to remove any excess air bubbles. Sprinkle the almonds on top, pushing them just slightly under the surface.

Bake in the preheated oven for 1 hour, or until a thin-bladed knife inserted into the middle comes out clean. Remove and let cool on a baking rack.

Nutritional Profile per Serving: Calories—184; % calories from fat—24%; fat (gm)—5 or 8% daily value; saturated fat (gm)—1; sodium (mg)—262; cholesterol (mg)—18; carbohydrates (gm)—33; dietary fiber (gm)—2.

# CHOCOLATE CHERRY AND ALMOND CAKE

※

*A friendly local restaurant recently announced in their dessert section that "the fat cake is back!!" They referred to a vast wedge of supermoist, midnight-brown chocolate cake— it didn't sell! "Do you know a creative alternative?" they asked. We set to work and this came out well at 4 grams of fat per slice compared to 36 grams in the "fat" cake.*

Time Estimate: Hands-on, 40 minutes;
  unsupervised, 20 minutes
Serves 8

## SPONGE CAKE

1/2 cup all-purpose flour
1/4 cup unsweetened cocoa powder
1 teaspoon baking powder
4 eggs, separated
1/2 cup sugar
1/4 cup nonfat milk
Olive oil cooking spray

## CHERRY CUSTARD

1 tablespoon unsweetened Dutch-process cocoa powder
2 tablespoons cornstarch
1¼ cups nonfat milk
1/8 teaspoon almond extract
1 cup fresh or frozen, pitted dark sweet cherries (if
  unavailable, canned sweet cherries may be used)
2 teaspoons sugar
1 teaspoon pure maple syrup
2 tablespoons slivered almonds

## GARNISH

1 tablespoon confectioners' sugar
5 cherries, cut in half

**The sponge cake:** Preheat the oven to 375°F (190°C). Sift the flour, cocoa, and baking powder into a medium bowl and set aside.

In a large bowl (preferably copper), over warm water, beat the egg yolks and sugar until the volume doubles, approximately 5 minutes. Add the milk and sifted flour mixture and mix at low speed with an electric mixer until well incorporated.

Clean and dry the mixer beaters. In a medium bowl, beat the egg whites at high speed until stiff but not dry. Fold the egg whites into the batter mixture. Pour the batter into a lightly greased 9-inch (23-cm) round cake pan. (I like to use the spray-type olive oils, ensuring the minimum added fat.) Tap the filled pan on the counter to release any trapped air bubbles. Bake the cake in the preheated oven for 20 minutes and turn out to cool on a rack.

**The cherry custard:** Combine the cocoa, cornstarch, and 1/4 cup of the skim milk to make a paste. In a medium saucepan, bring the remaining milk to a boil, stirring constantly to prevent scorching. Stir in the cocoa paste and remove from the heat. Stir in the almond extract, cherries, sugar, maple syrup, and almonds.

**To assemble:** Slice the cake horizontally into 2 even layers. Place one layer, cut side up, on a serving plate and spread with the filling. Cover with the second cake layer, cut side down. Garnish with a sprinkle of the confectioners' sugar and the cherry halves.

**To serve:** Cut into 8 wedges. No whipped cream or ice cream; the cherry custard should do the trick.

Nutritional Profile per Serving: Calories—183; % calories from fat—21%; fat (gm)—4 or 7% daily value; saturated fat (gm)—1; sodium (mg)—118; cholesterol (mg)—107; carbohydrates (gm)—32; dietary fiber (gm)—2. ⬇

# CRÊPES SUZETTE, TAKE II

The original Crêpes Suzette was made as a prop in a Paris stage show. I have always believed it to be "No, No, Nanette," but I haven't been able to confirm this. I named this version "Take II" because of its obvious changes. It will, nonetheless, win you a standing ovation! You can make the crêpes before dinner and cover them with a towel. You can also make the sauce and then add the crêpes to warm up and finish—a classic dessert without fuss!

Time Estimate: Hands-on, 30 minutes; unsupervised, 30 minutes

Serves 4

## CRÊPE BATTER

1 whole egg
1 egg yolk
1 cup 2%-fat milk
1 cup all-purpose flour
1/2 teaspoon vanilla extract
Grated zest of 1 lemon
1 teaspoon light olive oil with a dash of toasted sesame oil

## THE ORANGE SYRUP

1 teaspoon light olive oil with a dash of toasted sesame oil
1 tablespoon grated orange zest
1/2 cup de-alcoholized white wine
1 cup freshly squeezed orange juice
2 tablespoons freshly squeezed lemon juice
2 tablespoons brown sugar
1 tablespoon cornstarch mixed with 2 tablespoons strained yogurt (see page 288) (slurry)
4 oranges, peeled and divided into segments
1 teaspoon chopped fresh mint

**The crêpes:** In a small bowl, mix the egg, egg yolk, and milk. In another bowl, sift the flour and make a well in the center. Pour the egg mixture into the well and gradually stir together until the flour is fully incorporated. Add the vanilla and the grated lemon zest. Set aside in a cool place for 30 minutes.

Heat the oil in an 8-inch (20-cm) sauté pan over medium-high heat, then pour the excess oil into the crêpe batter. This makes the crêpes self-releasing. Pour 1/4 cup of the batter into the pan and swirl to make a round, thin crêpe. Cook until slightly brown—approximately 1 minute on each side. Place the cooked crêpes on a plate and set aside, covered with a damp towel.

**The orange syrup:** Heat the oil in a 10-inch (25-cm) skillet over medium-high heat. Add the orange zest and cook to extract the volatile oils, about 2 minutes. Add the wine and reduce until it is like a syrup, dark in color but not burnt.

Add 1/4 cup of the orange juice, 1 tablespoon at a time to keep the dark color. Slowly add the remaining orange juice, the lemon juice, and brown sugar. Stir until dissolved.

Strain the syrup, removing the zest. Return the syrup to the skillet. Slowly stir in the cornstarch slurry. Bring to a boil and stir until the syrup is well combined and slightly thickened.

Place one cooked crêpe in the syrup and coat well. Using a spoon and fork, fold the crêpe in half and in half again, so the crêpe is now in the shape of a triangle. Move the crêpe triangle to the side of the pan. Repeat the coating and folding process with the remaining crêpes. Spoon the segmented oranges and the mint into the syrup with the crêpes.

**To serve:** Place the crêpes on a warm plate and spoon the orange segments with syrup over the top.

Nutritional Profile per Serving: Calories—335; % calories from fat—17%; fat (gm)—7 or 10% daily value; saturated fat (gm)—2; sodium (mg)—66; cholesterol (mg)—111; carbohydrates (gm)—60; dietary fiber (gm)—4.

# Moravian Cake

⧉

*This delicious snacking cake is naturally moist but should be stored in a tightly lidded cake tin or a large sealable plastic bag. With a good cup of coffee, you'll have all you need for your next get-together . . . have fun!*

Time Estimate: Hands-on, 30 minutes;
  unsupervised, 35 minutes
Serves 8

2 cups all-purpose flour
1/2 teaspoon baking powder
1 teaspoon baking soda combined with 1 tablespoon
   warm water
1/4 cup sliced almonds
1 cup water
1 cup dark brown sugar
1½ cups seedless raisins, preferably the "flame" variety
1/3 cup margarine
1 teaspoon freshly ground cinnamon
1/3 teaspoon freshly ground cloves
1/4 teaspoon freshly grated nutmeg

Preheat the oven to 350°F (180°C). In a large bowl, sift together the flour and baking powder. Make a well and stir in the baking soda mixture and the sliced almonds. Set aside.

Pour the water into a high-sided saucepan over high heat. Mix in the brown sugar, raisins, margarine, and spices. Bring to a boil. Remove from the heat and pour into a bowl set in a larger bowl of ice water to cool slightly. (You don't have to cool it quickly; it can be set aside to lose heat naturally. But if you're in the kind of hurry that faces me each day, the ice helps!) Add the cooled syrup to the flour mixture all at once and stir well.

Pour the mixture into a 10-inch (25-cm) oven-proof skillet and spread evenly. Pop in the preheated oven and bake for 35 minutes or until the edges of the cake start to pull away from the sides of the pan. (Please be sure your skillet's handle is approved for this temperature. Be careful to drape a towel over it to remind yourself that it's hot!)

**To serve:** Wedges of this snacking cake are especially complemented by hot tea or coffee.

Nutritional Profile per Serving: Calories—455; % calories from fat—19%; fat (gm)—10 or 15% daily value; saturated fat (gm)—2; sodium (mg)—306; cholesterol (mg)—0; carbohydrates (gm)—89; dietary fiber (gm)—2.

---

If possible, always freshly grind your spices. For this recipe, you can grind the cinnamon and cloves in a coffee grinder or a blender. You'll need 1 (1-inch or 2.5-cm) stick of cinnamon and 6 cloves. The difference between these and the commercially ground product is the fineness of the grind. I prefer roughly ground for this recipe.

# New Book Pudding

*The classic recipe for Old Book Pudding, from one of my old television shows, was a real nutritional "shocker!" The Minimax version brings you the same luscious flavor with a greatly diminished risk factor. But it's the "toothpaste pump" idea that makes it truly memorable—see for yourself.*

*Time Estimate: Hands-on, 30 minutes; unsupervised, 1 hour*

*Serves 4*

3/4 cup strained yogurt (page 288)
2½ ounces (75 gm) dry coconut macaroons, crumbled in a food processor
8 tablespoons raisin purée (see sidebar)
4 drops almond extract
1/4 teaspoon ground cardamom
2 tablespoons unsweetened Dutch-process cocoa powder
1 tablespoon finely chopped almonds
6 egg whites
Pinch of salt

COCOA SAUCE

5 tablespoons water
4 tablespoons brown sugar
3 tablespoons unsweetened Dutch-process cocoa powder
1 tablespoon arrowroot

GARNISH

Plain yogurt
Lime slices
Fresh mint leaves

In a large bowl, stir together the strained yogurt and macaroon crumbs. Add the raisin purée, almond extract, cardamom, cocoa powder, and chopped almonds.

Beat the egg whites with the pinch of salt and a drop or two of water to help them whip and retain volume. Gently fold a third of the egg whites into the yogurt mixture, then fold in the rest. Put the mixture into a round, tubular mold such as a recycled, 1-inch (2.5-cm) diameter toothpaste pump that has had the top cut off and has been washed out and freeze until solid, about 2 hours.

**The cocoa sauce:** Pour the water into a small saucepan over medium heat. Add the brown sugar and cocoa, and stir until dissolved. Take out a tablespoon of the cocoa sauce and mix with the arrowroot to form a paste. Remove the saucepan from the heat. Add the arrowroot slurry, return to the heat, and stir until thickened.

**To serve:** Remove the pudding from the mold and slice into 1/2-inch (1.25-cm) pieces. Pour enough cocoa sauce to just cover a small plate. Spoon a little plain yogurt into a piping bag. Pipe thin, straight lines across the cocoa sauce, about 1 inch (2.5 cm) apart. Lightly drag a toothpick back and forth, at right angles to the yogurt lines, to make a "feathered" design. Lay New Book Pudding slices on top and garnish with the fresh lime slices and mint leaves.

Nutritional Profile per Serving: Calories—305; % calories from fat—21%; fat (gm)—7 or 11% daily value; saturated fat (gm)—2; sodium (mg)—280; cholesterol (mg)—2; carbohydrates (gm)—51; dietary fiber (gm)—3.

## Raisin Purée

Put 1/2 cup raisins in 1/2 cup of hot water; let sit for 30 minutes, then put the raisins and their liquid into a food processor or blender and whiz until smooth.

# Spiced Apple Pie

*Wherever there are apples, you'll find a variation of the apple pie, but nowhere in the world has it been enshrined as part of the national identity as in the United States. I set out to bake a big one with top and bottom crust and to try and keep it to our Minimax standards—it worked!*

*Time Estimate: Hands-on, 1 hour;*
  *unsupervised, 1½ hours*
*Serves 8*

### CRUST

1½ cups cake flour
1 teaspoon sugar
1/8 teaspoon salt
2 tablespoons light olive oil
4 tablespoons (1/2 stick) margarine, frozen for 15
  minutes
1 teaspoon distilled vinegar
4 tablespoons ice water
1 tablespoon 2%-fat milk
1 tablespoon sugar mixed with 1/2 teaspoon cinnamon

### FILLING

6 tart cooking apples, peeled, cored, and thinly sliced
1/3 cup dark brown sugar
1 tablespoon cornstarch
1/2 teaspoon cinnamon
1/8 teaspoon ground cloves
Zest of 1 lemon, grated
1/2 cup raisins
4 cups nonfat frozen yogurt

**The crust:** Put the flour, sugar, and salt in a large mixing bowl. Drizzle evenly with the oil and stir with a fork until it has a fine, sandy texture.

Slice the margarine into 1/8-inch (.5-cm) pieces. Stir it into the flour mixture just enough to coat the margarine and keep the pieces from sticking together. Sprinkle with the vinegar and water, and then, using 2 knives, cut in a crisscross motion to work the dough just until all the liquid is absorbed. Shape into a ball, wrap in plastic wrap, and refrigerate while you prepare the filling.

**The filling:** Put the brown sugar, cornstarch, cinnamon, cloves, lemon zest, and raisins into a large plastic bag. Seal the top and shake until well mixed. Add the apple slices and shake until the slices are coated with the sugar and spices.

Preheat the oven to 350°F (180°C). Divide the refrigerated dough in half. Gently form into 2 balls and roll the first one out to an 11-inch (28-cm) circle on a floured board. Transfer the dough to a 9-inch (23-cm) pie dish and fill with the apple mixture. Now roll out the other ball of dough and lay it over the apples. Seal the edges and crimp. Cut a few small vents in the top of the crust and brush lightly with milk. Sprinkle the top with cinnamon sugar.

Bake in the preheated oven for 1 hour and 15 minutes or until the filling is bubbling and the top is golden brown. Remove from the oven and cool slightly on a rack.

**To serve:** Cut the warm pie into 8 wedges and present each slice with 1/2 cup of nonfat frozen yogurt on top or on the side.

Nutritional Profile per Serving: Calories—393; % calories from fat—22%; fat (gm)—10 or 15% daily value: saturated fat (gm)—1; sodium (mg)—167; cholesterol (mg)—1; carbohydrates (gm)—75; dietary fiber (gm)—3.

# 30% calories from fat

⣿

# Appetizers
# &
# Soups

# HUMMUS

*You'll enjoy my version of hummus as a dip, but don't miss out on all its other possible uses—such as a great low-fat spread for sandwiches.*

*Time Estimate: Hands-on, 30 minutes*

*Serves 8 (makes 1 3/4 cups)*

1 (15½-ounce or 440-gm) can low-sodium garbanzo
    beans, drained and rinsed
3 tablespoons sesame tahini
1/4 cup water or stock
3 cloves garlic, bashed, peeled, and chopped
2 tablespoons chopped fresh parsley
2 tablespoons chopped fresh cilantro
3 tablespoons freshly squeezed lemon juice
1/8 teaspoon cayenne pepper
8 baby carrots
2 large celery stalks, cut into short sticks
1 red bell pepper, cut into strips
2 whole-wheat pita breads, cut into wedges and toasted

Purée the beans in a food processor. Add the remaining ingredients and whiz for 1 to 2 minutes or until it reaches a creamy smooth texture. The result will be a lovely, pale green color because of the parsley and the cilantro. If you prefer the traditional pale beige color of hummus, fold the two green herbs into the puréed mixture after processing.

**To serve:** Present the hummus in a bowl surrounded by the raw vegetables and toasted pita for dipping.

Nutritional Profile per Serving: Calories—143; % calories from fat—28%; fat (gm)—4 or 7% daily value; saturated fat (gm)—1; sodium (mg)—95; cholesterol (mg)—0; carbohydrates (gm)—22; dietary fiber (gm)—5. ⬇

You will see quite a bit of oil on top of the tahini when you open it. You can mix it back in, but if you pour it off, this decreases the fat. The liquid is easily replaced in the recipe by adding a little extra water or stock.

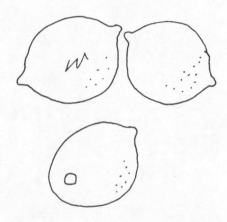

# POPCORN—
# SEASONED AND MAPLE

*I grew up in the European hotel business—a life utterly separated from popcorn. My first encounter with this ubiquitous American snack was developing these ideas for you. The question before us is "How can you enjoy serving popcorn without encouraging couch potato-itis in your family?" I suggest that you do the usual thing by putting your popcorn in a big bowl and bringing it out to the eager family sitting on the couch, but this time, don't turn on the television. Instead, try talking! It's tough at first, but wonderful when it catches on!*

*Time Estimate for both: Hands-on, 15 minutes*
*Serves 4*

1/4 cup popcorn kernels

SEASONED POPCORN

1 teaspoon light olive oil with a dash of toasted sesame oil
1 tablespoon freshly squeezed lime juice
1/8 teaspoon cayenne pepper
2 teaspoons brewer's yeast

MAPLE POPCORN

1/4 cup brown sugar
1 tablespoon pure maple syrup
1/4 cup water
2 tablespoons unsweetened grated coconut
4 tablespoons sliced almonds
1 teaspoon cinnamon

Pour the popcorn into an already heated hot-air popcorn popper (try saying that three times, fast!) and start popping, allowing the popped kernels to fall into a large bowl. Set aside.

**The seasoned popcorn:** Pour the oil and the lime juice into a large roasting bag and shake until evenly distributed. Add the popped kernels, trap air in the bag, and shake well.

Mix the cayenne pepper and brewer's yeast together. Sprinkle into the bag and shake again. Each piece of popcorn is now coated in a bright, spicy seasoning. A few pieces will be damp, but the flavor will compensate.

**The maple popcorn:** In a large skillet, over medium heat, stir the brown sugar, maple syrup, and water until it comes to a boil. Reduce to a thick syrup (234° to 240°F or 112° ro 115°C), the soft-ball stage on a candy thermometer. Test a drop of syrup in cold water. It should form a soft ball that flattens when removed and pressed between your fingers. Mix in the coconut and almonds.

Pour the topping over the popcorn, stirring gently to flavor each kernel. Sprinkle with the cinnamon. As it cools, the topping will harden. Before it cools completely, use your fingers to separate the popcorn kernels.

Nutritional Profile per Serving of Seasoned Popcorn: Calories—60; % calories from fat—25%; fat (gm)—2 or 3% daily value; saturated fat (gm)—.2; sodium (mg)—3; cholesterol (mg)—0; carbohydrates (gm)—10; dietary fiber (gm)—2.

Nutritional Profile per Serving of Maple Popcorn: Calories—165; % calories from fat—30%; fat (gm)—5 or 8% daily value; saturated fat (gm)—2; sodium (mg)—8; cholesterol (mg)—0; carbohydrates (gm)—28; dietary fiber (gm)—3.

# Shrimp Rolls 690

This is an excellent example of "East meets West": the blending of previously distinct cultures to come up with unique ideas. One of the masters of this craft is Jeremiah Tower, the chef/owner of several popular San Francisco restaurants, including 690 on Van Ness Avenue, where this is served. It needed very little adjusting to make it a great low-fat dish.

The idea is to serve these filled rice-paper packages as either a first course or a hot-weather main dish. They are literally bursting with aromas, colors, and textures.

*Time Estimate: Hands-on, 55 minutes*
*Serves 4*

1 cup coarsely chopped cooked small shrimp
1/3 cup strained yogurt (page 288)
1/2 teaspoon chili powder
Freshly ground sea salt, to taste
Freshly ground black pepper, to taste
1/2 cup fish stock (page 287)
1 teaspoon freshly grated gingerroot
2 (4-inch or 10-cm) lemon grass strands
4 tablespoons freshly squeezed lime juice
1 tablespoon low-sodium soy sauce
3 tablespoons light olive oil
1/4 teaspoon toasted sesame oil
1 small roasted red bell pepper (page 41), finely diced
1 small roasted green bell pepper (page 41), finely diced
1 roasted jalapeño pepper (page 41), halved lengthwise, seeded, and finely diced
1 tablespoon chopped fresh cilantro
1 cup warm water
1 teaspoon turmeric (optional)
4 (8- to 9-inch or 20- to 23-cm) dried rice papers
1 small cucumber, peeled, seeded, and cut into matchsticks
2 cabbage leaves, cut into fine strips
12 mint leaves, cut into fine strips

Mix the shrimp with the strained yogurt and the chili powder, and season to taste with salt and pepper.

In a small saucepan, bring the fish stock, grated ginger, and lemon grass to a boil and reduce by half. Strain the stock into a measuring cup. Whisk in 3 tablespoons of the lime juice, the soy sauce, oils, roasted peppers, jalapeño pepper, and cilantro. Set aside.

In a bowl, combine the warm water and the remaining tablespoon of lime juice. If you prefer a colorful set of rice papers, add turmeric to the bowl of warm water! Submerge the rice papers one at a time, until they start to soften—about 15 seconds. Transfer to a damp paper towel and cover with another damp paper towel. Repeat until all the papers are done. Keep them covered until ready to use—they dry out rapidly!

Fill each paper with shrimp mixture, cucumber, cabbage, and mint. Roll up loosely and place on individual plates.

**To serve:** Dollop with a spoonful of the sauce and delight your guests.

Nutritional Profile per Serving: Calories—155; % calories from fat—26%; fat (gm)—5 or 7% daily value; saturated fat (gm)—1; sodium (mg)—278; cholesterol (mg)—63; carbohydrates (gm)—18; dietary fiber (gm)—1. ⬇

---

Rice paper is simply a very thin, Southeast Asian pastry wrapper that you've probably eaten many times as "spring rolls." It will be easy to find at your local Thai market and is sold dried, in 1-pound (450-gm) packages, so you'll have enough sheets to experiment with many different fillings—you're only as limited as your imagination!

# Sooke Soup

*This is a remarkable example of micro-regional food. Sooke Soup is a dish that traces its creation to a very small area on the west coast of Vancouver Island in British Columbia, to the town of Sooke Harbour, which is indeed famous for the cuisine developed at the Sooke Harbour House by Sinclair Philip, his wife, Fredrica, and their superb team of chefs. Here you find the brilliance of invention coupled with the freshest of foods.*

*Time Estimate: Hands-on, 55 minutes*
*Serves 6*

YOGURT SAUCE

1/4 cup strained yogurt (page 288)
1 tablespoon de-alcoholized white wine
1/2 teaspoon chopped fresh thyme
1 teaspoon chopped fresh chives
1/4 teaspoon freshly ground black pepper
1/8 teaspoon freshly ground sea salt
1/4 teaspoon freshly grated nutmeg

SOUP

2 Granny Smith apples, cored and peeled
1 teaspoon light olive oil with a dash of toasted sesame oil
1/3 cup chopped onion
1 clove garlic, bashed, peeled, and diced
6 cups low-sodium chicken stock (page 286)
1/2 teaspoon chopped fresh thyme
4 cups frozen peas, thawed
2 cups curly kale leaves
1/4 cup cornstarch mixed with 1/2 cup nonfat milk (slurry)
4 ounces (115 gm) smoked black cod, chopped in small pieces

GARNISH

1 tablespoon chopped fresh chives
1 tablespoon chopped fresh thyme
1/4 teaspoon cayenne pepper

**The yogurt sauce:** In a small bowl, combine the yogurt, de-alcoholized white wine, thyme, and chives, stirring until all the lumps have disappeared. Stir in the pepper, salt, and nutmeg, and set aside.

**The soup:** Slice one Granny Smith apple and dice the other. In a large, high-sided stewpot, heat the oil and sauté the onion and garlic over medium-high heat for 2 minutes. Add the *sliced* apple, stirring to coat. Add the chicken stock and thyme, bring to a boil, and simmer for 10 minutes. Add the peas.

In a steamer, cook the kale leaves for 3 to 4 minutes. The kale will turn a beautiful bright green. Remove and cut into very fine strips. Keep cool for later use.

Pour the soup into the container of a food processor or blender and purée. Pass the puréed soup through a mesh sieve and return the sieved purée to the stewpot. Stir in the cornstarch slurry and bring just to a boil, stirring constantly until thickened. Add the *diced* apple, cod, and kale; heat through until the cod is firm.

**To serve:** Spoon the soup into individual serving bowls and garnish with the chives, thyme, and cayenne pepper. Dollop a spoonful of the yogurt sauce on top and enjoy!

Nutritional Profile per Serving: Calories—214; % calories from fat—25%; fat (gm)—6 or 9% daily value; saturated fat (gm)—1; sodium (mg)—335; cholesterol (mg)—12; carbohydrates (gm)—29; dietary fiber (gm)—6. ⬇

# THAI SOUP
## (TOM YUM GAI)

※

*This is a good example of the classic Asian Hot and Sour Soup: a thin, broth-styled liquid, chock full of aromatic seasonings that jostle each other for equal billing. It winds up not too spicy, not too sour, not too rich, but just right! Don't be put off by some of the exotic-sounding ingredients. Lemon grass, lime leaves, and galangal are fabulous fragrances that I think you'll want for experiments in many other dishes.*

Time Estimate: Hands-on, 30 minutes;
 unsupervised, 30 minutes
Serves 4

### SPICY CHICKEN STOCK

1 teaspoon light olive oil with a dash of toasted sesame oil
1 medium onion, peeled and coarsely chopped
1 stalk celery, coarsely chopped
2 large carrots, coarsely chopped
1 small bunch fresh thyme
3 whole cloves
5 whole black peppercorns
2 bay leaves
1 (3½ -pound or 1.6-kg) whole chicken
7 cups water

### THAI SOUP

4 cups prepared spicy chicken stock (see above)
1 lemon grass stalk*, crushed and cut in 1-inch (2.5-cm)
  sections
3 Kaffir lime leaves*
2 slices galangal*
1 teaspoon roasted chili paste* (hot, hot, hot!)
2 tablespoons fish sauce*
1½ tablespoons fresh lemon juice
1 green onion, sliced on the diagonal
1 cup fresh mushrooms, quartered
1 tablespoon chopped fresh cilantro
1 cup diced breast meat from the stock chicken

*Available at Asian markets.

**The spicy chicken stock:** This is a phenomenal chicken stock, quite different from any you've ever eaten. In a large stockpot, over high heat, pour in the olive oil. Add the onion, celery, carrots, thyme, cloves, peppercorns, and bay leaves, and cook for 2 minutes to release the flavors. Drop the chicken in on top. Pour 1 cup of the water over all and cover. Let the chicken steam, with its sinews cracking and exploding with flavor, 15 to 20 minutes. Add the remaining 6 cups of water, cover, and simmer gently for 30 minutes. Strain the chicken stock. Skin and debone the cooked chicken. Dice 1 cup of the breast meat to be added to the soup later and freeze the rest of the chicken meat for use at a later date.

**The soup:** Pour the strained chicken stock into a large saucepan. Do not pour in any of the sediment that has settled to the bottom. Add the lemon grass, Kaffir lime leaves, and galangal. (Don't try to chew the galangal, lemon grass, or Kaffir lime leaves—they are strictly for flavor.) Bring to a boil, cover, and boil for 5 minutes.

Stir in 1 teaspoon of the chili paste (no more—this is hot stuff), the fish sauce, lemon juice, green onion, mushrooms, cilantro, and the cooked chicken meat. That's it!

**To serve:** Ladle into bowls, inhale deeply, and savor the aromas!

Nutritional Profile per Serving: Calories—114; % calories from fat—28%; fat (gm)—4 or 6% daily value; saturated fat (gm)—1; sodium (mg)—423; cholesterol (mg)—27; carbohydrates (gm)—5; dietary fiber (gm)—1. ⬇

# 30% calories from fat

⌘

# Entrées

# BROILED SALMON STEAK AND CREAMY CUCUMBER SAUCE

⁂

*A few years ago, we had some very dear friends pay us a visit. I really wanted to do my best, but time was against an elaborate menu (sound familiar?). This recipe was the result. It worked perfectly—simple and delicious and just 30 minutes to do the whole thing!*

*Time Estimate: Hands-on, 30 minutes*
Serves 4

## SIDE DISHES: STEAMED NEW POTATOES AND ASPARAGUS

6 cups water
15 red new potatoes (about 1¼ pounds or 565 gm)
1 pound (450 gm) asparagus, stems cut off 2 inches (5 cm) below the tips
2 teaspoons chopped fresh dill

## CUCUMBER SAUCE

2 cups peeled, seeded, and diced cucumbers
1 tablespoon chopped fresh dill
1 teaspoon chopped fresh mint
1/8 teaspoon freshly ground white peppercorns
1/8 teaspoon freshly ground sea salt
1/2 cup de-alcoholized white wine
1 tablespoon cornstarch mixed with 2 tablespoons de-alcoholized white wine (slurry)
1 cup strained yogurt (page 288)

## SALMON

2 (12-ounce or 350-gm) skinless, boneless king salmon fillets
1 teaspoon light olive oil with a dash of toasted sesame oil
1/8 teaspoon freshly ground white peppercorns
1/8 teaspoon freshly ground sea salt

**The side dishes:** Pour the water into a large pot, bring to a boil, and steam the potatoes, covered, for 20 minutes. Remove and set aside. Steam the asparagus tips in the same pot, covered, for 5 minutes. Sprinkle with the dill just before serving.

**The cucumber sauce:** While the potatoes and asparagus are steaming, in a medium saucepan, combine the cucumbers, dill, mint, pepper, and salt, and cook over low heat for 10 minutes. Add the wine, increase the heat to high, and bring to a boil. Add the cornstarch slurry and stir until the sauce is thickened, about 30 seconds. Remove from the heat and let cool. Stir in the strained yogurt.

**The salmon:** Preheat the broiler. Pour the oil onto a plate and sprinkle with the pepper and salt. Season both sides of the salmon fillets by wiping them through the oil on the plate. Place the salmon on a foil-covered rack in a broiler pan. Arrange an oven rack 3 to 4 inches (8 to 10 cm) from the broiling element. Broil the salmon fillets for 5 minutes on each side. Transfer the cooked salmon to a cutting board.

**To serve:** Cut each salmon fillet in half. Spoon a bed of sauce onto each dinner plate and place one piece of salmon in the middle. Drizzle more sauce in a narrow band down the center of the salmon. Serve with the new potatoes and asparagus on the side.

Nutritional Profile per Serving: Calories—469; % calories from fat—29%; fat (gm)—15 or 24% daily value; saturated fat (gm)—3; sodium (mg)—374; cholesterol (mg)—92; carbohydrates (gm)—44; dietary fiber (gm)—4.

# BRITISH CLAY BOWL SALMON PIE AND SWEET CORN SAUCE

*Just to let you know that my birthright still means a great deal to me, I have invented the British Clay Bowl Salmon Pie, presented in a crust case that stays wonderfully crisp. Tender and tasty, pink, yellow, and white, it is a lunch pie with a tender, flaky crust.*

Time Estimate: Hands-on, 60 minutes;
  unsupervised, 30 minutes
Serves 4

1/2 recipe Basic Pastry Crust (page 289)

FILLING

1 (7½-ounce or 215-gm) can water-packed salmon
   (sodium free if possible), or 8 ounces (225 gm) fresh
   salmon
2 teaspoons capers
1 teaspoon chopped fresh dill
1/4 teaspoon freshly ground black pepper
1 cup cooked white rice
1/2 cup frozen corn

SWEET CORN SAUCE

1 cup frozen corn
1 cup de-alcoholized white wine
1 teaspoon cornstarch mixed with 2 teaspoons de-
   alcoholized white wine (slurry)
1/2 cup strained yogurt (page 288)
1 teaspoon chopped fresh dill

Roll out the pastry crust to fit your baking dish. Set aside.

**The filling:** Preheat the oven to 350°F (180°C). In a small bowl, mix the salmon, capers, half the dill, and half the pepper. In another bowl, mix the rice, corn, remaining dill, and remaining pepper. Spoon half of the rice mixture into a lightly greased, 5½-inch (14-cm) wide (2 cups in volume), ovenproof baking dish and press down firmly. Follow with half the salmon, the remaining rice, and finally the remaining salmon.

Cover the filling with the pastry crust. Roll and crimp the edges for a decorative look, cut a few steam vents, and bake the pie 50 minutes.

**The sweet corn sauce:** In a large saucepan, mix the corn and wine, bring to a boil, and remove from the heat. Strain, reserving the liquid and solids separately. Put all the corn in a processor or blender and add enough liquid to purée until smooth. Strain back into the saucepan, pushing gently on the solids to extract all the juices, and add the reserved liquid. Add the cornstarch slurry. Return to the heat, bring to a boil, and stir until thickened, about 30 seconds. Remove from the heat and let cool.

Put the yogurt in a small bowl and stir gently to remove the lumps. Add the cooled sauce and stir until completely incorporated. Stir in the dill.

**To serve:** Cut the pie into 4 wedges, place on warm serving plates, and serve with the sauce spooned on top.

Nutritional Profile per Serving: Calories—359; % calories from fat—29%; fat (gm)—11 or 18% daily value; saturated fat (gm)—2; sodium (gm)—214; cholesterol (mg)—30; carbohydrates (gm)—46; dietary fiber (gm)—3.\

# BAKED HERB-GARDEN SALMON

⋙

*I have found that there is a surprising shortage of information about how to bake a whole fish with its head and tail intact. Here is a delicious method for cooking whole fish, with a special note of guidance on salmon selection. You can also use this technique on any round-bodied whole fish, like red snapper, large trout, striped bass, grouper, ocean perch, rockfish, pompano (bream), drum, mullet, or white fish.*

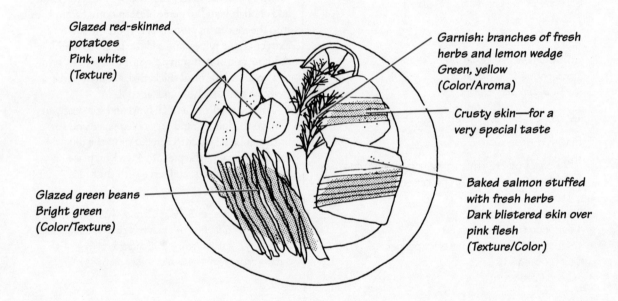

Glazed red-skinned
potatoes
Pink, white
(Texture)

Garnish: branches of fresh
herbs and lemon wedge
Green, yellow
(Color/Aroma)

Crusty skin—for a
very special taste

Glazed green beans
Bright green
(Color/Texture)

Baked salmon stuffed
with fresh herbs
Dark blistered skin over
pink flesh
(Texture/Color)

*Time Estimate: Hands-on, 45 minutes*
*Serves 4, with ample leftover salmon for other uses*

I whole (4- to 6-pound or 1.8- to 2.75-kg) salmon
I teaspoon light olive oil with a dash of toasted sesame
  oil
I tablespoon all-purpose flour
1/4 teaspoon freshly ground sea salt
1/4 teaspoon freshly ground black pepper
2 cloves garlic, crushed
I bunch fresh tarragon or 1/2 teaspoon dried
I bunch fresh rosemary

I bunch fresh thyme
I bunch fresh dill
I whole lemon, cut into1/2-inch (1.5-cm) slices

GARNISH

I lemon, cut into wedges
Sprigs fresh rosemary
Sprigs fresh thyme
Sprigs fresh dill

Preheat the oven to 450°F (230°C). Place the salmon in a sink filled with cold water. Using a small knife, brush the skin from tail to head, loosening and removing the scales. Run your hand back over the entire body, checking to make sure that all the scales are gone. Rinse under running water and place on a cutting board.

Sprinkle a little salt on a small soft piece of wet cloth; then wipe out the center of the fish so that no blood or discoloration remains.

For a delicious crispy skin, brush one side of the fish with the olive oil, making sure to work it well into the skin, and sprinkle with the flour, half of the salt, and half of the pepper, patting the seasonings firmly into place. Gently shake off any surplus, then place the fish back on the cutting board, prepared side up.

Using the back of a knife, make a lengthwise center guideline on the fish body, but do not cut the skin. Using a very sharp knife or a sharp clean razor blade, score diagonal incisions 1 inch (2.5 cm) apart through the skin only from the edges of the body in toward the center line almost to the belly. Make a final incision down the backbone so that the skin comes away easily when served.

Make a paste of the garlic, the remaining salt, and the remaining pepper, and rub into the incisions. Layer the herbs inside the fish. Lay the lemon slices down the center line.

Line a shallow baking pan with heavy-duty aluminum foil, shiny side up. Lift the prepared fish by the head and tail and place it so that the main body of the fish (at least) is in the pan. Wrap the head and tail in oiled aluminum foil. Be sure to fan the tail out so that it holds its shape. Bake the prepared fish in the preheated oven for 8 minutes per 1 inch (2.5 cm) of thickness.

Remove from the oven and take off the foil on the head and tail. Switch the oven to broil and pop the fish back in to crisp the skin for its table presentation, just until it blisters and browns, about 5 minutes.

**To serve:** Lift the fish out of the pan, still on its aluminum-foil bed, and onto a large oval serving plate, then slide the foil out from underneath. The bottom skin will usually come away with the foil. Slice by following the skin lines, serving slices from the back and belly, and garnish with pieces of the crispy skin. Save the pan drippings to drizzle over your side dishes. I recommend steamed green beans and new potatoes.

When the top layer has been served, simply remove the head to a large side plate, together with all the herbs and lemon, and pry up the backbone to reveal the remaining bone-free fillet. You may serve these pieces to your guests who don't want to eat the crispy skin.

| Nutritional Profile per Serving | | | |
|---|---|---|---|
| | Classic | Minimax | Daily Value |
| Calories | 667 | 378 | |
| Calories from fat | 55% | 26% | |
| Fat (gm) | 41 | 11 | 17% |
| Saturated fat (gm) | 15 | 2 | 10% |
| Sodium (mg) | 1,030 | 275 | 11% |
| Cholesterol (mg) | 237 | 56 | 19% |
| Carbohydrates (gm) | 13 | 32 | 11% |
| Dietary fiber (gm) | 1 | 5 | 20% |
| Classic compared: Whole Baked Salmon with Cucumber Sauce | | | |

# SMOKED SALMON WITH BARLEY PILAF

*One of the truly great taste experiences of the Pacific Northwest is the locally caught and lightly smoked salmon. I've used the same fish, but given it a light tea smoke and a Pacific Rim garnish that is a blend of Asian and European cuisine. This dish has great color, texture, and taste, with a definite aroma of fresh ginger.*
*When this recipe first appeared, I used black cod or sablefish. I have since found that black cod is extremely high in fat—too fat, in fact, to use in my kind of cooking. Salmon is lower in fat, but still plenty moist for smoking.*

Time Estimate: Hands-on, 35 minutes;
  unsupervised, 82 minutes
Serves 4

BARLEY PILAF

2 leeks, dark green tops only
1 teaspoon light olive oil with a dash of toasted sesame oil
1/8 teaspoon toasted sesame oil
2 cloves garlic, bashed, peeled, and chopped
1 cup uncooked long-grain brown rice
1/2 cup pearl barley
2⅞ cups water mixed with 1/8 cup fish sauce

SALMON

Basic Tea Smoke ingredients (page 40)
4 (4-ounce or 115-gm) skinless, boneless salmon fillets

MARINATED VEGETABLES

2 leeks, light green parts only (from above)
1/2 red bell pepper, seeded and cut lengthwise into
  1/4-inch (.75-cm) slices
1/2 green bell pepper, seeded and sliced lengthwise into
  thin matchsticks
1/8 large red onion, thinly sliced
4 sprigs Italian flat-leaf parsley
1/4 cup rice wine vinegar
1/4 teaspoon toasted sesame oil

4 cups water
1 (2 x 3-inch or 5 x 8-cm) piece of fresh gingerroot,
  bruised
White leek halves (from above)

**The barley pilaf:** Cut each leek into 3-inch (8-cm) pieces, separating the pieces into 3 groups: the white bulbs, the light green, and the dark green tops. Slice the white bulbs in half lengthwise; cut the light green parts into matchsticks; dice the dark green tops. In a small saucepan, heat the oils and sauté the diced dark green leek tops and garlic over medium-high heat for 2 minutes. Stir in the rice, barley, water, and fish sauce. Cover and cook over medium heat for 45 minutes.

**The salmon:** Prepare the smoke ingredients according to the directions on page 40. Cover the pan tightly and cook over high heat until the ingredients in the foil start smoking, about 5 minutes.

Put the salmon fillets on a steamer platform. Set the platform in the Dutch oven over the smoke ingredients, cover, and cook over high heat for 10 minutes.

**The marinated vegetables:** In a large bowl, combine the light green leek matchsticks, red pepper, green pepper, red onion, and parsley. Stir in the vinegar and sesame oil, and let rest for 15 minutes.

Pour the water into a steamer, add the ginger, and bring to a boil. Put the white leek halves on a steamer platform, place the platform in the steamer, cover, and steam for 12 minutes. As the leeks cook they begin to lose their form and will lie flat in the steamer. Remove them from the platform and set aside.

**To serve:** Place one-quarter of the steamed leeks on each dinner plate, arranging them in the shape of a raft, and cover with a piece of the smoked salmon. Spoon 1 cup of the marinated vegetables on top and serve with 1/2 cup of the barley pilaf.

Nutritional Profile per Serving: Calories—491; % calories from fat—26%; fat (gm)—14 or 22% daily value; saturated fat (gm)—3; sodium (mg)—119; cholesterol (mg)—71; carbohydrates (gm)—62; dietary fiber (gm)—8.

# THAI-STYLE SARDINES

*To my taste, this sardine salad purée in a crusty loaf is one of the great snacks of all time. I serve it with Herb Salad on the side . . . delicious!*

*Time Estimate: Hands-on, 25 minutes*
*Serves 4*

## SARDINES

1/4 cup water
Zest of 1/4 lime, cut into matchsticks and bruised
1 teaspoon light olive oil with a dash of toasted sesame oil
2 green onions, finely sliced diagonally
1 (14½-ounce or 415-gm) can peeled tomatoes, drained and chopped
2 dried red chili peppers, finely chopped
2 tablespoons finely chopped fresh mint
1 tablespoon coarsely chopped fresh cilantro
Juice of 1/2 lime
3 (3½-ounce or 100-gm) cans water-packed sardines, drained

## HERB SALAD

1 small head butter lettuce, cut into 1/4-inch (.75-cm) strips
1 plum tomato, cut into small dice
1 tablespoon finely chopped cilantro
1 tablespoon finely chopped fresh mint
1 tablespoon freshly squeezed lime juice
1/4 teaspoon freshly ground black pepper

## TOAST

1/2 French baguette (thin French loaf), hollowed out

**The sardines:** In a small saucepan, add the water to the lemon zest and bring to a boil for 1 minute. Strain and set the lemon zest aside.

In a large skillet, heat the oil over high heat and cook the blanched lemon zest and green onions for 2 minutes. Add the tomatoes, chili peppers, mint, cilantro, and lime juice, and cook for 2 minutes. Remove from the heat, lay the sardines on top to warm through, then toss them in the sauce until they break into pieces.

**The herb salad:** In a medium bowl, toss the lettuce, tomato, cilantro, mint, lime juice, and pepper.

**To assemble:** Preheat broiler. Remove half of the sardines and sauce to a bowl and mash well, reserving the remaining sardines for another use. Fill the hollowed-out baguette with the sardine mash and place under the preheated broiler until the bread is lightly toasted, about 2 to 3 minutes.

**To serve:** Cut the toasted sardines into slices and serve with Herb Salad on the side.

You may also like a lighter variation without the bread: Make a ring around the edge of a serving plate with the Herb Salad and spoon the sardines and sauce into the center.

Nutritional Profile per Serving: Calories—246; % calories from fat—26%; fat (gm)—7 or 11% daily value; saturated fat (gm)—2; sodium (mg)—459; cholesterol (mg)—29; carbohydrates (gm)—31; dietary fiber (gm)—2. ⬇

# Braised Chicken with Pepper Sauce & Polenta

⌘

*This is bistro food—succulent chicken braised in a sauce full of peppers, onion, garlic, and anchovy. It is served with polenta made rich with Gorgonzola cheese and colored with reds and greens.*

*Time Estimate: Hands-on, 45 minutes; unsupervised, 35 minutes*

*Serves 4*

## POLENTA

3 cups water
1 cup yellow cornmeal
1/4 teaspoon freshly ground sea salt
1/4 teaspoon freshly ground black pepper
2 ounces (60 gm) Gorgonzola cheese
1 red bell pepper, seeded and diced
1 tablespoon chopped fresh parsley

## CHICKEN WITH PEPPER SAUCE

1 teaspoon light olive oil with a dash of toasted sesame oil
4 (8-ounce or 225-gm) whole chicken legs
1 cup chopped onions
3 cloves garlic, bashed, peeled, and chopped
2 tablespoons low-sodium tomato paste
1 red bell pepper, seeded and diced
1 tablespoon chopped fresh rosemary
2 bay leaves
1/2 cup de-alcoholized white wine
4 anchovy fillets, finely chopped
2 cups low-sodium chicken stock (page 286)
1 tablespoon arrowroot mixed with 2 tablespoons de-alcoholized white wine (slurry)
1 teaspoon freshly grated lemon zest

## SIDE DISH: STEAMED GREENS

3 cups collard leaves, washed and thick stems removed
2 cups kale leaves, washed and thick stems removed
2 cups mustard greens, washed and thick stems removed

**The polenta:** In a large saucepan, bring 3 cups of water to a boil. Stir the water rapidly while sprinkling in the cornmeal. Add the salt and pepper. When it starts to thicken, pull it off the stove, cover, and allow to sit for 8 to 10 minutes. When done, the polenta will be a thick porridge that pulls cleanly from the sides of the saucepan and a spoon will stand up in it. Add the cheese, red pepper, and parsley, mixing well. Spread evenly into a lightly greased 9-inch (23-cm) round baking dish. Set aside to bake with the chicken.

**The chicken with pepper sauce:** Preheat the oven to 350°F (180°C). Heat the oil in a large oven-proof, high-sided skillet over medium-high heat and brown the chicken on both sides. Remove the chicken to a cutting board; take off the skin and discard, using paper towels to absorb any excess fat from the meat. Set aside.

Fry the onions and garlic in the same pan over medium-high heat until softened, about 2 minutes. Stir in the tomato paste and cook briskly until its color darkens. Add the red pepper, rosemary, bay leaves, and wine, scraping the bottom of the skillet to deglaze it. Add the anchovy fillets, chicken, and chicken stock, and bring to a boil. Place the pan in the preheated oven and bake 35 minutes. Place the polenta in the oven during the last 15 minutes of baking.

Transfer the cooked chicken to a cutting board. Trim off the exposed leg and thigh bones. Stir the arrowroot slurry into the pepper sauce, return to low heat on the stovetop, and stir until thickened. Return the chicken to the sauce. Stir in the lemon zest and heat through.

**The greens:** In a large pot with a steaming tray, steam the greens, covered, for 4 minutes.

**To serve:** Cut the polenta into wedges and set each on a warm plate. Place a chicken leg on each and spoon the sauce over the top. Serve the greens on the side.

Nutritional Profile per Serving: Calories—474; % calories from fat—29%; fat (gm)—15 or 23% daily value; saturated fat (gm)—6; sodium (mg)—615; cholesterol (mg)—97; carbohydrates (gm)—47; dietary fiber (gm)—7.

# CHICKEN FANTENGO

※

*Please note the way I've used chicken skin in this casserole. If you remove the skin, then stew the meat, it loses succulence. You've got to keep the meat whole and with the skin on to retain its juiciness. But if you do that, the fat drains out into the casserole and you can't remove it. My way of dealing with this issue is to cook the meat and vegetables separately.*

*Time Estimate: Hands-on, 45 minutes;
   unsupervised, 15 minutes*
*Serves 5*

4 (8-ounce or 225-gm) whole chicken legs
1 teaspoon light olive oil with a dash of toasted sesame oil
2 yellow onions, peeled and thinly sliced
2 cloves garlic, bashed, peeled, and chopped
1 (6-ounce or 175-gm) can low-sodium tomato paste
2 cups low-sodium chicken stock (page 286)
12 ounces (350 gm) Jerusalem artichokes, peeled and coarsely chopped
1¼ cups de-alcoholized white wine
1 tablespoon plus 1 teaspoon minced fresh oregano leaves
1/2 teaspoon freshly ground black pepper
1/4 teaspoon freshly ground sea salt
4 ounces uncooked spiral pasta
1 cup pitted black olives
1 tablespoon chopped fresh parsley

Preheat the oven to 425°F (220°C). Put the chicken pieces on a rack in a roasting pan and bake for 50 minutes.

Pour the oil into a large saucepan over medium-high heat and fry the onions and garlic until translucent, about 4 minutes. Stir in the tomato paste until completely incorporated, turn up the heat a notch, allowing the natural sugars in the tomato paste to go light brown and caramelize, about 10 minutes. Pour in the stock, artichokes, 1 cup of the wine, 1 tablespoon of the oregano, half of the black pepper, and the salt. Cover and simmer 8 minutes.

While everything else is cooking, cook the pasta according to package directions until just tender, about 9 minutes. Add the cooked pasta and olives to the sauce and heat through.

Remove the chicken from the oven and transfer to a flat surface. Pour off the excess fat from the pan. Put the pan on the stovetop, add the remaining 1/4 cup wine, and scrape up the pan residues. Pour into a fat-strainer cup. Allow the fat to rise to the top and pour the rest of the liquid into the sauce.

Remove the skin from the cooked chicken, using a bowl of ice water to cool down your fingers. It's about 3 seconds between dips for normal, 4 seconds for macho, and 5 seconds for super-macho. I must say that tongs don't do a good job: get in and let your fingers do the working. Separate into major meat pieces according to muscle lines and add to the sauce. Stir in the remaining teaspoon oregano and 1/4 teaspoon pepper.

**To serve:** Spoon into individual bowls and garnish with the parsley.

Nutritional Profile per Serving: Calories—386; % calories from fat—27%; fat (gm)—12 or 18% daily value; saturated fat (gm)—3; sodium (mg)—477; cholesterol (mg)—67; carbohydrates (gm)—43; dietary fiber (gm)—5.

# Chicken Kebabs with Peanut Butter Spreadin'dipity

⁂

*A wonderfully rich sauce of yogurt, peanut butter, and banana over broiled skewers of tender chicken breast—what an incredible combination! Add a tossed salad of greens, sliced mushrooms, and tomato wedges for a memorable meal.*

*Time Estimate: Hands-on, 22 minutes; unsupervised, 22 minutes*

Serves 4

## YOGURT SAUCE

1/2 cup strained yogurt (page 288)
1/3 cup unsalted creamy peanut butter
1 banana, peeled and mashed
2 teaspoons chopped fresh cilantro
1/4 teaspoon cayenne pepper
2 tablespoons freshly squeezed lemon juice
4 teaspoons low-sodium soy sauce

## CHICKEN KEBABS

4 cloves garlic, bashed and peeled
1/2 teaspoon sesame oil
4 teaspoons low-sodium soy sauce
4 (3½-ounce or 100-gm) boneless, skinless chicken breasts, cut into 1/2-inch (1.5-cm) cubes
4 cups hot cooked white rice

**The sauce:** In a small bowl, combine the strained yogurt, peanut butter, and mashed banana. Add the cilantro, cayenne, lemon juice, and soy sauce, and let it sit for 5 minutes.

**The chicken kebabs:** In a small bowl, mix the garlic, oil, and soy sauce. Brush the chicken pieces with the mixture until well coated and refrigerate for 10 minutes.

Preheat the broiler. Divide the chicken pieces equally among 4 skewers, place on a rack in a roaster pan, and broil for 5 minutes. Remove from the broiler, turn the skewers, brush the chicken with the sauce, and put back under the broiler for 2 minutes.

**To serve:** Lay the chicken kebabs atop a mound of fluffy rice on each plate. Spoon a little of the sauce over each one and serve the rest on the side for dipping.

Nutritional Profile per Serving: Calories—524; % calories from fat—25%; fat (gm)—15 or 22% daily value; saturated fat (gm)—3; sodium (mg)—601; cholesterol (mg)—55; carbohydrates (gm)—63; dietary fiber (gm)—3.

# CHICKEN POLESE

*This dish began many years ago in Sydney, Australia, at a truly wonderful Italian restaurant called Beppies, owned by Giuseppe Polese. The recipe has remained a favorite over the years, but especially this new version. Exceedingly fast to put together, it includes two of my favorite bright notes: the tang of anchovy fillet and the zing of piquant capers. I think you'll begin using them in many other recipes. I like pasta and green salad on the side.*

Time Estimate: Hands-on, 30 minutes
Serves 2

1/2 teaspoon light olive oil with a dash of toasted sesame oil
1 clove garlic, bashed, peeled, and chopped
2 (6-ounce or 175-gm) boneless chicken breasts, with skin
1/2 red bell pepper, finely diced
2 plum tomatoes, finely diced
1 tablespoon finely chopped fresh oregano
Freshly ground black pepper
1 tablespoon chopped fresh parsley
2 (1/2-ounce or 15-gm) slices low-fat mozzarella cheese
4 anchovy fillets
2 tablespoons capers
1/2 teaspoon arrowroot mixed with 2 tablespoons de-alcoholized white wine (slurry)

Heat the olive oil in a large skillet over medium-high heat and fry the garlic until just brown, about 2 minutes. Remove the garlic with a slotted spoon and discard. In the same skillet, fry the chicken breasts on medium-high heat for about 3 minutes on each side. Remove the skin and discard. Transfer the chicken to a plate and set aside.

In the same skillet over medium-high heat, fry the red bell pepper for 2 minutes. Add the tomatoes, oregano, black pepper to taste, 1 teaspoon of the parsley, and the chicken. Cover and cook for 2 minutes. Remove the lid and cover each chicken breast with a slice of the cheese, 2 crisscrossed anchovy fillets, and a sprinkle of the capers. Cover and cook until the cheese melts, about 2 minutes. Transfer the chicken to warm serving plates.

Remove the pan from the heat and stir in the arrowroot slurry. Return to low heat and stir until the sauce has thickened, about 1 minute.

Serve the chicken breasts in a juicy pool of the sauce, dusted with the remaining parsley.

Nutritional Profile per Serving: Calories—254; % calories from fat—30%; fat (gm)—8 or 13% daily value; saturated fat (gm)—3; sodium (mg)—445; cholesterol (mg)—86; carbohydrates (gm)—8; dietary fiber (gm)—2. ⬇

# CHICKEN YANKOVA

⁂

*Treena and I first ate this dish in Moscow back in 1970 B.G. (before glasnost). The original is a modified Chicken Kiev in which a chicken is smothered in butter and packed into a puffed-pastry envelope and slow-baked. Delicious, but 70 grams of fat per serving!!!*

*The crisp bread loaf is best served whole and cut slice-by-slice on a wooden board. A great dish to serve with a colorful salad.*

Time Estimate: Hands-on, 60 minutes;
  unsupervised, 15 minutes
Serves 4

12 ounces (350 gm) mushrooms, sliced
2 teaspoons light olive oil with a dash of toasted sesame oil
1 tablespoon freshly squeezed lemon juice
1/4 teaspoon cayenne pepper
1/2 teaspoon dried dill weed
1 French bread loaf (approximately 12 X 4 X 3 inches or 30 X 10 X 8 cm)
1/4 cup grated dry Monterey Jack cheese
4 (4-ounce or 115-gm) skinned chicken breasts
1 cup low-sodium chicken stock (page 286)
4 sprigs fresh tarragon, or 1 teaspoon dried
Freshly ground black pepper to taste
1/8 teaspoon saffron powder
1 tablespoon arrowroot mixed with 2 tablespoons de-alcoholized dry white wine (slurry)
Fresh parsley or tarragon sprigs

Put the mushrooms in a large bowl. Sprinkle them with half the olive oil, the lemon juice, cayenne pepper, and dill. Cover the bowl with a plate and shake it thoroughly. Now the mushrooms are evenly coated with the flavoring ingredients.

Cut lengthwise into the bottom of the French bread loaf at a 30-degree angle on both sides, taking a triangular section out of the loaf. Now cut the dough off the triangular section, leaving you with the crust, which you will use as a cap. Hollow out the rest of the loaf, leaving a practically dough-free loaf surrounded by crust. Sprinkle one-quarter of the grated cheese over the cap and the rest into the hollowed loaf.

Preheat the oven to 300°F (150°C).

Pour the remaining olive oil on a plate and mop it up with the chicken breasts into a large heated skillet and brown the chicken over medium-high heat for 4 minutes on each side (8 minutes total). Take the chicken out of the pan and set aside.

Drop the marinated mushrooms into the same pan and sauté for 2 to 3 minutes. Transfer the mushrooms to a plate. Take another plate of similar size and place it on top of the mushrooms. Now squeeze the plates together while holding them over a small saucepan. The juice should drizzle into the saucepan!

Pour the chicken stock into the skillet, scraping the residue off the bottom of the pan. Pour this deglazed sauce into the small saucepan with the mushroom juice and keep on low heat.

Set the chicken breasts into the bread loaf. Lay 1 long sprig of tarragon over each chicken breast. If you can't get fresh tarragon, then sprinkle with the dried.

Season the mushrooms with pepper and pack them in over the chicken. Place the cap on the loaf so that the filling is packed solid and enclosed. Cover with foil and bake in the preheated oven for 10 minutes, just to warm through. The crust should not become overcrisp.

**The sauce:** Stir the saffron into the sauce in the small saucepan. Remove from the heat. Mix in the arrowroot slurry, return to the heat, and bring it to a boil to thicken.

**To serve:** Carve the loaf with a good serrated bread knife and place a couple of 1-inch (2.5-cm) slices of Chicken Yankova on a plate. Drizzle with the sauce and garnish with the rest of the grated cheese and a sprig of fresh tarragon or parsley—enjoy!

Nutritional Profile per Serving: Calories—410; % calories from fat—27%; fat (gm)—12 or 19% daily value; saturated fat (gm)—5; sodium (mg)—672; cholesterol (mg)—77; carbohydrates (gm)—34; dietary fiber (gm)—3.

# CHICKEN ULTRABURGER

※

*As you'll see below, this delicious burger is topped with an equally delectable sauce that has two names. If you're serving a certified burger lover, call the sauce Minimax Burger Mayonnaise. However, if you're trying to impress an elegant friend, serve the burger without the bun, drizzled with what is now called Horseradish-Wine Sauce. Either way, you're bound to make a good impression.*

Time Estimate: Hands-on, 50 minutes
Serves 4

1 (3½-pound or 1.6-kg) whole roasting chicken
1 onion, peeled and quartered
4 tablespoons fresh parsley leaves
4 tablespoons fresh parsley stalks
2 tablespoons Dijon mustard
1/4 teaspoon freshly ground sea salt
1/4 teaspoon freshly ground black pepper
1 cup cooked long-grain brown rice
1 tablespoon light olive oil mixed with a dash of toasted sesame oil
4 whole-wheat hamburger buns
8 lettuce leaves
4 thick tomato slices

MINIMAX BURGER MAYONNAISE
   OR HORSERADISH-WINE SAUCE

1/2 cup de-alcoholized white wine
1/4 cup strained yogurt (page 288)
2 teaspoons prepared horseradish

**The chicken:** Remove all the skin from the chicken and trim off all visible fat. Cut off the meat—you should have approximately 16 ounces (450 gm). Chop the meat into small pieces and divide it into two piles, each with half of the breast meat and half of the leg and thigh meat.

Place the onion, parsley, parsley stalks, mustard, salt, and pepper in the food processor and pulse until the onion is minced but not puréed. Transfer to a large bowl and set aside.

Process the meat in the processor (one-half at a time, if necessary) 20 fast pulses. Transfer to the bowl with the onion mixture, add the rice, and stir until well mixed. Form into 4 patties of equal size. (This step is easier if you chill the chicken-rice mixture in the refrigerator for an hour.)

Heat the oil in a large skillet over medium heat. Add the chickenburgers and cook 4 minutes on each side.

**The Minimax Burger Mayonnaise (Horseradish-Wine Sauce):** Deglaze the skillet with the wine, scraping to loosen up the bits of pan residue into the liquid. Strain into a small bowl. Stir in the yogurt and horseradish, and set aside.

**To serve:** Place a chickenburger on each bun, top with the Burger Mayonnaise, passed through the same sieve used to strain the deglazing liquid. Top with the tomato slices and lettuce and the remaining bun half.

Nutritional Profile per Serving: Calories—364; % calories from fat—27%; fat (gm)—11 or 17% daily value; saturated fat (gm)—2; sodium (mg)—513; cholesterol (mg)—68; carbohydrates (gm)—35; dietary fiber (gm)—4.

# CRUNCHY-TOP TURKEY

*My father was a Scot, my mother, English, and I was born in London. I'm a Brit to my roots, and my love of savory pies of any kind confirms the fact! By using a crust only as a lid to set on top of the filling, I've substantially reduced the amount of fat in this recipe.*

*Time Estimate: Hands-on, 50 minutes*
Serves 4

1 recipe Wheat-germ Crust (page 290)

FILLING

1 teaspoon light olive oil with a dash of toasted sesame
   oil
2 onions, peeled and finely chopped
1 teaspoon caraway seeds
1 teaspoon dill seeds
12 ounces (350 gm) turkey thigh meat, fat trimmed and
   cut off the bones into large slices, following the muscle
   lines
1 cup low-sodium beef stock (page 286)
1 cup de-alcoholized red wine
4 ounces (115 gm) fresh mushrooms
1 tablespoon arrowroot mixed with 2 tablespoons de-
   alcoholized red wine (slurry)

SIDE DISHES

1 pound (450 gm) broccoli, florets trimmed and stems
   discarded
4 sweet potatoes, baked and kept warm

Preheat the oven to 425°F (220°C). Roll out the Wheat Germ Crust dough into a large circle and place a pie plate on top, upside down. Cut along the outside edge of the pie plate with a sharp knife to get the perfect size circle. Remove the plate, roll up the dough over the rolling pin, and unroll it onto a baking sheet covered with parchment paper. Score the dough with serving lines to make it easier to cut after it's baked. Bake in the preheated oven for 10 minutes and cut into 4 wedges, one for each person.

To a large skillet over high heat, add half the oil and cook the onions, caraway, and dill seeds, letting them sit without stirring for 2 minutes. Now that they're browning nicely, turn the heat down to medium and cook 3 minutes more. Transfer to a plate and set aside.

To the same skillet, add the remaining oil. Distribute the turkey, piece by piece, flat on the pan and brown for 2 minutes on one side. Add the cooked onions and stir until well incorporated. Cook over medium heat for 5 minutes, stirring occasionally.

Pour in the beef stock, scraping the pan residues completely into the liquid. Pour in the wine, stir well, and simmer, uncovered, for 15 minutes. Add the mushrooms and simmer 10 minutes more. Remove from the heat. Add the arrowroot slurry, return to the heat, and stir until thickened.

At the same time you add the mushrooms, put the broccoli on to steam until tender, about 10 minutes.

**To serve:** Place a baked sweet potato and steamed broccoli on each plate. Spoon on the turkey and vegetables, and top each serving with a pastry wedge.

Nutritional Profile per Serving: Calories—493; % calories from fat—29%; fat (gm)—16 or 25% daily value; saturated fat (gm)—3; sodium (mg)—221; cholesterol (mg)—53; carbohydrates (gm)—62; dietary fiber (gm)—9.

# Enchiladas Fina Cocina

*Norman Fierros is a man with a mission: to upgrade the tastes and appeal of classic Mexican food. His Fina Cocina restaurant in downtown Phoenix is proof that his new "pudding" is worth the eating. I've springboarded off one of Norman's ideas with one of my own. Now, why don't you do the same with mine?*

*Time Estimate: Hands-on, 45 minutes; unsupervised, 45 minutes*

*Serves 4 (2 enchiladas each)*

## TOMATILLO SAUCE

1 teaspoon light olive oil with a dash of toasted sesame oil
1 onion, peeled and sliced
2 cloves garlic, bashed, peeled, and chopped
1 pound (450 gm) tomatillos, peeled and diced
1 jalapeño pepper, seeded and finely chopped
1 cup water
1 cup low-sodium chicken stock (page 286)
3 tablespoons arrowroot mixed with 6 tablespoons water (slurry)

## ENCHILADAS

8 (10-inch or 25-cm) flour tortillas
1 teaspoon light olive oil with a dash of toasted sesame oil
1 red onion, peeled and very thinly sliced
1 red bell pepper, seeded and sliced
1/4 cup low-sodium chicken stock (page 286)
1 teaspoon cumin seeds
1 teaspoon cayenne pepper
8 ounces (225 gm) cooked chicken meat, preferably thigh and leg, without skin, fat, or bone
1 tablespoon chopped fresh cilantro
1 tablespoon chopped fresh parsley
Reserved arrowroot mixture (see above)
Chopped cilantro leaves

**The tomatillo sauce:** Heat the olive oil in a medium saucepan over medium-high heat and fry the onion, garlic, tomatillos, and jalapeño pepper for 1 minute. Pour in the water, bring to a boil, and boil for 7 minutes. Strain through a sieve (to remove the tomatillo skin and seeds) into a saucepan. Stir in the chicken stock, bring to a boil, and boil for 2 minutes. Remove from the heat and stir in 1 tablespoon of the arrowroot slurry. Return to the heat and stir over low heat until thickened, about 1 minute. Remove from the heat and set aside.

**The enchiladas:** Place the tortillas on a plate over a pot of hot water and cover with a clean towel. Heat the olive oil in a large skillet over high heat and fry the red onion and red pepper for 1 minute. Add the chicken stock, cumin seeds, cayenne pepper, chicken meat, cilantro, and parsley, and heat through. Remove from the heat and pour in the remaining arrowroot slurry. Return to the heat, and stir over low heat until thickened, about 1 minute.

**To assemble and serve:** Place a warm flour tortilla on a warm serving plate. Spoon the filling down the middle and roll it into a cylinder. Spoon the tomatillo sauce over the top and garnish with a sprinkle of the cilantro leaves.

Nutritional Profile per Serving: Calories—507; % calories from fat—26%; fat (gm)—15 or 23% daily value; saturated fat (gm)—3; sodium (mg)—478; cholesterol (mg)—50; carbohydrates (gm)—67; dietary fiber (gm)—5. ⬆

# Rock Cornish Game Hens & Pilaf Kirkland

*A rock Cornish game hen cannot be heavier than 2 pounds (900 gm). They are fed a diet of acorns and cranberries, which gives them a slightly "wild" taste and a fuller flavor than chicken. This dinner is quite easy but makes an elegant presentation. I usually serve a heap of steaming fresh-cooked spinach or Swiss chard on the side with a pinch of freshly grated nutmeg.*

Time Estimate: Hands-on, 45 minutes;
   unsupervised, 50 minutes

Serves 4

2 rock Cornish game hens

RICE PILAF

1 teaspoon light olive oil with a dash of toasted sesame oil
1 large yellow onion, peeled and finely diced
1 clove garlic, bashed, peeled, and chopped
1 cup mixed uncooked grains, preferably 1/2 cup Lundberg mixed long-grain rice, 1/4 cup pearl barley, and 1/4 cup wild rice
2 cups low-sodium chicken stock (page 286)
2 bay leaves
1 sprig thyme
1 sprig parsley
3/4 cup small green peas
1⅔ cups large mushrooms, cut into 1/2-inch (2.5-cm) thick slices

SAUCE

1/4 cup de-alcoholized white wine
1 tablespoon arrowroot mixed with 2 tablespoons de-alcoholized white wine (slurry)
1/2 tablespoon chopped fresh cilantro
1½ tablespoons chopped fresh parsley
1 red bell pepper, seeded and finely diced

Cut the Cornish hens in half: Make a cut on one side of the backbone. Make a second cut on the other side of the backbone. Take out the backbone and open up the bird. Cut through the breast bone from the inside. Remove the fine rib bones and cut off the wing tips. Save the wing and backbones for a stock. Dry the hens well with paper towels. Place them on a rack in a roasting pan.

Preheat the oven to 375°F (190°C). Heat the olive oil in a casserole set over medium-high heat and cook the onion and garlic until the onions are translucent, about 5 minutes. Add the rice and stir until well coated. Pour in the stock, lay the herbs on top, and cook, uncovered, in the preheated oven for 45 minutes. When done, remove the herbs, stir in the peas and mushrooms, and return to the oven to heat through, about 5 minutes.

Time the hens to bake in the oven, starting 15 minutes after the rice. Bake them for 30 minutes at the same temperature, 375°F (190°C). Remove from the oven and transfer the hens to a warm plate.

**The sauce:** Pour the wine into the roasting pan, then pour all the roasting juices into a fat-strainer cup. Let sit for a few moments to allow the fat to rise to the top, then pour the juice back into a saucepan through a fine sieve. You should have about 1/2 cup of juice. Pour in the arrowroot slurry and cook over low heat, stirring, until thickened. Stir in the cilantro, parsley, and diced red pepper.

**To serve:** Make a bed of the pilaf on each dinner plate and set 1 hen half on top. Coat everything with the colorful sauce.

Nutritional Profile per Serving: Calories—533; % calories from fat—28%; fat (gm)—17 or 26% daily value; saturated fat (gm)—5; sodium (mg)—147; cholesterol (mg)—104; carbohydrates (gm)—52; dietary fiber (gm)—6.

You may choose to skin these little birds before eating them. This is a bit fiddly but will save you 8 grams of fat, so it's worth the time if you want to be in the 20-percent category. If you don't eat the skin, the calories will be 441; percentage of calories from fat, 18; grams of fat, 9; grams of saturated fat, 2; and cholesterol, 83. Quite a savings all round, so think about it!

# ROAST BEEF & YORKSHIRE PANCAKES

⬦

*The change we've made to one of the all-time English favorites is that the traditional Yorkshire Pudding—loaded with fat—has been replaced with delicious, horseradish-spiked pancakes. An additional step of reducing the size of the meat portions trims down the classic dish's walloping 1,485 calories and 113 fat grams per serving to 202 calories and 6 grams of fat. Two lovely side vegetables would be steamed carrots and broccoli with a dusting of nutmeg.*

*Time Estimate: Hands-on, 45 minutes; unsupervised, 90 minutes.*

*Serves 8*

## YORKSHIRE PANCAKES

1/2 cup all-purpose flour
1 egg
1 egg yolk
1 cup nonfat milk
1 teaspoon light olive oil with a dash of toasted sesame oil
1 tablespoon chopped fresh sage
1 tablespoon chopped fresh mint
8 teaspoons prepared horseradish

## ROAST BEEF

2 pounds (900 gm) beef bottom round
Freshly ground black pepper
1 large clove garlic, peeled and sliced into 4 pieces
2 cups low-sodium beef stock (page 286)
1 tablespoon arrowroot mixed with 2 tablespoons water (slurry)

**The Yorkshire pancakes:** Sift the flour into a bowl and make a well in the center. Lightly beat the egg and egg yolk together and pour into the well. Gradually pour in the milk, beating the ingredients together until a smooth batter is formed. Let sit for 30 minutes.

**The roast beef:** Preheat the oven to 325°F (165°C). Cut all but a thin layer of fat from the meat and sprinkle with freshly ground black pepper to taste. Score 4 small knife cuts underneath the roast and push the garlic pieces into the incisions. Place the prepared roast on a trivet in a roasting dish, fat side up, and roast until you achieve your desired doneness: an internal temperature of 120°F (48°C) for rare; 140°F (60°C) for medium; 160°F (71°C) for well done. It will take around 1 hour. When the roast is done, turn off the oven, open the door, and let it stand for 20 minutes to set the juices before carving. Remove the roast to a carving board, leaving the meat juices in the pan.

While the roast cooks, finish cooking the pancakes: Lightly oil an 8-inch (20-cm) diameter crêpe pan with the olive oil, then tip the surplus into the batter and mix. This will make each pancake more "self-releasing." When the pan is hot, pour in sufficient batter just to cover the bottom. Sprinkle with the fresh sage and mint. Once bubbles appear on the surface and it goes dull and waxy, flip it over and cook 1 minute longer. Transfer the pancake to a plate and spread the plain side with 1 teaspoon of the horseradish cream. Fold it in half and in half again. Keep the prepared pancakes warm until ready to serve. Continue the process with the rest of the pancake batter. You should have 8 pancakes, one for each guest.

To make a gravy, pour the reserved roasting juices into a fat-strainer cup, scraping out all the brown residues. Add the beef stock and let the fat rise to the top, then pour the juices through a sieve into a small saucepan. Stir in the arrowroot slurry and cook, stirring, over low heat, until thickened, about 1 minute.

**To serve:** Carve the beef into thin 1/4-inch (.75-cm) slices. Place 2 slices on each plate and ladle with the gravy. Place the pancake on the side, with the vegetable of your choice.

Nutritional Profile per Serving: Calories—202; % calories from fat—25%; fat (gm)—6 or 9% daily value; saturated fat (gm)—2; sodium (mg)—87; cholesterol (mg)—114; carbohydrates (gm)—9; dietary fiber (gm)—1.

# SLOW BEEF CURRY

——— ✦ ———

*The curries of Thailand richly deserve to be as famous as the regional delicacies of India. This adaptation is a remarkable example of how low-fat but bright flavors work to stimulate the senses and cover up the changes made in both meat and fat content. Even if all the meat is removed, the vegetables remain utterly delicious.*

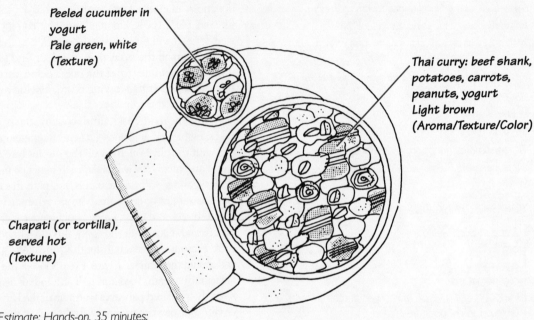

**Peeled cucumber in yogurt**
**Pale green, white**
**(Texture)**

**Thai curry: beef shank, potatoes, carrots, peanuts, yogurt**
**Light brown**
**(Aroma/Texture/Color)**

**Chapati (or tortilla), served hot**
**(Texture)**

*Time Estimate: Hands-on, 35 minutes; unsupervised, 3 hours*

*Serves 4*

## CURRY PASTE

5 small dried red chilies, with seeds
3 whole cloves
1 (1/2-inch or 1.5-cm) piece of cinnamon stick
1/2 teaspoon black cardamom seeds
1 teaspoon light olive oil with a dash of toasted sesame oil
7 cloves garlic, bashed, peeled, and chopped
7 shallots, peeled and very finely sliced
1/2 teaspoon grated gingerroot
1/2 teaspoon freshly grated nutmeg
1 tablespoon zest of lime, cut into fine matchsticks
2 tablespoons water
1/2 teaspoon coconut extract
3 tablespoons Thai fish sauce

## STEW

1 pound (450 gm) meaty beef shanks, or 8 ounces (225 gm) of another very lean stew meat, trimmed of all visible fat and cut into 1-inch (2.5-cm) pieces
1½ pounds (675 gm) new potatoes, scoured and cut into 1-inch (2.5-cm) pieces
1 pound (450 gm) carrots, peeled and cut into 1-inch (2.5-cm) pieces
1/2 cup water
2 tablespoons cornstarch mixed with 4 tablespoons water (slurry)
1 cup strained yogurt (page 288)
1/2 cup unsalted dry-roasted peanuts

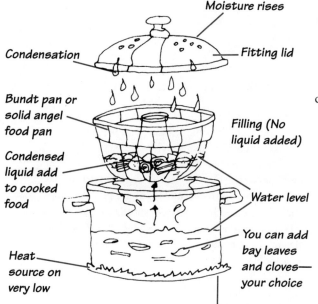

**Moisture rises**

**Condensation**

**Fitting lid**

**Bundt pan or solid angel food pan**

**Filling (No liquid added)**

**Condensed liquid add to cooked food**

**Water level**

**You can add bay leaves and cloves—your choice**

**Heat source on very low**

**The curry paste:** Place the chilies, cloves, cinnamon stick, and cardamom in a small coffee grinder and whiz for 30 seconds. As a precaution, press the mixture through a very fine sieve to remove any large, gritty particles.

Heat the oil in a large skillet over medium heat and cook the garlic and shallots until they are brown, about 5 minutes. Transfer to a small food processor, add the rest of the curry paste ingredients, and purée until the mixture becomes a well-blended paste, about 30 seconds.

**The stew:** In a large bowl, mix the beef, potatoes, and carrots with the curry paste, covering all the surfaces with the spices. Transfer to a Bundt or Kugelhopf pan and set it inside a large saucepan containing boiling water, so that the water comes half way up the side of the pan. Cover and simmer over very low heat until the meat is tender, at least 3 hours and up to 6.

Strain the cooking liquids from the meat and vegetables into a medium saucepan. Rinse the Bundt pan with 1/2 cup water and add this to the strained liquid in the saucepan. Bring the liquid to a boil, add the cornstarch slurry, and boil until thickened, about 1 minute. Remove from the heat and gently whisk in the yogurt. Return the meat and potatoes to the saucepan and cook until just heated through. The dish should not boil, otherwise the yogurt will "break" into hundreds of tiny flecks.

**To serve:** Ladle into bowls and sprinkle with the peanuts. I like to serve this dish with flat chapati bread or whole-wheat tortillas. A refreshing side dish could be peeled cucumbers in yogurt.

| Nutritional Profile per Serving | | | |
|---|---|---|---|
| | **Classic** | **Minimax** | **Daily Value** |
| Calories | 1237 | 440 | |
| Calories from fat | 59% | 26% | |
| Fat (gm) | 80 | 13 | 20% |
| Saturated fat (gm) | 47 | 2 | 10% |
| Sodium (mg) | 1,239 | 918 | 38% |
| Cholesterol (mg) | 151 | 31 | 10% |
| Carbohydrates (gm) | 72 | 60 | 20% |
| Dietary fiber (gm) | 2 | 7 | 28% |
| Classic compared: Thai Beef Curry | | | |

# SANCOCHO

*One-pot cooking makes so much sense, and this great Puerto Rican recipe is such a good example. At the heart of it must be a good meat broth and lots of fresh vegetables. In this recipe the meat is more a condiment than the star attraction.*

*Time Estimate: Hands-on, 60 minutes; unsupervised, 75 minutes*

Serves 6

1 teaspoon light olive oil with a dash of toasted sesame oil
1 large onion, peeled and diced
1 tablespoon minced fresh garlic
1 green bell pepper, seeded and cut into 1/2-inch (1.5-cm) cubes
2 red bell peppers, seeded and cut into 1/2-inch (1.5-cm) cubes
12 ounces (350 gm) bottom round steak, trimmed and cut into 1/2-inch (1.5-cm) cubes
8 ounces (225 gm) pork shoulder, trimmed and cut into 1/2-inch (1.5-cm) cubes
2 ounces (60 gm) ham, finely cubed
2 cups low-sodium beef stock (page 286)
Bouquet garni (see below)
1 (4-ounce or 115-gm) jicama, peeled and cut into 1/2-inch (1.5-cm) cubes
4 ounces (115 gm) fresh yams, peeled and cut into 1/2-inch (1.5-cm) cubes
4 ounces (115 gm) fresh pumpkin meat, peeled and cut into 1/2-inch (1.5-cm) cubes
4 ounces (115 gm) potatoes, peeled and cut into 1/2-inch (1.5-cm) cubes
1 large plantain, peeled and cut into 1/2-inch (1.5-cm) slices
2 cups cooked corn kernels
2 tablespoons arrowroot mixed with 4 tablespoons water (slurry)
1 tablespoon finely chopped fresh cilantro
1/4 teaspoon freshly ground black pepper

BOUQUET GARNI

3 sprigs fresh cilantro
1 bay leaf
1 teaspoon marjoram
1 teaspoon cracked black peppercorns
3 whole cloves

Heat the oil in a large Dutch oven over medium heat and sauté the onion, garlic, and peppers for 5 minutes. Remove the vegetables and set aside.

Increase the heat to high and add the beef, pork, and ham to the Dutch oven. When the meat is browned, return the vegetables to the pot. Pour in the stock and add the bouquet garni. Cover, bring to a boil, then simmer gently for 45 minutes. Add the jicama, yam, pumpkin, and potato. Cover and simmer for 30 minutes.

Add the plantain and corn, and simmer for 10 minutes. Remove the Dutch oven from the heat. Add the arrowroot slurry, return to the heat, and stir until thickened. Mix in the chopped cilantro and the pepper. Of course, remove the bouquet garni before serving.

**To serve:** Ladle into bowls and have at it!

Nutritional Profile per Serving: Calories—345; % calories from fat—22%; fat (gm)—8 or 13% daily value; saturated fat (gm)—3; sodium (mg)—186; cholesterol (mg)—59; carbohydrates (gm)—45; dietary fiber (gm)—5.

# Steak and Oyster Pie

⌗

*Nothing represents the best of British food as well as beef pies with kidneys, mushrooms, and oysters. I set out to bring some relief to the traditional levels of fat and cholesterol and find the results most pleasing.*

Time Estimate: Hands-on, 60 minutes;
  unsupervised, 90 minutes
Serves 8

PIE

1 recipe Basic Pastry Crust (page 289)
1 teaspoon light olive oil with a dash of toasted sesame oil
2 onions, peeled and cut into chunks
2 carrots, peeled and cut into chunks
12 ounces (350 gm) bottom round steak, cut into
  1/2-inch (1.5-cm) cubes
2 heaped teaspoons low-sodium tomato paste
12 ounces (350 gm) mushrooms, wiped clean and
  sliced, stems included
2 cups low-sodium beef stock (page 286)
8 shucked oysters (preferably medium-size "Pacific"),
  drained and chopped, liquid reserved
Bouquet Garni (page 289)
2 tablespoons oyster sauce
2 tablespoons arrowroot mixed with 4 tablespoons
  water (slurry)

SIDE DISHES: MASHED POTATOES AND
  STEAMED BROCCOLI

3 pounds (1.4 kg) russet potatoes, peeled and cut into
  2-inch (5-cm) pieces
1/2 teaspoon freshly ground sea salt
1 cup 1%-fat buttermilk
1/8 teaspoon freshly grated nutmeg
1/4 teaspoon freshly ground white pepper
3 pounds (1.4 kg) broccoli, trimmed and cut into florets

**The crust:** Preheat the oven to 425°F (220°C). Roll the pastry out to an 11-inch (28-cm) diameter circle and trim the rough edges. For a more attractive crust, you can crimp the edge as in an old-fashioned pie.

Transfer to a baking tray. Lightly score eight wedges in the dough without cutting all the way through. Brush lightly with the milk. Prick to help release steam during the baking process. Bake in the preheated oven for 12 to 15 minutes or until golden and crisp. Cool on a wire rack before cutting into wedges.

**The filling:** Heat the oil in a large, ovenproof casserole with a lid. Add the onions and carrots, and sauté for about 1 minute on high heat. Transfer the vegetables to a bowl and set aside.

Add the meat to the casserole and brown on all sides. Stir in the tomato paste, scraping the bottom of the pan so that all the juices and residue are mixed together, and cook 3 to 4 minutes.

Add the mushrooms to the cooked carrots and onions. Stir two-thirds of this mixture into the meat. Pour in the stock and reserved oyster juice all at once and stir. Add the bouquet garni and the oyster sauce. Cover and simmer for 1 hour.

**The mashed potatoes:** Bring the potatoes to a boil in a large pot of water, add the salt, and cook for 20 minutes. Drain, return to the same pot over low heat, cover with a kitchen towel, and let steam dry for 15 minutes. Mash together the potatoes, buttermilk, nutmeg, and white pepper. Keep hot while you finish the pie.

**Finishing the pie:** Preheat the oven to 400°F (205°C). Add the remaining mushrooms, carrots, onions, and the oysters to the mixture. Remove the pot from the heat and stir in the arrowroot slurry. Return to the heat and stir until thickened. Spoon the filling into a high-sided 9-inch (23-cm) pie plate. Place the cooked pie crust on top and bake for 5 minutes.

While the pie is baking, steam the broccoli for 2 to 3 minutes.

**To serve:** Using the scoring as your guide, cut a wedge out of the pie crust and set it over two large spoonfuls of the filling. Spoon the mashed potatoes alongside the pie with the broccoli on the other side.

Nutritional Profile per Serving: Calories—469; % calories from fat—25%; fat (gm)—13 or 20% daily value; saturated fat (gm)—2; sodium (mg)—569; cholesterol (mg)—50; carbohydrates (gm)—67; dietary fiber (gm)—8.

# Harvest Succotash

*Unfortunately there are only a few accounts of the origin of this classic food of the North American native. We do know that the Zuni tribe often made an all-in-one stew that they called a "Summer Succotash," which was thickened with ground sunflower seeds and garnished with a variety of summer vegetables. I call my version of this dish Harvest Succotash because the vegetables reflect a later time of year.*

Time Estimate: Hands-on, 45 minutes;
  unsupervised, 1 hour
Serves 6

3 acorn squash, cut in half and seeded
2 tablespoons sunflower seeds (for garnish)
2 teaspoons light olive oil with a dash of toasted sesame oil
12 ounces (350 gm) lean lamb shoulder, all visible fat removed and cut into 1/2-inch (1.5-cm) pieces
1 yellow onion, peeled and chopped
3 cloves garlic, bashed, peeled, and chopped
1 jalapeño pepper, seeded and chopped (with seeds if you like it spicy; without, if you like it mild)
3 red bell peppers, seeded and chopped
1 tablespoon mild chili powder
1 teaspoon ground cumin
1/2 teaspoon freshly ground sea salt
1/4 teaspoon freshly ground black pepper
2 cups low-sodium chicken stock (page 286)
2 (5-inch or 12.5-cm) sprigs fresh mint
3 cups fresh or frozen corn kernels
3 cups cut fresh or frozen green beans
2 tablespoons arrowroot mixed with 1/4 cup water (slurry)

GARNISH

3 tablespoons chopped fresh cilantro

Preheat the oven to 350°F (180°C). Place the squash halves facedown on a large baking pan and bake in the preheated oven for 1 hour. Scatter the sunflower seeds on a small baking pan and toast in the oven with the squash for 15 minutes. Set the seeds aside to use for garnish.

Heat 1 teaspoon of the oil in a high-sided skillet over high heat. When it is very hot, drop the lamb pieces into the pan to brown well, about 5 minutes. Transfer the meat to a bowl and set aside.

In the same pan, heat the remaining teaspoon of oil and fry the onion over medium heat for 2 minutes. Add the garlic and cook, stirring, for 30 seconds. Add the peppers and seasonings, and fry for 3 minutes. Pour in the stock and stir, scraping all the flavorful bits off the bottom of the pan. Add the meat and fresh mint, and simmer, covered, for 45 minutes. Remove the mint. Add the corn and beans, and simmer, uncovered, for 15 minutes. Remove from the heat, stir in the arrowroot slurry, and return to the heat to thicken.

**To serve:** Place a squash half on each warm plate and spoon the stew over the top, heaping it into the cavity. Sprinkle with the cilantro and toasted sunflower seeds for extra color and texture.

Nutritional Profile per Serving: Calories—304; % calories from fat—26%; fat (gm)—9 or 13% daily value; saturated fat (gm)—2; sodium (mg)—421; cholesterol (mg)—41; carbohydrates (gm)—43; dietary fiber (gm)—11. ⬇

# Hawke's Bay Lamb

*Treena and I lived in New Zealand, home to tens of millions of sheep, for over seven years. Our son, Andy, was born there and grew up with his sister, Tessa. During their school years, we used to prepare a great dish of lamb leftovers that Treena invented (largely because she loved to serve a creamy onion sauce with roast lamb). We used to double the sauce and use it as a blanquette (white-wine stew with a creamy finish). The kids loved it. They still do, now that I've done a fat reduction on it. So here goes . . .*

Time Estimate: Hands-on, 45 minutes;
   unsupervised, 20 minutes
Serves 4

## MASHED POTATOES

1½ pounds (680 gm) potatoes, boiled and mashed
1 cup nonfat buttermilk
1/8 teaspoon freshly ground nutmeg
1/4 teaspoon freshly ground white pepper
1/8 teaspoon freshly ground sea salt

## LAMB CASSEROLE

1 teaspoon light olive oil with a dash of toasted sesame oil
2 medium onions, peeled and sliced
1/4 cup all-purpose flour
2½ cups nonfat milk
1/4 teaspoon freshly ground white pepper
1/8 teaspoon freshly ground nutmeg
2 bay leaves
1 pound (450 gm) cooked roast lamb, cubed (preferably New Zealand spring lamb)
3 cups button mushrooms
1/2 cup de-alcoholized white wine
3 tablespoons chopped fresh parsley
1/4 teaspoon paprika

## SIDE DISH

1:2 cups water
20 ounces (575 gm) spinach leaves, washed, stemmed, and shredded

1/4 teaspoon freshly ground nutmeg
1/8 teaspoon freshly ground sea salt
1/4 teaspoon freshly ground white peppercorns

## GARNISH

Fresh parsley
Paprika

**The mashed potatoes:** In a large saucepan over low heat, mix together the mashed potatoes, buttermilk, nutmeg, pepper, and salt. Remove from the heat and cool just a bit. Spoon the cooled potatoes into a pastry piping bag.

**The lamb casserole:** in a large stewpot, heat the oil and sauté the onions over medium heat, stirring to prevent any coloring, until soft, about 5 minutes. Remove from the heat, stir in the flour, return to the heat, and gradually stir in the nonfat milk, pepper, nutmeg, and bay leaves. Bring to a boil, reduce the heat, and simmer 10 minutes.

Add the lamb and mushrooms, and simmer for 30 minutes more. Stir in the wine, parsley, and paprika.

**The side dish:** In a large pot, bring the water to a boil. Lay the spinach on a steamer tray and sprinkle with the nutmeg, salt, and pepper. Steam, covered, for 4 minutes.

**To serve:** Pipe the potatoes out of the pastry bag and onto a plate, making a nest shape. Place the steaming hot spinach in the center of the potatoes and spoon the lamb casserole on top. Garnish with the fresh parsley and paprika.

Nutritional Profile per Serving: Calories—561; % calories from fat—22%; fat (gm)—13 or 21% daily value; saturated fat (gm)—5; sodium (mg)—452; cholesterol (mg)—109; carbohydrates (gm)—63; dietary fiber (gm)—8.

# LAMB SHANKS IN A POLENTA PIE

*Two very important comfort foods come together here: braised lamb and polenta. Polenta is ground yellow cornmeal cooked until it becomes like a porridge, and is formed into a pie crustin this recipe .*

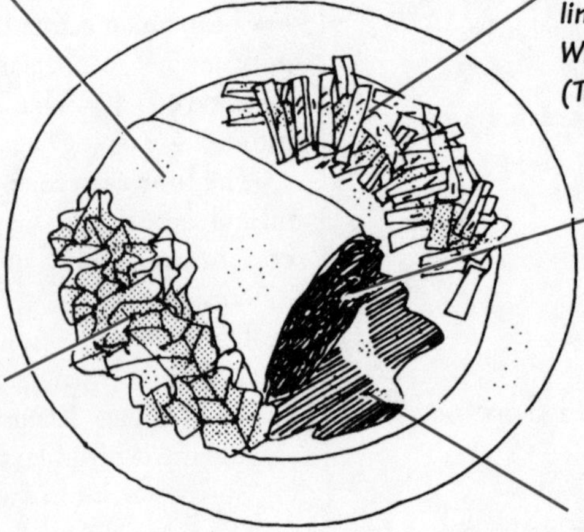

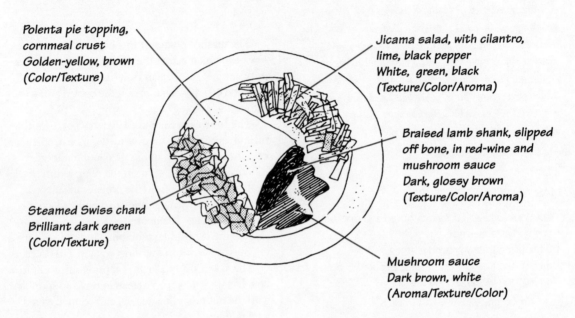

Polenta pie topping, cornmeal crust
Golden-yellow, brown
(Color/Texture)
Jicama salad, with cilantro, lime, black pepper
White, green, black
(Texture/Color/Aroma)
Braised lamb shank, slipped off bone, in red-wine and mushroom sauce
Dark, glossy brown
(Texture/Color/Aroma)
Steamed Swiss chard
Brilliant dark green
(Color/Texture)
Mushroom sauce
Dark brown, white
(Aroma/Texture/Color)


*Time Estimate: Hands-on, 90 minutes; unsupervised, 2 hours, 30 minutes*
*Serves 4*

LAMB SHANKS AND MUSHROOM SAUCE

1 teaspoon light olive oil with a dash of toasted sesame oil
1 large onion, peeled and cut into thick slices
3 large stalks celery, sliced crosswise into 1-inch (2.5-cm) pieces
1 large carrot, cut on the diagonal and partly turned after each cut
2 cloves garlic, bashed, peeled, and chopped
1 (3-ounce or 90-gm) can low-sodium tomato paste
4 (1/2-pound or 225-gm) lamb shanks
2 cups de-alcoholized red wine
1 (4-inch or 10-cm) sprig rosemary
12 medium mushrooms, sliced into thirds
2 tablespoons arrowroot mixed with 1/4 cup de-alcoholized red wine (slurry)
1 pound (450 gm) Swiss chard, steamed until just wilted
1 tablespoon freshly grated Parmesan cheese

POLENTA

3 cups cold water
1 cup fine-grain yellow cornmeal
1/4 teaspoon freshly ground sea salt
1/4 teaspoon freshly ground black pepper
2 tablespoons freshly squeezed lemon juice
1/4 teaspoon light olive oil with a dash of toasted sesame oil

**The lamb shanks:** Preheat the oven to 350°F (180°C). Heat the oil in a large stockpot on medium heat and sauté the onions, celery, and carrots for 3 minutes. Stir in the garlic and tomato paste, and cook until the mixture becomes deep brown, about 3 minutes. Add the lamb shanks and wine, making sure to scrape up any pan residues, and mix them in well. Add water until the liquid is level with the top of the lamb shanks. Gently nestle in the rosemary until it is completely buried, cover, and bake in the preheated oven for 2 hours, or until the meat slips easily off the bone.

**The polenta:** In a large saucepan, bring the water to a rapid boil. Stir in the cornmeal in a slow, steady stream, making sure the water does not stop boiling. When all the cornmeal has been added, sprinkle in the salt and pepper. Stir constantly, scraping the sides and bottom of the saucepan, until the polenta has a thick texture that pulls cleanly from the sides of the pan and a spoon will stand up in it. This takes about 5 minutes for the fine-grain variety. Lower the heat if the mixture starts to stick. Remove from the heat, stir in the lemon juice, and mix well.

Brush oil lightly over two dinner plates. Pour in the polenta, smoothing it out to make two circles, one 1 inch (2.5 cm) smaller than the other. Let cool until set, 1 hour at room temperature or 30 minutes in the refrigerator.

Transfer the cooked lamb from the pot to a large plate and trim off any fat. Gently pry the meat off the bone so that you end up with pieces still in their original muscle shapes and set aside.

**The mushroom sauce:** Strain the lamb cooking liquid into a fat-separator cup, discarding the cooked vegetables. You should have 2½ cups of liquid. Add enough wine or stock to come up to this level if you don't have enough. Pour the liquid from the fat separator into a medium saucepan, leaving the surface fat at the bottom of the cup. Stir in the mushrooms and gently warm through. Just before serving, pour the

| Nutritional Profile per Serving | | | |
|---|---|---|---|
| | Classic | Minimax | Daily Value |
| Calories | 954 | 706 | |
| Calories from fat | 46% | 30% | |
| Fat (gm) | 48 | 23 | 35% |
| Saturated fat (gm) | 14 | 8 | 40% |
| Sodium (mg) | 1,094 | 503 | 21% |
| Cholesterol (mg) | 312 | 209 | 70% |
| Carbohydrates (gm) | 12 | 50 | 17% |
| Dietary fiber (gm) | 2 | 7 | 28% |
| Classic compared: Lamb Shanks | | | |

arrowroot slurry into the sauce and stir over medium heat until thickened, about 2 minutes.

**To serve:** Slip the smaller polenta circle from the plate onto a large oval platter. Pile the meat in the center, cover with the wilted Swiss chard, and sprinkle with the Parmesan cheese. Top with the remaining polenta circle to make the upper crust of your "pie." If you are not going to eat the dish immediately, cover with aluminum foil and keep in the refrigerator. When ready to serve, bake at 300°F (150°C) for 30 minutes. The top can be browned slightly by brushing it with 1 teaspoon of oil and broiling for 5 minutes. The pie cuts neatly into wedges and looks terrific with mushroom sauce and Jicama Salad (see accompanying recipe) served on the side.

## JICAMA SALAD

1 (12-ounce, or 350 gm) jicama peeled and sliced into large matchsticks
8 cilantro leaves, finely chopped
2 tablespoons freshly squeezed lime juice
1/8 teaspoon freshly ground black pepper

Stir all the ingredients together in a bowl and refrigerate until ready to serve.

# MOUSSAKA

*Originally this classic was made in Romania, but it has become one of the greatest examples of Greek "food of the people." I have made several changes in order to lower the health risks.*

Time Estimate: Hands-on, 45 minutes;
  unsupervised, 15 minutes
Serves 6

1 teaspoon light olive oil with a dash of toasted sesame oil
1 cup finely diced onion
1 clove garlic, bashed, peeled, and minced
12 ounces (350 gm) ground lamb
3 tablespoons low-sodium tomato paste
1/4 cup bulgur wheat
1 teaspoon dried oregano
1 cup water
1 cup de-alcoholized red wine
1/8 teaspoon cinnamon
1 bay leaf
1/8 teaspoon freshly ground sea salt
1/4 teaspoon freshly ground black pepper
1 (12-ounce or 350-gm) eggplant, peeled and sliced
1/4 cup plus 2 tablespoons freshly grated Parmesan cheese

## SAUCE

1 cup nonfat milk
1/8 teaspoon freshly grated nutmeg
1/8 teaspoon freshly ground sea salt
2 tablespoons cornstarch mixed with 4 tablespoons water (slurry)
1 egg yolk, slightly beaten

## SIDE DISHES

1 recipe Pilaf Kirkland (page 242), without peas and mushrooms
3 cups frozen petit peas

Prepare the rice pilaf up to the point of adding the stock. Set aside. Preheat the oven to 350°F (180°C).

In a large wok or frying pan, heat the oil over medium-high heat and sauté the onions and garlic until the onions are soft and translucent. Turn out onto a plate and set aside.

In the same pan, brown the lamb. Add the tomato paste, bulgur, cooked onions, oregano, and water. Stir, scraping any residue off the bottom of the pan and into the mixture for added depth of taste. Add the wine, cinnamon, bay leaf, salt, and pepper.

Layer one-third of the eggplant slices on the bottom of a ceramic or glass soufflé dish. Cover with half the lamb and sprinkle with one-third of the 1/4 cup of cheese. Repeat with one-third of the eggplant, the remaining lamb, and one-third of the cheese, finishing with a layer of the remaining eggplant and the remaining cheese.

**The sauce:** In a small saucepan, heat the milk. Sprinkle with the nutmeg and salt. Gradually stir in the cornstarch slurry and bring to a boil, stirring until thickened. Remove from the heat. Pour a little of the sauce into the beaten egg yolk, then stir it back into the sauce. This will prevent the egg yolk from curdling.

Pour the sauce over the moussaka layers and sprinkle with the remaining 2 tablespoons Parmesan cheese. Bake in the preheated oven for 40 minutes. When done, the eggplant will separate from the sides of the soufflé pan, revealing the bubbling juices.

**Side dishes:** Stir the stock into the rice mixture, lay the herbs on top, and bake the rice pilaf with the moussaka.

During the last 5 minutes of cooking, boil the peas in 1/4 cup of water for 3 minutes. Drain and keep warm.

**To serve:** Slice moussaka into 6 even wedges and divide among the dinner plates. Scoop a spoonful each of pilaf and peas on the side.

Nutritional Profile per Serving: Calories—339; % calories from fat—30%; fat (gm)—11 or 17% daily value; saturated fat (gm)—5; sodium (mg)—313; cholesterol (mg)—40; carbohydrates (gm)—40; dietary fiber (gm)—8.

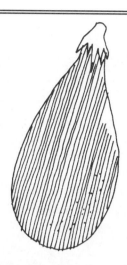

## SALTING EGGPLANT

A great many recipes call for salting eggplant slices liberally and then pressing them to reduce both bitterness and excess water content. The slices are then cooked in oil or lamb fat.

I chose to buy a smaller eggplant, not more than 3 inches (8 cm) in diameter, and simply peeled it, sliced it, and slipped it naked into the sauce—no salt, no oil, no bother, and no bitterness! I did add 1/4 cup (59 ml) of bulgar wheat to soak up surplus liquid.

The result of these efforts is clear from the numbers: an incredible drop of 57 grams of fat, 580 calories, and 4,473 mg of sodium—for each serving!

My local deli owner is Greek. The day after this recipe went on television he looked at me, bit his finger, and shook his head in mock bewilderment. Then he smiled!

# Hoppin' Skippin' John

⚜

*This is classic "soul food," especially around Charleston, South Carolina, where it is eaten with either a turnip-top salad or collard greens on New Year's Day for good fortune. I believe my new version takes "hoppin" John to the "skippin" level. You be the judge. I make it extra-lean by cooking the ham hock separately from the beans.*

Time Estimate: Hands-on, 45 minutes;
  unsupervised, 80 minutes

Serves 4

1 (2-pound or 900-gm) ham hock, trimmed of all
  visible fat
5 cups water
2 teaspoons light olive oil with a dash of toasted sesame
  oil
1 medium onion, peeled and finely chopped
1 stalk celery, finely chopped
1 tablespoon loosely packed fresh thyme leaves
4 whole cloves, freshly ground
2 bay leaves
1 cup uncooked long-grain white rice
1 cup dried black-eyed peas, soaked overnight and
  drained
1/4 teaspoon freshly ground sea salt
1/4 teaspoon cayenne pepper
1/8 teaspoon freshly ground black pepper

SIDE DISH

1 whole dried red chili pepper
1/2 lemon, seeds removed and thinly sliced
2 cups torn collard greens (2-inch or 5-cm pieces),
  washed and stems removed
1 tablespoon freshly squeezed lemon juice
1 tablespoon fresh chopped parsley
1 teaspoon grated lemon zest
Chopped fresh parsley, to taste

Put the ham hock in a saucepan with water to cover and bring to a boil. Boil for 2 minutes, then drain, discarding the water. Return the ham hock to the saucepan, cover with the 5 cups water, and bring to a boil. Cover, reduce the heat, and simmer for 1 hour. Strain through a sieve, reserving the ham hock stock—you should have 4 cups. Cut the lean meat from the hock and set aside.

In a large skillet, heat 1 teaspoon of the oil over medium-high heat and cook the onion until soft, about 3 minutes. Add the celery, thyme, ground cloves, bay leaves, rice, reserved ham hock meat, and the soaked, drained peas, and stir well. Pour in 3 cups of the reserved ham hock stock, cover, and simmer for 20 minutes over medium heat, until the rice is just tender. Discard the bay leaves; season with the salt, cayenne, and black pepper.

In a low-sided stewpot, heat the remaining teaspoon oil over medium-high heat and cook the whole chili pepper and lemon slices, just to release their volatile oils, about 2 minutes. Remove the lemon slices and chili pepper, and discard. To the same stewpot, add the collard greens and the remaining 1 cup of the reserved ham hock stock, cover, and simmer gently for 5 minutes.

Fold the cooked collards and their pot juices into the peas and rice. Stir in the lemon juice, 1 tablespoon parsley, and the lemon zest.

**To serve:** Spoon into individual serving bowls and garnish with the fresh parsley to taste.

Nutritional Profile per Serving: Calories—471; % calories from fat—24%; fat (gm)—13 or 19% daily value; saturated fat (gm)—4; sodium (mg)—538; cholesterol (mg)—26; carbohydrates (gm)—69; dietary fiber (gm)—13.

> To save time, an alternative to soaking the peas overnight is to place them in a large pot and cover with 4 cups of fresh water. Bring to a boil for 2 minutes, remove from the heat, cover tightly, and let sit for 1 hour. Drain, discarding the water, and they're ready to cook.

# PANCIT LUGLUG PALABOK
## (PORK & SHRIMP IN A RED SAUCE WITH RICE NOODLES)

⁂

*This is a popular dish in the Philippines. It uses readily available ingredients, and the simple two-pan method is almost as quick as a stir-fry. I've added finely diced bell pepper and cilantro to help with the color and texture.*

Time Estimate: Hands-on, 40 minutes
Serves 6

3 cups water
12 ounces (350 gm) small raw shrimp (weight with shells on)
12 ounces (350 gm) boneless pork loin chop, trimmed of all visible fat
1 teaspoon light olive oil with a dash of toasted sesame oil
4 cloves garlic, bashed, peeled, and chopped
1 teaspoon achiote or turmeric powder
1 teaspoon fish sauce
2 tablespoons arrowroot mixed with 4 tablespoons water (slurry)
2 green onions, chopped
1 red bell pepper, seeded and finely chopped
1 tablespoon chopped fresh cilantro
8 ounces (225 gm) firm tofu, cut into tiny dice
1/4 teaspoon freshly ground black pepper
12 ounces (350 gm) rice noodles (Bijon)

Pour the water into a medium saucepan and bring to a boil. Add the shrimp and simmer for 5 minutes. Strain, reserving the water. Plunge the shrimp into ice-cold water, then peel. Put the shells back into the reserved water to make a stock. Simmer the shells for 15 minutes, then strain off 2 cups to use later. Coarsely grind the shrimp.

Coarsely grind the pork chops.

Heat the oil in a large skillet or wok over medium-high heat. Fry the garlic and pork for 3 minutes. Add the shrimp and fry until just warmed, about 1 minute.

Stir in the reserved shrimp stock, the achiote powder, and the fish sauce. Remove the pan from the heat and stir in the arrowroot slurry until thickened. Add the green onions, red pepper, cilantro, tofu, and black pepper, and heat through.

Cook the rice noodles in boiling water until soft, about 3 minutes. You should stir them once, at the beginning, the moment they become flexible. This will keep them separated during the cooking process. Drain well.

**To serve:** Divide the rice noodles among 6 bowls and top with the shrimp-pork mixture.

Nutritional Profile per Serving: Calories—334; % calories from fat—25%; fat (gm)—9 or 14% daily value; saturated fat (gm)—2; sodium (mg)—129; cholesterol (mg)—90; carbohydrates (gm)—36; dietary fiber (gm)—2. ⬇

Achiote powder is made from the small, reddish seeds of the annato tree. It gives a lovely color to many dishes. Don't hesitate to go into a Latin American or Filipino grocery and ask for it. It's pronounced "ah-chee-OH-tay."

# ORANGE-BRAISED PORK CHOPS

※

*Orange zest gives interest and sophistication to this dish.*

Time Estimate: Hands-on, 25 minutes;
  unsupervised, 30 minutes
Serves 4

4 (4-ounce or 115-gm) boneless, center-cut loin pork
  chops
1 teaspoon light olive oil with a dash of toasted sesame oil
1 cup de-alcoholized dry white wine
1 cup low-sodium chicken stock (page 286)
8 ounces (225 gm) carrots, cut into matchsticks
8 medium fresh mushrooms, cut into quarters
8 ounces (225 gm) fresh green beans
2 teaspoons chopped fresh thyme
1/4 teaspoon freshly ground black pepper
1/4 teaspoon freshly ground sea salt
2 teaspoons shredded orange zest
4 ounces uncooked penne pasta
1 tablespoon arrowroot mixed with 2 tablespoons de-
  alcoholized white wine (slurry)
1 teaspoon minced fresh thyme

Preheat the oven to 400°F (205°C). Dab the meat with a paper towel to remove the surface moisture. Heat the oil over medium-high heat in a large, high-sided, ovenproof skillet and brown the chops for 2 minutes on each side. Transfer the chops to a plate.

Blot the pan with a paper towel to remove excess fat, then pour in the wine and chicken stock, stirring until all the pan residue has been scraped up into the liquid. Return the pork to the pan, add the carrots, mushrooms, and green beans, trying as much as possible to submerge them in the liquid. Sprinkle with the thyme, pepper, salt, and orange zest. Bring to a boil, cover, and pop into the preheated oven to bake for 30 minutes.

Cook the penne pasta in a large pot of boiling water for 10 minutes, drain and set aside.

Remove the pork dish from the oven. Drape a towel over the handle so you won't forget how hot the handle is after being in the oven. Transfer the pork to a plate. Stir the arrowroot slurry into the pan juices and cook over medium-high heat until thickened, about 30 seconds. Stir in the cooked pasta and reserved pork.

**To serve:** Divide the pork, pasta, and vegetables among 4 warm dinner plates. Cover with any sauce remaining in the pan and sprinkle with a whisper of the minced thyme.

Nutritional Profile per Serving: Calories—359; % calories from fat—27%; fat (gm)—11 or 41% daily value; saturated fat (gm)—3; sodium (mg)—228; cholesterol (mg)—66; carbohydrates (gm)—35; dietary fiber (gm)—4.

# ROAST PORK WITH FIESTA BEANS AND RICE

※

*Puerto Rican people have a wonderful celebration every year around Christmas and New Year's Eve, when they barbecue whole suckling pigs. Here you'll find the fullness of aroma, color, and texture—minus the whole pig. I've tried to capture the tastes in this new dish, dedicated to the vibrant Puerto Rican life-style and to Yvonne Ortiz, my culinary guide among her people.*

Time Estimate: Hands-on, 45 minutes;
  unsupervised, 90 minutes
Serves 12

PORK

1 (4-pound or 1.8-kg) pork loin roast
1 banana, peeled
1 tablespoon chopped fresh cilantro
1 clove garlic, bashed, peeled, and chopped
1/8 teaspoon freshly ground sea salt
1/4 teaspoon freshly ground black pepper

## FIESTA BEANS AND RICE

1 teaspoon light olive oil with a dash of toasted sesame oil
1/2 medium onion, peeled and finely diced
4 cloves garlic, bashed, peeled, and chopped
2 jalapeño peppers, finely diced
2 (28-ounce or 800-gm each) cans peeled plum tomatoes, with their liquid
2 tablespoons finely chopped fresh oregano
1 cup uncooked long-grain white rice
1 (15-ounce or 425-gm) can garbanzo beans, drained and rinsed
1/4 teaspoon freshly ground sea salt
1/4 teaspoon freshly ground black pepper
1 red bell pepper, seeded and diced
1 (16-ounce or 450-gm) can black beans, drained and rinsed
2 tablespoons finely chopped fresh cilantro

### GARNISH

1 banana, cut into 1-inch (2.5-cm) slices
Juice of 1/2 lime
1 tablespoon chopped fresh cilantro
4 sprigs fresh cilantro

**The pork:** Preheat the oven to 350°F (180°C). Cut the pork in half and place the pieces side by side on a cutting board. Lay the banana lengthwise on top and down the center of one piece and mark its outline. Cut a shallow trench the length and width of the banana and half its depth. Repeat the process on the other piece of pork. Reserve the pork meat that is cut out and set aside.

Sprinkle the cilantro and garlic down the pork trenches, then season both pieces of pork with the salt and pepper. Put the banana in the trench in one of the pieces and cover with the other piece. Using string, tie the halves together. Put the prepared pork on a rack in a roasting pan and cook in the preheated oven for 80 minutes or until a meat thermometer reads 160°F (71°C). Remove from the oven and let rest for 10 minutes before carving.

**The beans and rice:** Dice the reserved pork into 1/4-inch (.75-cm) cubes. In a medium stewpot, heat the oil over medium-high heat and brown the diced pork on one side. Add the onion and garlic, and cook until the onion is soft, about 5 minutes. Add the jalapeño peppers, tomatoes and their liquid, and the oregano, and simmer, uncovered, for 10 minutes. Add the rice, garbanzo beans, salt, and pepper and bring to a boil. Decrease the heat, cover, and simmer for 20 minutes. Gently stir in the red pepper, black beans, and cilantro, and heat through.

**The garnish:** Just before serving, mix the sliced banana with the lime juice and chopped cilantro.

**To serve:** Carve the pork into 1/2-inch (1.5-cm) slices. Put 1 slice on each plate with some of the fiesta rice and a spoonful of the banana garnish on the side. Top with a graceful green cilantro sprig.

Nutritional Profile per Serving: Calories—465; % calories from fat—27%; fat (gm)—14 or 21% daily value; saturated fat (gm)—4; sodium (mg)—411; cholesterol (mg)—97; carbohydrates (gm)—42; dietary fiber (gm)—6.

> Fiesta Beans and Rice can also be served on its own as a vegetarian main dish, *omitting the diced pork*; there's enough for 6 hearty portions, with 415 calories, 6 grams of total fat, and only 12 percent calories from fat per serving.

# ROAST LAMB WITH APPLE-ORANGE GRAVY

— ⌘ —

*You needn't give up gravy for Minimax roasts. My technique uses an appropriate liquid added to the cooking pan and then poured through a fat-strainer jug before thickening.*

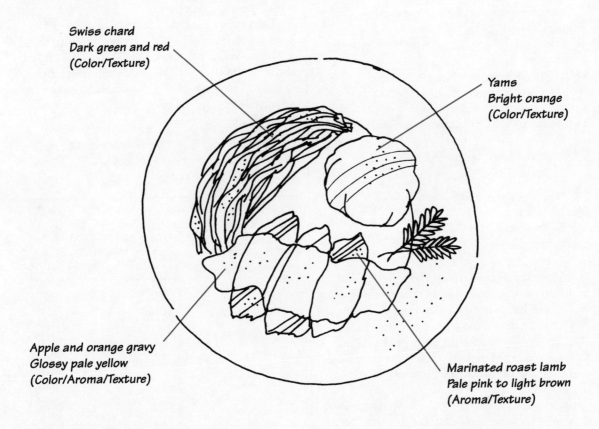

**Swiss chard**
**Dark green and red**
**(Color/Texture)**

**Yams**
**Bright orange**
**(Color/Texture)**

**Apple and orange gravy**
**Glossy pale yellow**
**(Color/Aroma/Texture)**

**Marinated roast lamb**
**Pale pink to light brown**
**(Aroma/Texture)**

Time Estimate: Hands-on, 15 minutes;
   unsupervised, 97 minutes
Serves 4

2/3 cup unsweetened apple juice
2/3 cup unsweetened orange juice
1 (3½-pound or 1.6-kg) leg of lamb
1 tablespoon all-purpose flour
1/2 cup water
2 tablespoons arrowroot mixed with 4 tablespoons
   water (slurry)

SIDE DISHES: MASHED YAMS AND
   STEAMED LEMON SWISS CHARD

6 medium yams, scrubbed
2 (16-ounce or 450-gm) bunches Swiss chard
1 tablespoon freshly squeezed lemon juice

Pour half the apple juice and half the orange juice into a medium saucepan, bring to a vigorous boil, and reduce to 1/4 cup, about 17 minutes. Remove from the heat and let cool.

Preheat the oven to 325°F (165°C). Pour the reduced juice into a flavor injector. Put the lamb on a flat surface and inject all over with small amounts of the juice. Dust lamb with flour, put on a rack in a roasting pan, and roast for 80 minutes. During the roasting time, add 1/2 cup of water to the roasting pan to keep the pan drippings from burning.

**The side dishes:** After the lamb has been cooking for 30 minutes, place the yams in the oven and bake for 40 minutes. Remove from the oven. Remove the flesh from the skins and mash. Keep warm until ready to serve. Just before you make the garvy, place the chard in a steamer and steam for 5 minutes; sprinkle with the lemon juice.

Remove the lamb from the roasting pan when done and set aside. Put the pan full of cooking juices on the stovetop over medium heat, pour in the remaining apple and orange juices, and completely scrape up all the residues. Strain and pour into a fat-strainer jug.

Pour the juices from the strainer into a medium saucepan, stopping when you get to the fat, and heat through. Remove from the heat and stir in the arrowroot slurry. Return to the heat and stir until thickened. Remove from the heat and set aside.

**To serve:** Carve the lamb into thin slices, put 3 slices (a 4-ounce [115-gm] portion) on each plate, and cover with the gravy. Spoon a mound of yams and one of chard on the side.

| Nutritional Profile per Serving | | | |
|---|---|---|---|
| | Classic | Minimax | Daily Value |
| Calories | 518 | 415 | |
| Calories from fat | 31% | 23% | |
| Fat (gm) | 18 | 11 | 16% |
| Saturated fat (gm) | 8 | 4 | 19% |
| Sodium (mg) | 344 | 320 | 13% |
| Cholesterol (mg) | 130 | 104 | 35% |
| Carbohydrates (gm) | 52 | 43 | 14% |
| Dietary fiber (gm) | 6 | 6 | 25% |
| Classic compared: Roast Lamb with Vegetables | | | |

# Rabbit Casserole

※

*If you've never owned a pet rabbit, this dish could become one of your all-time favorites! The meat is as tender as chicken, but succulent and richer in flavor. Rabbit adapts itself to many superb seasonings. This recipe is done very simply and tastes great. I always serve this dish with a purée of turnips, carrots, and parsnips, seasoned with nutmeg and parsley—a wonderful vegetable dish for almost every meat or poultry, stew or casserole. Add your favorite bread and nobody will leave the table dissatisfied.*

*Time Estimate: Hands-on, 60 minutes*
*Serves 4*

1 (2-pound or 900-gm) rabbit
1 tablespoon light olive oil with a dash of toasted sesame oil
8 medium onions, peeled
8 fresh mushrooms
1/8 cup lean ham
3 tablespoons low-sodium tomato paste
2 cups de-alcoholized red wine
1 cup ham hock stock (page 287)
1 bouquet garni (page 289)
2 carrots, peeled and chopped into 1-inch (2.5-cm) pieces
2 turnips, peeled and chopped into 1-inch (2.5-cm) pieces
2 parsnips, peeled and chopped into 1-inch (2.5-cm) pieces
1/4 teaspoon freshly grated nutmeg
3 tablespoons chopped fresh parsley
2 tablespoons arrowroot mixed with 1/4 cup de-alcoholized red wine (slurry)
1/8 teaspoon freshly ground sea salt
1/4 teaspoon freshly ground black pepper

Chop the rabbit into 8 pieces: hind legs, thighs, half saddles (the long strip from the shoulders to the thighs), and shoulders.

Preheat the oven to 350°F (180°C). Pour the oil into a low-sided, ovenproof casserole over high heat and brown the rabbit pieces, turning to expose all the sides, about 5 minutes. Remove and set aside.

In the same casserole, brown the onions and mushrooms. The mushrooms will brown in about 30 seconds; remove them and set aside, keeping the onions in the casserole until they're done, about 5 minutes. Add the ham and tomato paste, and cook until the tomato paste darkens in color, about 5 minutes. Add the browned rabbit pieces, the wine, the ham hock stock, and bouquet garni. Bring to a boil and remove from the heat. Cover and put in the preheated oven to bake 10 minutes.

While the rabbit casserole is baking, steam the carrots, turnips, and parsnips until soft, about 12 minutes. Transfer the vegetables to a food processor or blender, add the nutmeg and parsley, and purée until combined but not smooth like a sauce. Spoon into a bowl and keep warm until ready to serve.

Remove the casserole from the oven. Transfer the rabbit pieces to a bowl and discard the bouquet garni. Stir the arrowroot slurry into the casserole liquid, place over medium heat, and stir until thickened. Season with the salt and pepper.

**To serve:** Place the rabbit pieces on a serving plate and drizzle with casserole liquid. Serve the puréed vegetables on the side.

Nutritional Profile per Serving: Calories—519; % calories from fat—28%; fat (gm)—16 or 25% daily value; saturated fat (gm)—5; sodium (mg)—298; cholesterol (mg)—132; carbohydrates (gm)—41; dietary fiber (gm)—9.

# Rogan Josh

*The cuisine of Northern India is heavily influenced by the Aryan peoples of their northern borders. This is where their yogurt and lamb comes from. When you smell the combination of garlic, ginger, and the sweet, warm spices, then you always know exactly where you are!*

*Time Estimate: Hands-on, 45 minutes;*
  *unsupervised, 75 minutes*
*Serves 6*

2 teaspoons light olive oil with a dash of toasted sesame oil
4 cloves garlic, bashed, peeled, and finely diced
2 cups chopped onion
1 tablespoon freshly grated gingerroot
1/2 teaspoon cayenne pepper
1/4 teaspoon powdered nutmeg
1/2 teaspoon turmeric
1/4 teaspoon mace
1½ teaspoons paprika
1 teaspoon garam masala (page 3)
1½ pounds (680 gm) lean leg of lamb, cut in 1-inch (2.5-cm) cubes
1 tablespoon dried coriander
2 cups peeled and chopped tomatoes
1/8 teaspoon freshly ground sea salt
1 tablespoon cornstarch mixed with 2 tablespoons water (slurry)
3/4 cup plain nonfat yogurt
3/4 cup water
1 tablespoon chopped fresh cilantro
3 cups cooked rice

Heat half the olive oil in a large (11-inch [28-cm]) wok over medium-high heat. Stir in the garlic, onions, ginger, and cayenne pepper. Sauté until the onions are slightly softened and appear translucent, about 2 minutes. Stir in the nutmeg, turmeric, mace, paprika, and garam masala. Turn off the heat.

Put another large (13-inch [33-cm]) pan on high heat and add the remaining olive oil. Drop the lamb cubes in around the edges, allowing them to brown fully on one side. Add the dried coriander. Stir in the cooked onion mixture. Now add the tomatoes and the salt.

Blend in the cornstarch slurry, yogurt, and water. Bring to a boil and stir until thickened. Reduce the heat, cover, and simmer for 1 hour. Uncover and cook another 30 minutes. Sprinkle with the chopped cilantro.

**To serve:** Spoon 1/2 cup of the rice on each plate and top with the Rogan Josh.

Nutritional Profile per Serving: Calories—360; % calories from fat—25%; fat (gm)—10 or 15% daily value; saturated fat (gm)—3; sodium (mg)—139; cholesterol (mg)—79; carbohydrates (gm)—37; dietary fiber (gm)—3. ⬇

# SOUL-FOOD PORK ROAST WITH GLAZED VEGETABLES

⌗

*What to do when you're not serving a gravy: try a glaze!*

*Time Estimate: Hands-on, 15 minutes;*
*unsupervised, 25 minutes*

Serves 4

1½ quarts ham hock stock (page 287), using 2½ quarts
water; ham hock meat coarsely chopped and
reserved
1 cup dried black-eyed peas
1 teaspoon light olive oil with a dash of toasted sesame oil
1/4 teaspoon freshly ground black pepper
4 (4-ounce or 115-gm) center-cut pork chops
1 (16-ounce or 450-gm) bunch collard greens, to yield 8
ounces (225 gm) of leaves after trimming
2 cups frozen corn
1 tablespoon freshly squeezed lemon juice
1/4 teaspoon cayenne pepper
2 tablespoons arrowroot mixed with 4 tablespoons
water (slurry)
Freshly ground black pepper to taste

In a large saucepan, combine 3 cups of the ham
hock stock with the black-eyed peas and bring to a
boil. Reduce the heat to low and simmer until tender,
about 25 minutes.

Preheat the oven to 350°F (180°C). Pour the oil
on a dinner-size plate. Sprinkle on the freshly ground
pepper. Place an 11-inch (28-cm) ovenproof pan
over medium-high heat. Dredge both sides of each
pork chop in the oil. Place the pork chops in the
heated pan and brown on one side, about 2 minutes.
Turn the chops over, put the pan into the preheated
oven and cook the chops for 15 minutes. Remove the
chops from the pan and keep warm.

Pour the remaining 3 cups of the ham hock stock
into the pan with the roasting juices and cook on the
stovetop over high heat, scraping the pan residues for
1 minute. Pour into a fat-strainer cup.

In a large saucepan, heat the pan juices from the
fat-strainer cup, add the collard greens and the
reserved ham hock meat, and cook over medium heat
for 4 minutes. Add the cooked black-eyed peas, the
corn, lemon juice, and cayenne pepper. Remove from
the heat and add the arrowroot slurry. Stir gently
until thickened. Cover and just heat through. Don't
stir too roughly, or you'll break the peas.

**To serve:** On dinner plates, make a mound of the
vegetables and set a chop in the center. Scatter a
spoonful of glazed vegetables over each chop and
sprinkle with the freshly ground black pepper.

Nutritional Profile per Serving: Calories—511; % calories
from fat—28%; fat (gm)—16 or 24% daily value; saturated
fat (gm)—5; sodium (mg)—298; cholesterol (mg)—83;
carbohydrates (gm)—52; dietary fiber (gm)—16.

# TOLTOTT KAPOSZTA
## (HUNGARIAN STUFFED CABBAGE)

⌗

*This is Hungarian "food-of-the-people" fare. It's relative-*
*ly simple to fix and makes an occasion out of very plain*
*food. The center of the cabbage is relatively small, so the*
*rest of the filling winds up as a sauce. Whipped potatoes*
*and a hunk of dark rye bread are great accompaniments.*

*Time Estimate: Hands-on, 40 minutes;*
*unsupervised, 30 minutes*

Serves 6

12 ounces (350 gm) pork loin, cut into 2-inch (5-cm)
cubes
1 cup chopped onion
2 cloves garlic, bashed, peeled, and chopped
8 ounces (225 gm) mushrooms, coarsely chopped
1 cup low-sodium chicken stock (page 286)
1/4 cup bulgur wheat
1 medium cabbage, trimmed, with damaged leaves
removed
1 teaspoon light olive oil with a dash of toasted sesame oil
3 tablespoons low-sodium tomato paste

1 tablespoon plus 2 teaspoons paprika

1/2 teaspoon caraway seeds

1/8 teaspoon freshly ground sea salt

1/4 teaspoon freshly ground black pepper

1/4 cup strained yogurt (page 288)

1 tablespoon chopped fresh parsley

2 tablespoons cornstarch mixed with 2 tablespoons water (slurry)

GARNISH

Fresh parsley sprigs

Mince the pork, onion, garlic, and mushrooms in a meat grinder.

Bring the chicken stock to boil, add the bulgur wheat, and simmer 5 minutes. Remove from the heat and set aside for later use in the sauce.

In a large saucepan, cover the whole cabbage with water, bring to a boil, and cook for 30 minutes. Remove the cabbage from the pan and cool quickly with cold water. Drain.

Heat the olive oil in a medium wok or large frying pan and cook the ground pork mixture. When there is no pink left in the pork meat, add the tomato paste. Sprinkle in 1 tablespoon of the paprika and the caraway seeds, and stir well. Remove and set aside.

Place the cabbage, core side down, on a board. Peel back the leaves without pulling them off at the core. Pull back as many cooked leaves as possible, leaving a round inner head about 4 inches (10 cm) in diameter. Hollow out the top of this inner head. Fill the hollow with a third of the pork filling or until packed solid. Set the leftover pork filling aside. Carefully re-fold the cabbage leaves in their original order and position. Wrap securely in muslin or cheesecloth.

Place some marbles in the bottom of a Dutch oven or large covered casserole. Put a steamer tray on top of the marbles. Add water to just above the base of the steamer. Place the wrapped cabbage on the steamer, cover, and cook on high heat for 30 minutes. If you hear the marbles clanking against the Dutch oven, you know it's time to add more water!

While the cabbage cooks, put the remaining pork filling in a nonstick skillet over low heat, cover, and

simmer. Add additional stock if needed to keep it from sticking.

When the cabbage is done, lift it out of the pan with a couple of wooden spoons. Place it in a bowl just large enough to hold it, with the core facing upward. Cut the muslin or cheesecloth away from the cabbage and fold it over the sides of the bowl. Cover the bowl with a plate and, holding it firmly, turn it upside down. Remove the bowl, strip off the muslin or cheesecloth, and you've got a big, steamed cabbage sitting right side up!

Add the strained yogurt, the remaining 2 teaspoons paprika, and parsley to the filling. Remove from the heat and stir in the cornstarch slurry. Return to the heat, bring to a boil, and stir until thickened.

**To serve:** Slice the cabbage in wedges like a cake and serve in a small pool of sauce. Garnish with the parsley.

Nutritional Profile per Serving: Calories—219; % calories from fat—26%; fat (gm)—6 or 10% daily value; saturated fat (gm)—2; sodium (mg)—114; cholesterol (mg)—37; carbohydrates (gm)—24; dietary fiber (gm)—6.

# VEAL HAMPSHIRE

*Treena and I visited the small Canadian city of Victoria on Vancouver Island off the west coast, and found a very pleasant little restaurant in Oak Bay called the Hampshire Grill. This is one of their special dishes, which we have since worked on together.*

Time Estimate: Hands-on, 70 minutes;
  unsupervised, 75 minutes

Serves 6

3 pounds (1.4 kg) boneless veal loin, cut slightly longer into the flap or skirt, butterflied, pounded to 1/2-inch (1.5-cm) thickness

## STUFFING

1 onion, peeled and diced
1 green bell pepper, seeded and diced
1 red bell pepper, seeded and diced
1 cup chopped mushrooms
2 cups raw spinach leaves, washed with stems removed
1 teaspoon light olive oil with a dash of toasted sesame oil
1 cup bread crumbs
1 tablespoon fresh thyme
1/8 teaspoon freshly ground sea salt
1/4 teaspoon freshly ground black pepper
1/8 teaspoon allspice
1 tablespoon Dijon mustard
1 ounce (30 gm) Canadian bacon, cut into fine strips
1/2 medium apple, peeled, cored, and sliced

## FRUIT SAUCE

2 cups veal stock (page 286)
1 tablespoon freshly squeezed orange juice
1 cup unsweetened apple juice
1 tablespoon arrowroot mixed with 2 tablespoons water (slurry)
1/8 teaspoon freshly ground black pepper

**The stuffing:** Grind the onions, peppers, and mushrooms through a meat grinder. Drain to separate juices from vegetables, reserving the juice. (I tried to use it as a super vitamin drink, but it tasted awful—so it gets added to the stuffing later on!)

Steam the spinach for 2 to 3 minutes. Put it into a cheesecloth, press out the excess juice, and discard the juice.

In a low-sided stewpot, heat the oil over medium-high heat and fry the ground vegetables until the onions appear translucent, about 3 minutes. Add the bread crumbs and the reserved grinding juices, stirring constantly so that the ingredients bind together. Add the thyme, salt, pepper, and allspice.

**To assemble:** Preheat the oven to 375°F (190°C). Place the veal on a cutting board and spread with the mustard. Spoon the cooked vegetables on top. Next, lay the pressed spinach over the vegetables. The Canadian bacon slices are next, topped with the apple slices. Fold or roll the veal so that the filling is encased by the meat. Wrap the veal in butcher's net or tie with kitchen twine. Place the meat on a trivet in a roasting pan and roast in the preheated oven for 1 hour.

**The fruit sauce:** Drain off any surplus fats from the low-sided stewpot and blot the surface with a paper towel. Deglaze the stewpot with the veal stock. Turn into a small saucepan along with the orange juice and apple juice, and reduce over high heat by one-third. Remove from the heat and add the arrowroot slurry. Return to the heat and stir until thickened. Season with the pepper.

Remove the veal from the oven and let sit about 20 minutes.

**To serve:** Carve the veal into slices and serve on a pool of the fruit sauce.

Nutritional Profile per Serving: Calories—402; % calories from fat—28%; fat (gm)—13 or 19% daily value; saturated fat (gm)—5; sodium (mg)—395; cholesterol (mg)—198; carbohydrates (gm)—19; dietary fiber (gm)—2.

# Fondue and Salad

*I'm really excited about this idea. I've now designed a Fondue and Salad with plenty to eat that contains only 16 grams of fat per serving, including the fondue, croutons, and the salad dressing. This concept of adding sweet potatoes could spark a renewed interest in this Swiss specialty.*

Time Estimate: Hands-on, 40 minutes;
  unsupervised, 60 minutes
Serves 4

## CROUTONS

1 teaspoon dried basil
1/4 teaspoon dried tarragon
1/8 teaspoon freshly ground black peppercorns
1 (6-inch or 15-cm) piece French baguette, about 2 ounces (60 gm), cut into 1/2-inch (1.5-cm) cubes
1/4 cup low-sodium chicken broth (page 286)
4 teaspoons freshly grated Parmesan cheese

## MUSTARD VINAIGRETTE

1/4 cup cider vinegar
2 tablespoons olive oil mixed with a dash of toasted sesame oil
1/8 teaspoon freshly ground black peppercorns
1 teaspoon chopped fresh basil
1/2 teaspoon dried tarragon
1/2 teaspoon Dijon mustard
1 teaspoon maple syrup

## FONDUE

1 clove garlic, peeled
1 cup low-sodium chicken broth (page 286)
1 cup de-alcoholized dry white wine
1¾ pounds (800 gm) sweet potatoes, cooked, peeled, and pulp mashed
1 tablespoon cornstarch mixed with 2 tablespoons chicken broth (slurry)
2 ounces (60 gm) extra-sharp cheddar cheese, shredded
1/8 teaspoon freshly ground sea salt
1/4 teaspoon freshly ground black pepper
1 tablespoon freshly squeezed lemon juice
1/2 loaf French bread, broken into small chunks
2 apples, peeled, cored, and sliced, dipped in lemon juice

## SALAD

1 medium apple, peeled, cored, and chopped
3 stalks celery, chopped
2 tablespoons finely chopped fresh basil
1 small head tender butter lettuce

**The croutons:** Preheat the oven to 350°F (180°C). In a small bowl, combine the basil, tarragon, and pepper. Place the bread cubes in a pie pan, arranging them white side up (not crust side). Using a pastry brush, coat the cubes with the chicken broth. Sprinkle with the mixed herbs and the Parmesan cheese. Bake on the middle rack of the preheated oven for 20 minutes. Remove and set aside.

**The mustard vinaigrette:** In a dressing jar or small bowl, mix the vinegar, oil, pepper, basil, and tarragon, and shake or whisk to combine. Add the mustard and maple syrup and shake or whisk again. Set aside.

**The fondue:** Heat a nonstick wok or heavy saucepan over medium heat and rub the clove of garlic around the inner surface. Pour in the chicken broth and the wine. Add the mashed sweet potatoes and whisk together until smooth and warmed through. Add the cornstarch slurry and cheddar cheese, and stir to thicken.

Strain the fondue by spooning it into a sieve over a large bowl. Rub the solid portions through with a wooden spoon. Return the fondue to the same heated wok, stir in the salt, pepper, and lemon juice and heat through.

**The salad:** Just before serving, combine the apple, celery, and fresh basil in a large bowl. Drizzle the vinaigrette over the top and mix well. Now add the lettuce leaves and croutons and toss until well coated.

**To serve:** Transfer the fondue to a fondue pot or serving bowl. Gather your friends and family around the pot, giving each a skewer to dip the bread chunks and apple slices into the fondue. Serve the salad on the side—a great time for all!

Nutritional Profile per Serving: Calories—572; % calories from fat—25%; fat (gm)—16 or 24% daily value; saturated fat (gm)—5; sodium (mg)—684; cholesterol (mg)—17; carbohydrates (gm)—95; dietary fiber (gm)—9.

# Golden Threads Squash

*What a great natural invention: the so-called spaghetti squash has a unique internal threadlike structure—and bright golden color!*

*Time Estimate: Hands-on, 45 minutes; unsupervised, 80 minutes*

Serves 6

1 (4½-pound or 2-kg) spaghetti squash
1 teaspoon light olive oil with a dash of toasted sesame oil
2 cloves garlic, bashed and peeled
2 medium carrots, peeled and cut into matchsticks
1 red bell pepper, seeded and cut into matchsticks
1 green bell pepper, seeded and cut into matchsticks
1/4 cup low-sodium chicken stock (page 286)
1½ tablespoons finely chopped fresh basil
4 tablespoons freshly grated Parmesan cheese
Freshly ground black pepper
1 tablespoon arrowroot mixed with 2 tablespoons chicken stock (slurry)

GARNISH

1 sprig fresh basil
1/2 ounce (15 gm) cracked filberts

Prick the squash on one side, allowing it to "breathe." Place it on a baking sheet and bake it at 325°F (165°C) for 80 minutes. Remove and dip it in an ice-water bath to prevent it from overcooking by retained heat.

Put the squash on one side and cut a long lid. Remove the lid and scoop out the seeds and discard. Carefully scrape the spaghetti like threads out of the shell. Put these golden threads on a plate and set aside.

Put the empty squash shell on a serving platter. If the shell won't stay in place, scoop out some of the pulp from the sides, and put it on the plate as a base to hold the shell stable.

Heat the olive oil in a wok over medium heat and fry the crushed garlic for 30 seconds. Add the carrots, peppers, and chicken stock, then gradually stir in the golden threads of reserved spaghetti squash. Sprinkle with the basil, half of the grated cheese, and some freshly ground black pepper, and stir lightly to mix.

Now remove from the heat and add the arrowroot slurry. Return the wok to the heat and stir until thickened.

Tip the mixture into the squash shell and garnish with the remaining cheese, the filberts, and the basil sprig.

Nutritional Profile per Serving: Calories—184; % calories from fat—27%; fat (gm)—6 or 9% daily value; saturated fat (gm)—1; sodium (mg)—100; cholesterol (mg)—3; carbohydrates (gm)—33; dietary fiber (gm)—10. ⬇

# SPAGHETTI CARBONARA

※

*The first time I ate this classic Italian dish was in Rome. It was served in the "Golden Room" at the Hosteria dell 'Orso, prepared on a golden lamp with a golden spoon and golden fork . . . well . . . you get the picture. My new version leaves the flavors intact but reduces the calories from 900 per serving in the classic to just 413. If you really need to reduce your cholesterol, use liquid egg substitute instead of the whole eggs.*

Time Estimate: Hands-on, 35 minutes
Serves 4

8 ounces (225 gm) spaghetti
3 teaspoons light olive oil with a dash of toasted sesame oil
4 ounces (115 gm) Canadian bacon, diced
1/8 cup pine nuts
2 eggs, lightly beaten
1/8 teaspoon freshly ground sea salt
1/4 teaspoon freshly ground black pepper
2 tablespoons chopped fresh parsley
2 tablespoons snipped fresh chives
1/4 cup freshly grated Parmesan cheese
3 sun-dried tomato halves, ground to yield 1 tablespoon

In a large pot of boiling water, cook the spaghetti according to package directions for al dente, or just tender, about 10 minutes. Drain in a colander set over a large serving bowl. Pour the cooking water out of the bowl, leaving it nicely heated.

While the spaghetti is cooking, heat 1 teaspoon of the oil in a large skillet over medium-high heat and cook the Canadian bacon and pine nuts until lightly browned, about 5 minutes. Use a slotted spoon to transfer the mixture to the heated serving bowl, mentioned above. Pour the remaining oil into the same skillet, scrape the residue off the bottom of the pan, then pour it into the heated serving bowl. Pour the eggs, salt, pepper, parsley, chives, cheese, and ground sun-dried tomatoes into the serving bowl. Add the cooked spaghetti and toss until the spaghetti is well covered. The eggs will be cooked by the spaghetti's heat. Season with additional salt and pepper to taste.

Nutritional Profile per Serving: Calories—363; % calories from fat—27%; fat (gm)—11 or 17% daily value; saturated fat (gm)—3, sodium (mg)—608; cholesterol (mg)—18; carbohydrates (gm)—48; dietary fiber (gm)—3.

# ROASTED VEGETABLE QUESADILLAS

⬥

*There is nothing quite as luscious as a roasted (actually, broiled or grilled is more accurate) sweet bell pepper—regardless of its color. When it is combined with the sweetness of plum tomatoes and the pungency of sliced red onions, you've got the makings of a truly great appetizer! A whole meal with golden saffron-tinted rice on the side (page 176), salsa (page 63), and an ear of sweet corn on the cob.*

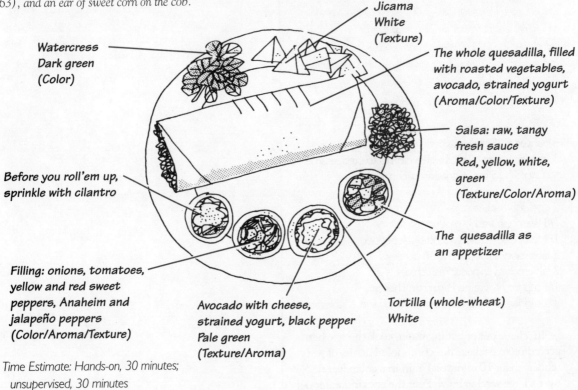

**Jicama**
**White**
**(Texture)**

**Watercress**
**Dark green**
**(Color)**

**The whole quesadilla, filled with roasted vegetables, avocado, strained yogurt (Aroma/Color/Texture)**

**Salsa: raw, tangy fresh sauce Red, yellow, white, green (Texture/Color/Aroma)**

**Before you roll'em up, sprinkle with cilantro**

**The quesadilla as an appetizer**

**Filling: onions, tomatoes, yellow and red sweet peppers, Anaheim and jalapeño peppers (Color/Aroma/Texture)**

**Avocado with cheese, strained yogurt, black pepper Pale green (Texture/Aroma)**

**Tortilla (whole-wheat) White**

*Time Estimate: Hands-on, 30 minutes; unsupervised, 30 minutes*
*Serves 4*

6 large plum tomatoes, halved and seeded
2 red bell peppers, top and bottom sliced off and reserved for salsa recipe (page 63), seeded and quartered lengthwise
1 green bell pepper, top and bottom sliced off and reserved for salsa recipe (page 63), seeded and quartered lengthwise
2 yellow bell peppers, top and bottom sliced off and reserved for salsa recipe (page 63), seeded and quartered lengthwise

2 Anaheim chili peppers, seeded
1 red onion, peeled and sliced in 1/4-inch (.75-cm) rings
1 large avocado, peeled, pitted, and mashed
3 tablespoons strained yogurt (page 288)
1 tablespoon freshly grated Parmesan cheese
1/8 teaspoon freshly ground black pepper
4 whole-wheat tortillas
Cayenne pepper (optional)
Jalapeño pepper, finely chopped (optional)
3 tablespoons chopped fresh cilantro

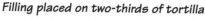
Filling placed on two-thirds of tortilla

Leave uncovered or slightly dampened with avocado.

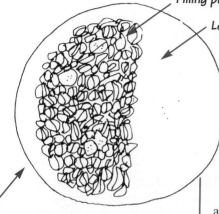

Roll this edge over to
cover filling tightly, until
it is enclosed and the
fold is underneath.

The quesadilla can then be cut
into bite-sized hors d'oeuvres.

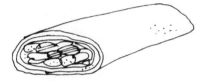

Preheat broiler. Place the tomatoes, peppers, and onion directly on a baking sheet, skin side up, within 2 inches (5 cm) of the heating element. After about 5 minutes, remove the tomatoes, turn the onions, and broil 5 minutes. The pepper skins will be blistered and black. Set the onions aside with the tomatoes. Transfer the charred peppers directly to a paper bag, seal, and let cool for 20 minutes. Peel off the charred black pepper skins.

Mix the mashed avocado with the strained yogurt, Parmesan cheese, and black pepper, and spread evenly over the tortillas.

Preheat the oven to 400°F (205°C). Cover two-thirds of each tortilla with layers of the roasted vegetables in the following order: onions, tomatoes, red, green, yellow, and Anaheim peppers. If you have the same asbestos-lined tongue as my wife, and "like it hot," then at this stage a little cayenne pepper or finely chopped jalapeño pepper will light your fire. Sprinkle with the cilantro and roll the quesadillas from the filled side to the empty flap. Transfer the quesadillas to a shallow baking pan, cover with foil, and bake for 10 minutes.

**To serve:** For an appetizer, cut each quesadilla into 1-inch (2.5-cm) pieces and present with a bowl of salsa (page 53) on the side. You can garnish the platter with watercress, cilantro, and finely cut discs of jicama . . . or just "set 'em out 'n' watch 'em go."

| Nutritional Profile per Serving | | | |
|---|---|---|---|
| | Classic | Minimax | Daily Value |
| Calories | 1,058 | 323 | |
| Calories from fat | 67% | 28% | |
| Fat (gm) | 79 | 10 | 15% |
| Saturated fat (gm) | 42 | 2 | 10% |
| Sodium (mg) | 1,787 | 372 | 16% |
| Cholesterol (mg) | 204 | 2 | .1% |
| Carbohydrates (gm) | 45 | 54 | 18% |
| Dietary fiber (gm) | 6 | 11 | 44% |
| Classic compared: Well-Filled Quesadillas | | | |

# Cannelloni

⌗

*The classic cannelloni from Pappagallo in Bologna, Italy, has been a high standard of eating pleasure for as long as I can remember. There are major changes in my version, but the result is truly tasty and enough of the unique flavors, textures, and aromas are still there to make it a prized recipe. I always serve a crisp green salad with lots of herbs and some good, fresh, crusty bread on the side—sublime.*

Time Estimate: Hands-on 45 minutes;
   unsupervised, 15 minutes
Serves 4

## RED SAUCE

4 ounces (115 gm) turkey Italian sausage
1/2 teaspoon light olive oil with a dash of toasted
   sesame oil
1 cup chopped onion
2 cloves garlic, bashed, peeled, and chopped
2 tablespoons low-sodium tomato paste
1¾ cups canned, low-sodium tomatoes, chopped, juice
   reserved
1 cup low-sodium tomato sauce
1 tablespoon chopped fresh basil
1 tablespoon chopped fresh oregano

## WHITE SAUCE

2 teaspoons Dijon mustard
3/4 cup strained nonfat plain yogurt (page 288)
1½ tablespoons cornstarch
1 cup low-sodium chicken stock (page 286)

## PASTA AND FILLING

8 large manicotti
1/2 teaspoon light olive oil with a dash of toasted
   sesame oil
1/2 cup finely chopped onion
2 cloves garlic, bashed, peeled, and chopped
1 cup canned low-sodium white beans
1 cup low-fat ricotta cheese
1/2 cup chopped fresh spinach
1 cup finely chopped zucchini
1 tablespoon chopped fresh basil
1 tablespoon chopped fresh oregano
1 tablespoon Dijon mustard

## GARNISH

2 tablespoons freshly grated Parmesan cheese
2 tablespoons chopped fresh parsley

**The red sauce:** Preheat the oven to 400°F (205°C). Break up the sausage into a very hot medium skillet and brown well. Tip into a bowl and set aside, wiping out any grease left in the pan. Add the oil to the same skillet, toss in the onions, and cook over medium-high heat for 1 minute, then add the garlic and cook for 1 more minute. Pull the vegetables aside, spoon in the tomato paste, and cook until it begins to darken, about 3 minutes. Now add the meat, the tomatoes and their juice, tomato sauce, and fresh herbs. Simmer for 20 minutes.

**The white sauce:** Combine the mustard and strained yogurt in a small bowl. Whisk together the cornstarch and chicken stock in a medium saucepan. Bring to a boil and stir until it thickens, about 30 seconds. Place two ice cubes in the broth to cool it quickly, then add the yogurt to the thickened broth, stirring until you achieve a smooth sauce. Set aside to use later.

**The pasta and filling:** Cook the manicotti in a large pot of boiling water for 6 to 8 minutes. Drain and cool in cold water. Cook the onions and garlic in the oil in a small skillet over medium-high heat until the onions turn transparent, about 2 minutes. Whiz the beans in a food processor until they form a smooth paste. Add the ricotta cheese and pulse just to mix. Scrape the bean/cheese purée into a mixing bowl and mix well with the rest of the filling ingredients including the cooked onions and garlic. Spoon carefully into the cooled manicotti using about 1/3 cup in each. Don't worry if they tear, the filling will hold them together while they bake.

**To assemble:** Spread 1/2 cup of the red sauce on the bottom of a 9 X 13-inch (23 X 33-cm) baking dish. Gently place the filled manicotti on top of the sauce and cover with the rest of the red sauce. Pour the white sauce over the middle of each manicotti leaving a little red showing on each end. Sprinkle the grated Parmesan cheese over the white sauce and bake in the preheated oven for 15 minutes to heat through and brown slightly.

**To serve:** Lay 2 filled manicotti on each warm plate and sprinkle parsley over the top.

Nutritional Profile per Serving: Calories—380; % calories from fat—27%; fat (gm)—11 or 18% daily value; saturated fat (gm)—5; sodium (mg)—649; cholesterol (mg)—44; carbohydrates (gm)—42; dietary fiber (gm)—6.

> An attractive way to serve this dish is to cook the manicotti in small, individual, oval ovenproof dishes and then serve it bubbling hot from the oven, setting the dish directly on a dinner plate.

# TORTELLINI METROPOLITAN

*At the Metropolitan Diner in Victoria, British Columbia, brothers Ford and Matt MacDonald serve this as an appetizer. We've tweaked it to go the distance as a main dish and brought the nutritional numbers into line for special needs.*

*Time Estimate: Hands-on, 30 minutes*
*Serves 4*

4 quarts water
2 (9-ounce or 250-gm) packages spinach tortellini with cheese filling

CREAMY CASHEW SAUCE

3 tablespoons cornstarch
1 cup strained yogurt (page 288)
8 ounces (225 gm) evaporated skim milk
1/4 cup de-alcoholized white wine (I prefer a somewhat sweet variety)
1 teaspoon light olive oil with a dash of toasted sesame oil
1 tablespoon finely chopped onion
1 teaspoon minced garlic

1/4 cup shredded Swiss cheese
1 tablespoon freshly grated Parmesan cheese
1 teaspoon chopped fresh tarragon
1 tablespoon toasted unsalted cashew pieces

GARNISH

1 tablespoon freshly squeezed lime juice
1 tablespoon toasted unsalted cashew pieces
1 teaspoon fresh tarragon
1 teaspoon chopped fresh chives

Bring the water to a boil. Add the spinach tortellini, bring back to a boil, and cook according to package directions, about 8 minutes. (Note: Dried tortellini takes about 20 minutes.) Drain the tortellini and set aside.

In a bowl, combine the cornstarch with the strained yogurt. Add the evaporated milk and the wine.

Heat the olive oil in a saucepan over medium-high heat and sauté the onion and garlic for 2 minutes. Remove the saucepan from the heat and add the cornstarch-yogurt mixture. Return to the heat, bring to a boil, and stir until thickened. Add the Swiss and Parmesan cheeses, tarragon, and cashews to the sauce.

Pour the sauce into a large skillet. Add the tortellini and toss until well coated.

**To serve:** Spoon the tortellini onto a plate and garnish with the lime juice, toasted cashews, tarragon, and chives.

Nutritional Profile per Serving: Calories—476; % calories from fat—25%; fat (gm)—13 or 21% daily value; saturated fat (gm)—5; sodium (mg)—769; cholesterol (mg)—125; carbohydrates (gm)—54; dietary fiber (gm)—2.

# 30% calories from fat

⊠

# Side Dishes
# &
# Vegetables

# Split Spun Salad

*It's a fantastic tool that I have used a salad spinner here to spin off excess salad dressing. This leaves the salad ingredients perfectly coated with flavor, without excess calories and fat. Naturally, this works best with a liquid rather than a creamy dressing.*

Time Estimate: Hands-on, 20 minutes;
 unsupervised, 30 minutes
Serves 4

## HARD INGREDIENTS (VEGETABLES)

8 green onions
 4 plum tomatoes, cut into eighths
 1 cucumber, peeled, seeded, and thinly sliced
 1 carrot, cut into matchsticks

## DRESSING

2 tablespoons canola oil
1 teaspoon toasted sesame oil
1/2 cup rice wine vinegar
2 tablespoons brown sugar
1/4 teaspoon freshly ground black pepper

## SOFT INGREDIENTS (GREENS)

1/2 head iceberg lettuce
2 Romaine lettuce leaves

## GARNISH

Freshly ground pepper to taste

**The hard ingredients:** Chop the green onions in two where the green stem starts turning a dark color. Chop the white bulb coarsely and set aside. Coarsely chop the dark green tops diagonally and set aside separately. Put all the hard ingredients except the dark green onion tops in a large serving bowl and toss well.

**The dressing:** In a small bowl or blender, beat the dressing ingredients together—you'll have about 2/3 cup of dressing. Add to the hard ingredients, toss well, and let sit 30 minutes. Drain off and reserve the dressing: you now have about 1/2 cup dressing.

Put the hard ingredients in a salad spinner set over a bowl and spin about 20 turns. You will spin off an extra 1/8 cup of the dressing. Now you have only 1/8 cup of dressing on the hard ingredients. Transfer these vegetables onto a plate and set aside.

**The soft ingredients:** Tear the salad greens into small, 2-inch (5-cm) pieces—a size that's easily handled with a fork—and wash them well. Put into the salad spinner and spin 20 times to remove excess liquid. Add the reserved green onion tops to the salad greens.

**To assemble:** Just before serving, put half the greens in the salad spinner, followed by the vegetables, and finally the remaining greens. Pour in the dressing and spin 10 times. You extract about 1/2 cup of the dressing in this process, leaving total of only a 1/4 cup coating the salad ingredients. Transfer the salad to a large bowl, sprinkle with the pepper, and toss well. The surplus dressing can be stored in the refrigerator for another day, but should be used before the week is out. The recipe makes enough for 12 servings when spun off in this way.

**To serve:** Divide among individual plates. Be sure to toss the vegetables with the greens at the last moment. This will protect the leaves from wilting.

Nutritional Profile per Serving: Calories—78; % calories from fat—30%; fat (gm)—3 or 4% daily value; saturated fat (gm)—4; sodium (mg)—28; cholesterol (mg)—0; carbohydrates (gm)—13; dietary fiber (gm)—3.

# STIR-FRIED SALAD

⁂

*This herbal salad can be used with many, many variations. Do try to fix it with your own favorite vegetables and herbs.*

*Time Estimate: Hands-on, 45 minutes;*
*unsupervised, 4 hours*
*Serves 4*

## LIME-GINGER DRESSING

1/2 cup rice wine vinegar
2 tablespoons light olive oil with a dash of toasted
    sesame oil
2 tablespoons low-sodium chicken stock (page 286)
2 tablespoons brown sugar
1/4 teaspoon cayenne pepper
2 tablespoons freshly squeezed lime juice
3 thin quarter-size slices fresh gingerroot
2 cloves garlic, bashed, peeled, and finely chopped
6 fresh basil leaves, finely sliced
6 fresh mint leaves, finely sliced

## STIR-FRIED SALAD

1 teaspoon light olive oil with a dash of toasted sesame oil
1/2 small yellow onion, peeled and thinly sliced
1 clove garlic, bashed, peeled, and finely chopped
2 large carrots, sliced diagonally
5 green onions, sliced
1/2 cup green beans, sliced in half lengthwise
1/4 cup finely sliced fennel bulb
4 thin quarter-size slices fresh gingerroot, finely chopped
1/2 cup red bell pepper, seeded and cut into fine matchsticks
1/2 cup green bell pepper, seeded and cut into fine matchsticks
2 stalks celery, sliced diagonally
1/2 cup finely sliced jicama
1/2 cup finely sliced cucumber
12 leaves of assorted salad greens, rinsed and dried

**The lime-ginger dressing:** In a blender, combine the vinegar, olive oil, chicken stock, brown sugar, and cayenne pepper. Add the lime juice, ginger, garlic, basil, and mint, and mix on high speed for 45 seconds. Strain into a bowl.

**The salad:** Heat the olive oil in a medium casserole over medium-high heat and fry the yellow onion, garlic, and carrots for 3 minutes. Add the green onions, green beans, fennel, ginger, peppers, celery, and jicama, and cook until just warmed through. Remove the warmed vegetables and place in a large bowl. Add the cucumbers to the mixture and set aside.

Pour the vinaigrette into the casserole, dredging up the residue from the bottom and edges. Heat the vinaigrette slightly and then pour over the vegetables. Marinate for about 4 hours.

Strain the vegetables over a bowl, catching the excess vinaigrette. You should have about 1/2 cup of excess vinaigrette.

**To serve:** Place the salad greens in a bowl, pour in 1 tablespoon of the excess vinaigrette (save the rest for another salad), and toss well. Add the marinated vegetables and serve!

Nutritional Profile per Serving: Calories—139; % calories from fat—33%; fat (gm)—5 or 8% daily value; saturated fat (gm)—1; sodium (mg)—73; cholesterol (mg)—0; carbohydrates (gm)—23; dietary fiber (gm)—6. ⬇

# Tomato and Endive Salad

The tomatoes really need to be in season for the success of all the flavors. In winter, substitute with your seasonal favorites. Brilliant orange slices would be phenomenal.

Time Estimate: Hands-on, 15 minutes
Serves 4

## TREENA'S VINAIGRETTE

1 clove garlic, bashed and peeled
1/2 white wine vinegar
1/2 teaspoon dry mustard
2 tablespoons brown sugar
1/8 teaspoon cayenne pepper or 1/4 teaspoon if you like it hot (like Treena does)

## SALAD

2 large beefsteak tomatoes, cored and cut into 8 thick slices
1/4 teaspoon freshly ground black pepper
2 heads Belgian endive, ends trimmed and leaves separated
1 green onion, finely chopped

Make Treena's Vinaigrette by beating all the ingredients together in a blender until the garlic is dissolved, about 1 minute. Layer the tomato slices in a pie plate. Pour in the vinaigrette, sprinkle with the pepper, then turn the top layer over so the pepper gets distributed throughout both layers, and let it sit for 5 minutes.

Arrange the tomatoes in an overlapping line down the center of a long serving platter. Put the Belgian endive leaves in the dressing and toss until coated. Tuck the endive leaves along either side of the tomatoes. Scatter with the chopped green onion and serve.

Nutritional Profile per Serving: Calories—86; % calories from fat—31%; fat (gm)—3 or 5% daily value; saturated fat (gm)—5; sodium (mg)—54; cholesterol (mg)—0; carbohydrates (gm)—14; dietary fiber (gm)—5.

# 30% calories from fat

⌗

# Brunch
# &
# Breakfast Dishes

# ARNOLD BENNETT OMELET

⚏

*There aren't many savory puffed omelets, but this is a delight-
ful exception—excellent brunch, lunch, or dinner fare.*

*You might be horrified to see the percentage of fat in this
recipe. Look again—this high percentage is one of those
anomalies that happens when the calories in a dish are
very low. There are only 5 grams of fat in this dish which
means it is well within the lowest fat parameters, and
probably yours too!*

Time Estimate: Hands-on, 25 minutes
Serves 2

1/4 cup dry-pack sun-dried tomatoes
4 ounces smoked black cod, salmon, haddock, or
  whitefish
2 green onions, finely chopped
2 large whole eggs
1/8 teaspoon freshly ground sea salt
1/4 teaspoon freshly ground black pepper
1/8 teaspoon cayenne pepper
1/2 teaspoon dried tarragon
4 large egg whites
1/4 teaspoon cream of tartar
1 teaspoon light olive oil with a dash of toasted sesame oil
1 tablespoon freshly grated Parmesan cheese
1 tablespoon chopped fresh chives
4 slices whole-wheat bread, toasted
4 tablespoons reduced-sugar jam
1/2 canteloupe, peeled and sliced

Soak the sun-dried tomatoes in boiling water for
10 minutes to soften, then drain and chop.

Remove any skin and bones from the fish and
flake into a bowl. Add the chopped green onions and
half the chopped sun-dried tomatoes.

Beat the whole eggs in a bowl and add the salt,
pepper, cayenne pepper, tarragon, and the other half
of the sun-dried tomatoes.

Beat the egg whites until foamy, add the cream of
tartar, and continue beating until they peak. Stir one-
third of the egg whites into the seasoned whole-egg

mixture to lighten. Fold in the remaining egg whites
just until the whites are evenly colored.

Preheat the broiler and set the rack 4 to 5 inches
(10 to 13 cm) from the heating element.

Set a 9½-inch (24-cm) nonstick pan over medium
heat and when hot, add the oil. When the oil is hot,
add the egg mixture all at once and stir quickly, using
a spatula and making a figure-eight motion. This
helps expose the eggs to the bottom heat. Bang the
pan on the heating element a couple of times to set-
tle the mixture. Smooth the surface with your spatula
and gently sprinkle the filling ingredients over the
top of the omelet. Dust with the Parmesan cheese.
Continue cooking on the stove top for about 2 minutes or until the omelet starts to come away from the
sides of the pan and air holes start to appear on the
top. Now slide the pan under the hot broiler and
cook until a brown color appears on top and the
omelet has risen, 2 to 4 minutes. Remove from the
oven, loosen the edges carefully, and shake the
omelet out of the pan with a spatula onto a cutting
board.

**To serve:** Cut the omelet in half, place on warm
plates, and sprinkle with the chopped chives. Serve
with the warm toast, jam, and canteloupe slices on
the side.

Nutritional Profile per Serving: Calories—241; % calories
from fat—26%; fat (gm)—7 or 11% daily value; saturated fat
(gm)—2; sodium (mg)—639; cholesterol (mg)—114;
carbohydrates (gm)—34; dietary fiber (gm)—3. ⬇

# FILLET OF BEEF BENEDICT

*Just think of it: beef so tender it melts in your mouth, a hint of Canadian bacon peeking through egg and mozzarella cheese, all together on a sourdough English muffin! Could a brunch dish so delicious be on a healthy Minimax menu? You bet! Make a salad with fresh spinach leaves and orange sections to accompany this dish.*

*Time Estimate: Hands-on, 25 minutes*
Serves 4

2 (4-ounce or 115-gm each) beef tenderloin fillets, fully trimmed
Freshly ground black pepper
3 ounces (90 gm) Canadian bacon, cut into 6 very thin slices
1/8 teaspoon cayenne pepper
1 cup liquid egg substitute
1/2 teaspoon light olive oil with a dash of toasted sesame oil
2 teaspoons prepared horseradish
2 sourdough English muffins, cut in half and toasted
2 ounces (60 gm) part-skim mozzarella cheese, cut into 4 thin slices
Freshly ground pepper

SAUCE

1/2 cup de-alcoholized white wine
1/2 teaspoon arrowroot mixed with 1 tablespoon de-alcoholized white wine (slurry)

GARNISH

1 tablespoon chopped fresh parsley
Paprika

Cut each fillet in half and pound with your fist or a mallet until it is just a little larger in diameter than the English muffin. Sprinkle with the freshly ground black pepper, to taste. Mince 2 slices of the Canadian bacon and mix with the cayenne pepper and egg substitute. Lightly grease 4 nonstick poaching cups or glass custard cups with half of the oil. Divide the egg mixture evenly between them. Set into a skillet of steaming water to poach. Cover and set the timer for 3 minutes. When they have cooked for 3 minutes, give them a gentle stir and cook, covered, 3 minutes more. Spread the horseradish on the toasted muffins.

Preheat the oven on broil. Brush a medium skillet with the remaining 1/4 teaspoon of oil and heat over medium heat until almost smoking. Brown the fillets for 1 to 2 minutes on each side. Transfer the fillets from the pan onto the toasted English muffins. Quickly fry the remaining Canadian bacon, 30 seconds on each side, and lay it on top of the fillets. Slide the cooked eggs out of the poaching cups onto the bacon and top with a slice of the cheese. Season with freshly ground white pepper. Pop the muffins under the broiler for 1 minute, or just until the cheese melts.

**For the sauce:** Pour the wine into the same pan in which the meat cooked and scrape up any brown bits from the bottom of the pan. Remove from the heat and slowly stir in the arrowroot slurry. Return to the heat and stir until clear.

**To serve:** Pour the sauce over and around the broiled muffins and sprinkle with the parsley and paprika.

Nutritional Profile per Serving: Calories—256; % calories from fat—32%; fat (gm)—9 or 14% daily value; saturated fat (gm)—4; sodium (mg)—570; cholesterol (mg)—50; carbohydrates (gm)—16; dietary fiber (gm)—1.

# McKerr Muffins

—— ✦ ——

*"Oh, what a beautiful morning . . ." when you start it with a brunch for family and friends and feature a delicious and healthful dish like this. I like this with a chunky fruit salad on the side.*

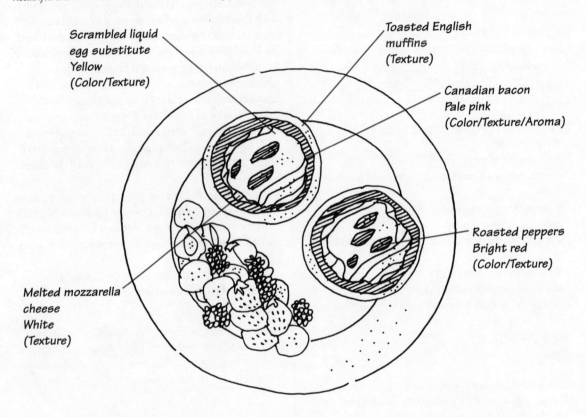

Scrambled liquid egg substitute Yellow (Color/Texture)

Toasted English muffins (Texture)

Canadian bacon Pale pink (Color/Texture/Aroma)

Roasted peppers Bright red (Color/Texture)

Melted mozzarella cheese White (Texture)

*Time Estimate: Hands-on, 25 minutes*
*Serves 2*

2 teaspoons Dijon mustard
2 English muffins, split and toasted
4 paper-thin slices Canadian bacon
1 large red bell pepper, roasted and peeled (page 41), or 1/2 cup roasted red pepper from a jar
1/2 teaspoon light olive oil with a dash of toasted sesame oil

1 cup liquid egg substitute
2 teaspoons chopped fresh chives
2 teaspoons chopped fresh parsley
2 teaspoons chopped green onion
1/4 teaspoon freshly ground black pepper
1/16 teaspoon cayenne pepper
4 (1/2-ounce or 15-gm) slices part-skim mozzarella cheese

Spread the mustard on the toasted muffin halves and lay out on a baking sheet. Place one slice of the Canadian bacon on each and cover that with one-quarter of the roasted pepper. Turn the oven on to broil.

Heat the oil in a small nonstick skillet over medium-low heat. Combine the egg substitute, chives, 1 teaspoon parsley, green onion, pepper, and cayenne. Pour into the warm pan and when it starts to set on the bottom, push gently, moving it into a mound in the center of the pan. It should keep a moist, glossy sheen to assure proper texture. When the egg is done, divide it among the muffin halves. Lay a slice of cheese on the egg and sprinkle with the remaining teaspoon parsley. Pop under the broiler to melt the cheese. Serve immediately.

If you give liquid egg substitutes special handling, they do a creditable job of replacing the scrambled egg for breakfast. The first factor is to cook them over medium-low heat so they don't get tough. The second thing is to pour the egg substitute into the warmed pan and leave it there for about 60 seconds to warm through and begin to set. The third and most important trick is to push them gently to the center of the pan with a spurtle or spatula as they set. They just don't take kindly to being scrambled madly with a fork. The surface must remain moist and the stored heat will complete the cooking on the way to the table.

| Nutritional Profile per Serving | | | |
|---|---|---|---|
| | Classic | Minimax | Daily Value |
| Calories | 602 | 313 | |
| Calories from fat | 79% | 26% | |
| Fat (gm) | 53 | 9 | 14% |
| Saturated fat (gm) | 29 | 4 | 20% |
| Sodium (mg) | 796 | 843 | 35% |
| Cholesterol (mg) | 565 | 23 | 8% |
| Carbohydrates (gm) | 15 | 34 | 11% |
| Dietary fiber (gm) | 1 | 4 | 16% |
| Classic compared: Eggs Benedict | | | |

# 30% calories from fat

⁂

# Desserts

# STEAMED MARMALADE PUDDING

*I created this dish in 1987 on a visit to Scotland. It still has lots of appeal for a cold, blustery winter's day. I prefer the Seville orange marmalade because Seville oranges have a fascinating and complex sweet-sour taste.*

*Time Estimate: Hands-on, 20 minutes; unsupervised, 1 hour, 35 minutes*

*Serves 8*

1/2 teaspoon plus 3 tablespoons light olive oil with a dash of toasted sesame oil
1/4 cup orange marmalade, preferably Seville
1/2 cup light brown sugar
1/4 cup liquid egg substitute
3/4 cup nonfat milk
1 teaspoon vanilla extract
1¼ cups all-purpose flour
1½ teaspoons baking powder
1/2 cup unsweetened frozen raspberries, unthawed

## SAUCE

1 cup unsweetened frozen raspberries, thawed
3/4 cup freshly squeezed orange juice
1 tablespoon honey
1 tablespoon arrowroot

Lightly grease a 6-cup pudding bowl with 1/2 teaspoon of the olive oil. Spoon the orange marmalade into the bottom of the bowl, smoothing it out evenly with the back of a wet spoon to cover about one-third of the inner surface. This will become the cap on the pudding.

In a bowl, beat together the remaining oil, brown sugar, egg substitute, milk, and vanilla. Combine the flour and baking powder, and sprinkle into the liquid mixture. Mix gently with a wire whisk just until smooth. Just as in a cake, the less mixing, the better the eventual texture of the pudding. Pour half the batter into the prepared bowl over the marmalade.

Drop in the frozen berries and top with the rest of the batter.

Cover the pudding with a sheet of waxed paper and a 14-inch (35-cm) square cotton dishcloth. Tie a piece of string around the lip of the bowl securing the cloth. Now bring the opposite corners of the dishcloth over the top of the bowl and tie them together. This creates a marvelous handle to pull the pudding bowl out of the steamer.

Place the pudding bowl in a large pan of boiling water. The water should come halfway up the sides of the pudding bowl. Cover and steam gently over medium heat on top of the stove for 1½ hours. Keep the water at a gentle boil. Remove the pudding bowl from the steamer and let it set for 5 minutes before unmolding. When you are ready to unmold it, run a thin-bladed knife between the pudding and the bowl. Place a plate on the top, hold it firmly in place, and turn the bowl upside down. The pudding should drop neatly onto the plate.

**The sauce:** Push the raspberries through a fine sieve. Mix with the orange juice, honey, and arrowroot in a small saucepan and heat, stirring, until the sauce thickens slightly.

**To serve:** Puddle 2 tablespoons of sauce on each plate and place a slice of pudding in the sauce.

Nutritional Profile per Serving: Calories—266; % calories from fat—26%; fat (gm)—8 or 12% daily value; saturated fat (gm)—1; sodium (mg)—121; cholesterol (mg)—0; carbohydrates (gm)—47; dietary fiber (gm)—2.

# The Basics

# Basic Chicken, Turkey, or Duck Stock

*Yields 4 cups*

1 teaspoon light olive oil with a dash of toasted sesame
  oil
1 onion, peeled and chopped
1/2 cup coarsely chopped celery tops
1 cup coarsely chopped carrots
Carcass from a whole bird and any meat, fat, or skin
  scraps
1 bay leaf
2 sprigs fresh thyme
4 sprigs fresh parsley
6 black peppercorns
2 whole cloves

Pour the oil into a large stockpot over medium heat. Add the onion, celery tops, and carrots, and fry to release their volatile oils, about 5 minutes. Add the carcass and seasonings and cover with 8 cups water. Bring to a boil, reduce the heat, and simmer for 2 to 4 hours, adding water if needed. Skim off any foam that rises to the surface. After 1 hour, add 1 cup cold water—this will force fat in the liquid to rise to the surface so you can remove it.

Strain; use with relative abandon.

The best way to get rid of excess fat is to chill the stock, let the fat rise to the top and harden, and then pick it off the top.

# Basic Beef, Lamb, or Veal Stock

*Yields 4 cups*

1 pound (450 gm) beef, lamb, or veal bones, fat
  trimmed off
1 teaspoon light olive oil with a dash of toasted sesame oil
1 onion, peeled and coarsely chopped
1/2 cup coarsely chopped celery tops
1 cup coarsely chopped carrots
1 bay leaf
2 sprigs fresh thyme
6 black peppercorns
2 whole cloves

Preheat the oven to 375°F (190°C). Place the beef, lamb, or veal bones in a roasting pan and cook until nicely browned, about 25 minutes. The browning produces a richer flavor and deeper color in the final stock.

Pour the oil into a large stockpot over medium heat and fry the vegetables for 5 minutes, to release their volatile oils. Add the bones and seasonings and cover with 8 cups water. Bring to a boil, reduce the heat, and simmer 4 to 8 hours, adding more water if necessary. Skim off any foam that rises to the surface. Strain and you've got a marvelous tool.

If you chill the stock in the refrigerator, the fat will harden on top and you will be able to pick it off.

# Quick Beef Stock in a Pressure Cooker

*Yields 4 cups*

Same ingredients as for Basic Beef Stock (page 286),
minus the carrots

Brown the bones in the oven as for Basic Beef
Stock.

Pour the oil into a pressure cooker over medium
heat and fry the onion and celery tops for 5 minutes.
Add the browned bones and the seasonings and
cover with 6 cups of water. Fasten the lid, bring to
steam, lower the heat, and cook for 40 minutes from
the time when the cooker starts hissing.

Remove from the heat, leave the lid on, and let
cool naturally, about 30 minutes. Strain; you will
have about 4 cups of stock.

*Note:* Whenever you're using a pressure cooker,
check your manufacturer's instruction book for maximum levels of liquids, etc.

# Basic Ham Hock Stock

*Yields 6 cups*

1 pound (450 gm) ham hock
1 bay leaf
3 whole cloves

In a pressure cooker, cover the ham hock with 2
quarts cold water. Bring to a boil, remove from the
heat, and drain, discarding the water. Put the ham
hock back in the pressure cooker and add the bay leaf
and cloves. Pour in 2 quarts water, fasten the lid, and
put over high heat. When the cooker starts hissing,
turn the heat down to medium-low and let simmer
30 minutes. Carefully skim the fat off the hot soup or
chill it thoroughly and pick the hardened fat off the
top. Strain and have at it.

# Classic Fish or Shrimp Stock

*Yields 4 cups*

1 teaspoon light olive oil with a dash of toasted sesame oil
1 onion, peeled and coarsely chopped
1/2 cup coarsely chopped celery tops
2 sprigs fresh thyme
1 bay leaf
1 pound (450 gm) fish bones (no heads) or shrimp
   shells (see Note)
6 black peppercorns
2 whole cloves

Pour the oil into a large saucepan over medium
heat and sauté the onion, celery tops, thyme, and bay
leaf until the onion is translucent, about 5 minutes.
To ensure a light-colored stock, be careful not to
brown.

Add the fish bones or shrimp shells, peppercorns,
and cloves, and cover with 5 cups water. Bring to a
boil, reduce the heat, and simmer for 25 minutes.
Strain through a fine-mesh sieve and cheesecloth.

*Note:* Salmon bones are too strong for fish stocks.

# BASIC VEGETABLE STOCK

⁂

*Yields 4 cups*

1 teaspoon light olive oil with a dash of toasted sesame
    oil
1/2 cup coarsely chopped onion
2 cloves garlic, bashed and peeled
1/2 teaspoon freshly grated gingerroot
1/2 cup coarsely chopped carrot
1 cup coarsely chopped celery
1 cup coarsely chopped turnip
1/4 cup coarsely chopped leeks, white and light green
    parts only
3 sprigs fresh parsley
1/2 teaspoon black peppercorns

   Pour the oil into a large stockpot over medium
heat, add the onion and garlic, and sauté for 5 minutes. Add the rest of the ingredients and cover with 5
cups of water. Bring to a boil, reduce the heat, and
simmer for 30 minutes. Strain, and great flavor is at
your fingertips.

# BASIC STRAINED YOGURT

⁂

*Yields 3/4 cup*

1½ cups (354 ml) plain nonfat yogurt, no gelatin added

   Put the yogurt in a strainer over a bowl—or you
can use a coffee filter, piece of muslin, or a paper
towel—and place in a small sieve over a bowl. Cover
and let it drain in the refrigerator for 5 hours or
overnight. After 10 hours it becomes quite firm and
the small lumps disappear, which makes it ideal for
use in sauces. The liquid whey drains into the bowl,
leaving you with a thick, creamy "yogurt cheese."

# EASY, QUICK, ENHANCED CANNED STOCKS

⁂

Canned stock (low-sodium if possible)
Bouquet garni

   Pour the canned stock into a saucepan and add
the appropriate bouquet garni. Bring to a boil, reduce
the heat, and simmer for 30 minutes. Strain and
move forward, enhanced, of course.
   *Basic Bouquet Garni:* For ease of operation, I suggest you use our basic "bunch of herbs": 1 bay leaf, 2
sprigs fresh thyme (1 teaspoon or 5 ml dried), 6 black
peppercorns, 2 whole cloves, 3 sprigs parsley.
   *For poultry:* Add a 4-inch (10-cm) branch of tarragon (2 teaspoons or 10 ml dried) or 6 sage leaves
(1 teaspoon or 5 ml dried).
   *For fish:* Use either a few small branches of fennel
or of dill, incorporated into the basic bunch of herbs.
   *For beef:* Use a few branches of marjoram or rosemary incorporated into the basic bunch of herbs.
   Remember: canned stocks are often loaded with
sodium. Please check the label if you are sodium sensitive.

# BOUQUET GARNI

*For ease of operation, I suggest you use my basic "bunch of herbs."*

BASIC BOUQUET GARNI

1 bay leaf
2 sprigs fresh thyme, or 1 teaspoon dried
6 black peppercorns
2 whole cloves
3 sprigs parsley

To make a bouquet garni, cut a 4-inch (10-cm) square piece of muslin or cheesecloth, put the ingredients in the center, and tie the four courners securely to form a tight pouch. Hit the bouquet garni several times with a mallet or the back of a knife to bruise the herbs and spices, helping them to release their volatile oils.

I let my herb bunches go around twice when I use them to flavor a canned broth. After the first use, put it into a sealable plastic bag and keep it deep-frozen until its next appearance. Do be sure to label it: frozen herb bags could be a disappointing late-night microwave snack for twenty-first-century teenagers!

# BASIC PASTRY CRUST

*Yields two 8-inch (20-cm) crusts*

1½ cups cake flour
1 teaspoon sugar
1/8 teaspoon salt
2 tablespoons light olive oil
4 tablespoons (1/2 stick) margarine or butter, frozen for 15 minutes
1 teaspoon distilled vinegar
4 tablespoons ice water
2 tablespoons 2%-fat milk

Put the flour, sugar, and salt in a large mixing bowl, drizzle evenly with the oil, and whisk together with a fork until it has a fine sandy texture.

Remove the margarine from the freezer and slice it into 1/8-inch (.5-cm) pieces. Stir it into the flour mixture just enough to coat the margarine and keep the pieces from sticking together. Sprinkle with the vinegar and water, then use two knives cutting in a crisscross motion to work the dough just until all the liquid is absorbed. Shape into a ball, put in a small bowl, cover with plastic, and refrigerate for 10 minutes before rolling. The longer it sits, the more the liquid will spread throughout the dough, making it easier to roll. Brush with milk after rolling.

## Tips and Hints

- Use cake flour. It has less protein than all-purpose flour, which reduces the production of gluten and makes for a more tender crust.
- For an even tenderer crust, remove 1 tablespoon of each cup of flour and replace with 1 tablespoon cornstarch. This reduces the protein yet again.
- For sweeter crusts, add more sugar or very sweet fruit purée (like prunes). The sugar prevents gluten from forming by keeping two of the proteins from combining.
- Since my family is trying not to have saturated fat, I use a good solid stick margarine—not the soft tub, which has added water and is difficult to cut into uniform pieces.

# Wheat Germ Crust

*Covers the top of a 9-inch (23-cm) pie*

1½ cups all-purpose flour
1/4 cup wheat germ
6 tablespoons polyunsaturated stick margarine, cut into
    12 small pieces and well chilled in the freezer for 2
    hours
5 tablespoons ice water
1 tablespoon 2%-fat milk

Sift the flour into a bowl and stir in the wheat germ. Pinch the margarine pieces into the flour with the tips of your fingers until it's completely distributed.

Pour in the ice water and mix the dough with your fingers until it sticks together and forms a small ball.

Preheat the oven to 425°F (220°C). Turn the dough out onto a floured board and roll into a long rectangle, about 1/8 inch (0.5 cm) thick. Fold the bottom third over the middle and the top third over that and repeat the process twice more. Finally, roll the dough out into a circle and place pie plate on top, upside down. Cut along the outside edge of the pie plate with a sharp knife to get the perfect size circle. Roll it up over the rolling pin and unroll it onto a baking sheet covered with parchment paper. If you're making a pie top with the dough, you might want to score the dough with serving lines that make the crust easier to slice after it's baked. It does make a very crisp, flaky crust. Bake in the preheated oven for 10 minutes.

# Index

bread, 101
fig, 105, 107, 110–111
fruit tart, 117
pizza, 153
rice, 29, 94
Wheat Germ, 290
Crystallized Violets, 130–131
Cucumber Raita Salad, 85
Cucumber Sauce, 228
Curry
paste, 244–245
pork, 171
Custard(s)
cherry, 215
Crème Caramel, 113
poached apple, 126–127
Trifle, 130

Dal, 196
Desserts
with 10% calories from fat,
100–132
with 20% calories from fat,
212–219
with 30% calories from fat, 284
Dosa, 2, 3
Dough
pirogen, 172
seed roll, 86
Dressing(s)
for bean and pasta salad, 70
for Chou Chou Salad, 84–85
for greens and vegetable salad, 274
lime-ginger, 275
See also Vinaigrette(s)
Duck Stock, 286
Dumplings, fish, 13
Dutch Pancakes, 202

Eastern-Exposure Squid, 15
Easy, Quick, Enhanced Canned
Stocks, 288
Egg Foo Yung Scramble, 204–205
Eggplant, salting of, 253
Eggs
chicken omelet, 206
savory puffed omelet, 278
Egg substitute, 279, 280–281
Mexican scrambled, 97
scrambled, 204–205
Enchiladas Fina Cocina, 241
English muffins, 279, 280–281
Entrées

with 10% calories from fat, 9–83
with 20% calories from fat, 140–189
with 30% calories from fat, 228–272
Evil Jungle Princess, 155

Fat
10% of calories from, xi
appetizers and soups, 1–8
brunch and breakfast dishes,
92–98
desserts, 100–132
entrées, 9–83
side dishes and vegetables, 84–91
20% of calories from, x
brunch and breakfast dishes,
200–210
desserts, 212–219
entrées, 140–189
soups, 134–137
30% of calories from, ix
appetizers and soups, 222–226
brunch and breakfast dishes,
278–281
dessert, 284
entrées, 228–272
side dishes and vegetables,
274–276
and food in future, xii–xiii
middle-of-road position, xiii
stretching percentages, xii
Fava Bean Soup Procaccini, 4
Fennel Risotto, 177
Fettuccine, 38, 148
Fierros, Norman, 241
Fiesta Beans, 257
Fig Crust, 105, 107, 110–111
Fillet of Beef Benedict, 279
Fillet of Beef Meurice, 163
Filling(s)
angel food cake, 108, 109
apple pie, 219
cheesecake, 104, 105, 107, 110, 111
cottage cheese, 103, 104, 105, 107,
110, 111
cottage pie, 53
crêpe, 152
Dutch pancake, 202
fruit tart, 117
lasagne, 188
manicotti, 270
masala, 2, 3
Minimax Pirogen, 172
oyster and bacon, 142, 143

potato pie, 94
quiche, 208
salmon pie, 229
seafood, 14
seafood pie, 29
squash, 104, 105
steak and oyster pie, 247
strudel, 102
tortellini, 78
turkey pie, 240
Fish. See Seafood; specific fish; specific
recipes under Fish
Fish Dumplings, 13
Fish 'n' Chips 'n' Peas, 140
Fish Stock, 287
Flan, 116
Flank steak, 167
Fondue and Salad, 265
Food Preference List, xv–xvii
Food processor, 28
French Rarebit, 203
Fresh Tuna in Nectarine Sauce, 16
Fruit Sauce, 264
Fruit Tart, 117
Fu Yung Gai, 206

Garam masala, 3
Garbanzo beans, 222, 257
Garden Burgers, 72
Garlic and Herb Yogurt Spread, 200
Garlic Herb Spread, 2
Ghivetch, 72–73
Ginger, 95
Ginger Cheesecake, 104–105
Ginger Garlic Marinade, 39
Ginger Pumpkin Cups, 115
Glazed Green Beans, 194
Glazed Halibut Fillets, 17
Glazed Potatoes, 85
Glazes
lime, 33
pear, 175
Goat cheese, 76, 156
Golden Bran and Raspberry Muffins,
92–93
Golden Threads Squash, 266
Gold Medal Beans and Rice, 183
Goulash, 61
Granola, 207
Gravy
apple-orange, 160–161, 258–259
for roast turkey breast, 46
See also Sauce(s)

Let's Stay In Touch!

Dear Reader,

Thank you so much for taking the time to read this book—all the way to the back cover!

I've been especially thrilled to bring you these recipes and hints for an exciting and healthy way of making food that's both delicious and good for you!

If you'd like to be part of the continuing process, please drop me a line with your comments and send it with the form below—or just send in the completed form so that I can get back to you with updates on new ideas, recipes, and culinary products.

From my kitchen to yours,

With love and thanks,

Graham Kerr

*Detach and mail to:* The Kerr Corporation, P.O. Box 1598, Dept. F, Stanwood, WA   98292

# "I want to stay in touch!"

**YES!** I want to stay in touch and receive information about new ideas and products from Graham Kerr.

Please check:  ☐ Under 40
☐ 40-59
☐ Over 60

My Name

Address

City                                                        State/Zip

Phone Number (Optional): (          )
Area Code

**MAIL TO:** The Kerr Corporation, P.O. Box 1598, Dept. F, Stanwood, WA   98292